GATHERING NO MOSS

This is the autobiography of a possibly autistic child, born in 1925, who, idiosyncratically educated, grew up to see out, as a member of the Colonial Service, the end of the British Empire in East Africa. In later service with the United Nations Food and Agriculture Organisation he witnessed novice states exulting in new-found independence. His last appointment, as deputy director of the Centre for International Briefing, at Farnham Castle in Surrey, was in an organisation devoted to inculcating, in those going 'abroad', better understanding of cross-cultural relations. Post-retirement, he keeps an eye, Pooter-like, on our changing world.

For Hilary and Jeremy

and

Beryl,

1929–2012.

GATHERING NO MOSS
The autobiography of a rolling stone

Alan Hall

ARTHUR H. STOCKWELL LTD
Torrs Park, Ilfracombe, Devon, EX34 8BA
Established 1898
www.ahstockwell.co.uk

© Alan Hall, 2021
First published in Great Britain, 2021

The moral rights of the author have been asserted.

All rights reserved.
No part of this publication may be reproduced
or transmitted in any form or by any means,
electronic or mechanical, including photocopy,
recording, or any information storage and
retrieval system, without permission
in writing from the copyright holder.

British Library Cataloguing-in-Publication Data.
A catalogue record for this book is available
from the British Library.

Arthur H. Stockwell Ltd bears no responsibility
for the accuracy of information recorded in this book.

ISBN 978-0-7223-5086-7
Printed in Great Britain by
Arthur H. Stockwell Ltd
Torrs Park   Ilfracombe
Devon EX34 8BA

CONTENTS

1.	First Apprehensions and Family Roots	7
2.	We Leave the Garden of Eden	19
3.	Our Parents: Life in Cambridge	25
4.	Burridge Heath	30
5.	Tankerton: King's Leigh School	37
6.	Plashet Road	48
7.	Ardrishaig	60
8.	Breaking Out	71
9.	Shocking News	80
10.	Active Service	91
11.	Inactive Service	102
12.	Student Life	114
13.	Andover	130
14.	Tanganyika	144
15.	Songea	157
16.	Upheaval at Sontob	173
17.	Letters from Songea	185
18.	Fighting on Two Fronts	200
19.	Approaching Marriage	205
20.	Marriage, Jeremy and Oxford	218
21.	Uhuru	235
22.	Changing Direction	250
23.	Mauritius	265
24.	Mauritius Diary, 1964	275
25.	Hilary and a Granny She Never Knew	299
26.	Rome	310
27.	FAO	329
28.	Iran	343
29.	Back to Rome	357
30.	The Centre for International Briefing	373
31.	Gatehouse of Fleet	384
32.	Russia	391
33.	Goodbye to Gatehouse	401
34.	Leigh and the World Beyond	407
35.	Getting a New Hip	416

36.	Winding Down	424
37.	India Diary, 2001	428
38.	Man of Letters	439
39.	Beryl	448
40.	Tatsfield	453

PHOTOGRAPHS

The author's father	257
The author's mother	258
The author in 1926, aged one	259
The author about to join the Colonial Service	259
Beryl Mungavin, personal assistant	260
Alan and Beryl on safari	260
Beryl with Jeremy in Mauritius	261
Hilary and Jeremy in Rome	261
Hilary, the author, Jeremy and Scally at Bracciano	262
Nikfarjan, the author and Haddad at Iran village meeting	262
Hilary in France	263
Three generations at Leigh	264
Alan and Hilary before pensioners' reunion	264

1 – FIRST APPREHENSIONS AND FAMILY ROOTS

My earliest recollections are of Caxton, near Cambridge, and the house there to which my parents had moved from a neighbouring village, Bourn, shortly after my birth on 23 September 1925. On that day my father wrote to my mother at the Brunswick nursing home, Cambridge, a letter that I didn't see until forty-three years after his death.

> The 1st Epistle of Sam to the Pudding since before 23rd December [the date of their marriage]
>
> Bourn, Nr. Cambridge
>
> My darling darling girl.
>   I was kind of flummoxed this morning and did not tell you all that was in my heart. But I was so relieved to see you well my angel. I honestly didn't sleep a wink, & I think I rather look like it now! I had that great big bed all to myself. . . . I kept wondering if it had come along and if my poor girlie was having a cruel time. So that today, my precious one, I'm all of a heap, just devoutly thankful that you've come through it all right . . . and the young Sam [me] seems a good chap. His looks will improve every day . . . and the nine months to the day tickles me immensely.
>   Kiss Puck for me [Puck being me, I suppose – they obviously hadn't yet decided on a name for me]. I'll come in tomorrow evening.

It was perhaps typical of my father that he should regard my arrival with somewhat clinical detachment, and reserve his emotion and pride in the occasion for the fact that my mother had survived her first confinement well. It was a matter for which they were both to be congratulated, having produced this 'young Sam', who seemed to be 'a good chap', and whose looks (by implication none too pleasing) would no doubt 'improve every day'.

I don't know when we moved to Caxton (only a mile or so from Bourn), but we were to live there for the first five years of my life – five very happy years. Dene House and its garden were substantial, but unremarkable. Indeed, I recall my feeling of disappointment on seeing it more than thirty years later: a square ochre-coloured house with a slate roof, big front door and four high sash windows in each wall; it stood bleakly in a large, featureless garden, with a couple of racehorses in two or three acres of paddock behind. Could this have been the house described so unfavourably by William Cobbett in the *Huntingdon Journal* on 21/22 January 1822? He did not think at all highly of Caxton, nor of the house, if indeed it was the same one:

> The village of Caxton resembles nothing English, except some of the rascally rotten burroughs in Cornwall and Devonshire, on which a just Providence seems to have entailed its curse. The land just about here does seem to be really bad. The face of the country is naked. . . . All is bleak and comfortless; and, just about the most dreary part of this most dreary scene, stands almost opportunely, 'Caxton Gibbet', tendering its friendly arm to the passers-by. . . . Not far from this is a new house, which, the coachman says, belongs to a Mr Cheer, who, if report speaks truly, is not, however, notwithstanding his name, guilty of the sin of making people either drunkards or gluttons. Certainly the spot on which he has built his house, is one of the most ugly that I ever saw. Few spots have everything that you would wish to find; but this, according to my judgement, has everything that every man of ordinary taste would wish to avoid.

For my part, neither William Cobbett's description nor my own later view of the place were how I remembered it as a child, and still remember it.

For a start, the 'paddock' was not a paddock – it was a *field*; and although we had a number of rambling old stables behind the garage (formerly a coach house or cart shed, I expect), there had been no racehorses in our time – at most, a couple of kids (i.e. goats) tethered to stakes. No doubt, Father had bought them in one of those spontaneous moments that he loved to indulge: some patient or other had probably offered them to him as 'a good way to keep down the grass'; and Father would have enjoyed coming home to announce, out of the blue, that he had bought two goats – just as, some years later, after we had moved to London, he came back from his round of visits one day with, of all things, a banjo that he had bought 'for only three pounds' from a local junk shop (Mother made him take it back). We children (my two brothers and I), were not very keen on the kids – aggressive little brutes – even though a supplementary (propitiatory) reason for their acquisition had been 'for the children'.

Our greatest joy, in that field, was to clamber over the wrecks of two old cars of my father's that had been 'disposed of' in the long grass: a green Morris Cowley with a dicky, and a blue car of even earlier vintage that had conked out from natural causes. The Morris Cowley had met its end after having performed a spectacular somersault one evening for no apparent reason – at least, no reason that I was to discover. There was Father in bed one morning, all tied up with bandages and sticking plaster, but remarkably cheerful nonetheless, describing with gusto how he had been catapulted out on to the grass verge near the village war memorial, and 'What good fortune it was that the car hood had been folded back!' No other vehicle was involved, and the whole episode seemed to have been something of a triumph, especially as we children subsequently inherited, so to speak, the remains of the Morris Cowley.

For the first five years of my life we lived in an ideally happy world. After one year, my brother David had appeared (saluted, I am told, by a smack in the face from me); and two years later, Hamish. It was our 'golden age', to which we all, parents included, were accustomed to look back with affection and some nostalgia. Yet now, at a distance of ninety-five years, it seems to me that there was something not exactly too good to be true about life in our village, but it had nevertheless a beguilingly attractive resemblance to the BBC's Toytown. There was the church; the school (to which we did not go); the village policeman, complete with bicycle, trouser clips and a square flash lamp on his belt; and the postman with his mailbag and military-style cap, which would have looked perfectly in place at the Battle of Waterloo. The village shop sold everything you might need from day to day – especially a range of sweets in big glass jars. Our neighbour, Mr Dawson, whose garden was separated from ours by a sunken, rutted lane leading to hedge-enclosed farm fields, lived in a thatched cottage and kept bees in his orchard. In May we had dancing round the maypole; and tea parties on vicarage lawns, with cucumber sandwiches, occurred with great regularity throughout the summer months. As Father's practice included several villages, all with their respective churches, we were taken along to many of these interesting but sometimes bewildering events. Children were much more 'in tow' than they are nowadays, trailing round while their parents had a good time. (Today the position seems to be reversed.)

There was a retired General Henley who, too, lived in a thatched house and who annually invited the village children to a Christmas party. David and I (who were not 'village children') were included, but sat separately, also on the floor, together with a family of girls and the General's grandson, Godfrey. The class distinction was marked and considered in those days to be quite natural – not that we thought of ourselves as superior, just different. In fact, to hear them singing carols that we had not yet learned put us somewhat in awe of the Caxton schoolchildren, with whom we had practically no contact at all on other days of the year. People knew their place, and Mother knew with whom we might suitably mix. She often took us several miles out to nearby farms, sometimes combining this with Father's visits, and occasionally to the home of Gertie, our maid, where the standard fare was thin bread and butter, and jelly, and where ten or fifteen people would sit down to afternoon tea at a long table in the farmhouse kitchen. We stoically accepted the bread and butter as an unavoidable preliminary to the jelly.

Another farm was the Shillitoes', whose daughter, Joan, a bit older than we were, had a fat white pony, on which two or three children would be piled at the same time. We loved to poke around the farm buildings, standing at a safe distance watching cows being milked (by hand), piglets tumbling over each other to get at a great fat slumbering sow, and huge shire horses being harnessed up, or straining between the shafts of a heavy cart through the mire of a rick yard.

The sights and smells and ways of the countryside were our earliest education, consciously encouraged by our parents, and fostered also by the two other adults who had most to do with us: our Nanny, who took us for 'walks' every day, almost regardless of the weather; and Sewell (I didn't know his first name – to me he was just 'Sool'), the gardener, who was our best friend, and to whom we must sometimes have been pests more troublesome than rabbits or greenfly. Nanny was Sewell's best friend, too, and eventually they married. For our walks we would be buttoned up in leggings, or jodphur-like trousers with numerous small buttons all the way up the leg which had to be fastened with a buttonhook, a fiddly, time-consuming business. There was very little traffic and no danger walking on the main road, either through the village or the other way, out towards Caxton Gibbet. Arriving at this rather insignificant yet awesome relic at the limit of our personal reconnoitring in that direction was like coming across a warning notice: 'Go No Further! Beyond This Place Be Robbers and Thieves'. Nanny cheerfully described that black, gnarled wooden post with its overhanging arm as "where they hung highwaymen to be an example to other folk". Grown-ups were curiously insensitive to the emotional impact on children of words and actions which might have a lasting effect on young minds. I remember almost as if it were yesterday, in the dark archway leading to a cobbled yard at my godmother's house, a gaunt old man known to us as Uncle Ernest threatening me jokingly (he thought) with 'the bogeyman' if I was not a good boy. Mother would not have approved of that. She was the most loving, conscientious and protective parent a child could hope to have.

Born Amelia Smith in the manse at Kilchoan, Ardnamurchan, my mother's early life in a wild and remote corner of Western Scotland could hardly have been more different from the conventional middle-class existence of a country doctor's wife in Cambridgeshire. The second youngest in a family of three sons and three daughters, her early education was provided by her father, probably the only 'educated' man in an area where contact with the hinterland (one could almost say mainland – there was no road out) was limited to the arrival of a fortnightly steamer. Life in Ardnamurchan for its population of crofters and fishermen was elemental. They were almost entirely self-sufficient. Their houses of stone, wood, turf and straw (only the manse, a handsome, grey stone house, and the church, I think, would have been slated) were sometimes almost primitive, blackened inside from peat fires, and with only the smallest of windows for light. Their food they grew, reared or fished for themselves. Even the minister, my grandfather, and his family lived a semi-farming life, with pasture and a few acres of wheat or oats to be hand-harvested and milled locally for their own use; and behind the manse was a byre and a couple of cows to keep them in milk and butter.

Life in the Western Highlands at the beginning of the last century was hard, but full of interest and natural opportunities for developing a girl's skills and means of self-expression: baking, curing, pickling, gutting fish, skinning rabbits and plucking fowl, to say nothing of helping to care for a variety of livestock as well as the conventional household duties. The Smiths were devoted to the community in which they lived, and to which my grandfather ministered. They seem to have been a very happy family, and Mother would often speak of Ardnamurchan and the settled, orderly ways of their upbringing.

At the age of fourteen or thereabouts my mother went off, as an elder sister had done before her, to the Ministers' Daughters' College (later renamed Esdaile) in Edinburgh. This was her only experience of society outside the Western Highlands until, partly in preparation for her marriage, she travelled down to Cannock, near Birmingham, to keep house for her eldest brother, John, newly established there in medical practice. It was from there that she wrote to my father the only letter between them that has survived from the time (about fifteen months) before they were married in Birmingham on 23 December 1924. Until I saw this letter, and that of my father, above, I had never thought of my parents as lovers. Reading them now, in my ninety-fifth year, is strangely affecting – how one-sided is a child's view of his mother and father! I reprint parts of them here to redress the balance, and to give a more rounded picture of my then young parents, whose affection for each other we children, perhaps obtusely, never really saw as extending much beyond the sort of love they gave each one of us:

> Clarmont, Sim Lane
> Cannock, June 19th '22
>
> My dearest and most loveable Sambo
>   So glad old man you took it into your head to write here — for here I still am. Your letter, darling – so repentant and self condemning was beautiful. Of course I've forgiven you sweetheart. I know I'm a spoilt kid and have always had too much of my own way — but I'll try not to be so trying to you. Goodness, Sam darling, my love is far too great for it to be all blown away in a few minutes just 'cos my poor beloved got annoyed – and I'm just not going to think of it any more. Our 18 days together were and are a sort of glorious dream to me now. You made me so happy dear. . . .
>   Och, I don't know what it is. At any rate I love you darling with my whole heart and will never cease to love you. To me you seem so wonderful – so kind and good. & if you do at times lose your temper, well, I don't wonder for I'm sure I'd try a saint sometimes – though I'll really try not to be bad. But darling I want you so much – & I'm fed up 'cos I can't – Some day tho' perhaps, beloved. Hope you're enjoying life, darling & don't be miserable over me sweetheart, 'cos I've forgotten all that & live over the wonderfully glorious time we had. With every little teeny weeny bit of my love
>   Your very own affect. & loving Amelia.

Although, from the evidence of this letter, my parents were clearly in love, I doubt whether they had much opportunity, beyond brief meetings, to get to know each other before they married. My father was a fellow medical student of another brother of my mother's, Alasdair, and met her during a vacation at Kilchoan. Although a perfect match, they were of very different temperament and character. Both came from an identical social background, but their respective families could hardly have differed more. Both my grandfathers were ministers of the Church of Scotland, and probably had similar aspirations for their children, yet only the Smiths conformed with what one might expect of a traditional family of the Kirk: happy, united, good-living, high-thinking, and strongly knit into their community by duty and affection. While it would not be wholly true to say that the Halls, at Banchory, on the other side of Scotland, near Aberdeen, were unhappy, disunited and quarrelsome, I think there can be no denying that my father grew up in a domestic atmosphere which perhaps reflected his parents' incompatibility with each other.

My paternal grandfather came from an Aberdonian family in a line of journeymen recorded, in descending order from 1821, as crofter, quarryman and builder. The only concrete fact about his early life related of my grandfather was how, as a student, he would trudge to Aberdeen University with a sack of oatmeal on his back – his main sustenance during the term. He eventually graduated, and a handsomely bound copy of the Psalms of David (in metre) and the *Scottish Hymnal* – which I have among the several books inherited from him – establishes the precise date of his ordination and induction to the parish of Banchory Ternan: 'Presented to the Reverend James Hall . . . by the Ladies of the Congregation' on 6 September 1884. Whether any of those ladies was subsequently disappointed when, eleven years later, he married Christina (Chrissie) Jamieson of Aberdeen, I do not know; but she was certainly a handsome catch. One of the daughters of the famously eccentric Reverend Dr George Jamieson, senior minister of Old Machar Cathedral, my paternal grandmother inherited much of her father's individuality and character.

George Jamieson, as described by Mrs Katherine E. Trail in her *Reminiscences of Old Aberdeen*, was a man of 'impressive appearance and powerful voice, with piercing eyes under very bushy eyebrows . . . and his beard must have reached very nearly to his waist. He offended many of his congregation by his strong individuality and his gift for saying the wrong thing.' He devoted much of his time to writing 'ponderous volumes on philosophical subjects, in which he propounded his theories of the universe'. No one, apparently, wanted to buy them and 'Had it not been for the generosity of his son [William, who was one of the discoverers of the Broken Hill mine in Australia] he would not have been able to publish them.' In his sermons 'He used to promulgate the most extraordinary theories, such as whether Cain and Abel were twins (the sum and substance of his address was that we do not know, and that it does not matter very much anyway). In his prayers he would amuse his congregation by occasionally coining words – and then explaining them to the Deity – such as "Give us, oh Lord, *revealment* – that is to say, the power of understanding." He was keenly interested in current affairs and not afraid to take an independent line. During the Ashanti War he prayed "for the safety of our soldiers in that far-off land – although, oh Lord, we are in two minds whether they should have been sent there in the first place".

I have been able to identify twelve children of Dr Jamieson, although he himself memorably remarked on one occasion, as if that were her department, not his, "My wife tells me that she has had sixteen babies."

Of these, my grandmother was one of the youngest of what seems to have been a remarkable brood. Her eldest brother, Andrew, was professor of electrical engineering at Glasgow; another, Fife, was a scientist of great promise who worked with Michael Faraday but died tragically young; two others emigrated to Australia, one of them making a considerable fortune there; a daughter, Isabelle (known as Mary), married a doctor who was knighted as one of the founders of the London Hospital for Tropical Diseases; another daughter, Alice, had the misfortune to be remembered simply as 'a pauper'. In marrying a clergyman my grandmother struck a middle course between the extremes.

London Granny (as we came to call her, since she moved there after the death of her husband) was bright, humorous and, for a minister's wife, almost outrageously unconventional. Her interests were in art, fashion and society. Occasionally, tired of the dull routine of the manse, she would take herself off to London or Paris for a refreshing change with friends or relatives who lived a more exciting life. In an age when she would have been expected to be a model of domesticity she was quite uninterested in housekeeping and, as a mother, allowed her maternal instincts to run on a very loose rein. My father used to say that the porridge at their table had "a skin thick enough to stand on and lumps as big as golf balls". To a man of my grandfather's dour temperament, the not exactly slapdash, but casual, performance of her duties by his wife must have been extremely irksome.

He was a Scot of severe and introverted disposition who appeared to love books more than his fellow human beings. His library was heavy with classical writers, philosophy, history and theology, but leavened also with poetry and lighter works discriminatingly, but cautiously, chosen. If he thought a writer worth reading, it was usually one whose reputation had already matured in public esteem, such as George Eliot or Byron, or Carlyle. He would then buy the complete set of their works – even, in the case of Sir Walter Scott, when they mounted to all forty-eight volumes. He was at his most contented in his study. His two sons, James* (my father) and George, judging by the stories they told of their childhood, were probably a great nuisance to him, except when they were perfectly behaved.

From all accounts, the brothers were high-spirited, mischievous children who were usually anything but well behaved – at least, according to Grandfather's exacting standards. Paternal 'thrashings' were a regular occurrence, usually administered with some ceremony, but sometimes in anger. There was the story, told many times, of Grandfather being in an exceptionally good mood and buying some ice cream for the boys, but, trudging home with it up the brae, he had the misfortune to meet his two sons careering towards him on a home-made go-cart. Their father had to leap aside to avoid serious injury to all of them. He turned round, quivering with fury, dashed the ice cream to the ground and proceeded to stamp on it, shouting at the top of his voice, "You *shan't* have it! You *shan't* have it!"

Another story, typical of those told by my father, was about James and George 'tracking' their father as he went about his parish visits. As everyone knows, this is a duty that entails the consumption of vast quantities of tea; so it was Grandfather's custom, whenever necessary, to relieve himself shortly before going on to another house. Unfortunately, on this occasion he turned back to choose a bush behind which George had just

---

* Although named James, my father was always in later life called Sam by all except his parents.

then resourcefully hidden himself. The wretched boy had no alternative but to remain crouched there, and receive the contents of his father's bladder sprinkled leisurely over his head, while his elder brother, safely ensconced some way behind, was bursting himself with silent laughter. (Of course, it is more than likely my grandfather had been fully aware what he was doing, and was enjoying it, having deliberately chosen that bush.)

In spite of the Victorian severity, therefore, Father always spoke of Banchory life with humour and a sort of rueful affection. There was also the Victorian routine of family prayers – in which the maids also joined – which must have provided, however much my father might later mock religion, some token of daily reconciliation to offset the frequent quarrelling. Nevertheless, it seems that there were occasions when his parents were not speaking to each other for days and weeks at a time. James and George would then make themselves scarce, go out fishing, roam the woods and get into scrapes with other boys. Not exactly neglected (although holey socks and out-at-elbows jerseys were spoken of), the boys took refuge in the exceptional liberty that parental hostilities offered them. A strong bond developed between the brothers, which lasted throughout the course of their two very different lives.

Both went to Aberdeen Grammar School, after which my father proceeded to the university and George, who appears to have got himself into what was referred to in the family as 'trouble with a local girl', took himself off to Australia. My father was an outstanding student, being dux of the school and taking the gold medal and prize for surgery and anatomy. Yet this impressive start was to be blighted by physical disability – a tubercular knee, which not only frustrated his ambition to specialise, but prevented his acceptance for war service. Famously convivial and full of fun, my father was mortified to see his friends and fellow students going off to do their war service and leaving him behind – this at a time when white feathers marked out young men thought to be shirking their patriotic duty. Three times he volunteered, and three times he was rejected as unfit. It dealt him a psychological rebuff which I believe he never fully came to terms with. And not just psychologically (we children were shielded from that): Father's disability plagued the first years of our parents' marriage.

Over a period of perhaps eight years, he was in and out of hospital, ultimately having to give up his new Cambridgeshire practice altogether and devote himself to performing odd locum and hospital duties in the periods of intermission while Mother and we children were lodged separately as best he could arrange.

During all this, what must have been a wretched time for both my parents, and in spite of the initial shock of leaving Caxton (at least for me, if not for my brothers) we accommodated ourselves remarkably well to what was to prove an unsettled period in our domestic life as a family. And even when it did finally settle, it was to be in a place wholly uncongenial to my mother.

Note: I believe my father's characterisation of *his* father as a somewhat grim parent may derive from the stories he chose to tell about him. A more than dutiful obituary in the local paper (which I cannot immediately put my hands on) wrote of his kindliness and of the affection in which he was held by his parishioners.

2 – WE LEAVE THE GARDEN OF EDEN

In Caxton we lived an ordered life, surrounded by love, affection and considerate behaviour, until – with a sense of shock I can feel even today – we suddenly moved. At this distance it is impossible to tell whether my dismay at leaving, if not the first, the only home I ever knew, derived somehow from an apprehension of our parents' distress (I suspect it was) or whether it was the change in our circumstances that unsettled me. My father's tubercular knee had been getting progressively worse, to the extent that the joint had to be removed and it was feared that he could no longer manage the active life of a country doctor.

Out of the blue, one day, a man arrived with a 'FOR SALE' sign, which he proceeded to put up in the hedge along the roadside below our garden. I watched him curiously, as we watched everything in our little world. There had been no preparation for this; and it was our questioning about this man and his intrusive sign that elicited from our mother the alarming news of impending departure from our Garden of Eden. (The anagram of Dene House and Eden is apposite.)

Shortly after that we found ourselves installed in a fairly large semi-detached house in St Barnabas Road, Cambridge, a displacement all the stranger with our father's absence in hospital. We still had our nanny though; we still had our regular 'walks' and maintained in our new environment the ordered routine so important for a child's feeling of security. These elements of continuity were reinforced by the presence of familiar things that had come with us from Caxton: the Dene House furniture, the heavy garden roller and the large quantity of my grandfather's books which Father had inherited. It could be said, perhaps, that these weighty tomes, which took up two walls of our dining room wherever we happened to be, were also part of the 'furniture'.

In St Barnabas Road we had *electricity*. After the oil lamps, and irons heated on the kitchen range at Caxton, this was something entirely new in our experience. David one day stuck his fingers into a power plug, instantly jerking them out again with a startled expression on his face.

"It feels funny when you do that," he said.

Not willing to take his word for it, and anyway wanting to know what *sort* of funny feeling, I put my fingers in too. The jolt of electricity through my arm convinced me that he was right. I don't know how we didn't kill ourselves.

Next door lived a grim old widow (or so she seemed to us) called Mrs Wilder – an appropriate name. She objected to the noise we made, playing in the garden, and was driven to particular fury whenever a ball landed on her side of the fence and, trembling, we had to ask could we please have it back? Beyond her was a boy called John Smart, with whom we maintained relations of cautious enmity across the boundaries of our respective gardens, Mrs Wilder being an unfriendly buffer state, so to speak, between us. My best friend, however, was Darrel Cruikshank, who lived further up the road, nearer the Cambridge Railway Station at the end of it.

Darrel possessed an enormous quantity of Meccano. While I had only a small set of struts, nuts and wheels, Darrel had boxes and boxes of them – much bigger struts, larger wheels, girders, pulleys and other impressive accessories – with which he made wonderful cranes, bridges and working vehicles. They put my own puny constructions totally in the shade. The most exciting thing about Darrel, though, was his expertise in digging holes in his father's garden. With his brother's help, and then with mine, eagerly volunteered, he would get down to a depth of about eight or ten feet (or perhaps that's just what it seemed like – much deeper than our height, anyway). Darrel would be at the bottom, digging away with a spade or trowel, filling a bucket which I or his brother would then pull up with a rope. I thrilled to this rugged adventuring; yet, when my turn came to go down the hole, as often as not the brothers would prevent me from getting out again, holding me prisoner at the bottom until I had humiliatingly performed some barbaric rite of self-abasement.

In spite of this and other ordeals undergone at the hands of my friend and some of his larger neighbours (such as being stuffed into a dog kennel with a stink bomb), my abiding memory is of the joy and excitement when two or three of us would spend a whole afternoon in one of the larger of these excavated caverns, covered over from the daylight. With a candle, a few old boards, a couple of biscuits and a length of string, we created adventures in a world of our own imagining, completely apart from the real one above our heads.

My own brothers did not join in these games. Hamish, three years younger than me, was 'too small' (a disadvantage which the youngest in a family tends to suffer for more years than is really fair). David, one year younger, made his own friends, who included an undesirable young tough named Alfie Sennett. Mother, ever alert to the 'suitability' of our associates, attempted to discourage David from going over to this boy's house – without success, until one day Alfie pushed David through the French windows of our dining room. That was the end of Alfie so far as we were concerned.

When I was six years old – much later than is common now – I was sent to a kindergarten, Kimway School, on the town side of Parker's Piece, run by two Scottish sisters named MacLeod: tweedy middle-aged spinsters of earlier vintage than Miss Jean Brodie. Theirs was a regime in which effort, tidiness, observation and conduct featured quite as prominently as arithmetic, drawing, spelling, etc. I think I quite enjoyed my days there, judging from the three reports which have survived (thanks to brother David, who, some fifty years later, sent them on to me). My first term report noted that I was 'very good indeed' at singing, but 'rather slow and dreamy . . . very keen, polite and helpful, but rather too noisy'. The complaint of being noisy, in fact, recurs throughout my reports, although the final one, for the summer term of 1933, expresses itself rather more diplomatically: 'has a cheerful, happy nature, but his sense of sociability makes him too talkative'. In retrospect this surprises me.

During the holidays and some weekends I would occasionally

be taken by the mother of one of my little friends – or perhaps it would be more accurate to say the boy who sat next to me in class – to stay at their home near Histon, just outside Cambridge. His name was Jimmy Rowley, a tall boy for his age, lanky, boisterous and dominating, though he couldn't have been much more than six, as I was. Theirs was a large manor house, approached by a long tree-lined drive. I remember it having a coat of arms above the main entrance – apparently the family, some generations back, had provided a Lord Mayor of London, or something important anyway. Mother no doubt considered Jimmy a very suitable friend. Had she known that this boy (with whom I shared a double bed) enjoyed forcing me to join him in a game of 'doggies' that he had invented, she might well have revised her judgement of him.

Fortunately, there were other things to do. Jimmy's father was a farmer with many acres, and we two boys spent most of our time walking the hedgerows, poking about in tractor sheds, talking to the farmworkers. The Cambridgeshire countryside is not outstandingly beautiful, but it was on Jimmy Rowley's father's farm that I consciously discovered an abiding contentment in the English rural landscape; it was the first time I had been, so to speak, let loose in it. To tramp across fields and stand at a headland, looking up the straight furrows of newly turned soil towards a distant clump of ancient elms, to hear the country noises – the dry rustle or flutter of some small animal or bird nearby, the moaning of a tractor working some way off, or country voices carried now and again in my direction – to fill up my senses with immediately perceived impressions of sight, sound and smell – this was to me then, as it is now, to feel *alive*.

Mrs Rowley used to call me a 'dreamer', not in any way approvingly. "Wake up, Dreamy!" she would say, and "What a dreamer that boy is!" This rather persistent jollying criticism (which echoed Miss MacLeod's observation) made little impression on me, probably because I could make no sense of it. Children often become absorbed in whatever it is they are doing, whether playing with a toy or just staring at something. The Rowleys were, I see now in retrospect, an extrovert family, and probably thought it unhealthy for a boy to concentrate on 'nothing'.

Mrs Rowley taught me how to eat toast at breakfast: you broke it up and buttered each piece immediately before conveying it to your mouth. You did *not* spread the whole slice; nor did you cut it into fingers, as we had done for us at home. And Mr Rowley taught me how to drink water from a bottle.

It was threshing time, and Jimmy and I walked over to the yard to watch what was in those days the most exciting activity in the farm calendar. At one end of the stackyard stood a great steam engine, its huge flywheel spinning, from which a massive flapping and smacking belt, at least five inches wide, linked up with the 'drum', driving a series of wheels, belts and cogs. The whole contraption, pink in colour but covered in dust and as big as a double-decker bus, vibrated, rattled, groaned, squeaked and hummed in multi-geared response to the wheezing and chugging of the engine. Farm carts pulled by horses, with ladders fore and aft, loaded with sheaves to a height of at least twelve feet, were drawn up beside the drum; and one by one the sheaves would be pitchforked across (or up, depending on the progress of unloading) to the single man on top, whose job it was to cut the twine round each sheaf, and feed the loosened stalks of wheat into the drum's maw. It could be a dangerous task – or so we were told, illustrated by a horrifying tale of some unfortunate 'feeder' who forgot to let go of a sheaf and toppled in with it! This story was often retold, and usually embellished with lip-smacking descriptions of 'strawberry jam' coming out with the grain.

The man I felt sorriest for, though, was the poor devil who was put on to bagging the chaff. Crouching at the rear end of the drum, deafened by the clatter of its riddles and the squealing, clicking elevator that carried the straw waste up to the stack, he was obscured by choking clouds of dust and chaff. Yet under the sack that he wore over his head and shoulders his eyes shone out from a grimy face with such a cheerful expression that I felt grateful to him for moderating my childish sympathy. I expect he was just pleased to be noticed. I innocently thought the purpose of threshing was to produce the stack of straw, which certainly looked as if it were what all this activity led to. The little cascades of grain emerging from one side of the drum took so long to fill a sack – much less impressive. Later in my life, after the end of the Second World War (whose seeds, of which I was equally innocent, were already beginning to germinate in Europe), I would have a go myself at building a stack. Now I simply marvelled at the skill of the men up there, how they built up the sides so straight, then gradually brought them in, tramping on layer upon layer, higher and higher, until one remaining man stood on the top of what was virtually a solid straw house. Later it would be thatched, almost as carefully as if it were indeed the roof of an actual house.

It was hot work, too. Jimmy took a swig from a bottle of water, expertly letting in a stream of bubbles as he drank. I waited my turn (there was no question of guests first), then, eager to prove that I, too, could drink from a bottle, smartly vacuumed my lips and tongue to the glass. Mr Rowley, seeing me starting to choke, pulled the bottle away, deliberately soaking me in the process. I gasped and spluttered to a chorus of utterly insensitive coarse laughter. In this, Jimmy and his father were at one with the farmworkers, standing round guffawing, jeering almost, at my discomfiture. There was no malice in their rough humour, but that little episode was my first experience of real humiliation. It was not simply that my pride suffered; I was quite unprepared for the shock of finding myself alone and hurt by grown-ups.

3 – OUR PARENTS: LIFE IN CAMBRIDGE

For most of the year or more that we lived in Cambridge, Father was in hospital. We missed him, but accepted his absence as small children accept most obvious facts – as part of the natural order. Our father had anyway played a fairly remote part in our lives. His relationship to us – even when we were very young – had been in the nature of man to man rather than adult to child. But what excitement when, quite unexpectedly one morning, Mother announced that Daddy was coming home! And then, one or two long days after that, we woke up and found him home in bed, as if miraculously transported there during the night, with an enormous plaster cast on his right leg, which we were invited to tap as hard as we liked.

My father's outstanding characteristic was his joviality. His great bellowing laugh, although occasionally used to cover embarrassment, was a genuine expression of the amusement that he derived from almost any circumstance or aspect of daily life. He often poked fun, but was never malicious; on the contrary, he was one of the best-natured men I have known. (And although you may say this observation comes from an affectionate son, it is nevertheless high praise, because ill nature, where it exists, will always display itself first within a family.) This quality of affability he shared with his brother, George – both had attractive outgoing personalities. Father would address anybody – even when he had just set eyes on them – as if he had known them all his life, occasionally with disconcerting effect; and he relished his reputation for being outspoken. Women, especially, would go into shrieks of laughter – "Oh! He's an awful man!" – as, disdaining euphemisms or conversational niceties, he would mention the unmentionable with zestful aplomb. This is not to suggest that he was in any way coarse or vulgar; far from it. He deprecated vulgarity. But it was an article of faith with him to say exactly what he thought – and what his interlocutor, too, was thinking, if that did not come out straight.

This easy sociability of my father's equipped him well for his work as a GP, and he was very popular with his patients, many of whom held him in great affection and esteem. Perhaps this is a common experience with doctors – at least, the good ones. One of his colleagues told my mother once, "Your husband has mother wit," meaning he understood his patients and their needs as a mother understands her own child.

He was also very conscientious. A doctor's commitment may be judged, I think, by his (or her) reaction to being called out at night. Usually I would not hear the night bell; we would simply learn at breakfast that Father had been called out at two or three in the morning. Occasionally, though, I would waken to hear him throwing up the bedroom sash window at our house in London, and saying in a deep, serious voice, "What is it?" (In those days, few of his patients had a phone, and so they would have to come round physically to the house.) There would follow a muffled response as the caller attempted to speak through the speaking tube at the front door. Although the other end of the tube came out by Father's bed, he never used it. So these night-time conversations tended to be a comical interlocution, with my father's restrainedly irritated head shouting down to the backside of a visitor obtusely addressing himself to a hole in the wall. However, once the nature of the emergency (and it had better be an emergency) had been established, Father would put on his dressing gown, socks and shoes – and gloves – and go out immediately, in his pyjamas, with perfectly good grace. He never grumbled about a disturbed night.

Mother told me on several occasions that my father considered himself to be a failure. He had aimed to specialise and go on to achieve great things in a particular branch of medicine. With one already famous uncle as an example, and his own excelling record as a student, he had had every prospect of professional success. Yet circumstances had forced him to settle for general practice. That, at any rate, was the family-accepted reason why Father had not ended up with a consulting room in Harley Street, trailing glory in one of the great London teaching hospitals. He was indeed very much the great man manqué – his general demeanour was lordly, and he had the personality to carry it off. He was not an extravagant man – our parents rarely entertained and, apart from regular devoted visits to the Theatre Royal in Stratford, rarely went out – but he had expensive tastes. His tailors, Pope & Bradley, and later (when that august establishment showed a reluctance to make suits for a man with a stiff leg) Boyd Cooper, were among the very best in London. And once a month he would travel up to Regent Street to have his hair cut at Austin Reed's, rather than use the local barber that we were sent to for a 'fourpenny back and sides'. Father was always impeccably groomed – apart from when on his nocturnal call-outs, that is.

It may be surprising that I should write at greater length of my father as a doctor than as a father. Although this was not deliberate, it does, I believe, accurately convey his own order of priority. He depended immensely on my mother and, I am sure, dearly loved his three children; but just because he did so depend on her, we were in *her* department. In this respect he was rather Victorian – head of the family and not to be bothered too much with domestic matters (which were expected to run smoothly and with his own requirements taken fully into account – as indeed they were). I cannot recall him ever playing with us, apart from joining in the occasional sing-song around the piano. Partly this may be explained by the unremitting calls on his time imposed by his practice. (Remember, a GP had no clerical assistants or nurses in those days; and he had no partner.) But chiefly, I think, he would have regarded playing with his children as frivolous – children should be encouraged to make their own amusements, and that, so far as possible, should be *outside* the house.

"What are those boys doing indoors?" he would say.

Partly, it must be admitted, Father was a rather selfish man, but his selfishness – or perhaps 'self-indulgence' is more accurate – was more than mitigated by his good nature, his generosity to others and his strong sense of duty.

He was utterly devoted to my mother. In an age when wives were expected to be 'dutiful' before all else, Mother was everything a wife and mother should be. A shy woman, with beautiful deep-brown eyes, fiercely certain in her beliefs and judgement, her upbringing in a Scottish manse had instilled in her a faith and view of the world which our eventual translation to the East End of London did not alter a whit. She had been trained for marriage and motherhood in a way that girls would now find almost demeaning. But her native roots were a source of great strength to her and, as I now recognise, to our family. In spite of financial anxieties and a period of upheaval and uncertainty in our domestic arrangements, the atmosphere in our house (wherever it happened to be) was always comfortable, ordered and secure.

Our parents were strict. Rules of behaviour were to be obeyed, and Father occasionally, though rarely, gave one or other of us – usually David – the belt. That was when we were still quite small. There was a strong moral climate in the house: we came to know very clearly what was acceptable and what was not tolerated, so that very soon it was simply our parents' approbation or disapprobation which governed our conduct. In matters of behaviour generally, Father was inclined to be fairly liberal: he was tolerant of most human failings except lack of consideration for other people. Mother was more conventional, judging people by her own very high standards, but with an attitude to 'what may be good enough for *other* people' which sometimes verged on arrogance, as she herself confessed.

At this early stage of my life, these subtleties were not yet apparent to me. I was surprised and gratified to find that we had the best mother and father in the world – other children's parents just did not match up to them.

While we were still in Cambridge, Mother discovered that I had a promising voice. She began coaching me with a view to being entered for a chorister's scholarship at King's College. Every afternoon I would stand by the piano, singing up and down the scales. Apart from having a good soprano voice herself, Mother had taken her musical studies to quite an advanced stage, and before her marriage used to play the organ in Kilchoan Church. My singing lessons, therefore, were quite professionally undertaken – but, alas, to no avail.

On the day of the 'audition', Mother took me to King's, where I was grievously unprepared for what I was to undergo. A large, gloomy and cavernous hall was full of boys sitting at refectory-style tables, where we were put to work on mathematical sums that were wholly incomprehensible to me. This sudden exposure to an alien environment where one was expected somehow to 'perform' was altogether too much; and, from utter nervousness, I was sick over the boy next to me before being led out to sit wretchedly on a stone doorstep until Mother could be found to gather me up. The audition, which I did eventually do in front of five old (to me) men in gowns, was at least accomplished. But I was judged to be 'too young', and Mother advised to bring me back 'next year'. The day concluded with a concert by the choir in the magnificent chapel, where relief at having survived mingled with wonder at the sound of organ and voices soaring up into the vastness of its Gothic architecture.

By the time 'next year' came round, however, we were no longer in Cambridge. The expense of renting our fairly substantial house must have eaten into the family savings to the point when it could no longer be afforded. We left Barnabas Road for the – to us – much more interesting destination of Burridge Heath.

4 – BURRIDGE HEATH

There may have been more to Burridge Heath than the six acres in Wiltshire leased to my Uncle George, but so far as we were concerned his poultry farm *was* Burridge Heath. George and Molly (who encouraged us to drop the 'Uncle' and 'Aunt', if indeed Molly ever was regarded as an aunt) having returned from Australia, had invested whatever money they had in this poultry farm. They had taken up residence there in a long, low, daub-walled and thatched cottage at least 300 years old. Not much appeared to have been done to it during that period, beyond the ravages of time, though no doubt it had been occasionally rethatched. There was no running water – only an old iron pump in the kitchen – and of course no electricity. In those days it seemed as remote a part of rural England as you could imagine: far off the main road (itself a minor road), down an overgrown lane to a jumble of farm buildings and a bleak ill-kept farmhouse belonging to a man called Wilcox, set against a wide field bounded on the far side by dense woodland. George and Molly's cottage stood two or three hundred yards along a track at right angles to the lane, opposite a muddy duck pond and jostled by decrepit outbuildings and a yard ankle-deep in mud and manure. This (the cottage, not the yard) was to be our home for the next six months. For our parents, and especially Mother (Father was away working as a house surgeon in a mental asylum), this must have been an especially trying time. For me and my brothers it was paradise.

Accustomed in Caxton to a country life, and then rather bewilderingly constrained in suburban Cambridge, we now found ourselves with more freedom and scope to explore than we had ever known – and there was so much of interest on every side in this ideal retreat. We soon discovered that the neighbouring farm's cows were much more interesting than George's hens. Collecting eggs – albeit something of a treasure hunt at Burridge Heath – could not compare for excitement with the thrill of helping (unasked, of course) to drive the cows in for the afternoon milking. We quickly ingratiated ourselves with Leonard Wilcox, the farmer – a laconic, gumbooted countryman with a strange accent – and would accompany him out to the field, imitating as closely and loudly as we could his "Ceomon! Ceomon!" and then skipping along behind the ambling herd with our own little sticks, giving an occasional furtive thwack to the odd straggler. We would hang about the dairy during milking (Leonard growl: "Jes yew sty artsoid, then!"), leaning on the doorway, totally absorbed by the sights, sounds and smells within. Those great beasts – so much bigger to a small boy – tethered in their stalls, humphing and snorting as Mr Wilcox and his cowman, each crouched on a stool, head against flank, expertly milked them into gleaming buckets. And there was always the possibility that one of them would lash out with a hind leg, provoking the milker into equally vicious retaliation.

We made wary contact, too, with Mr Wilcox's son when he came home from school. He taught us how to play 'kit-kat' with three sticks, two long and one short, which he cut from the hedgerow with a much-envied penknife. Our best friend at Burridge Heath, though, was Charlie, the amiable, rather slow-witted youth who divided his time between the farm and helping out with Uncle George's 2,000 hens. An archetypal yokel, Charlie was the only person there (apart from Mother) who was always prepared to put up with our endless questions, attention and 'help'; and we boys were probably the only audience prepared to listen appreciatively to his ignorant pontification on any subject at all within the range of our joint experience of the world – admittedly pretty slender on both sides. And if some of his tales were 'absolute nonsense', as Mother averred, it was great fun listening to him talking about calves born with two heads, and being treated, for once, on equal terms with an adult.

The best time for conversation with Charlie (as distinct from hanging about pestering him while he worked) was when he took his lunch. Being an early riser, Charlie broke off for this ritualistic repast about an hour before our own midday meal, just as we were getting peckish ourselves. We would watch fascinated as he produced his small haversack and, sitting himself down against a straw stack, draw out a bottle of cold tea and a single round cottage loaf cut in half and filled with a large slab of cheddar cheese. Charlie was fully aware of the effect the sight of this man-sized meal had on our saliva glands, and he took a grotesque relish in its deliberate consumption, smacking his lips and telling us how good it was. But, being a good-natured lad, he would as a concession sometimes take a small piece of cheese and plant it firmly in the nearest cowpat or piece of horse dropping (he always seemed to sit down near some), offering it magnanimously to whichever of us had the nerve to take it out.

The cottage at Burridge Heath, charming as it was, with roses straggling round the door, was not really big enough for two families. Downstairs at one end was the stone-flagged kitchen, which led into a sort of living-cum-dining room, which we shared rather uneasily with Molly and George. We used it while Molly and George were out and about on their chores, and made ourselves scarce when they came in. Beyond this middle room was a sitting-room-cum-office-cum-egg store. A ladder-like staircase led straight up into a bedroom, where Hamish slept with Mother, and through which Molly and George passed to their own bedroom. David and I had mattresses on the floor of a 'room' on the other side, above the kitchen, access to which was through a doorway little bigger than a serving hatch, through which we had to crawl on our hands and knees. The ceiling of this room was less than five feet high – just enough for a child to stand up. Great! There was no bathroom, all washing being done in the kitchen. The lavatory was a malodorous pit privy in an outhouse.

George and Molly lived in this ancient country residence with seven cats and a playful collie aptly named Gyp, plus the odd chicken strolling in for temporary accommodation or looking for somewhere to lay its egg. George was a lean, muscular man with a rugged moustache and brown as a nut, every inch the Australian jackaroo that he used to be – until Molly's restlessness brought them home again. Their first venture on returning to Britain had been as a ghillie/housekeeper partnership in a Welsh fishing or shooting lodge belonging to a member of the aristocracy. My father had received an urgent communication from his brother: 'I have taken a job as ghillie. Please send me a book on Fishing.' As Molly's housekeeping skills were best described as slapdash (my parents said 'slovenly') and George's fishing skills had progressed little beyond the illegal guddling of salmon as a boy, their combined efforts did not entirely meet the standards required by Lord and Lady Whoever-it-was. However, as my uncle and aunt seem to have charmed themselves into the position in the first place – assisted by their clerical connections and George's youthful proximity to the Dee – they succeeded also in charming their way out of it without too much loss of face. Between then and starting up at Burridge Heath on the strength of a small legacy, they led – or rather, continued to lead – an avant-garde life in left-wing circles. George wrote three novels, none of which found a publisher, and sold the *Daily Worker* on the streets of London. They went to Russia, on a tour organised by the British Communist Party, just about the time Stalin was massacring kulaks in hundreds of thousands, and returned with their enthusiasm for 'The Party' undimmed. In extenuation, one must remember these were the thirties, when young men and women, fired by the Spanish Civil War and the rise of fascism, fiercely espoused left-wing causes and saw (however vainly, as we now know) their hope for Europe's future in Soviet Russia.

None of this, of course, touched us at Burridge Heath; nor, I believe, were our parents much exercised by world events. There must have been a curious contrast between their middle-class conventionality and the carefree bohemianism of Molly and George. While Father was away working at a mundane job to support his family, I have an abiding memory of Uncle George one day returning from his morning round of the henhouses carrying two pails laden with eggs that he had just collected, suddenly putting them down and, for no reason at all, pelting them at the attendant Gyp, the bitch barking and leaping about as her master, with equivalent noises and roaring with laughter, hurled egg after egg at her.

The contrast was most strongly marked between Mother and

Molly, both of them daughters of clergymen, yet wholly different in character and outlook. Molly, at that time childless, was intellectual, artistic, fluent and witty, contemptuous of much that my mother esteemed; Mother was the very embodiment of homely virtues, with a strong respect for tradition, and her interests were almost entirely devoted to her family. Her relations with Molly were friendly only through the exercise of much tact and self-restraint. Separate domestic arrangements – cooking and eating in relays, so to speak – no doubt helped. Nevertheless, Mother was appalled at the, let us say, relaxed lifestyle of her brother- and sister-in-law. She especially resented having to clear up cats' mess because Molly just didn't seem to notice, or didn't care. And the piles of dirty dishes for Mother to wash up after our meals would nearly always include George and Molly's. This was fair enough, perhaps – we were, after all, being accepted into their house with a great deal more forbearance than many another family of two would show towards a sister-in-law and three young children. But still, it was irritating to have to do these chores while Molly lay back reading a novel. Father and George, on the other hand, easily spanned the gulf between the personalities of their respective wives. I loved to see them together, loud in conversation and laughter. Both were entirely without affectation.

How long did we stay at Burridge Heath? Certainly above six months. I recall Mother teaching me reading and maths, sitting on a bench outside the cottage, among the hollyhocks, with Gyp snoozing at our feet in the sunshine; then later, after I had broken a leg falling out of a tree ('a beautiful spiral fracture', Father said), I recall David pulling me on a home-made sledge on the ice of the frozen pond, with my leg still in plaster. So I am sure we must have spanned a summer and winter.

I think it must have been while I was still convalescing that Father took me back with him to spend a few days at his mental hospital. Where it was exactly I don't think I ever knew; it seemed a long way, in another world entirely. There was a long drive up to it, through imposing wrought-iron gates to red-brick buildings. Inside there were long, cold corridors, but a warm, friendly staffroom where a bulky Irish doctor (who was later to take his own life) engaged me in mystifying conversation. It was comforting, though, that my father's colleagues seemed to know who I was, even though I had never met them before. The only contact I had with the patients was when playing ball with a porter in the garden it accidentally flew over the wall separating staff from inmates. Perhaps I had been asking questions about these people who had to be kept 'inside', and my playmate thought here was a good opportunity for an 'introduction'.

"Go on – just you ask for it back," he said, no doubt preparing himself for an interesting confrontation between Innocence and Insanity.

With some trepidation I climbed up enough to peer over. The garden on the other side was much the same as the one on ours, except that there were about twenty men and women sitting on the grass or wandering between the trees and shrubs. It all seemed pretty normal, except that these people were not congregating, but sat or walked about on their own. One old lady, as soon as my head poked over the wall, came rushing up with the ball clasped tightly in both her hands, her face wreathed in smiles.

"I've got 'im, I've got 'im," she piped up.

Although she was running towards the wall, she didn't look at me, even when I nervously asked, "May I please have my ball back?"

She went on chuckling, "I've got 'im, I've got 'im."

Then she suddenly stopped smiling and threw the ball awkwardly back over the wall, still without a glance in my direction. She just stood staring in the direction she had thrown it, as if waiting for it to come flying back over again. I felt sorry for the old woman, and the memory of that pang of childish sympathy has stayed with me. But I kept the ball.

My friend the porter told me about 'padded cells for really dangerous lunatics', conjuring visions of tormented beasts in human form, with superhuman strength and malevolent intent hurling themselves impotently at the walls of a windowless subterranean dungeon. Later my father's explanation of that shocking information removed some of my fascinated horror, and did so in a way that chimed with my own perception, gained from my encounter with 'the lady over the wall', of how things really were with the inmates of that place.

"They are poor fellows," he said. "Am I frightened? No, I just say, "Hullo, George – how are you today?"

I wished that I had thought to say "How are you today?" to the old woman. That I did not was, perhaps, an early instance of the diffidence or awkwardness prompted in me by an acute sensitivity to people and circumstance.

The last of several operations performed on Father's knee while we were still at Cambridge had involved removal of the actual joint (at least, that was how we understood it at the time). He would drive over to Burridge Heath in a little buff-coloured Morris Minor on his free days or weekends, wearing a cumbersome calliper attached to an enormous boot which we all anticipated he would have to wear for the rest of his life. For more than eighteen months he lived with that expectation, and became more or less reconciled to being 'crippled' – to use an expression that is now frowned on, but at that time was used (like 'lunatic') just as naturally as we now, more kindly but obscurely, say 'physically disabled' (or 'mentally ill'). On walks round the farm we became accustomed to Father, first with the aid of two sticks, then with one, swinging his massive iron-girt leg with ungainly but increasingly confident strides. So it was astonishing when he one day appeared on one of his brief visits *minus the calliper!* In explanation, he demonstrated by standing on one leg that the bones had indeed actually united. My brothers and I thought that the loss of the big boot was rather disappointing, but gathered from our parents' manifest delight at the transformation that a stiff leg was perhaps even better than a big boot.

5 – TANKERTON: KING'S LEIGH SCHOOL

I was now eight years old, and both David and I were in need of a wider and more systematic education than that which Mother had done her best to provide, buoyed up with the conviction that a 'good grounding' in the Scottish manner was our first essential requirement. She did her conscientious best in this respect, and indeed it seems that, stuck out in the wilds of Burridge Heath, she thought there was little alternative to home tutoring. How my parents finally decided to send me to King's Leigh School at Tankerton, in Kent, I do not know. For us it was enough that we were going to live 'at the seaside'.

Tankerton, whatever it may be now, was not then really a town; it was a sort of overflow from Whitstable, stimulated by the seaside holiday business – boarding houses, bungalows and shops selling sticks of rock and naughty postcards – creeping along the coast towards Herne Bay. It had a stretch of concrete esplanade with long metal pipes for railings, and a pebbly beach intersected at intervals by deeply embedded breakwaters, their heavy, slimy baulks encrusted with barnacles and seaweed. Further along, the shore became abbreviated by cliffs surmounted by grassy downs, where elderly holidaymakers in ones and twos braved the wind to make their ozone-seeking perambulations, and locals took their dogs for exercise.

Mother had rented a small cottage in the grounds of a larger house known as South Lodge, itself in what had once been land belonging to an ancient castle, all that remained of which being an old gateway leading into municipal gardens further along, adjoining ours. South

Lodge was a dark, square house surrounded by gloomy trees and evergreen shrubbery. It stood sentinel near two venerable wrought-iron gates waiting vainly for their next coat of paint. A short drive almost completely overhung by spindly unclipped privet and holly led up to the cottage, which was festooned by creepers – probably Russian vine – and backed on to a high wall.

Our landlord was a Dr Haygate, who had been a distinguished engineer in his time but was now about ninety years old – and did in fact die shortly after our arrival. He was looked after by two spinster daughters, who lived with him, Miss Hilda and Miss Ann.

Miss Hilda was very much in charge. She was a thin, sandy-haired, freckled woman in tweedy clothes, for ever picking at invisible flecks and pieces of fluff on her skirt, making little clicks of annoyance which we transliterated as "Toddy! Toddy!" We used to have great fun impersonating Miss Hilda, twisting ourselves into exaggerated contortions to flick away at our bottoms, or staggering about, straining to reach inaccessible parts of our anatomy, all to a strenuous accompaniment of "Toddy! Toddy! Toddy!"

Miss Ann Haygate was not quite 'all there' – at least in our opinion. We did not see much of her, and when we did she just used to giggle when addressed.

The grounds of South Lodge had something wonderful waiting to be discovered. In a far corner of the large garden, beyond a wide lawn full of plantains, daisies, dandelions and other assorted weeds, stood, like monsters from another age, two great steam engines and two enormous four-wheeled caravans, each the size of a small railway carriage. These splendid machines, all the more impressive for being seen by small boys through the long grass and briars which grew up through their wheels and superstructure, had been hand-built many years previously by Dr Haygate. They had been used by him, before the age of motor cars, to trundle his family and servants around the countryside, very much in the vanguard of modern domestic tourism. Now they stood silently rusting away in his garden. Somehow I find this a rather more comforting picture in my mind than if they were to have been carted off to a museum (as, eventually, they very likely were) and spruced up, to be goggled at by the public at large.

My first day at school was wretched. King's Leigh School was one of those privately run prep schools which, before the war, flourished or struggled in unregulated profusion, especially in that part of Kent known as the Isle of Thanet. Accommodated in one half of a large three-storeyed house (later taking in the other half) with a two-storeyed, flat-roofed extension, it was owned by a dignified old gentleman with mutton-chop whiskers, who might well have stepped out of Dickens' *Pickwick Papers* (one of his favourite books). For most of his life Mr Lincoln Taylor had been a master at Clifton College in Brighton. The headmaster of King's Leigh was his son, whom I now know to have been a well-meaning fraud, but at that time was encouraged, like all the boys there, to venerate as some kind of superman.

E. Lawrence Taylor (I can still visualise his frequently executed signature) was a tall ('six foot three', it was impressively revealed) heavily built man, rather thin on top. He prided himself not only on phenomenal physical fitness, but on being good at pretty well everything, but in retrospect I realise that his intimidating proficiency in all spheres was probably confined to sporting activity (including the driving of fast cars). It certainly did not include the normal subjects of a school curriculum.

We were to spend five years at King's Leigh. Academically, they were five almost wasted years. Inevitably, we picked up smatterings of knowledge, but the teaching was quite eccentric and haphazard. How our parents did not discover this earlier, and remove us to a school that taught its pupils properly, I can only put down to the very definite, and perhaps attractive, school ethos – and perhaps also to the charm of Mr Lincoln Taylor. Yet they did suspect the quality of the teaching. On one memorable occasion, goaded by our sycophantic praises of the headmaster, Father retorted, "It's a rubbishy school!" – a remark which Hamish took an early opportunity of passing on to other boys. Naturally, it soon reached the ears of Mr Lawrence Taylor, who, outraged at this profanity, at once phoned home for an explanation. Discovering with lightning speed latent political skills, my father did not actually deny having said it was a rubbishy school, but chided the head for taking any notice of "third-hand tittle-tattle from a child". Nevertheless, the episode somewhat wrong-footed my father, whose worries at that time were not confined to the proper education of his children.

So far as I remember, I had no preliminary interview with the headmaster; I simply found myself, that first day, abandoned in a room full of noisy children, one of whom, older than the rest, kept yelling "Keep quiet!" at the top of his voice, with absolutely no effect other than adding to the din. One or two of the boys sniffed around David and me, seated disconsolately together in one large wooden armchair.

"Are you new boys?"

We nodded cautiously.

"Hey [snigger], these two are new boys!"

I felt the same emotions of anxiety and bewilderment that had afflicted me at King's College, but help was at hand.

Panic (and the shouting) subsided when a head poked itself round the door and asked, in quite a different tone, "Are the new boys here?"

Several boys at once rushed to introduce us: "Yes, sir. Here, sir! Here they are, sir! These are the new boys, sir!"

From being objects of derision, we became suddenly individuals of consequence. There was no question, Mr Lawrence had a way with boys.

We soon discovered, however, that the power behind the headmaster was his mother. Mrs Taylor (abbreviated by the boys to 'Misst') was short and dumpy, with grey hair piled up on top of her head and secured there by a large comb. She was the art teacher, filler-in for other subjects and chief disciplinarian – and woe betide the boy to whom she took a dislike. Follow the rules and you got on well with Mrs Taylor; rebels, such as my brother David was to become, got a rough time.

The two remaining members of the family who contributed something, though not much, to the school were Mr Lawrence Taylor's brother, Frank, who taught maths – or rather, occasionally did so, since he was a chronic invalid – and his Aunt Nelly, known to us as Miss Green. Mr Frank Taylor we hardly ever saw; Miss Green we only got to know (and dislike) after we became boarders. Poor Miss Green (I am obliged in fairness to be charitable) was at least sixty years old, and looked ninety. She had a spinal curvature, so she could only look at us sideways, like an ancient bird. With her musty old-fashioned clothes and shambling gait, she looked every inch a witch. Our antipathy towards this old crone was induced not simply by her personal appearance, but also by the circumstances when we came under her care – that is to say, when we went out for 'walks', and when we were ill and she was in charge of 'the San'. The walks were the most painful. In our royal-blue blazers, and caps with a very large peak, we would trail along in an embarrassingly conspicuous crocodile, two by two, Miss Green lolloping along at the rear like a transmogrified sheepdog, and be mercilessly ridiculed by the council-school boys.

"Yah! Penguins!" they shouted as we passed.

"Take no notice, boys," said Miss Green in her quavery voice. As if we could!

That was bad enough. However, Miss Green achieved maximum prominence and almost equal unpopularity when there was some kind of 'epidemic', such as flu or a tummy bug, and a number of us boarders would be confined in a separate room and fed by her with a revolting warm bread-and-milk mush. She insisted that all windows be tightly closed or, if opened, that we put our heads under the blankets. This stifling regime could last for days, and almost certainly prolonged the period of convalescence.

All three of the active members of the family ('staff' seems an inappropriate word) had a personal passion which each in his or her own way was determined to impart to the boys of King's Leigh; and it was probably our parents' perception of this sincere objective that helped to stay their hand when their better judgement urged them to remove us from this eccentric school. Mrs Taylor taught art both systematically and well. Whole lessons would be devoted to making simple brushstrokes, which later might extend to the petals of a flower. There was no nonsense about 'self-expression'. Even the smallest boys did still-life drawing. Turner and Constable were held up as examples to venerate, and we painted innumerable sunsets and fireworks, which were then dispatched to our parents with our weekly letters home. All the boys in their various age groups were entered for the Royal College of Art exams every year, gaining innumerable certificates and the occasional bronze or silver star. These results were largely due to the inspired teaching and encouragement of Mrs Taylor.

Mr Lincoln Taylor's passionate concern was to implant in us a love – if that is not too emotive a word for us philistines – for the works of Charles Dickens, and for some of the better-known bits of Gilbert and Sullivan. He could not abide hearing boys stumbling through *The Pickwick Papers*, and therefore would read the book to us instead, to our great enjoyment. But in singing lessons, when it came to *The Mikado*, he presided at the piano and we – the whole school – did the singing. However narrow its application, the cultural emphasis of the elder Taylors was an adult one, and testified to their seriousness and dedication.

Mr Lawrence Taylor no doubt considered himself equally dedicated, but he was a lazy man who, however well he related to boys, had no real aptitude for teaching, nor, I think, much interest in it. His only qualification – apart from *his* passion, sport – was that he was the son of his parents.

At the slightest excuse for missing a French lesson (for which he, with rigid adherence to a textbook, was responsible) he would shout up the stairs, "Form Four, get on with revising your French verbs."

Of course, Form Four did nothing of the kind, since they knew very well that he would not remember (or perhaps even know) what it was they were supposed to have revised.

From time to time an assistant master would appear at the school and briefly introduce a syllabus of his own, before inexplicably giving way to somebody else, who was quite likely to teach a different subject, or ignore what we had already covered. There was Mr Edghill, whose favourite expression in class was 'blithering idiot'! He was a seasoned teacher – of what I cannot remember – from many previous schools. He sometimes took us swimming, and was himself a strong swimmer, striking out with flailing arms and such force that the whole of his body above his waist surged right out of the water. He soon enough disappeared over the horizon, however, and was, after a gap of a term or two, replaced by a Mr Hodson, who taught German – an addition to the curriculum at no extra charge. He was a pleasant young man, but we were convinced he was a spy. We must have been hot on his trail because he, too, disappeared after a couple of terms, which was the end of our German lessons. No matter. A former pupil named Frazer was introduced to teach – wait for it – carpentry! but this time as an 'extra'. There was also a very dapper ex-sergeant-major who came weekly for a term to give us PT (as PE was known then) up on the flat roof. This was the sum total of the staff in my time, apart from a matron with very little authority (Mrs Taylor called the shots) and one or two domestics.

In spite of its educational failings, I was quite happy at King's Leigh, both as a day boy and then later, after we had moved to London, as a boarder. Mr Lawrence Taylor and his parents were genuinely interested in children, and believed strongly in the development of 'character'. In some respects the headmaster was quite advanced, treating favoured boys almost as equals. At table, when not discoursing in a friendly, authoritative manner on the batting average of county cricketers, or the qualities of Bassett-Lowke model railway engines, he would relish entertaining those of us mature enough to appreciate his sense of humour, with stories caricaturing aspects of social behaviour, about which we were invited, by implication, to feel superior. He commended P. G. Wodehouse to us, and *Punch* – in particular, the cartoons of Bateman showing moronic individuals committing gross solecisms of behaviour – people who said (with a Cockney accent) things like "Ooh, it did give me a turn!" or "It broke in me 'ands, Mum" were favourite subjects of mealtime jocularity. I don't suppose this was intended to turn us into supercilious little prigs, but no doubt it went some way towards that.

A push in much the same direction was provided by the encouragement of competition between the boys for 'honour'. Honour was achieved by doing anything for a member of the Taylor family, such as "May I have the honour of filling your glass of water, sir?" or receiving a favour, such as "Would you do me the honour of signing my ruler, sir?" A boy named David Lindsell, having had the honour of cleaning the headmaster's football boots, produced a clod of dried mud, which he had taken from them, and, with self-conscious pleasure at having thought of something really original, proudly asked for the honour of having it signed – which Mr Lawrence graciously did. One almost imagined the clod (meaning the lump of mud) being thereafter placed for posterity in a glass case. Father did once expostulate, after having received one of our (censored) letters home reporting the honour Mr Lawrence did us in allowing us to clean his car.

Yet the most effective reproach was delivered by a boy who, in retrospect, I see as the only one of us who had the guts to stand up against this preposterous nonsense. This was Austin – he didn't seem to have a Christian name – who transferred to King's Leigh from the council school. That apprenticeship, and his Kent accent, marked him: he was the ugly duckling, not ostracised but treated as an outsider. (How despicable we were!) Were it not that he was a tough lad and handy with his fists, he would have fared worse than he did. One day, as we were preparing to troop off to the cricket ground (a rented field, some way off), there was the usual chorus of "May I have the honour of carrying your bat, sir?" and "May I have the honour of walking beside you, sir?" and "May I have the honour of carrying your pads, sir?" and ". . . the ball, sir?"

Austin, from the rear, piped up, "May I 'ave the honour of carrying yer top 'at, sir?"

There was a horrified silence, punctuated by suppressed sniggers.

The headmaster was thunderstruck, but managed to choke out, "That boy is in Coventry. He is a piece of furniture!"

And so he was, for the next several weeks, 'Piece of Furniture', referred to as such by staff and boys alike whenever it was necessary to mention him or (rarely, and anyway forbidden to us) actually address him. He ceased to be Austin; he was 'Piece of Furniture'. It was not a unique punishment; indeed it was a popular form of disgrace (for all except the guilty party, that is) whenever any of us offended grossly against good behaviour, and thus 'let down the honour of the school'. But never was it exercised with such sadistic and prolonged intensity as it was against the infidel Austin. It was a tribute to his sturdy character that he bore the isolation stoically, without complaint or apparent rancour. I think many of us secretly admired him, as indeed he deserved to be.

Although I can remember the names of at least fifteen of my fellow pupils (apart from my brothers), I never met any King's Leigh boy in later life. I mention some of them briefly, simply to give an idea of the friends and fellow pupils who shared our experience of this weird school over a period of some five years.

The boy who had been ineffectually yelling "Keep quiet!" on our first arrival, Alan Lindsell, left at the end of that term as head boy – more an unpaid assistant master than pupil – having set the tone for his successor, a beefy boy named Douglas Hunter, who terrified me on the rugby field with his ferocious charges. (Bear in mind it took practically the whole school to produce two fifteens, so we had six- and seven-year-olds being bowled over like ninepins by lanky adolescents as standard practice – very good for character building.) Alan Lindsell and his brother, David, were especially favoured boys, being the sons of a colonial governor in Nigeria – a piece of information extremely useful for dropping into the headmaster's conversations with prospective parents. David Lindsell was the only boarder who had a room of his own, to which he would invite a few of us to sing the latest 'hits', of which we would have been entirely ignorant but for him. There was no wireless at the school, and we certainly didn't listen to 'frivolous' music at home. So, with David Lindsell thumping out the tunes on his baby grand, teaching us the words as we went, 'Red Sails in the Sunset' and 'South of the Border' entered my repertoire.

There were several families benefiting, like us, from generous fee discounts. Three Tibbett boys, sons of a widow living in a small pebble-dash bungalow, were all exceptionally clever. Their mother scraped and sacrificed to give them a good education! Fortunately, all three – Nick (vicious bowler), John (cheerful, cheeky, round-faced), and David (a sickly intellectually brilliant boy) – were self-motivated and sometimes seemed, in their respective forms, almost to have their own private curriculum. The three Crick brothers were boarders, and we were later to join them in the ten-bed dormitory: Tim, a fat boy with asthma; Bob, a sweet-looking mischief-maker; and Jim, another invalid, very frail. The family lived on a barge on the Medway, which was very romantic – especially as they sometimes actually sailed away on cruises. We visited them once, but discovered that the idea of living on a barge was more captivating than the reality of it, tied up to a rather humdrum wharf. The Cricks more or less paralleled our own ages.

Hamish joined us while we were still day boys. He, too, had been much upset by his first-day encounter with King's Leigh, and decided after about half an hour that he had had enough, and bolted. I was sent in pursuit, to bring him back. Our house was only about 300 yards away, along the road and up a gravel lane to the gates of South Lodge, but Hamish had a lead on me. I caught up with him just as he reached his sanctuary, by which time two senior boys on bicycles had joined the chase. Family loyalty then came to the fore – this harrying of my young brother was too much. Greatly daring, I heaved the heavy gates shut, and with thumping heart braved the threats, entreaties and imprecations of the two prefects, who, fortunately for us, respected our territory. They could easily have pushed through. So the harriers were foiled and retired baffled. It was left to Mother to lead us both back. Hamish's period of liberty was brief.

My best friend, as a day boy, was John MacLean. He and I tried, mainly for the money – fourpence a week – to get ourselves accepted as choirboys at the local church, All Saints. We turned up on choir-practice evening, only to be chased off by the choirboys already there, who didn't want outsiders queering their pitch. John had an uncle in the Royal Northwest Mounted Police in Canada who sent him real RNWMP badges. Whew! An uncle in the Mounties! That was really something. We had toy pistols, belts and plastic Mountie cuffs and would take ourselves off to the countryside outside Tankerton to act out fantasies of cops and robbers. A favourite spot was a small reservoir, where we made a raft with planks and three or four empty oil drums (or perhaps it was a raft that we happened to find there) on which we floated out to the middle, blissfully ignorant of the reservoir's depth. Mother would have been horrified to find us there. We could easily have drowned.

Other friends were Skellet, the school team wicketkeeper, who had an enviably large Hornby train set, taking up the whole of one room in his parents' house; Fitt, whose father owned the local garage, and whose sister I was quite keen on in an offhand sort of way; and Bott, who had an aunt whom the headmaster was *very* keen on. Bott's aunt was responsible, indirectly, for much revision of French verbs, and did in fact eventually become Mrs E. Lawrence Taylor, by which time our parents had moved to London.

Having been introduced as day boys, boarding was not the wrench it might otherwise have been. The school had a family atmosphere (and how!) and the food was not too bad; apart from the inevitable loss of freedom, David and I adjusted to the change reasonably well, though Hamish was often homesick and never really came to terms with boarding. Our free time, especially in the evenings, was very likely more productively employed than it would have been at home. One particular reflection strikes me on looking back: there was always something to do, and nothing we did was done *casually*. Whether it was making model aeroplanes, playing billiards (on a miniature table), ping-pong, draughts, chess, whist, pontoon, rummy (for matchsticks) or shove-halfpenny – let alone games practice and school-organised recreation – we did it with enthusiasm and passion. I never knew what it was to be bored.

6 – PLASHET ROAD

It has always been a mystery to me why, when he decided to go back into general practice, my father should have chosen the East End of London. In those days medical practices were bought and sold, with patients, house and surgery included in the deal. It may well be, therefore, that it was a simple matter of cost, and that Father settled on Plashet Road because it was available at a price he could afford. Yet I feel there may have been more to it than a tight budget, and that, disillusioned with the way his career had so disappointed his hopes, he may even have made a deliberate decision to isolate himself from people whose background was similar to his own. Here he was, more than fifteen years after having qualified, and he had not yet become properly established. In any event, my parents had apparently agreed that a return to the country would have been too strenuous, and that it had to be a town practice. No doubt the location of our school (from which we could nevertheless have been profitably withdrawn to another) had some influence on the decision. But Father alone scouted out the possibilities, decided on Plashet Road, and – I am sure with Mother's compliance – concluded the negotiations.

Arrangements were made to terminate the lease of South Lodge Cottage and to put us into King's Leigh as boarders. Our furniture, which had been in store since our departure from Cambridge, was removed and transported to the new home. When all of this had been completed, and we boys were safely in the care of Mrs Taylor, Father drove down to Tankerton in a brand-new Austin Ten (CMF 904) and conveyed Mother and the remainder of our possessions to London. That was the first she saw of 49 Plashet Road – and she hated it.

Plashet Road was part of the tram route between Stratford East and the two Hams (West and East). No. 49, known as Dacre Lodge, was the largest among a collection of houses which comprised the local shopping area (in days when there were no supermarkets, remember, and most shops had to be within walking distance). On the left-hand side of quite an imposing porch supported by two pillars, about five yards back from the road, behind stubby iron railings, were the bow windows of what was to be our sitting room, and my parents' bedroom above. On the other side, to the right, with its own separate door, was the surgery; and to the right of that, high green-painted wooden gates to a narrow driveway leading past the house to the garage. It was not so much the house which dismayed Mother, but the neighbourhood: the grinding and clanging of trams; the butcher's shop next door, with great carcasses of meat hanging in the window; the dog-fouled pavement; the pub opposite, and its huddle of depressed-looking men waiting for opening time; and the smell of the dust, soot and grime that were to be Mother's enemies for the next twenty-five years. She made her tour of the house with a sinking heart.

Through the entrance hall, to the left, past the sitting room, was the dining room, with French windows leading down some steps to about thirty yards of garden, mostly lawn. Beyond the hall a short passage led into the kitchen, a scullery and pantry (there were no fridges then), with the back door on to the driveway. Upstairs, a bathroom and five bedrooms led off the main landing. The garage had originally been built for a coach and horses; what had been a hay loft above it was now a sort of outdoor box room (which my brothers and I were to make good use of as our 'headquarters').

The surgery side of the house comprised a little vestibule with a 'pinging' doorbell (to let the Doctor know when somebody had come in), a waiting room, a consulting room and a small dispensary – all very neat and practical (purpose-built, in fact) for a doctor and his family. Mother, I feel sure, struggled to see the best of it; but unfortunately her resolution was undermined by the discovery that, while she and my father were touring the house, thieves had made off with two large trunks (containing many of the family valuables) that had been strapped to the back of the car. My parents emerged to find an empty boot, the leather straps slashed with a knife. As Mother told us, much later in our lives, that was the last straw. Retiring to the house with its bare-walled rooms and furniture placed as it had been left by the removal men, she sat down on a packing case and wept.

"What sort of place have you brought me to, Sam?"

What sort of place was it? Upton Park, in the County Borough of West Ham, was the historic name for an area which stretched from the Municipal Park (so named) at the Stratford end of Plashet Road to where Plashet Road met Green Street at the other end, and then along Green Street in the direction of the docks as far as the Barking Road – roughly one and a half miles from one side to the other. About the only bit of Upton Park that anybody who doesn't live there knows about is the West Ham United football ground, at the Barking end of Green Street. We were on the other, 'quiet' side of Upton Park. The Green Street side was lined with shops all the way along. That was where the banks were, Marks & Spencers, Woolworth's (the 'Sixpenny Store', as it was known – nothing cost more than sixpence), a dingy cinema (where I saw *Snow White and the Seven Dwarfs* twice through at a sitting) and, next to a busy street market, Upton Park Underground Station on the District Line, which we always used when going 'up to town'.

Some of our neighbours said we lived in Forest Gate (Epping Forest), but, properly speaking, Forest Gate was half a mile north of us; and anyway, the forest had long since retreated over the Wanstead Flats towards Woodford. Yet my father had patients who remembered the time when Upton Park was countryside – really a park (or demesne, perhaps) – and not merely the civic garden that we knew under the jurisdiction of West Ham Borough Council. In our immediate area the names of the roads – Selwyn, Cecil, Dacre, Stopford, Neville, Boleyn – recalled the not so distant feudal ownership of the land.

Unlike East London boroughs, such as Bethnal Green, Stepney or Poplar, Upton Park had no traditions of urban manufacturing or trade going back through the ages. The rows of identical houses had been built mostly after the end of the nineteenth century. Yet it would be inaccurate to describe our area as little more than London sprawl. These, to an outsider, boringly indistinguishable grey streets with their tiny front gardens and ochre-brick, two-storeyed side-by-side houses with back-to-back gardens more than just dockland dormitories and homes of the working class. Yes, some of those front 'gardens' were little more than rubbish traps, perhaps with an unclipped privet hedge, or just a single large dusty hydrangea (which, miraculously surviving neglect, might bloom valiantly nevertheless every summer). But the back gardens, hidden from view – except from your own back windows – reflected everything of the individuality and diversity of the East Enders among whom we had come to live. Washing lines were prominent, of course (so was ours on Mondays).

On the sunny side of the dividing fences some people grew vegetables. You would see an occasional greenhouse, rabbit hutches, a dog kennel, a dilapidated garden shed with a splendid rose bush rambling over half of it and the neighbour's fence, and an apple or cherry tree taking up too much space, but occasionally rewarding its owner with a bounteous crop. We had expert growers of chrysanthemums, wizards of French-bean cultivation, trainers of greyhounds, pigeon fanciers and racing cyclists, all of whom used the precious space behind their houses in an interesting variety of ways (not always pleasing to the eye) which belied the monotonous uniformity of their main-road frontage.

Many of the people living round there were second- or even third-generation residents. Old Mr Speed, who used to be a tram driver and who helped out in our garden from time to time, lived in one of the original almshouses, beyond Fred Pratt, the butcher. The almshouses, a row of about six squat cottages, alone of all the houses in Plashet Road, stood well back from it; and their variously cultivated, allotment-like gardens were a charming if sad reminder of what the process of urbanisation had overtaken or surrounded. They were a little oasis.

Next to us, on the other side of our narrow driveway (which Father reversed up so skilfully), were the Scotts, and daughter Molly, a roly-poly girl with whom we were alternately friendly or scornfully indifferent (on both sides). Mr Scott, a very dignified white-moustached former merchant-navy officer, had the ironmonger's shop and – in the tradition of *Open All Hours* – every morning would lay out on the pavement his piles of buckets, flue brushes, bundles of bamboo canes, packets of coal briquettes, kindling, etc.; and every evening he would bring it all back in again. Next door but one (George Wilson's tiny sweet shop was in between) the greengrocer did the same with his fruit and vegetables. Alf Bevan, or his brother Albert – who vended some of this produce along the back streets from a pony and cart – would go off at five in the morning to Covent Garden for their supplies. I was often sent to Alf's by Mother, with a large carrier bag, for 'a shilling's worth [five pence] of potatoes'. For that we would get about five pounds – enough to fill the bag, anyway. The purchase of meat and fish was always done by Father, partly because he insisted on getting the best of everything, and partly because he succeeded in getting it.

If the Sunday joint was considered to be 'from an old beast' (our meals were always appreciatively discussed, never taken for granted), Father would have no hesitation in saying to Fred Pratt, "That was a terrible piece of meat you gave us, Fred."

To this Fred would likely reply that it was the best bit of sirloin in the shop, "cut special for you, Doc".

We all had our chores when we were at home. Helping with the washing-up – with rivalry to wash up, dry or put away – was a regular obligation (frequently avoided by David, having to go 'urgently' to the lav). Shoe-cleaning, weeding and washing and polishing the car, as well as running messages to Forest Gate or Green Street for shopping that could not be done locally, were all duties that we accepted as being unavoidable (except by guile, which didn't always work). There was never any question of protest or complaint.

As there were three of us, we did not lack company, although the times when all three were in harmony were fairly infrequent. Hamish, only two years younger than David, was still very much 'the youngest'; and David was more inclined than either of his brothers to seek companionship outside the family. He was friendlier with Frank Bevan, Alf's son, than I was; also with Con Collins, son of the publican who leased the big Charrington's pub across the road. So he tended to learn the ways of the world and bad language quicker than the rest of us. There was a railed-off area with cobblestones where the beer-keg wagons drawn by heavy shire horses were offloaded, and the barrels manhandled on to a chute down into the pub cellars. There we, but especially David, would use the rails for acrobatic somersaults, along with any other of the street kids who happened to be around. Mother did not like us playing in the street, and we were constantly encouraged or instructed to go to the park. Getting roller skates added to the park's attractions: its asphalt paths were beautifully smooth, although we had to dodge the bowler-hatted park keepers, with their admonitory whistles, on the garden paths where rollerskating was forbidden. (Pedestrians had to dodge *us*.)

The routine of our life at Plashet Road revolved around Father's work: he held a surgery in the morning from nine till eleven. At nine precisely, Mother would open the surgery door, placing an old smoothing iron against it to prevent it closing. Sometimes there would be a little queue waiting outside; but however early patients might arrive, the door was never opened before time. From then on we all had to be very quiet. Indeed, the only loud voice that could be heard was Father's booming "Come!" followed by the burble of the next consultation, in which my father's side was often clearly audible: "Are your bowels open?" or "Say 'Ah'!" or How on earth did you manage to do that?"

Then, when the last patient had been seen, Father would emerge for a cup of tea and a cigarette before going off on his rounds.

All our meals were taken en famille, and we would wait for Father to return before sitting down to lunch, though he would do his best to be in on time. What was left of the afternoon after he had completed his rounds, until teatime, was sacrosanct to 'resting': Mother, who would often be completely exhausted by then, usually went upstairs; Father would read a book in his armchair in the sitting room, periodically nodding off, picking up his book with a start and nodding off again. After tea, before the evening surgery, there was the dispensing of medicines to be done. This was before the National Health Service, and half the patients came privately. Prescriptions were written for the 'Panel' patients, but for the remainder Father made up the prescribed medication himself. His dispensary was like a small apothecary's shop, with bottles of every size and shape arrayed on shelves against the wall. The firm of Allen & Hanbury was as familiar to us as is Boot's to the average family today. A boy named Charlie delivered the pills, ointments and medicines, all neatly wrapped in white paper and sealed with red wax – itself a time-consuming task, which Father performed for each package. Up to ten or so were wrapped daily – meticulously.

Although we did have a maid, Ivy, who lived in, housework – especially for a perfectionist such as Mother – was unremitting. Clean-air Acts have since then immensely improved the quality of London's atmosphere; but in the thirties, when all heating was by unimproved coal fires, and factory chimneys belched out filth and noxious fumes, dust and soot descended like a suffocating blanket, leaving a grey powdery film over everything, even inside the house with the windows closed (Father, with his passion for fresh air, did not help much in that respect). Every piece of furniture, every window sill, ledge, mantelpiece and exposed ornament had to be dusted every day; floors and staircase were swept throughout, and carpets were gone over with a sweeper (no Hoover then) in every room. Grates had to be cleaned out, coal and coke brought up from the cellar, fires set or rekindled. All washing was done by hand – I cannot recall a washing machine in all the time we were at Plashet Road. Mother's first electric iron was a topic of conversation for days. Added to all the cleaning, washing and polishing were the mending of shirts and darning of socks (which thrift and custom imposed on most wives then); all the cooking, baking and food preserving; plus, for good measure, the de facto duties of a receptionist. It is no wonder our mother was drained.

Although Father had no partner, and therefore had the whole responsibility of his practice twenty-four hours a day, seven days a week, he belonged to a panel of six doctors who took it in turns to do duty for the others on Sundays and Thursday afternoons (when there was no surgery). On these free days, when the weather was fine, we would drive out to Epping Forest for a picnic; and these expeditions to the country (which our parents continued to make while we were at school) became an established outing that we all looked forward to – and especially to the possibility that we might come across one of the peak-capped Eldorado or Wall's ice-cream sellers pushing a little icebox cart on their three-wheeled bicycle. Sometimes the weekly trip to the country was extended to include a visit to a farm near Waltham Abbey to buy really fresh eggs and, in season, large quantities of tomatoes or strawberries.

The Essex roads were relatively free of cars – hardly anybody in our area had one. Our ability to escape the noise and dirt of London, to breathe what we thought of as the fresh air of the countryside, and to bring back in triumph fresh produce from the farm, was a privilege – a luxury that few of our neighbours could enjoy. Hop picking in Kent was the nearest to seeing the country that some of them got. The present A104, skirting Loughton (where we were to go to school) to Epping, at weekends had more cyclists on it than cars. If we found more than three where we parked ours we thought the place crowded. In the forest we could even lose ourselves, and sometimes did.

Much as my brothers and I enjoyed these outings, for our parents they were almost a necessity – a periodic release from a treadmill of urban life that we for the most part did not have to share. Being away at school, we were never fully integrated into the Plashet Road community. It was like a foreign posting: we lived there, but did not belong. Only Father, in his professional capacity, was really at home. He had the good fortune to be able to combine the conduct of his practice with wide social acquaintance; his life in that respect was complete. Many of his patients were his friends, of whom he was genuinely fond, and they of him; but he did not seek friends of his own standing, and, apart from my mother and his brother George, there was nobody with whom he had a close personal relationship. He had no hobbies or recreations – apart from fishing in Scotland – but he loved the country and the open air.

However, the Plashet Road that we boys were escaping from was not, for me at least, simply the physical place where we lived; it was also the family atmosphere I associated with it, or, to be specific, the contrast between Mother's controlled loathing of her environment and Father's apparent contentment. Even as a boy of ten or eleven, while I was still at King's Leigh, I sensed the dichotomy between their deep affection for each other and the unshared fulfilment of Father's life. He had evidently succeeded in coming to terms not only with having to scale down his career ambitions, but also with living and working where he now was. But circumstances were now about to change all our lives in a way that cut through everything.

It did not happen all at once. First I was to be put through the hoops again. Ever aiming at the best, Father put me in for a scholarship at Westminster School. Mr Lawrence Taylor was duly warned, and for a few fraught weeks I was given special attention and some extra tuition in a vain attempt to make good five years of almost totally inadequate teaching. My recollection of the scholarship examination is similar to my King's College experience: brought along by Mother, and left with a large number of boys about my own age, chattering and larking about as if this were just a normal school break. How was it that only I was new and nervous with apprehension? I probably wasn't the only one, but that is how I felt. There were several papers the details of which are mercifully obliterated from my memory, except that I resourcefully dealt with the Latin paper (which was quite incomprehensible) by writing in the few words that I knew and putting dashes for those I didn't. Thus, for example, *Timeo Danaos et dona ferentes* I would translate as '---- ---- and ---- ----'. At the end, there was an interview, this time with the headmaster – again, gowned and kind (how I learned to mistrust headmasterly benignity!). Mother told me later that they had been unable to judge from my papers what I knew. I assume that was a kind way of saying they knew what I did *not* know.

It was probably then that the magnitude of our educational incompetence came fully home to our parents. They began scouting about for another school – not just for me, but for all three of us. The possibility of our going to the council school 100 yards along the road I am sure did not enter their minds, and it is intriguing to wonder how things might have turned out had they so decided. But middle-class prejudice, and the undoubted disparity in educational opportunities between state and most reasonably adequate private schools in England before the war, led them to choose Loughton School, in Essex, about eight miles away. As we were now to be day boys again, this involved a tram ride to Stratford Station, and then a slow, stopping train to Loughton.

Loughton was pleasantly situated, out beyond the London suburbs, below Buckhurst Hill and within easy reach of Epping Forest. The town's coat of arms (and our school's, too) was a notched lopping axe. Loughton School was a private boys' school with about 140 day boys and a handful of boarders. The owner and headmaster was O. G. Johnson, MA (known to the boys as Oggy), a thoroughly professional teacher, but his general demeanour conveyed the impression that he regarded most of his pupils with distaste if not actual repugnance. This probably did him an injustice: I believe he was a more humane and understanding man than we gave him credit for. But he was totally lacking in a sense of humour; and that put him at a disadvantage which he possibly recognised and was alert to counteract, either through a stifling exercise of authority, or through occasional laboured attempts at his own idea of humour, followed by guffaws in his highly imitable (and often imitated) laugh – "Warf! Warf! Warf!" – in which nobody else joined.

From the first, I was struck by the professionalism of Loughton: this was a proper school. In contrast with the homely informality of King's Leigh, the Loughton School morning assembly was most impressive, remarkable for the complete silence in which the main school classes, led by the form master of each, filed into the hall. We then waited, still without a sound (other than a desk creak, cough or sniffle), for the headmaster to make his entrance. The interval of silence might last three or four minutes before Oggy strode in, Bible in hand, gown flowing, thin nose twitching, as if his neat military moustache had been impregnated with something mysteriously malodorous. With a great clatter of seats the sixth form and remove (who shared the hall, divided normally by a folding door screen) stood up; the little boys of the first and second forms, who were seated on the floor in front, struggled to their feet; and the third, fourth and fifth, standing at the rear, stopped nudging and pushing each other. Oggy took his place at a lectern and announced the hymn that always preceded prayers. Flanking him on the platform, the masters, similarly gowned, looked untypically relaxed, not yet braced for the rigours of the day.

There was 'Boris' Bone (sixth form), science and maths, florid face, fierce bark, small bite; 'Pat' Kane (fifth form), geography and English literature, a good-natured, humorous Irishman, passionately interested in the latter subject but mostly convinced he was casting pearls before swine; 'Toofy' Morrow (fourth form), Latin and English, like a bird of prey with pince-nez and buck teeth, the finest teacher of them all, feared by sluggards but venerated by older boys who came to know him for what he was – a kind-hearted man who genuinely loved boys who were prepared to work, but who gave short shrift to those who were not; 'Jumbo' Jennings (remove), French, whose bellowing attempts at keeping order and trumpeted admonitions were equally unavailing – as, indeed, were his attempts at teaching us French, until the proximity of exams compelled more serious attention.

It was ironic that poor Jumbo was in charge of probably the most obstreperous class in the school. I myself was in the remove (a name redolent, for me, of the Frank Richards stories about Greyfriars School, Billy Bunter, Harry Wharton, Bob Cherry et al.). I do not remember much about the junior form masters, apart from tubby little 'Moses' Mossley (first form), who played the harmonium, but who in most other respects was not taken seriously by anyone outside his class of infants. He made up for this by having an outsized ego, displayed to comical effect whenever he was asked to play the piano at a school concert: he would refuse to start playing until there was absolutely dead silence – which could take some time to achieve – during which Moses worked himself into a towering rage of indignation, which he took out on the unoffending piano. Oggy himself taught history in a manner that induced the most suffocating boredom, but at least he was conscientious and sufficiently feared to keep us up to the mark.

This somewhat light-hearted introduction to our new school does not, however, accurately reflect my first weeks at Loughton, which were anything but carefree. I was a serious pupil, fond of reading to a fault, and anxious to get things right. Unfortunately, King's Leigh's relaxed standard of tuition (if it can be called tuition) had cocooned me in a false sense of security. Mr Lawrence Taylor's reports had always been glowingly optimistic: 'Alan has made great strides this term with his [what shall I put this time?] . . . French. He now has a good mastery of the Irregular Verbs. He did well, too, in the match against St. Cuthbert's, but he *must* learn to keep his elbow up when playing forward.' The Westminster exam had been a shock which not only banished any complacency I may have felt, but it also severely weakened my self-confidence. Sometimes during that first term at Loughton (which I believe we entered halfway through) sheer bafflement and incomprehension reduced me to silent weeping at my desk. Nor did it help much when, on receiving our first end-of-term reports, Father became, untypically, furious at the dismal results, and upraided David and me for our 'backwardness'.

"Look at this! *Fifteenth* in geography!"

"But there were two boys lower than me, Father."

"It doesn't matter who came bottom – you should be *top*!"

It was most unfair, and no doubt part of my father's anger was really against himself for not having arranged our early education better.

7 – ARDRISHAIG

I did not hear Neville Chamberlain's broadcast, four days after my thirteenth birthday, in which he said, "How horrible, fantastic, incredible it is that we should be digging trenches and trying on gas masks here because of a quarrel in a faraway country between people of whom we know nothing. . . ." Had I done so I would certainly have agreed with him that trying on gas masks was 'fantastic', but not that it was horrible, nor incredible, because we actually had been fitted out with gas masks (a choice of large, medium, or small) and had much enjoyed making rude noises with them at each other. After that first try-on, Mother had packed them away in their little cardboard boxes (with a string to hang them over your shoulder), ready if there really was going to be a war. The exercise which filled Mr Chamberlain, and most thinking adults, with horror was, for me, in the same category of experience as the thrill of suspecting Mr Hodson of being a German spy – part of a boy's fantasy world.

We were on our summer holidays when fantasy turned to reality. It all seemed to happen very quickly. One day, impelled by our parents' evident preoccupation with the news, we were grouped round our little wooden wireless in the Plashet Road sitting room, Father as usual in his armchair beside it, Mother on the other side of the fireplace in hers, darning socks probably (sitting down in the morning for anything other than the eleven-o'clock cup of tea would have been unnatural for her without a useful reason for it), listening to the dry tones of the Prime Minister's announcement that no response had been received from "Herr Hitler" to the British ultimatum (to withdraw his troops from Poland) and that consequently we were now "in a state of war with Germany".

I remember feeling a tingle of excitement. War! Did that mean London was going to be bombed? Clearly our parents thought so: they had made plans in advance to remove us from danger if war did break out. Winston Churchill's war memoirs record that Mr Chamberlain 'had scarcely ceased speaking when a strange, prolonged wailing noise . . . broke upon the ear'. I do not myself remember that. But it was the very next morning that we did have our first experience of an air raid – and by then we had already been evacuated!

I woke at early dawn to see a low-beamed ceiling above my head, and daylight coming through an unusually small window. A shrill, persistent noise reached me, emanating from beyond a wide lawn surrounded by vaguely familiar trees. Where were we? What was that noise?

"Quickly! Quickly! Get up. It's an air raid!"

With thumping heart I clambered out of bed, and we hurried downstairs in our pyjamas, shepherded by two old ladies in frilly dressing gowns. My life seemed to have gone suddenly into rewind, and then, just as abruptly, into fast forward. From our cosily familiar, undemanding seaside boarding-school routine, we had been translated unexpectedly, via a dreary part of London (our new home) and a new school in Essex, back to rural Cambridgeshire – en route, it transpired, to Scotland.

But it was not yet Scotland, that September morning in 1939, hearing the ARP warden vigorously blowing his whistle as he bicycled past the gate at the end of Miss Banton's rectory garden. Within twenty-four hours we had been bundled off to Kingston, near Cambridge, only a few miles from our original home at Caxton. The Reverend Peake Banton and his two elderly sisters, as patients and friends of Father's, had been part of the background to our golden early life. David and I had often been taken with him by Father when visiting in that direction. The Bantons had a lovely old walled kitchen garden behind the house, and it had always been a great treat to be taken in to see what nice things there might be to eat – raspberries, strawberries, ripe gooseberries, loganberries or perhaps, rather disappointingly, a tomato or carrot.

Both Miss Bantons played the violin, and their brother, I believe, the clarinet. Mother (who was also a student of the violin) used to join them on the piano; and Father, who had little appreciation of music, was persuaded to join them on the drums. As he never did anything by halves, he bought a complete set of them – side drum, big foot-drum, cymbals, the lot. (They too followed us to Plashet Road, where, except for fooling about by us, they remained in a cupboard or the 'hay loft' – unused relics of happier days.) I never heard this little quintet perform, but apparently they were good enough – or bold enough – to give concerts at various local functions.

Whether the all-clear sounded or we got tired of waiting for the bombs to fall, I can't remember. (The warning, throughout Britain, had been set off by a single German reconnaissance plane flying at high altitude over the Kent coast.) Indeed, the only other concrete fact that I recall from this brief revisiting of our childhood scene is the enormous dish of small boiled onions that we had, with white sauce, as an important component of lunch one day. Their memorably laxative effect caused all of us to spend more time than might otherwise have been necessary in the rectory's interesting triple-seated pit privy.

Mother, having left us temporarily at Kingston Rectory, went back to Plashet Road to pack and make arrangements for our journey north. She then returned and accompanied us up to Scotland, where we were to stay with her sister, our Aunt Sis, in Ardrishaig. To this day I recall the feeling of inexplicable depression I experienced on the train from Glasgow to Gourock, before taking the steamer round the Kyles of Bute into Loch Fyne. No doubt it had something to do with our sudden displacement (Mother's return ticket; ours one-way only); or our view through a grubby carriage window of the grey, wet tenement buildings of the Glasgow suburbs, past which the train was slowly clanking and grinding; or the recent brief reminder of what our life had been, before schools, uncertainty and war broke everything up. Perhaps I was just tired after a long journey.

Aunt Sis was a large, capable woman of intimidating personality.

A great talker (in the manner of many Scotswomen) and generally of cheerful disposition, she was nevertheless none too pleased to have three young nephews landed upon her, more or less 'for the duration'. I understand that Mother gave her one pound ten shillings a week (fifty pence each) for our maintenance. While this apparently modest contribution reflects the decline in money value since then, it also denoted Mother's firm belief that she and her children had just as much right to living space at Calman, her father's house, as did Aunt Sis and her daughter, Isha. Calman, a good-sized grey stone house, had been left by my grandfather Smith as a home 'for any member of the family who needed it' – a somewhat ambivalent legacy, having regard to the wife and six adult children he left behind him.

In practice, after my grandmother Smith's death, shortly before the war (a much respected matriarch, she was blind and an invalid for most of the time I knew her, on our periodic visits up north) it was understood that legal title was in the name of the youngest son, Duncan – known to us as Uncle Will. Although then living unmarried in Edinburgh, where he worked as a dental mechanic, he had been born deaf and, with a cleft palate, had additional speaking difficulty. The remaining two sons and three daughters were all married, with the exception of the middle daughter, Isobel, who was a physiotherapist (known then, innocently, as a masseuse) in Trumpington, just outside Cambridge. My uncles John and Alasdair were both doctors in Birmingham. Unfortunately, Aunt Sis's husband deserted her and their infant daughter shortly after her birth, and went off to Australia, where he died many years later. Isha probably never knew her father.

Anyway, the result of all this was that Aunt Sis and Isha took up residence with Granny at Calman. The arrangement apparently suited everybody: Sis had a house when she needed one, Granny had someone to look after her in her declining years, and Will had a place to come and spend his holidays, and he would ultimately retire there. Until our arrival, none of the other members of the family had laid any claim to shelter at Calman, and, after Granny died, Sis had come to regard the home – naturally enough, I suppose – as hers.

If you look at a map of the Kintyre Peninsula you will see that the Crinan Canal runs parallel with the shore of Loch Gilp in a northerly direction from Ardrishaig, until it veers west, across the neck of the peninsula, to Crinan and the Sound of Jura on the other side. Calman, which is actually midway between Ardrishaig and Lochgilphead (a distance of three miles), is therefore boxed in, so to speak, by the loch and its coastal road in front, and the canal behind. In fact, the elevation of the canal at the point it passed the house was such that we could see the masts and funnel of the puffers (small coal boats) glide past our garden at the level of the chimney pots. The garden, sloping away from the canal, down towards the loch, was about half an acre, part rough orchard, part lawn and flower beds (our job to weed); and on the other side of the house was a wide drive, some neglected trees and shrubs, and a good kitchen garden. A gate at the rear led to a flight of steps up the canal bank and on to the towpath. Along it the stately progress of a single horse, pulling against sixty yards of taut rope and its inertly attendant barge, was for us an everyday sight. A man in a rough blue jersey would be idly cradling the tiller as the long, low, dirty hulk moved silently along at walking pace, hardly rippling the water. As small children we were forbidden to go unattended on to the canal bank. Dark tales were told of people drowning, sometimes from suicide, so the Crinan Canal still has, for me, sinister connotations. No matter how many times we took the towpath to Ardrishaig or Lochgilphead, in preference to the road, its lifeless green-brown water and steep stone edge flanking unknown depths were always incongruously menacing in that lovely countryside.

Once Mother had settled us in and returned to London we soon became fully at home with Aunt Sis as maternal substitute. Having Isha already at Lochgilphead Higher Grade School helped when David and I were also enrolled there (Hamish went to the primary school next door to it). Partly for that reason, and partly owing to the nature of state education in Scotland (which is much more the norm there than it is in England), I experienced none of the trauma suffered on starting (or false-starting) at my previous schools. The Scottish way of doing things was somehow reassuring, ordered and understandably *basic*. And school life linked seamlessly with life at home in a way it never had before. I was happier (and perhaps learned more) at Lochgilphead Higher Grade School than in any other school I had attended.

All children who lived too far away to go home for lunch (as we did) had to bring a 'piece' with them to school: a sandwich consisting of two thick slices of white, floury bread, with egg, cheese, sardines, or sometimes dates. It was not very much, but enough to keep us going until we got home in the afternoon. The school bus picked us up at the end of the drive on its way from Ardrishaig, which had only a primary school. There was something about this rattly old bus stopping outside our house and Aunt Sis's home-made sandwich to be eaten in the midday break which was oddly comforting. Our school here was not a faraway place, another world from life at home calling for constant adjustment and readjustment as we shifted from one to the other. It was, if you will pardon the pun, all of a piece.

I was placed in Class Three, under Miss Speed, a thin middle-aged lady with large spectacles and a pleasantly smiling expression, who nevertheless brooked no nonsense. Hers was the only classroom in 'theatre' style, with the desks raked up in steps – which made throwing pellets from the rear down on to target necks below much easier. Unfortunately, it made the detection of such horseplay easier, too. Miss Speed's subjects were geography and history – Scottish history, naturally. All pupils were issued with a slim blue 'Dates' book, in which the year of each event, starting with the landing of St Columba in Iona (563) and progressing relentlessly year by year, via the birth of Robert the Bruce (1274) and the Act of Union (1707) to the Battle of Culloden (1746), was throughout each term duly recorded, set for committing to memory, revised, retested and, in short, hammered into us until even the dullest pupil could reel off great wodges of 'history' in accurate sequence. Needless to say I can recollect virtually none of this now. However, as I am confident that every bit of conscientiously absorbed information, every experience and tiny perception is duly logged by the brain and tucked away for life – even if apparently forgotten – I am sure this rigorously documented panorama was immensely valuable. I may now have only the vaguest notion of what the Battle of Bannockburn (1314) was all about, who Bothwell (1535–78) was, or where exactly

William Wallace (?–1305) came in, but my idea of Scotland, my feelings about it, and where I fit in myself are compounded of a lot more than simply personal experience. Miss Speed and her 'Dates' book gave depth to it, and so made a little notch in the pattern of my own identity.

The system was for each teacher to have his or her own classroom, access to which was from the central hall of the school; so instead of teachers changing places as the subjects changed in the timetable, the whole class moved bodily out on the clanging of a 'period' bell. The noise and exuberance as five or six classes simultaneously decamped and criss-crossed the hall to their respective destination classrooms can be imagined, with 'accidental' bumping, pushing and barging being the accepted means of progress across the floor. Only occasionally might this anarchic transmigration be brought to order by a whiplash voice cutting through the din: "You! What's yer name? Yes, YOU! Come here, boy!" And there would be Jimmy Stewart, the headmaster, standing outside his office, a large, heavy man in a brown suit, transfixing some unfortunate lad with a menacing stare through his small gold-rimmed spectacles; and crooking a slow, beckoning forefinger, he would 'invite' the wretch to draw closer.

Jimmy Stewart inspired fear, and with reason. All the teachers had recourse to the strap and used it in class quite frequently: a delinquent boy or girl – but usually a boy – would be called up to the front, made to cross his hands one above the other, palms upward, and then walloped. Kind-hearted teachers, such as Mr Mitchell, might connive at a jersey pulled down over the palm, but there was no question of that with Jimmy Stewart. "Pull your sleeve up, boy! Pull it UP!" And he would bring the strap down with all his force. I have seen a boy with weals right up the inside of his forearm, his wrist and fingers swollen after such exemplary punishment.

During the weekends and the holiday periods, when we had been released from chores such as sweeping out the 'garage' (Aunt Sis had no car), chopping sticks for the fire, weeding (groan), getting in the coal, or perhaps gutting fish or plucking a hen, the seaside was our playground. Loch Gilp is a shallow loch, about half a mile across from one side to the other; and when the tide goes out, almost the whole of the loch – nearly as far as Ardrishaig – becomes sandy mudflats. Unsalubrious as it certainly was, with Calman's sewer dribbling or intermittently gushing some pretty disgusting effluent on to the large stones and boulders high up the beach below the road, this was our territory. We knew every rock and low-tide pool, and eagerly scoured the shore to see whatever may have been left there by the latest tide. Each new piece of jetsam was inspected – a shattered wooden crate with significant lettering stencilled on one side such as 'AGILE' or 'S WAY UP', a length of old rope or a rusty tin can – to see what use it might be put to in our games of 'shipwreck' or 'pirate's lair'. The pervading smell of decayed seaweed and feculence was no deterrent, and anyway you only really noticed it when the wind wasn't blowing off the loch; and it usually was. Chipping away at a shaley slab of rock with a stone and rusty nail, I could lose myself in the laborious construction of miniature roads that twisted through miniature mountains, valleys and plains.

At low tide, barefooted and keeping a sharp lookout for razor shells and jellyfish, we would range far out, following the receding waters, or keep pace back with their returning swirls, totally free under the sky in the wide, wet domain between 'our' shore and the other side. With only ourselves for company (rarely Isha), we three brothers took to the expanse of rippled muddy sand, with its shallow pools and mucilaginous seaweeds that splashed, popped and slithered as we ran over them, shouting as if in our native element. The water was always freezing, even in summer, when we dared each other to leap straight in from a rock at high tide (walking into waves of shallow water excruciatingly prolonged the agony!). We did it and, recklessly immersed, would gasp out, "It's *freezing*!" or, with perhaps less conviction, "It's *lovely*!" (There was nothing in between.) After thrashing about for a few minutes we would climb out, blue with cold and teeth chattering.

Aunt Sis did not appear to worry about the possibility of one of us drowning – or it may be that her warnings not to go out too far went unheeded. The only really dangerous place was near the canal 'overflow', about 200 yards along from Calman. This large duct, about two and a half feet in diameter, operated on the same principle as an automatic flush: when the level of water in the canal got too high, a release mechanism caused a huge jet of water to gush through this duct, under the road and out on to the shore, with tremendous force, shooting out with a great thumping, swooshing noise. An ancient notice and sagging strands of barbed wire festooned with seaweed and other unpleasant detritus warned against getting too near. We treated the overflow with respect, but became quite expert, by listening to the rumblings and splashings in the control house below the bank, at predicting when this monster was going to belch forth.

In spite of our English accents we were not teased or ragged at school, and gradually made friends. My own popularity received a boost after a fight I got into with a boy named Victor Sorella, an Italian Scot whose father owned a Continental-style bar in Lochgilphead. Victor was a dark, curly-headed, squat little ruffian, precociously developed physically, a little older than I was, and much stronger. He was generally regarded, wisely, as being too tough to get into an argument with. Out in the playground one day, Victor decided to pick on me as a conveniently weedy victim on whom to vent his customary belligerence. Foolishly, not wanting to lose face in front of my classmates, who quickly gathered round this interesting confrontation, I pulled off my spectacles and handed them to another boy.

"Hold these!" I said, and with ridiculous bravado struck up a pugilistic pose, defiantly quavering. "All right, then, if you want a fight!"

Victor could hardly believe his luck. Unzipping his brown corduroy jerkin to give his shoulders more room, a spiteful grin on his brown face, he pranced at once into a practised counterpart of my own bobbing and weaving (as taught in E. Lawrence Taylor's dining-room boxing lessons). Egged on by the cheers and jeers of the spectators, we flailed about without either of us landing a proper blow – until Victor took an almighty swipe at my head, missed, and smashed his fist into the school wall. That effectively put an end to the fight.

As I took my spectacles back, Victor snarled, "What are you trembling for?"

Noting his bleeding right hand, I retorted vigorously, "I'll give *you* something to tremble about!"

And Victor slunk away.

I was amazed at the esteem I acquired from this rather absurd encounter. Boys patted me on the back or stopped me in the street later.

"I hear y'gave Sorella a hiding. Good f'you, boy!"

One or two of the teachers even – who had apparently been watching – gave me unmistakable glances of commendation. Because he was an unpopular boy, it passed into legend that I had given Sorella a thrashing. As for me, I found this version of events too flattering to wish to deny it; so I didn't. It was an instance of people believing what they want to believe, but I did not fool myself into thinking it was anything other than a lucky escape.

I remember with affection, as if it were yesterday, Gordon MacNeil and Douglas Williamson, friends of mine whom I was never to see or hear of again after we had left Ardrishaig (almost eighty years ago). Gordon was a stocky, solid, unemotional boy with short, fuzzy fair hair and a wonderful capacity for getting into scrapes. Although not especially unruly, it was always Gordon who was caught in the act of throwing a rubber in class, Gordon who invariably merited the strap, whatever the misdemeanour, and who bore punishment without flinching. Douglas was from Edinburgh and formerly, like us, privately educated. He was a clever boy, elegantly thin and (I thought) capable of being excruciatingly funny – especially in class, when we were not supposed to laugh. With Miss Speed at the blackboard brightly talking about the Battle of Killiecrankie, Douglas, sitting next to me, would mumble from the side of his mouth in an exaggeration of his Edinburgh accent, a sort of parallel running commentary on the activity of some fictional character of his imagination to whom he might give a name such as, say, Bottythweilus, the mere enunciation of which could put us into paroxysms of suppressed mirth. Douglas did not take his lessons seriously, and at the end of our first year he found himself kept back when the rest of the class moved on up. He was mortified to find himself suddenly confronted, unfortunately too late, with the need sometimes to be serious.

Gordon and I found ourselves in the school choir. How he got chosen goodness knows. He was tone-deaf and had a range of about five notes, the bottom and top of which gave the impression, respectively, that he was either about to be sick or experiencing mortal fright. The school speech day was the great occasion that our choir practice led up to – the pinnacle of its achievement – coached by the headmaster himself. Now it had arrived, and there we were, arrayed in two ranks on the platform of the local cinema, arms stiffly at our sides, with Jimmy Stewart himself standing at the rear like an avuncular giant among pygmies (the avuncular bit put on specially for the benefit of the assembled parents in the audience). Jimmy had a good tenor voice, and knew it. He regarded himself as Lochgilphead's answer to Nelson Eddy, and had no intention of passing up an opportunity of demonstrating his control of the occasion. In the middle of something like 'Scots, Wha Hae wi' Wallace Bled' the headmaster leaned over towards Gordon and was distinctly heard to growl into his ear, "Stoap sengen', boy."

Gordon was not offended by being told to stop singing, but was aggrieved at having had to endure so many practice sessions, in our own time, all to no purpose. Not that 'our own time' was particularly exciting. Breaks and the lunch hour were opportunities for playing marbles, exchanging cigarette cards (to make up a set, usually fifty), conkers (in season), desultory ball games on the dusty gravel-and-remains-of-asphalt playground, or just loafing about until the loud ringing of a handbell had us racing into our queues, like parallel rugby line-outs in front of the duty teacher. The bigger children (which included me) were allowed into the town at midday and, if we had any money, might supplement our piece by buying a hot fourpenny pie, kicking front doors as we ran along the street to the shop.

8 – BREAKING OUT

The Lochgilphead school was, of course, co-educational, although during school hours it was de rigueur for boys not to display the slightest interest in the girls. Out of school hours was another matter, and the school bus provided me with an opportunity to develop closer acquaintance with a – well, yes – fat girl named Margaret, commonly known as Pie – spelt π, to make it acceptable to her. It was a friendship of the mind, conducted chiefly through a furtive exchange of notes, as one or other of us clambered on or off the bus. The notes became letters which, at the high noon of our relationship, were passed along the bus by complicitous fellow passengers, impressed by a *liaison dangereuse* conducted under the very nose of Mr Mitchel, who rode shotgun and would have been expected to stamp severely on anything remotely verging on hanky-panky. We may have been exceptionally innocent (though not entirely), but we never so much as held hands on the occasional Sunday walk we took along the canal bank as far as the Lochgilphead cemetery – keeping a sharp lookout against the awful possibility of being sighted.

Nor did we ever walk alone – our Sunday promenades were foursomes. David, not to be outdone, struck up a parallel friendship with Pie's friend, another Margaret, a tall girl with bobbed hair whom he decided for no particular reason to call Kim. It was a perfunctory affair, not to be compared with mine; his real interests were focussed elsewhere.

On the opposite side of Loch Gilp, extending up as far as Loch Fyne, was land of the Kilmory Estate, owned by the Pelham-Burn family; and we had quite often seen two buxomly adolescent girls riding their ponies out from there towards the beach, or across the sands. David, always the more adventurous, struck up a friendship and, before long, found himself invited over to Kilmory Castle. Then, following one of Mother's visits and negotiations between her and Mrs Pelham-Burn, he was actually invited to stay there for a period. Jean Pelham-Burn, the only daughter of the house, was probably about sixteen and, having now left school, completely at a loose end (the other girl, her cousin, having been merely on holiday). The arrangement suited Aunt Sis fine – one mouth less to feed, and the most troublesome member of the household under somebody else's care for a change. Thereafter, for a period of some weeks or months, the two riders galloping full tilt across the sands were Jean and my brother David. We kept in touch by yodelling to each other across the loch.

Stranded as we were on that isthmus between Lochgilphead and Ardrishaig, with the canal behind us and the loch in front, I was now thrown back on comradeship with my youngest brother (Pie's mother having meanwhile intercepted one of my letters and put a stop to any further correspondence between us, which effectively ended our interest in each other). Hamish at home had been a protected species; now, under Aunt Sis's jaundiced supervision, he had to fight his own corner, and accordingly, as underdog, developed qualities of resilience and determination which were to stand him in good stead. Although a slow learner who never acquired decent handwriting, he was irritatingly good at mental arithmetic, and used to win at games of Monopoly and whist with a regularity all the more infuriating for being accepted smugly (by him) as his due, when as often as not the blighter had improved his chances by cheating. He could not bear losing.

With David at Kilmory, Hamish and I would go fishing, each with a plumbed line, under Ardrishaig Pier. We climbed down rusty iron rungs on to the slimy green baulks of timber, the brown-grey water of the harbour heaving up, pausing, subsiding, the sounds of great sloshes and gurgles magnified from enclosure by the decking above. On rare calm days we could see right down into the water, where a myriad fish – *pyuchkies*, as they were contemptuously called – swirled about our bait. There was a tremendous thrill in being able to watch one actually take it, then haul it in all gleaming, slippery wet.

Our Uncle Alasdair had a small sailing boat which he kept at Ardrishaig and which Aunt Sis sometimes lent (or let) to other people but, very sensibly, never allowed *us* to use. This boat happened one day to be left invitingly on the shore by whoever had last been out in it. The temptation was too much to resist. Heavy as it was (it was about fourteen feet long), Hamish and I managed to drag it to the water and set sail. What exhilaration! The sail filled and, with me at the tiller and Hamish admiringly perched on the bow, we spanked out to sea before a good stiff breeze, in the general direction of Loch Fyne and the Firth of Clyde. As the wind got stronger out on the loch, Ardrishaig Pier began to recede alarmingly fast.

"Hadn't you better turn back, Alan?"

The captain had the same thought. Yes, now . . . what was it you did? To turn the thing you pulled over the tiller. Right, here goes. . . . The boat swung half round, and with a ghastly lurch the sail hit the water with a smack.

"No, no, Alan, it's too dangerous!" shouted the first mate in shock.

The captain had the same thought. Better get the sail down. We fought it down, battling its flapping, wet embrace in a tangle of rope and canvas. By sheer luck the oars were in the boat – heavy oars, but just within our strength to row (I had served my apprenticeship in that department on the ponds of Wanstead Flats and Whipps Cross). We began to row – or rather, *I* began to row, desperately urging the now blubbering first mate to *push* on the other side. In that choppy, rolling sea we made virtually imperceptible progress, and were it not that we managed to reach a single large black rock at the mouth of Loch Gilp we might have given up from utter exhaustion. We scrambled panting on to the slippery, barnacled outcrop, keeping a tight grip on the boat's painter (a precious lifeline) while we got back our breath. It may be that the incoming tide helped us back, eventually, to the harbour; I have no recollection of the last stretch, except that we made it – with blistered hands, dog-tired and very scared. Fortunately, nobody had missed us, and nobody ever discovered our nearly disastrous little expedition.

David's sojourn with the Pelham-Burns eventually came to an end – he and Jean were too independent for each other – and it then became my turn to receive patrician hospitality. A small flotilla of Royal Navy motor anti-submarine boats (MASBs) was based at Ardrishaig, and with it a fair number of naval officers, petty officers and ratings with nothing much to do in their spare time. Jean seemed to prefer the ratings, and her mother evidently wanted to keep her out of harm's way by corralling with her, during the holidays, an approved companion – first David, then me. It was my first and only experience of the sort of country-house life one reads about in books such as P. G. Wodehouse's *Code of the Woosters*, or Siegfried Sassoon's *Memoirs of a Fox-Hunting Man*, or almost any novel of Anthony Trollope's – with the difference that this was wartime 1940.

Kilmory House (only the Lochgilphead people and Ordnance Survey called it Kilmory Castle) was a large stone partly crenellated building, not exactly grand, but with an impressive appearance of early Victorian prosperity deriving from the time when many Glasgow families became very rich indeed, and liked nothing better than to acquire land and property in the Highlands. It stood on a site which may at one time have afforded splendid views over Loch Fyne, but was now denied pre-eminence by the quantity of tree planting that had been carried out by previous owners apparently without regard to its ultimate effect on the landscape and vistas from the house. Entering by the drive at the Lochgilphead end, through a series of paddocks and parks, requiring much opening and shutting of gates, one arrived after about half a mile at the imposing front with an archway giving on to a central courtyard and the principal doors of the house. The main wing was to the right, servants and services to the left. The high dimly lit entrance hall, its walls graced with one or two large oil paintings, and a multitude of guns, spears and trophies, suggested a family that had made its mark here for centuries; yet the Pelham-Burns were relatively recent arrivals and had, so it seemed, impoverished themselves by the extent of modernisation and refurbishment they had effected throughout this house of at least fifty rooms, some of them quite grand.

Captain Pelham-Burn was a tall, lean, craggy man with a jutting nose and sardonically mournful expression. His commission had been in the Seaforth Highlanders, and much of his career had been spent in Ceylon (Sri Lanka), possibly as a military attaché. He was currently officer commanding the Lochgilphead Home Guard, which had necessitated revised orders being issued to the domestic staff that henceforth he was to be addressed as *Major* Pelham-Burn. He divided the world into two types of people: gentlemen and people who were not gentlemen.

On one occasion, on returning from some games in Ardrishaig that he had taken Jean and me to – at which the navy had turned out in force to challenge local worthies at high jumping, tug of war, etc., joining an audience there of half the town and many people from other parts too – he recounted with some astonishment to his wife, "And do you know, Vaux [captain of the naval base] and I were the only gentlemen there!" Then, as if conscious of an implied insult to me, he hastily added, "And Alan too, of course."

I have to admit it was most agreeable being a gentleman. I had a large bedroom and bathroom to myself (not that I had much time for the bathroom), and, kitted out in somebody else's jodhpurs, I quickly became as if to the manner born, riding out on a mild white pony, with Jean on her larger, more spirited Bubbles. Jean was a tomboy with fair hair and ruddy cheeks. I would help her to groom the ponies and muck out the stables, laying in fresh bedding. I learned how to look at the ponies' hooves and teeth, and how to check the quality of their droppings. She also taught me how to use a two-handled scythe – on thistles, docks and nettles – and how to set a snare for rabbits, and later patrol the run to see what we had caught. I didn't much like that part, squeamishly recoiling from the sight of a wretched animal helplessly kicking and jerking itself tighter in the noose as we approached. Grasping it firmly, Jean quickly finished it off with a sharp practised chop on the back of its neck. She was a great, strong, healthy girl, and took some pleasure in putting me to shame. While I am not now discomfited at being thought a wimp (a nasty, clever word not then coined) since the opposite of wimpishness strikes me as being infinitely more unpleasant, Jean's scorn pierced me.

A day or two later, having just come down to breakfast, and as I was peckishly debating with myself whether to have the kedgeree *and* devilled kidneys, I was startled by a deafening explosion. Emerging quickly from behind the serving screen, I beheld Captain Pelham-Burn standing by an open window, calmly removing a cartridge from his smoking shotgun.

"Go and finish it off, Alan," he commanded casually.

Through the window I could see a rabbit on its back, kicking convulsively on the lawn. With a beating heart and shaky legs I ran out, knowing that I was being tested. I grabbed the probably dead, but still kicking rabbit and whacked it two or three times hard on the ground – not quite the approved manner, but good enough. Jean's father took the pathetic and now definitely dead creature from me without a word, but I was conscious of having passed the test. In truth, fear of his contempt had given me courage. But he was a hard taskmaster. He took me out shooting grouse in the hills – he with a gun, me carrying his pouch of about thirty cartridges. Tirelessly he strode the heather in his tweed jacket, cap and plus-fours, banging off at the occasional bird as I staggered in attendance, until, satisfied eventually that I had reached the limit of my endurance without complaint, he would take the pouch and send me off back with whatever he had so far bagged.

Jean's brother, Hamish, also a captain in the Seaforths, and occasionally home on leave from his regiment, had inherited something of his father's spartan qualities – and taken them a stage further. I was told he enjoyed beating people – not in the sense that *my* brother Hamish enjoyed beating me at Monopoly, but beating people physically, with a cane – for the pleasure of which he was apparently prepared to pay ten shillings (fifty pence), which was quite a lot of money in those days. I was indirectly sounded out as to whether being a candidate for this treatment appealed to me, but had no compunction in funking that one. Later, Gordon MacNeil told me that he had agreed to, and undergone, a beating, and that it was the most painful experience of his life.

With a rather exclusive little group of children, David and I joined a regular dancing class arranged by Mrs Pelham-Burn at Kilmory. It was conducted in the normally deserted ballroom by a pernickety little man named MacLellan. His method of instruction was so technically precise, concentrating tediously on the exact positioning of our feet, that he managed to remove whatever pleasure we might have derived from dancing. Nevertheless, we did eventually put on a performance of eightsome reels, Gay Gordons, and Dashing White Sergeants, etc., for the benefit of admiring relatives – but not ours. The irony of us door-kicking hooligans tripping lightly in our pumps over the polished parquet floor at Kilmory was unlikely to have been appreciated by any of those present.

Actually, David, who had chummed up with some of the Ardrishaig sailors (and incidentally got hooked on the navy), was more interested in joining them at the local hops.

"Isha goes – why can't I?" he plaintively asked the impassively forbidding Aunt Sis.

"You're not going and that's the end of it."

But David, seeing his cousin, hair in curlers, pressing her frock ready for an evening do, found this (sensible) obduracy hard to bear, and managed, one wild night, to give our aunt the slip – temporarily. When, of course, she discovered he was not in his bed, her anger at being disobeyed was such that, knowing full well where he had gone, she immediately went in pursuit. On went her brown rustling raincoat, on with her plastic pixie hat; and snatching up her umbrella, she charged out into the rain. I did not witness what then transpired, but from Aunt Sis's, Isha's, and David's subsequent accounts – from understandably different points of view – a vibrant picture presents itself to my imagination.

Inside the blackout-shrouded village hall the Ardrishaig hop was fully into its collective stride and going like billy-o, full of noise, vigour, fun and general commotion: feet stamping, kilts flying, sailors leaping about – everybody having a wonderful time. The perspiring accordionist vied with two fiddlers and a drummer, whose energetic syncopation was almost drowned by the hubbub.

Timing her entrance with precision – the drum roll had just signalled the end of the previous dance, and there was a momentary lull as the dancers got their breath back – Aunt Sis's furious voice (offstage) could be heard distinctly: "NO! I'm *not* here for the dancing. I don't *need* a ticket. It's that boy I'm looking for – I know he's here."

Brushing past the doorkeeper, she burst belligerently into the hall, her umbrella grasped like a weapon. The astonished gathering then witnessed the extraordinary sight of one rather large lady in a plastic pixie hat and dripping brown raincoat making a beeline for a small boy in the crowd, and proceed to chase him round the floor, brandishing her umbrella and shouting, "You come here, David [gasp]! You're a naughty boy [gasp]! You should be in bed!"

David, sprinting in and out of the bemused spectators, managed at first to evade his enraged aunt, but there was little room for manoeuvre. After two or three thrilling laps she finally managed to collar him and drag him protesting out into the street. It was more than a mile back to Calman, during the course of which David, held by the scruff of his neck, let loose against his captor a more or less continuous stream of invective, no holds barred, employing all the swear words recently learned from his new friends. But for all the effect they had on Aunt Sis, they might have been raindrops bouncing off her shiny raincoat and pixie hat. She marched straight on, looking grimly ahead, with David scampering beside her like a barking puppy snapping at her ankles.

This episode was naturally reported back to our parents, and no doubt lost no detail of David's disobedience and uncontrollability in the telling. It may well have contributed to their decision to bring us back to London. Hitler's bombing of the capital (particularly severe in the East End) had markedly abated in 1941. Mother's explanation was different: on her last visit she had been appalled by our physical condition and generally neglected appearance. We were all three very thin, apparently, with long uncut hair; and David had impetigo. I cannot honestly say we *felt* neglected. Aunt Sis was a good cook, and we had our meals at regular times, though I was often hungry (as boys at that age are) to the extent that I would sometimes raid the press (store cupboard) for 'cap' biscuits. One has to bear also in mind that many items of food were rationed – even at Kilmory, where there was plenty of game and much living off the land, we had our own little pats of (rationed) butter, and would use up our bacon ration for a week in a single meal.

Nevertheless, it was undeniable that Aunt Sis's behaviour had of late become somewhat lax. She had been a regular attender at

Lochgilphead Parish Church (where a great uncle of mine had been the minister for many years), and the better part of our Sunday mornings was always taken up with the morning service (where we sat beside the pulpit, in front of the whole congregation). But then, without any explanation, Aunt Sis (and perforce we, too) started going to the 'Wee Free', where Jimmy Stewart held forth in the choir. I suppose she had fallen out with the Reverend Beaton (the parish-church minister). After a while, though, her church attendance even at the Wee Free began to be less regular: we would be sent off with Isha, while Aunt Sis had other commitments. She began entertaining rather more frequently. Mr Dargie, the livestock auctioneer, was an old friend who came in regularly for a blether and an evening of whist, at which two of us were usually brought in to make up the foursome. Mr Dargie, a rotund, jolly old fellow with a rich broad-Scots voice (which we loved to imitate), was almost one of the family: his weekly visits were part of the domestic routine. But then new friends – Canadian forestry men – began coming to the house, with whom Aunt Sis was quite surprisingly unbuttoned, so to speak, to the extent that our presence was an irritant. We were introduced, if it were necessary to mention us at all, as 'my evacuees from London', which did rather suggest that our appearance was indeed something for which she did not wish to be known as having any particular responsibility.

So Mother may have been right in her judgement. In any event, she never forgave her sister for, as she put it, 'starving' us. So far as I know, she never met or spoke to her again. As for Aunt Sis, she was no doubt glad to be shot of us.

9 – SHOCKING NEWS

We returned to London in September 1941, by the night train from Glasgow. The dim blue lighting and blacked-out, netted windows of the carriage grimly presaged our entry into the 'war zone'. Compared with the bombing of 1940 and the first part of 1941, air raids on London were then relatively light, and it was not until June 1944 that the rocket attacks (V-1s, or doodlebugs, and V-2s) brought a return of sporadic danger to the civilian population of East London. As for us, we were bundled off almost immediately to boarding school – David to the boys' naval training ship *Mercury* on the River Hamble, Hamish and I back to Loughton. It was the first time we had been separated – the beginning of a family dispersal that would eventually take each of us off to a different part of the world and into entirely different careers.

Strangely, I find the detail of this period – roughly two years, from the time of our return from Scotland to my enlistment in the army – has almost entirely erased itself from my memory. I had sprouted during our time in Ardrishaig into a lanky adolescent, bespectacled, painfully shy and socially maladroit. Perhaps many boys are at that age yet won't admit it, and so act out a loutish role – a mixture of bombast and facetiousness – to cover their feelings of insecurity. In my small circle of friends at school I acquired a reputation for waggish humour and cultivated eccentricity. But bombast was alien to my nature (not confident enough), much as I might wish to assert myself. Life in Scotland, for all the unpopular domestic regime at Calman and our headmaster's ferocious discipline, had been relatively unrestrained. Aunt Sis and Jimmy

Stewart, in their respective spheres, were more concerned to keep boisterous behaviour within bounds than to direct it towards a definite objective. As a result, almost anything that did not positively annoy them – which included much that *would* have annoyed them had they known of it – was permissible, provided we could get away with it. We had been like foals in a very large field, free to roam in it, occasionally breaking out, but submitting meekly enough to being stabled at night. Uncultured, half wild, it was not surprising that I should feel gauche and out of place among the suburbanites of Loughton. My earlier brief experience at the school, in showing up my 'backwardness', had not been a happy introduction.

The school that we had left two years previously, after so briefly attending it, felt quite a different place. Hamish and I were, of course, now boarders, because London was still a potentially dangerous place to live. I had a bedroom somewhere up in an attic, together with a boy named Durrant, memorable chiefly for his extraordinary gait (when walking, his head did not bob up and down like most people's; it maintained a course precisely parallel with the ground, rather like Groucho Marx, but without the moustache, spectacles and cigar). Hamish was in the main dormitory, along with the other junior boys (about twelve in all), including the senior boarder, Gerald Boreham. Boreham was a prefect and in charge of the juniors (though he seemed to spend most of his time in the evening talking to the headmaster's daughter, Cynthia). Another difference was that the school now had about twenty *girls*, although none boarding (apart from Cynthia Johnson). They were of various ages and some of them disconcertingly good-looking. I was hopeless with girls (Pie did not count).

Schoolwork was my salvation. I was not exactly a swot, but, being now much better prepared, enjoyed my lessons – with the exception of science. This bears out my theory that children's dislike of particular subjects can often be put down to poor teaching. Boris Bone was a hopeless teacher, and may even have recognised this himself, since he brazenly helped us to cheat at exams.

When invigilating, he would say in a loud voice, for example, "Anyone wanting the SODIUM SILICATE for the SECOND PART OF QUESTION FOUR will find it on THAT SHELF."

Everyone then immediately recognised what question four was after.

Toofy Morrow said I had a facility for languages, which was a generous assessment considering we only did Latin and French. In those days you worked for the Cambridge or Oxford School Certificate, followed by matriculation if you were going on to university. If you did well enough in the School Certificate, you were exempt from matriculation. I had no interest in sport, but was compelled to participate in games nonetheless.

The school cadet corps, under 'Major' Bone, was moderately appealing; and, kitted out in a fifth- or fifteenth-hand First World War tunic (too long in the sleeves) with brass buttons, and threadbare khaki trousers smartly wound round the calves with puttees, I climbed the ranks to become, eventually, a sergeant. I believe promotion went according to height. Anyway, we couldn't have a prefect, as I was by then, taking orders from a non-prefect corporal, could we?

At home, my father's work as a family doctor had in the meantime shifted from the normal duties of his practice, since most of the children and some of the adults had been evacuated to the country; much of his time now was taken up with regular attendance at the Upton Park Civil Defence Casualty Centre. He was on the roster there as duty medical officer and always on call for emergency assistance. Everywhere around us tidy piles of rubble and bare plots of land between the houses – where once a house, pub, church or shop had been – bore witness to the intense bombing our parents, and so many others, had undergone, night after night, never knowing whether 'the next one' was for them. Several of our neighbours had Anderson shelters in their gardens – little excavated retreats dug into the ground and roofed over with curved corrugated iron – effective enough against all bar a direct hit, but not very comfortable on a wet winter's night, though many people were most resourceful in making a little nest in there. Of course Father, as usual, had his own solution to the problem of parental self-preservation, which furnished equal security with a great deal more comfort. One end of the cellar was completely cleared and turned into a bunker, with a wooden partition to separate the occupants from the coal. The two beds (in which my parents slept every night, regardless of whether an air-raid warning – those dreadful wailing sirens – had sounded) were placed directly under a massive steel girder which Father calculated would protect them from being crushed, even if the house collapsed. Fortunately, this calculation was never put to the test.

It made me proud to see evidence of Father's absorption in the Civil Defence organisation of our area: his steel helmet, official gas mask (no cardboard-boxed civilian thing, but a proper service one) and the big sticker, 'DOCTOR', on the windscreen of his car. Mother told me that his work at the casualty station, often in the thick of an air raid, or clambering with his stiff leg over the rubble of a bombed building, had been immensely fulfilling. I believe it did much to assuage the humiliation of his rejection for active service in the First World War, and I rejoiced to see Father's manifestly valuable contribution to our 'war effort'.

When Mother had first told me, about five years previously, that my father was addicted to morphine, the shock was like a blow to the solar plexus. Even now, as you may see from my delayed introduction of the subject, it is painful to dwell on and I have debated with myself whether I should mention it at all. But if these memoirs are to be more than mere entertainment, they must be a truthful record; so there is no avoiding it. I remember the exact circumstances. We had only recently settled in at Plashet Road and were on holiday from King's Leigh. I was standing in the scullery doorway, lounging against the wall, watching Mother toasting Welsh rarebit under the grill. She was talking a propos of nothing in particular about one of the several members of Father's family who had 'succumbed to drink'. I had probably heard it before.

Suddenly she said, "I think you are old enough to know now that Daddy also has had to go into a nursing home to withdraw him from morphine and alcohol addiction."

I was devastated. I felt the blood draining from my face. I broke out in a sweat and felt physically sick.

Mother, seeing the effect her words had on me, reacted completely out of character: "Come on – pull yourself together," she said roughly.

I sensed that she was afraid that Father, out on his rounds, would come in and see me in this collapsed state. She quickly made me a cup of tea and half pushed, half led me into the sitting room.

"I thought you were old enough to know the truth," she said, still resentfully, as if I had let her down (as indeed I had). But, having started, she went on and told me the whole story.

It was quite simple really. While in hospital with his tubercular knee, Father had been given morphine to ease the pain; and, over long periods of hospitalisation, repeated administrations of the drug had led to addiction. An ordinary lay patient would have been weaned off it and that would have been the end of it. Unfortunately, Father was not an ordinary lay patient – he was a medical practitioner with easy legal access to morphine.

No one who has not the experience of drug addiction can fairly pass judgement on those who have.

Father had much going for him to assist his rehabilitation: a loving wife and a close medical friend. Perhaps they were too close; perhaps the essential discipline needed to kick the habit calls for a measure of impersonality rather than love and understanding. An addict knows only imperatives – indeed he positively *plays* on better feelings and understanding – which is what my father did.

Dr Vivian was an unconventional doctor. (She had been at university with Father; I never met her.) A writer and something of a mystic, she owned and managed a nursing home in Bournemouth; and she could do the trick. Two or three painful weeks at Vivian's, apparently, and Father would be 'clear', usually accompanied by a heavy cold – one of his reactions to withdrawal. But after a period of months (sometimes a year or two) he would relapse. At the time Mother spoke to me, he was clear, so it was possible for her to conclude her account on a cautiously optimistic note. When Father came in for lunch, all was back to normal. I had recovered my composure.

But of course I had *not* recovered (nor, as it later proved, had Father). For me, nothing was to be the same again. My world had turned upside down. My father, who was not only a hero to me, but the very model of what a man should be, was suddenly revealed – or so it then appeared – to have feet of clay. Yet, looking back now after so many years, if the truth be told, it was I who had the feet of clay. My mother had sought to share the burden of her distress with me, and I had failed her. There are excuses I can find for myself: I was little more than eleven years old at the time; I was totally unprepared for what she told me. Bear in mind also the unforgiving nature of middle-class respectability at that time. However snobbish the idea might be thought nowadays, one felt – certainly my mother felt – one had a 'position' to maintain. She had shared with me what for her – and therefore necessarily for me too – was a shameful secret. And it was not only Father's addiction that was to be a secret; my own knowledge of it was also to be a secret from *him*. The brevity of Mother's revelation had concentrated so much tragedy into a few words. It had been like a pistol shot: not much to be seen, but doing a lot of damage.

The irony, or perhaps the real tragedy, was that so much of the pain and distress was self-inflicted, not so much by Father on himself (though it was) but by Mother on *herself*. To her, Father's addiction was not an illness to be treated; it was a moral weakness to be fought (of course) and, above all, to be concealed. Father had a phenomenally strong constitution. His use of morphine was noticeable only to Mother, who said she could detect a certain quality in the light of his eyes. It did not impair his intellectual capacity (it may even have sharpened it) and he seemed able to maintain his consumption at a steady level. His professional capacity was unaffected. In an earlier age, little was thought of the 'responsible' use of opium (from which morphine is derived); Samuel Taylor Coleridge and Thomas De Quincey made no secret of their indulgence. And the same did apply to my father's consumption of whisky. He did not get drunk; and indeed I can remember only one occasion, at a family sing-song around the piano one Christmas, when his boisterous singing seemed to owe something to alcohol.

Our lives, therefore, continued normally. On the surface nothing changed. Below the surface, Mother's life was a nightmare of anxiety which she lived with day in, day out, and it was no less tormenting for the periods of intermission. As for me, being away at school or, latterly, in Scotland, I was able to shut off the nightmare, bury it at the back of my mind, and, when alone, bury myself in books and reading. But I had lamentably lost confidence. And it was characteristic of this skeleton-in-the-cupboard aspect of our family drama that Mother and I rarely spoke of it. I do not know when my brothers got to know of it, nor when Father learned that we knew.

I had always been something of a bookworm; now I became a book addict. Apart from the nursery books that had been read to us, such as the German *Shock-headed Peter* (terrifying) and Beatrix Potter's *The Tale of Peter Rabbit* et al., my first independent reading, at Tankerton, was *The Rainbow*, a twopenny comic, from which I graduated to *Film Fun*, a series of cartoon stories about funny actors such as Laurel and Hardy, Harold Lloyd, Schnozzle Durante, The Three Stooges, Joe E. Brown and possibly Arthur Askey (or did he come later?). King's Leigh had a modest library (shared with the sports gear) of standard boys' books of the age, including books by G. A. Henty, R. M. Ballantyne, H. Rider Haggard, Captain Marryat, etc., and several reflecting Mr Lawrence Taylor's own taste: *Psmith*, *Vice Versa*, *Three Men in a Boat*, the Father Brown stories, Sydney Horler, Edgar Wallace, Leslie Charteris and Dorothy L. Sayers. These I devoured avidly, as well as the popular Biggles books, and tales of the master detective Sexton Blake (Sherlock Holmes came later) – fifty or sixty pages of close reading at fourpence a time. In spite of Mr Lawrence Taylor's warm recommendation, I did not start reading P. G. Wodehouse until I had access to the West Ham Public Library, after our return from Scotland (where my weekly fare, eagerly looked forward to, was *The Hotspur*. Every week during the Loughton school holidays I would walk across West Ham Park (dodging the roller skaters) with my quota of four books. The Tankerton thriller writers led on to yet more books by the same authors, plus Sapper's *Bulldog Drummond* (now somewhat deprecated as being unpleasantly right wing), Baroness Orczy's Scarlet Pimpernel series, the Richard Hannay adventures by John Buchan, and (delightfully different) the very many William books by Richmal Crompton. Anything by any of these authors I scooped up and settled down with in my place at the window end of the sitting-room sofa – total immersion, oblivious to what was going on around me.

Although television had just been introduced in Britain, very few people had a set before (or during) the war. There was never one in the house while I was still under my parents' roof. We did, however, increasingly find ourselves going to the pictures, as the cinema was called (just as radio was called the wireless). The staple fare was cowboy films – Buck Jones and Tom Mix – and the slapstick humour of Will Hay, George Formby and other *Film Fun* favourites (Charlie Chaplin and the Keystone Cops were old hat). At first we would go to the morning children's shows in a rather grubby Stratford cinema, where there was a rush to sit in the front rows; then increasingly to the normal afternoon continuous showings, when we might well see one of the films, or even the whole programme, through twice. In addition to the Stratford fleapit, we had a choice of four cinemas quite close: two at Forest Gate (the Odeon and the Queen's, next door to each other) and two in Green Street. Our parents hardly ever went – Mother virtually never, and Father I can remember going on only one occasion. The film was nothing special – it must have been a wet Thursday. Thursday afternoons were not the busiest time of the week at the Odeon. We were ushered into rather more expensive seats than usual, but we – I think it was Hamish and I – quickly scuttled down the empty rows of seats to places nearer the screen, leaving Father by himself at the back.

By the time the performance had come full circle and we looked round for Father, he had disappeared. So, having satisfied ourselves that he must have got fed up with the film and gone home (which was quite possible), we made tracks there ourselves. Sure enough, there he was, but not in very good humour.

"What on earth happened to you boys?" he demanded in his usual loud tone.

"Nothing, Father. The film only just finished."

This was not a satisfactory answer.

"But where did you *go* to?"

"Nowhere, Father. We just came home."

This was equally unsatisfactory.

We continued, totally at cross purposes, Father insisting that we *must* have moved from our places at the front, we equally adamant that we had not budged.

With irritation mounting on Father's side, and mystification on ours, he at length said, "Well, it was a rotten film anyway. I don't know why you waste your time on . . ." And he went on to elaborate on just why it was so rotten a picture.

"But, Father, that picture was on at the *Queen's*; we were at the *Odeon*."

Father looked momentarily nonplussed, then threw back his head and roared with laughter. He had apparently gone out for a drink (no alcohol at the cinema, of course), then made his way back to the neighbouring cinema instead of the one we had first entered. He had waved aside the commissionaire – "It's all right, I've got a ticket" – and the man had respectfully opened the door for him. The incident appealed to Father's sense of humour.

His talent for doing things his own way, and insistence on unconventionality verging sometimes on eccentricity, often attracted attention in public places. Most men looking for a public convenience will move up close to a likely informant and murmur, "Excuse me – is there a Gents here somewhere?"

With Father, from a distance of five or ten yards it would be, "Where can I go to have a pump-ship, George?" – or whatever name came into his head. He was, or appeared to be, quite unselfconscious.

On another occasion, unusually for him (he said he'd had enough religion in his youth to last him the rest of his life) accompanying us to our local church, St Peter's in Upton Lane, he spotted during the hymn at the offertory that the sidesman was a patient of his. Instead of putting his collection in the plate, he grasped the astonished man warmly by the hand and shook it vigorously, articulating in a loud stage whisper, "How are you, Wilkins? Good to see you here."

Of course, it should have been Wilkins who was pleased to see *Father* there.

I had just left school and was about to enter the army when a grievous blow, totally unconnected with the war, struck our family. David and Hamish had gone off on their bicycles to Trumpington (just outside Cambridge) to see our Aunt Isobel, and incidentally to collect a supply of plums from her garden. It was August

1943, and a journey of about fifty miles – we often used to do it. I remember standing in the sitting room when Mother went to answer the phone. The phone was constantly ringing in our house and I paid no particular attention to it.

But she returned with disaster on her countenance and, her voice fighting through tears, said, "Hamish has had an accident."

I felt a pang of fear and apprehension.

Father said, "Oh, my God! Where are they?"

It had been David on the phone. He was somewhere between Ongar and Chigwell, and Hamish had been taken to the Middlesex Hospital. David himself was in a state of shock. They had been on their way back, with their bicycle baskets full of plums. Apparently David had been ahead at a certain point, as they were passing a stationary vehicle, with Hamish following. As he negotiated his way past this vehicle, the weight of plums over his front wheel caused him to lose balance, and he toppled over into the path of an oncoming lorry. He attempted to crawl to the opposite side of the road, but there was no time. The lorry driver slammed on his brakes; Hamish went under the locked wheels, and was dragged along with the vehicle until it came to a halt.

Father went at once to the phone, and eventually, after the usual infuriating delays (it was a 'toll' call; no SDT then), managed to get through to the emergency ward of the hospital. He listened, and we could hear his grave voice saying, "Yes. . . . Yes. . . . Yes. . . ." And finally: "I must be guided by you. . . . Yes."

He had given permission for Hamish's right leg to be amputated, and it was typical of my father that he made the decision, when it had to be made, unhesitatingly, by himself. It would have been cruel to have involved my mother in it, and it would not have occurred to him to do so. He recognised the responsibility as his. No doubt being a doctor helped.

It was now evening, beginning to get dark. We did not know properly how to get to the Middlesex Hospital, so we got Bill, whom Father used when his own car was off the road, to take us in his big Austin Six. At some point we may have picked up David – I can't remember. He had been taken in by a woman who saw or heard the accident from her house. She sat him down and gave him a cigarette (he'd already covertly started smoking).

At the hospital I was left in the car with Bill, so concerned and sympathetic, while Mother went in with Father. Bill and I made conversation that neither of us paid much attention to. After about ten or fifteen minutes, my parents reappeared out of the darkness, very solemn and subdued. Hamish was still unconscious after the operation. The left leg had also been badly damaged, but the doctors believed it could be saved. Bill drove us home in almost complete silence.

The next day, or possibly later, Father had to break the news to Hamish. Mother was with him and gripped Father's arm to prevent him breaking down as he sought to soften the blow.

All Hamish said, in a surprised voice, was "Not . . . off?" and there were some brief tears. He was amazingly brave.

Days and weeks passed. I believe I was still at school, doing an extra term to fill in time, but cycling there and back, no longer boarding. Although I was keen to see Hamish, I have no recollection of visiting him in hospital. There may have been a logistical reason for this surprising omission; but any anxiety I may have felt at the prospect of seeing my youngest brother minus one leg was at once banished on Hamish's return, very much his old self only calmer, more assured, and with a suggestion of maturity that lifted him from his former lowly status of 'the youngest' to now more level terms with David and me. He was a brick. His plucky attitude to the personal calamity that he had suffered helped us all, and we admired the way he got to grips with the business of stump-socks, crutches and, eventually, an artificial leg. But by the time he had reached that stage I was in the Royal Engineers.

10 – ACTIVE SERVICE

I did not wait to be called up, but volunteered for the army, hoping to kill two birds with one stone – to get into active service as soon as I could, and also to make progress with a career in engineering. A War Office scheme sought to attract recruits for commissions in the Royal Engineers, and I was accepted for that. First, though, I had to undergo six weeks of initial military training at Maryhill Barracks in Glasgow. This was a grim establishment of granite buildings interspersed with wooden huts and wide asphalt squares resounding to the yells of drill sergeants and the clattering tramp of marching recruits. Having had two years in the Loughton School cadet corps, square-bashing was not new to me, but the *speed* at which everything was done jolted us rookies abruptly into the army culture.

"Come on, come on – jildy, jildy! MOVE yourselves – you're not in Civvy Street now!"

Soldiering in the mid-twentieth century still had many attributes of the nineteenth (or even the eighteenth): a spartan activity ordered by drill, bugles and non-commissioned officers. Starting with reveille and cold showers at six in the morning, the programme was an unremitting sequence of drilling and physical training. We marched to meals; then "HALT!" and "Get fell out!" to shuffle along in line, like prisoners of war, past a row of cooks, each sloshing or plumping his contribution of army rations into our hopefully proffered mess tins. Nobody had a good word to say about the food, but there was rarely any complaint to the orderly officer on his round of the tables. Typically, a self-consciously benign young captain with a swagger stick under his arm would be followed by the orderly sergeant with his red sash and glaring expression, as if to say, "You may think this officer is a pushover, but it's *me* you've got to reckon with."

"Any complaints? Food all right?"

Mumble, mumble.

British soldiers, like farmers, throve on grumbling, and resented any suggestion that grievances might somehow be redressed.

With many of my comrades, soldiering was an unwelcome interruption to the course of their normal lives; yet I, who was later to find the army a tedious waste of time, at first found it challenging and full of interest. I have – or had – a yen for a new experience, even when it might be unpleasant. Taken in the right spirit, it enlarges the mind and, with luck, add to one's fund of wisdom. I even took pride in spit and polish, boning my parade-cum-walking-out boots with the handle of an old toothbrush to a deep, gleaming black. That, and the polishing of brasses and the blancoing of webbing were sternly enforced spare-time duties, with frequent inspections to make sure they were properly done.

"You call them brasses polished, you 'orrible creature! What are you? 'Orrible, that's what you are. They're effing filthy!"

The smack of discipline, like the early morning showers, was refreshing and somehow reassuring. You knew where you were with the army.

Apart from drilling and PT, Maryhill taught me the anatomy of the Bren gun. A favourite exercise (of the sergeant armourer) was to have us down on groundsheets, dismantling and assembling these machine guns at speed, with praise for the first to finish and savage humiliation for the last. We were also introduced to the private soldier's personal weapon, the Lee–Enfield .303 rifle – not, of course, for firing ammunition, but for purposes of sloping, ordering and presenting arms. We never saw ammunition for either of these weapons, and our bayonets were purely for fixing. The stage of hurling ourselves at sacks of straw, screaming with simulated rage, was still ahead of us.

Our platoon was a mixed bunch. Among those I remember were a Westminster School boy who tried (unsuccessfully, I'm ashamed to say) to convince me that classical music was worth listening to;

a shambling young Austrian Jew whose family had been harassed in Vienna by the Nazis, and who had himself made a hair-raising escape across Europe to enlist in Britain; and a dissipated-looking rake, also from one of the public schools, whose main interest was in finding girls to chat up. I suppose that could have been said of most of them (I almost wrote 'us', but it would not then have been true of me) – that and frugal beer drinking (its consumption necessarily limited by the very low rate of army pay). Some of us got a kick simply out of walking out in uniform – which was itself a new experience – and trawling round whatever charity canteens in the town might have something to offer. A bowl of soup and a bun were good value in exchange for participating in a bout of hymn singing.

After Maryhill I was transferred under my scheme to the Royal Engineers at Clitheroe, in Lancashire, where the trainees were quartered in an old cotton mill. Here at least we had bunk beds, instead of straw-filled palliasses on the floor. The RE had their own distinctive esprit de corps, fortified by a band whose main duty it was to lead the training battalion to and from church on Sundays. During the week we developed skills of, this time, trench digging, derrick rigging, wireless telegraphy, handling explosives, heaving telegraph poles about and, of course, bridge building. The Bailey bridge was one of the great inventions of the war – something like Meccano, only much larger. Even to ourselves it was almost miraculous how, in forty-five minutes, we could throw a bridge capable of bearing a squadron of tanks over the Ribble (I think it probably was). At the end of my sapper training I had my WOSB (Wozbee – War Office Selection Board): two or three days of being put through the hoops, with everybody striving to demonstrate 'leadership potential' at the expense of his fellows – not my scene. But in any event, when it became clear that I was ignorant of 'stresses and strains', retaining walls and abutments, then all the rest (the intelligence tests, discussion groups and field conundrums to test resourcefulness and initiative) counted for nothing. I just did not know enough (all right, anything) about the technical side of engineering. It was yet another false start.

A week after the Allied forces landed in Normandy (6 June 1944) I was transferred to the Essex Regiment, with a recommendation (as

I discovered later) that, after infantry training, I should go before another WOSB. My service in the REs had been just four months, but I had enjoyed it. The Sappers had a perky confidence and pride in their technical proficiency, and getting to know some of it was a fascinating experience I was glad not to have missed – in spite of not being able to make anything more of it.

Although now in the Essex Regiment, my infantry training was undertaken not very far from Clitheroe – I was stationed in a commandeered holiday camp at Blackpool, where we were billeted in chalets. There were no famous Blackpool lights, of course, and Billy Butlin was away for the duration. We were back to square-bashing and PT. A month or two later I was again transferred, to somewhere near Yarmouth, lodged in an ordinary house that had been taken over by the army (as were all the platoons of the unit; our company headquarters was in a former hotel). But that didn't mean any degree of comfort – we were back to the straw-filled palliasses on the floor. Our training, however, now bore some relation to fighting an enemy: map reading, foot patrols, forced marches, firing live ammunition, and yes (echoes of Waterloo and Passchendaele), fixing bayonets and hurling ourselves, screaming with simulated rage, at bags stuffed with straw designated as GERMANS. We were out in all weathers – and my memory (probably inaccurate) is that it was raining most of the time – day and night. There was some excitement in these exercises, and we all understood that within a matter of weeks we were likely to be shipped over to an active-service unit on the Continent. I (foolhardily) looked forward with enthusiasm to the prospect of doing some real soldiering. Although I hoped to get a commission, that was not my overriding ambition. So when my company commander told me, at the end of our training period, that he was sending me on for 'the draft', I was elated. Captain Woolcote (or something like that) was a deadly serious civilian soldier who, in retrospect, puts me in mind of Apthorpe in Evelyn Waugh's *Men at Arms*.

Sitting behind his table at company headquarters, he addressed me with the look of a man putting a name to a face for the first time: "Ah yes . . . Hall. I see you are down for a Wozbee. Well, no doubt you will have an opportunity for that at your unit. In the meantime I'm recommending that you go forward for the draft." His expression said plainly that if I was officer material he would surely have noticed me before now.

But when I said, "Yes, sir, I would prefer that," he almost looked as if he would change his mind.

I sometimes wonder how my life might have been different if I had done more to press for that WOSB, instead of remaining, if not exactly content, at least passively willing to accept my status as a (not so humble) squaddie. Although I was now reasonably educated for my age, I appeared to lack gumption (*must* have lacked gumption). I was excessively diffident, and weakly made a virtue of having no military ambition other than to play a part in the war effort. I remember being home on leave at the same time as David, who, although not yet commissioned in the Royal Navy, had clearly set his sights on it. We were seated at table and I had been displaying some reverse snobbery on the lines of "What does it matter what rank you are so long as you do your bit to the best of your ability?"

David said, crassly, but getting under my skin nevertheless, "We have enough sheep; we need more leaders."

Useless to protest that I was neither sheep nor leader – that was sheer sophistry, and it begged my own question. I was *not* doing my bit to the best of my ability. By aspiring to nothing, I did not exactly waste but dissipated four precious years at a critical period of my life. Apart from the exertions and rigours of training, and a few brief weeks at 'the front', it was for me a stretch of virtually unstimulated passivity. Culturally I was to become almost moronic.

Loaded down with equipment, we boarded the ship at night for the Channel crossing – a mixed collection of men bound for different units in France, or was it Holland? We did not know. We did not even know which port we sailed from (probably Dover). Careless talk cost lives – the less we knew the better. I spent the crossing in the bowels of the ship, on some sort of bunk, with other bunks above and below, the engines thudding, nobody talking much. It was difficult to tell when we moved off, or when we arrived. One was conscious only of changes in the ship's vibration. I was tense with excitement. This was IT!

After about sixteen hours of anticipation, dozing and periods of just waiting, we eventually docked in France – Calais, I think – and disembarked into a grey day on to grey docks with cranes and railway lines, where marshalling officers were bustling about with clipboards, and military police stood about, looking completely at home on the French side of the Channel and, unusually for them, almost friendly. From the ship we boarded a train; then, after a slow trundle across Northern France, transferred on to trucks which eventually delivered us to a hutted 'holding unit', stiff, tired and completely in the dark as to where we were. In the army that was quite normal. Here (wherever it was) I met up with three young men with whom I was to associate, in the same platoon, for the remainder of my time in France, Holland, Germany and, ultimately, Italy. We were all destined for posting to the Second Battalion of the Essex Regiment, the 'Pompadours': Fred, a square-jawed stolid lad from Stoke; Bob, a rather effeminate, sensitive boy from Billericay; Victor, short, puckish, shrewdly humorous (I forget where from); and of course myself, a faintly gormless misfit from West Ham, or Kent, or Scotland (I didn't really know which). We were thrown together by the accident of war, with not a great deal in common other than our immediate destination, but we were to stay together as friends in the same unit for the final six months of the war in Europe. That was one of the benefits of the army: it shoved you up close to people whom otherwise you might encounter only cursorily (or even go out of your way to avoid, for that matter). Fred and Victor were working class – a description one doesn't often use nowadays, but what's wrong in acknowledging class difference? In cultural terms it's real enough. I read Anthony Trollope; you watch *Coronation Street*. Who is to say one is superior to the other? Both novel and soap are vehicles for social observation and commentary. Yet don't we all find ourselves constantly making dismissive judgements about the sorts of thing other people like, or do, or think, or say? Instead of valuing cultural differences, we disparage them, and so demean ourselves. Class tribalism is the bane of the English. Fred was a butcher's boy in Civvy Street, having left school at fourteen. He didn't know anything about Caesar's Gallic Wars, but he was a more mature character than I was.

We were in the holding unit for only a day or so – hardly long enough to get a few hours' proper sleep and eat a couple of meals before being transported in the back of a three-tonner to where the Pompadours' rear unit was billeted, in a rambling chateau a few miles outside Amiens (yes, I had now discovered more or less where we were). There was nothing very grand about the accommodation we had though – about ten men crammed into what had probably been a single bedroom. There were no beds, of course (what there were had been snaffled by the NCOs), but sleeping rough was to be routine for the next few months. Yet, after the nervous tension of our baffling journey over from Blighty to 'somewhere in France', it was as if cattle destined for somewhere rather nasty had found themselves transported instead to a nice green field. The quiet and faded tranquillity of that old chateau, standing in wooded grounds, was almost an anticlimax, but it was magical. Snow had started to fall, and everything was shrouded in a layer of white. Sounds were muffled. There was a feeling of relaxation and, strangely, peace. Accustomed to the stern discipline of a training battalion, we now found procedures in the Second Essex to be markedly easier. My first evening was spent in a local café, getting acquainted with cheap French wine. A few days later, with my new mates, I walked the five or so miles into Amiens along a straight, straight road lined with poplar trees, just as I imagined it would be. I believe we went to the cathedral, but I have no memory of it. The following week we were at the front, in Holland.

For the first time, we joined men who had experience of enemy action. Some of them had been wounded, recovered and returned to the front; one or two had been decorated or mentioned in dispatches, a tiny oak-leaved insignia worn above the left-hand breast pocket of a sallow youth giving an unexpected air of low-key nobility to an otherwise unprepossessing character. The company commander, Major Holmes, had himself been wounded in an action for which he was awarded the Military Cross. Still absent, he was spoken of by the men of A Company (ours) with veneration. Our platoon sergeant, an educated man named Tyrrell, had received the Military Medal.

Large areas of Holland had been flooded by the retreating Germans. Our reconnaissance patrols (the main activity then) were night-time exercises undertaken partly in Ducks (amphibious vehicles) and partly wading – hazardous in the darkness, with water all round and little cover or features to guide one. The object was for a section of about nine men to make for a certain objective – say a railway signal box – and *listen* for sounds of the enemy (thought to be, literally, within yards), always bearing in mind that he was somewhere there listening out for you. If we didn't hear them (I never did) we returned and reported nothing heard. Occasionally, a patrol would trip a booby trap and somebody would get a shower of shrapnel. A private in our platoon got hit one night by mortar fire (he caught up with us again three months later, sporting a 'wound stripe' on his sleeve). Mostly, though, it was machine-gun fire that stuttered out – background noise, sometimes close, sometimes far distant. It was easy to distinguish the 'Brrr! Brrr! Brrr!' of the Germans from our own 'Rat-tat-tat-tat!'

My own courage was never seriously tested, even when we moved forward across the Rhine at Nijmegen, and on into Arnhem (where the British First Airborne Division had some months earlier fought a doomed, gallant action to capture the bridge ahead of our troops, who never got through to them), and we came under sporadic artillery fire. But, as we filed cautiously through the ruined streets, keeping alert for snipers and booby traps, it was a fool's sense of invulnerability that had my nerves tingling with excitement rather than fear. The devastation in Arnhem was appalling – everywhere destroyed or damaged houses with gaping windows, craters, and lamp posts knocked askew. In the rubble of one building I found three silver teaspoons and put them in my pocket. I have them still, and an uneasy conscience.

The Germans were now in full retreat, and for the next movement forward – to Zeiss – we piled into open three-tonners. Arnhem had been deserted, but the contrast along our route was astonishing: the Dutch people came out of their houses, smiling, waving and cheering with frenzied enthusiasm. After four years of German occupation, and recently disappointed hopes, now they really were free of them. The spontaneous joy and welcome of the Dutch were, for me too, almost intoxicating; yet I observed that some soldiers displayed an almost blasé acceptance of their role as liberators, riding through this tumultuous civilian reception with little visible emotion. Was it insensitivity, or a weak intuitive understanding of what the Dutch had been through? Or is it just that British men hate to show emotion unless sanctioned by the pack?

Later, in Zeiss, with the Germans still making distance between us, we four musketeers, off duty, met up with three pretty girls in the park, innocently delighted to talk to us. They invited us to the home of two of them, who were sisters, to meet their parents, equally delighted. Their father, who was a silversmith (a day or two later he made me an inscribed ring), brought out a bottle of schnapps, and we all toasted each other with great friendliness. During the remaining few days in Zeiss, where I think we were probably resting, we again walked out with the girls, linking arm in arm in chummy chains – which helped to fudge the possibilities of pairing off (just as well).

We were somewhere between Arnhem and Münster when the war in Europe ended. The line at our end, in the north, had been static for some days. With our company headquarters in an isolated house, our standing patrols a few hundred yards ahead of it were in close touch with the enemy. Our trenches had been dug on either side of a hedge, along which, at the far side of the same field, the Germans were similarly dug in. The countryside was littered with tripwires, mines and booby traps. Billeted somewhere at the back of the house, we could smoke, talk and generally fill in the time between our turns of creeping forward to change places with those in the trenches – no smoking or talking there, just listening, and breathy whispering if we thought we heard or saw something. The renewed tension, after glorious relaxation at Zeiss, was no longer a stimulant; it was a nervy irritation. After crossing the Rhine and sweeping up into Germany, we all felt that the end of German resistance must be close. And it was.

On a day much like any other, word went round the company that there was to be an important announcement. Those that were not standing to were to get themselves into the hall. There was hardly room. Men were crammed not only into the entrance hall of the house (which was moderately big), but clustered all the way up the staircase and round the balustrade of the landing too. Somebody from company headquarters was fiddling with a wireless set. I forget who it was who made the announcement. Montgomery? Perhaps just the BBC? But after the preliminary hissing and spluttering and snatches of unwanted music we finally got it: there was this crackly voice, and then one tremendous cheer of exultation and relief as the news sunk in. All the nagging anxieties at the back of our minds were banished at a stroke. It was over! It was over! For us the war had ended. We were about to become an army of occupation.

Yet our battalion was still constantly on the move. I remember passing through Osnabrück, taking over from American troops in a farmhouse – all those Coca-Cola tins, and *water* in tins, too; they even had centrally heated cans of soup! Somewhere near there we were guarding a German arms store – the floor of one room piled high with surrendered pistols and revolvers, still for the most part in excellent working order. We helped ourselves ad lib. I took a splendid Luger and a small snub-nosed automatic pistol, and as much ammunition for both as I could conveniently carry. For the next few weeks I got a buzz with these lethally sexy weapons, taking random potshots at any object that took my fancy – as nearly everybody was doing. So long as you 'got fell in' and 'stood to' when you had to, and didn't fall asleep on guard duty, cowboy antics off duty were tolerated.

Germany at the end of the war bore every manifestation of a defeated country: shattered buildings, a shabby, reserved civil population and little traffic – except the ubiquitous Allied military vehicles. Food and fuel were in short supply, and it was not long before less-principled Germans were seeking to ingratiate themselves in various ways with the occupying forces. The army issued strict orders that there was to be 'no fraternising', but recognised that men who had been in action needed a bit of respite and relaxation. Those who had served longest were put on a waiting list for 'local leave' in Brussels – which seemed to be code for three days there in bars and brothels (I didn't get to go, so cannot speak with first-hand knowledge).

For a time we were stationed outside Hanover, where efforts were made to keep the men occupied and moderately contented. The normal practice was to pile on the 'training', but there seemed to be little immediate appetite for resuming this, and much of our time was devoted to 'housekeeping', army-style, and games (usually football, which we played in our army boots). Although we received NAAFI rations, free cigarettes and chocolate, etc., I don't recall any NAAFI concert or even a canteen – it was always 'other buggers' that got them. The nearest thing to luxury was when a field laundry turned up and we got to have a hot shower (if the water didn't run out) and could simply *exchange* our dirty socks and underwear for clean, instead of having to wash them for ourselves. After one of these infrequent field-laundry visits, our corporal celebrated his unaccustomed super-cleanliness by 'scoring' with a local girl, and described to us in some detail how she spent part of the time in his amorous embrace eating NAAFI cake that he had brought her. I don't think the non-fraternisation order was ever formally annulled, but it was increasingly disregarded.

During the battalion's next posting, to Berlin, nearly everybody was at it. Even I, still nervous with girls, but egged on by the example of my comrades, had a go at striking up a friendship. Her name was Heidi, and she was a round-faced, cheerful girl of about seventeen or eighteen. She was chaperoned at the dance hall we went to by her father, a mousey little man, demoralised by the German defeat and civil privation. I impressed her by leaping over a chair to claim a dance. This possibly uncharacteristic action on my part was nevertheless absolutely necessary, since the women were massively outnumbered by men – chiefly British soldiers, whose idea of chivalry, if it ever existed, was simply to get there first.

"Ah," exclaimed Heidi, "you yump over the sit!"

From then on there was no holding me back.

11 – INACTIVE SERVICE

Dreary as it was – long, empty streets with the occasional forlorn tram – Berlin still had cafés, beer cellars and dance halls keen enough for Allied custom. My off-duty life there was a fairly regular routine of trawling the haunts popular with British troops, mainly around the Kurfürstendamm – large, cavernous rooms filled with a cosmopolitan variety of noisy soldiery, with different units usually seated or standing round separate tables, smoking, talking, shouting and laughing while consuming immoderate quantities of lager. This would often lead to a brawl that was smartly stifled by the military police, who would appear from nowhere, grab the obvious miscreants, or innocent bystanders, and throw them into the back of a truck, while the remainder of those involved escaped by achieving sudden sobriety. I also began visiting Heidi at her parents' flat, where they would considerately (and, I now feel, irresponsibly) leave us alone in their living room while they made do with the kitchen. Sometimes we would go dancing.

Among other places, it was our company's responsibility to guard the official residence of Sir William Strang, the British Commissioner in Berlin – a very grand house that was formerly the home of Hermann Göring (who probably still owned it, although he himself was at the time residing in a Nuremberg jail). I admired the solidity of its construction, the thick walls, the handsome woodwork, the feel of 'quality' in the cloakroom – which was as far as I got inside. But usually guard duty was boringly uneventful. I even welcomed the opportunity of snapping to attention and saluting the occasional officer passing in or out. Four tiddly subalterns pushing their car to make it start was likely to be the most exciting incident on an unexceptional night.

It was from Berlin that I had my first period of home leave, memorable chiefly because on my return I was to discover that, during my absence, a corporal from the REME (Royal Electrical and Mechanical Engineers) had supplanted me in Heidi's affections. Heidi was duplicity itself. On two occasions I believe she was entertaining both me and my (ultimately successful) rival in separate rooms, one of which (not mine) must have been a bedroom – unless her parents had utterly abandoned their daughter to the mercies of two British soldiers at the same time, vacated the kitchen and gone to bed themselves. Heidi told me (she had beautiful eyes, and I almost believed her) how tedious 'this corporal' was in pressing his attentions on her – and no doubt, more truthfully, she was saying the same about me to him. But she was not a convincing liar, and I was resentful that this man had come into the picture at all. On my final visit to her parents' flat I was very drunk and climbed the three flights of their cold stone staircase singing at the top of my voice. It was the Corporal who opened the door to me. He didn't waste many words. So far as I remember, he said something to the effect that Heidi did not want to see me any more, and that if I came to the flat again he'd break my bloody neck. It was a convincing demonstration of his attitude towards me; and, not being in any condition to argue with him, I shambled off, still singing, in the direction of the nearest bar, humiliated but determined to display, albeit sozzled, equanimity. My final recollection of that unfortunate evening is of myself swaying into a dance hall and taking no more than three steps inside the door before I was seized unceremoniously by two British soldiers. They turned me round and frogmarched me out into the street, with a bellowed warning in terms similar to those used by the REME corporal.

I had been fond of Heidi – seriously enough to have taken her photograph home with me to show my parents. Her rejection of me was painful; and the manner of it, in the clear light of day, was positively mortifying. I could not understand how, when we had parted so cordially before my home leave, she could have thrown me over for this considerably older man, within the space of little more than a fortnight! Many German girls took up with Allied soldiers for what they could get out of them by way of cigarettes or food (army cooks were especially popular). Naively, and idiotically, I had imagined that Heidi genuinely liked me. The thought that she (and her parents) might have a covetous motive in being friendly simply had not entered my head. On one occasion I did give her a packet of ten cigarettes for her father – an exhibition on my part of positively Aberdonian generosity, which may, to her, have suggested rather that I was a tight-fisted, thoughtless nitwit. In turning over in my mind this whole brief, unedifying relationship with Heidi, I burned with shame.

A few months later, no longer in Berlin, I wrote her a letter to apologise for my last disastrous visit, and to enquire how things were with her. (Curious? Hopeful?) She replied very pleasantly and kindly: thank you, she was very well, and was shortly to be married – to this corporal. I suppose it was true.

The rapidity with which units of the British Army of Occupation were moved around must have some rational explanation. In my platoon the general opinion, amounting almost to a grievance, was that it was to prevent us getting our feet too comfortably 'under the table'; but, if so, it was not entirely effective, and took little account of Tommy Atkins' amazingly swift footwork. As it happened, when we moved to Einbeck, a small town about twenty miles north of Göttingen, the table I got my feet under was in our own company office. I was made company clerk – one of those 'old soldier' jobs, such as storekeeper, company runner (so-called) and, of course, batman, conferring (unofficially) perks or privileges beyond the reach of ordinary soldiers. Naturally, having an education marginally better than most of my comrades' had nothing to do with my selection. I just happened to be friendly with my predecessor, who put in a good word for me.

As company clerk, I was exempt from most of the parades and training exercises. While my comrades were doing arms drill outside in a biting wind, I was sitting in a warm office drinking tea with the Company Sergeant Major (CSM). From there one saw one's company – indeed, the battalion – from a completely different point of view. Officers now were informal and friendly –

even the CSM turned out to be human – and my work, such as it was, proved to be light and undemanding. My most serious efforts were devoted, under the signature of the company commander, to a continuous battle with the battalion quartermaster for 'supplies'. This individual, a well-fed captain who was rarely seen in the open air, believed that the most effective way of achieving economy in the use of 'stores' was to ignore requests for their replenishment. A certain measure of resourcefulness was therefore called for when indenting for whatever equipment or supplies might be needed by the company. For example, after submitting several fruitless requests for stationery, I decided to type out an indent in the usual form, but on a sheet of toilet paper (which I signed myself on behalf of the company commander), headed 'URGENT'. This secured an immediate and satisfactory response.

Krista was a fair-haired, blue-eyed, Hitler-youth prototype of a girl, complete with pigtails and frilly frock. I met her at a football match, where she had gone to find a suitable *Englander* with whom to improve her English. With my round steel spectacles and generally unsoldierly appearance, I looked just the type she was looking for.

She gave me a brilliant smile: "You come to watch the football, *ja?*"

Actually, I was on much the same sort of expedition as she was, but for practical purposes I agreed that, *ja*, I had come to watch the football. We neither of us needed any prompting to ignore the football from that point on. However, for all her vivacity and enthusiasm, I observed that Krista was very afraid to be seen talking to an English soldier. Among a football crowd she did not feel vulnerable, but walking out with me, as she later did, made her distinctly uneasy; and as for inviting me to her home, that was quite out of the question. Meeting me was, for her, a furtive assignation, never definitely agreed, always subject to her being able to detach herself from her everyday life without attracting suspicion.

Ultimately, as she got to know me better, Krista plucked up courage to tell her mother about me, which made things easier for her. We gradually developed a pattern of behaviour. It was summertime, and in the evenings I would look out for her from my billet – a house on the outskirts of Einbeck – and when I saw her coming I would start out on the road, slowly walking away from the town, giving her time to catch up with me, out of general view. After the tedious routines of army life, our walks together in the country were delightful. Oddly, although I had much more in common with Krista than I had with Heidi – or perhaps for that reason – there was no messing about. Occasionally I did half-heartedly try (displaying how thoroughly I had absorbed the prevailing army morality, lout that I was), but was always amicably but firmly resisted. Her English was much better than my German; nevertheless, we both made progress. We talked about our families (on reflection, I'm not sure she did talk about *her* family), our plans for the future (we both wanted to go to university), and the future of defeated Germany. At that time, neither of us knew much about the German concentration camps, and nothing of the Nazis' diabolical attempt systematically to eliminate the Jewish race. Krista acknowledged that Hitler had led her country to destruction, but maintained that the German people had not properly understood where they were being taken. I remember the day when we walked through a forest to a ruined tower, and climbed up it to the top, from where we could look out over the trees to the surrounding countryside in every direction. We stayed there, talking religion and philosophy, until the evening faded almost to darkness, and in the course of conversation our two national identities merged into common humanity.

My friendship with Krista was interrupted by a period of home leave, this time under a scheme which allowed farmers in Britain to get servicemen to help them with their harvest.

My Uncle George, who had spent most of the war as a prisoner of war in Austria (having been captured in Crete), and was thus released from the army early, had bought a small farm in Suffolk. Now he applied, with my enthusiastic support, for me to come and assist him. This was approved by my battalion for a period of one month, subject to possible extension. Off I went, leaving the company office to take care of itself.

Working on a Suffolk farm (of which more anon) was for me, at harvest time, a delightful interlude which I was only too keen to prolong, so when my uncle asked for an extension of this 'harvest leave' I stayed on with him in anticipation of receiving formal approval. Unfortunately, before this came through, a general recall of all troops currently on leave from Germany was broadcast over the radio. Did this apply to me? I had to assume that it did. I put in a quick farewell visit to Plashet Road and made for Victoria Station. What happened then is best related in a letter I wrote home shortly before arriving back at my unit.

R.H.U.
September, 1946

My dear Mum, Dad, Ham and David,

    I am sorry I have not written to you before this, but it has been impossible. About half an hour after you left me, David, I was lying on a wooden bed in a C.M.P. cell, feeling more than a little depressed. It happened like this.

    I joined the queue going onto No. 11 Platform (you remember, David) and, as I had expected, was stopped by the M.P. [military policeman] at the gate. What I was not expecting, though, was for the chap to place me under immediate Close Arrest. I told him that it was quite unnecessary, as it was obvious that I was going back, but it wasn't any good. There were two of these Red Caps on the gate, and one of these escorted me back to this lock-up in Whitehall. It was an underground place, and electric light was the only light I saw for the next two days.

    As soon as I got in there I was marched into an Office and had several particulars taken down, and from there into a guard room where I was thoroughly searched, and every article in my possession taken away from me, except the clothes I stood up in (though they made me give up my shoe laces, belt and tie) and a towel, tooth-brush and soap.

    The police there, used, no doubt, to handling the lower orders of Army men, shouted, bullied and made things generally unpleasant for me. But when I first went in, I thought it all rather a good joke and everything went in one ear and out the other. Then, clutching my washing gear in one hand, and holding up my trousers with the other, I was marched into the cells, and depression. The door clanged (It really did clang) and I was alone, harbouring something of a grudge against the M.Ps.

    The only time I got out was to wash in the morning and to do voluntary scrubbing of the floors. I asked them if I could have the two books which I had in my case, and after about half an hour I was marched out and told to take them out myself. Undoubtedly those books relieved what would have been otherwise utter boredom. The P.G. Wodehouse book I passed through a hole in the wall of the cell, to the chap in the cell next door. I hope Jean [my cousin] doesn't want it back, but this fellow's need was greater than hers might be. Our food was brought in to us, cooked by the N.A.A.F.I. on the top of us – quite good food but not enough.

During the time I was in there I had three different cell mates. The first was a young kid, only a few days adrift, an illiterate who talked absolute nonsense for fifteen hours continuously – I was quite glad when he went out. The next chap was twenty-eight, and without any exaggeration I thought he was forty at least. He was the opposite of the other fellow, I think he was absent for about eight months, he seemed very worried and slept most of the time. The third one was a sailor from Chatham, caught out without a pass. He came in about ten o'clock at night, just as I was trying to get to sleep, and kept me awake for an hour telling me all about it. The next morning I was out. You can immagine [sic] how eagerly I got out my cigarettes as soon as I was out of the place.

Four of us were escorted by a Cpl. from the Irish Guards and four guardsmen, to the transit at Harwich. This escort was jolly decent to us, buying us anything we wanted from the canteens, sharing their haversack rations with us, and generally treating us as 'poor mates in misfortune'. At the Harwich camp we were behind barbed wire, but had cigarettes and matches.

We were escorted to here (near Bad Deymheusen) by fellows returning from leave, again a good lot, who paid for our N.A.A.F.I. rations out of their own pockets, as we had no money (I gave my 2/6 to St Dunstans). I was charged here this morning and was released without prejudice, but I will still be charged back at the Unit. I must stop now as we get locked up in a couple of minutes (I don't get released until 0900). I'll finish this off in a later letter under happier circumstances.

With fondest love from Alan

'Released' to rejoin my company at Einbeck, I received profuse apologies from my company commander; but it was ironic, and characteristic of the army, that I had to be put on a charge to receive this expression of regret.

In my last year of army service the Second Essex were posted to Northern Italy, first to Trieste, then Mestre (just outside Venice) and, ultimately, Padua. It was while the battalion was at Padua that I personally was posted to Cortina d'Ampezzo. This famous ski resort had been taken over – hotels, bars, ski lifts, the lot – by the British Army as a rest and recreation centre, where privileged personnel (chiefly officers and NCOs) could apply to spend their local leave. My commanding officer wrote a testimonial for me, about this time, which partly explains the circumstances:

> 14442414 Pte. A.S.M. Hall
>
> The above-mentioned soldier . . . has shewn himself to be a hard-working, keen and sober man. I have found him to be very willing and correct in his behaviour. I sent him to the Winter Sports Centre at Cortina, so that he would have the opportunity of having a responsible job on his own. He has done well from reports I have received.
>   G.S. McMillan, O.C. 'A'Coy. 2nd Essex

It was a great stroke of luck, due largely to having my feet under the table at the company office. The 'responsible job' was to be ski-storeman at one of the hotels – an undemanding function which required me to check out basic skiing equipment (boots, skis and sticks were just about all we ran to) from about eight till ten in the morning, and to check in the returned gear late in the afternoon. As there were two of us on duty, this meant that one of us could go off skiing all day, while the other could only do it from ten till about three thirty. During the three or four months I remained in Cortina, I progressed from the nursery slopes to some of the more difficult runs, and managed also to do a bit of slaloming and rough cross-country skiing. In the fresh air and bright sunshine it was gloriously distant from the tedious barrack-room life I had so fortuitously left behind at Padua. With relatively few skiers – mostly men – one could not only enjoy uncluttered skiing, but had space and time to drink in the peace and beauty of the mountain slopes. How many skiers are today so fortunate?

    The evenings would usually find me in one of the many bars, and latterly in a nightclub that had been newly set up with a floor show. The band, which included a fascinating girl who played the drums, was noisy and not very good; but apart from the floor show – which included the army's version of striptease, in which there was a great play of tantalisingly removing veils, but with the girls ending up, nevertheless, with most of their clothes still on – there was little dancing. And although the troupe did double time as 'hostesses', the good citizens of Cortina were evidently not going to allow their daughters to associate themselves, beyond any call of duty, with the lower orders of British soldiery starved of female company on recreation leave. The hotel chambermaids and cooks wisely did not hang about after hours.

Carousing over cheap wine or beer, and the serious playing of cards for low stakes, I got to know, and became quite friendly with a man of unusual character, a stocky, heavy-jowled Brendan Behan lookalike. Ben was about ten years older than me, foul-mouthed (as, to be fair, were most soldiers) and overbearing in manner – not at all the sort I would normally take to – yet he had an arresting personality and was acutely intelligent. Sometimes I thought him quite brilliant. In other circumstances, had he not been brought up in the backstreets of Liverpool, he would certainly have found himself in a position of authority – managing director of a business, perhaps, or, more likely, a film or media impresario. Compared with some of the occasionally skittish officers on leave at Cortina, he was massively more impressive; yet, like me, he was a ski-storeman (in one of the other hotels) and, like most old soldiers, confined his ambition to making life here and now as comfortable for himself as possible. At this he was, on his own terms, completely successful.

Ben played chess with me (usually winning). His closest mate was an ex-commando named Martin. Both of them had done time in the glasshouse (military prison). One evening, playing cards – it was usually poker or pontoon – in a drunken argument Martin hit me so hard he knocked a tooth through my lip. He and Ben then remorsefully shepherded me back to our billet and tenderly put me to bed. It was the hard drinking of these two engaging reprobates that was eventually to be my downfall. There was an evening game that we played occasionally, something like a round of twenty questions, but played only once, after which the loser was required to drink a cocktail of grossly incompatible drinks – for example, half a litre of lager seasoned with a glass of white wine and tots of kümmel, Campari and cherry brandy. As several of us were involved, I managed for some time to avoid losing; but when, inevitably, I ultimately lost and had to pay the penalty, the effect was sufficiently powerful to keep me snoring in bed (which I must somehow have reached or been delivered to) until about ten o'clock the following morning, when I blearily opened my eyes . . . to find a ghastly apparition – in fact two ghastly apparitions: the orderly officer and regimental sergeant major standing at the foot of my bed in full regalia of inspection, and expressions of astonishment and outrage on their respective faces. Instead of two tidy beds with neatly laid-out equipment, there was one tidy bed and . . . one fully clothed but dishevelled, unshaven, unwashed soldier, with his boots on *actually in* the other bed! The army does not waste words in these circumstances.

"That man is on a charge, Sar' Major!"

"Wot's yer name? Right, you're on a charge!"

Before the day was out I was RTU (returned to unit) – i.e. back to my battalion in Padua. That was my only punishment, but it was mortifying to have lost, through my own stupidity, what must have been one of the pleasantest and cushiest jobs in the British Army in Italy. Yet, as it happened, the battalion was shortly afterwards moved back to its headquarters at Warley Barracks, near Brentwood in Essex. The Pompadours had come back home. As for me, I was posted on to Colchester to serve out my time, along with hundreds of others awaiting their turn for demobilisation. It was easy for me now to hitch-hike home to Upton Park, and most weekends saw me thumbing a lift to spend a couple of days away from the austerities of army life in the warmth and comfort of my family.

Throughout all the time I was away I had written home weekly, and every week Mother had written to me – as indeed she had to all of us when away from home. Only one of these letters (reproduced above) has survived. Had I been able to consult them, this rather bald account of my four years in the army might have appeared in a different light. As it is, I have recorded those parts which stand out in my memory of it.

Two further opportunities arose while I was in Germany for me to go in for a commission.

"I think you would make a good officer," said Major Holmes generously one day, out of the blue. "I've put you up."

Then he was posted to another unit and nobody – certainly not me – followed it up.

Later, while we were in Trieste, where we were billeted in long white stuccoed buildings surrounded by palm trees, there was a general call for 'volunteers' to be considered for commissions.

"Right," growled our platoon sergeant, "any man what wants to be an officer: one step forward, *march!*"

Of course, nobody stirred. Even had I the courage to face the scorn and ribaldry of my comrades, which I hadn't, once the war in Europe was won I had no further interest in the army. From then on I was freewheeling. In retrospect, I realise that my lack of ambition was indeed moral cowardice: I *was* afraid, partly from persistent shyness, to stand out from my 'mates' as a potential officer, and so preferred to stay in the herd. I was not a sheep, perhaps, but a pretty dumb animal just the same.

Life at Colchester was a tedious sequence of five days between weekends, occupied by anything the CO or company commander could think up to keep the men busy – men whose own thoughts were concentrated on the prospect of returning to Civvy Street. There was PT, arms drill, route marches, training even; or when they ran out of ideas, kit inspections. Kit inspections, so characteristic of army traditions, underlined its discipline, its pride (those silver drums, the regimental colours, the dusty flags in the battalion depot chapel celebrating past campaigns and battle honours), its tremendous sense of duty and its sometimes boneheaded punctiliousness. Our blankets had to be folded in a precise manner on the bed, and every item of officially issued equipment – from our rifle and gas mask down to our spare underpants and socks – had to be laid out in exactly the same way by each man; not only were the beds lined up, but every toothbrush and each piece of webbing was presented, similarly in line, meticulously cleaned, polished, oiled or blancoed, ready for inspection.

My last memory of service life is a felicitous illustration of my attitude to the army after the war was done, and of the army's attitude to me. About a fortnight before my demobilisation, I happened to be the barrack-room orderly, whose duty it was to remain behind and make sure that everything was neat and tidy, ready for the daily barrack-room inspection. Having done my sweeping-up, and having flicked the odd sock or tube of toothpaste out of sight, I settled down on one of the beds to read a newspaper. I did not pay any attention to a soldier who whistled in for his fags, found one left, screwed up the empty packet and dropped it on to the floor. Nor did I notice the orderly officer with his attendant CSM until they had entered the barrack room to find me calmly reading my newspaper when I should have been springing to attention. Yet, were it not for that screwed-up cigarette packet, I might just have passed muster, but there it was, in full view, ON THE FLOOR! The orderly officer, already irritated by my apparent insouciance, needed look no further.

"Barrack room in a filthy condition!" he bellowed. "Put that man on a charge, Sar' Major!"

Up before the commanding officer the next morning, I tried to explain.

The CO sighed deeply. "Oh dear, Hall. I really don't know what we're going to do with you," he said sadly, shaking his head as if I were some wretched reprobate for whom there could indeed be little hope of redemption in this world.

Although this was the first time he had ever set eyes on me (or I on him for that matter), it was nevertheless a fitting comment, which could have been justly applied to most of my time in the army. I had largely wasted it, and they hadn't really known what to do with me.

12 – STUDENT LIFE

I was released from the army on 16 September 1947, a week before my twenty-second birthday, and it may surprise you to learn that my military conduct was officially noted as 'exemplary – a well-mannered and -spoken soldier, who is interested in a journalistic career'. The latter piece of information I must have volunteered myself; and indeed the looming need to decide on a career increasingly imposed itself on me. Some weeks prior to my demobilisation my father had secured for me an interview with the master of Downing College, Cambridge. These were the days when admittance to a university (and there were not nearly so many then as there are now) was through sitting a matriculation exam, taken at your school, and then an interview – at which your proficiency at games or the fact of your father having attended the same college was likely to be an equally (or more) important deciding factor.

The master, whose name I came across several times in later life, but which I have now forgotten – something like Booth-Clibbon – had his room, at the top of a winding staircase, filled with books. There were books on his desk, books on the floor, books piled on chairs, and the walls lined with books. It was a very civilised and amiable chat that we had, talking mainly about myself and my plans for the future. He was rather more than middle-aged, a stocky man with – somewhat incongruously, I thought, for an academic – a clipped military moustache. He led me on artfully to reveal in all its emptiness the blank at the pinnacle of my ambitions. What career did I have in mind?

"Oh, I rather thought I would like to be a doctor, like my father."

Could any reply have been more ridiculous from a man who had clearly not thought it through, and who obviously had no idea of what this college could do for him? I believe a letter was written to my father suggesting, in a kindly fashion, that I should sort out my ideas if I was to profit from university training.

Yet there had been a good chance of getting a place at Downing if I had prepared myself better for that interview. I had passed my School Certificate exams at Loughton with 'credit' in nine subjects and a simple 'pass' in one (science, my least-favoured subject). They were good results and secured me exemption from matriculation, yet the gormlessness and generally lackadaisical attitude that had kept me in the ranks throughout my army career had almost certainly shown through in that interview. But it was also – and this was more fundamental to the early development of my character – a paralysing shyness which refused to allow me to express myself in any way that caused me to stand out as an individual. Following one's father was a motivation that should not call for any explanation; to say that I wanted to become a journalist (if that is what I did want) would require *explaining*, justifying a choice (which in truth I had not made, in any direction), sticking my neck out. I have always mistrusted introspection, believing that we tend to give ourselves the answers we feel we can happily live with; but shyness – the attribute that dominated my early adulthood – has always intrigued me. Is it fear? Modesty? Extreme sensitivity? An inferiority complex? Surely it can't be an inferiority complex – that applies only to *other* people! Whatever the explanation, it was a disability I lived with, and the commonplace business of ordinary social intercourse was a constant burden to me.

Cambridge written off, I returned to journalism. Father knew the editor of the *Stratford Express*. Journalists were not then expected to have a university degree: you went in at the bottom, were prepared to learn shorthand, and cut your teeth in the local magistrates' courts, reporting cases of burglary, brawling, road accidents and the more newsworthy aspects of shopkeeping misdemeanours. The editor agreed to see me, but was either unimpressed or was not looking for a cub reporter. He suggested I apply to the *Daily Telegraph*. I think it was Mother who, sensing that this initiative was running into the sand, suggested I study economics, as being perhaps the sort of subject that is suitable for somebody who is interested in everything but can't put his finger on anything in particular. The nearest institution offering a course of study leading to a London University degree in economics was the South-West Essex Technical College and School of Art (more commonly known as Walthamstow Tech). I applied for enrolment and was accepted.

Walthamstow Tech was distinguished architecturally only in that it occupied an impressively large site in an area that was otherwise characterised by streets and houses very similar to those of Upton Park. It was a big white stone-faced building standing in an expanse of roughly mown grass; its uniform rows of windows looked out upon uniform rows of suburban houses. The Tech was an establishment of the thirties, brashly out of place in its rather dingy old-fashioned neighbourhood. It had a wide and imposing flight of steps, American-style, leading up to a faux-classical portico and entrance hall; but apart from that it might have been a government office building: a long oblong box with a lot of windows. Nor was there much of a collegiate atmosphere. Large numbers of students arrived each morning by bus or bicycle or on foot, like an army of clerks arriving for work, and settled down almost at once to their studies.

Academic work was organised in departments, and within each department students were grouped according to the course of study they were following. My course was similar to the Oxford PPE (philosophy, politics and economics), and about fifteen of us were reading various aspects of it. Our lecturers were pleasant and diligent, but in our first year did little more than amplify the standard textbooks and discuss our written work. I found I got almost as much from my fellow students. Latterly, however, perhaps shaking off the lingering effects of wartime conditions, there was a gradual introduction of more imaginative teaching: classes were enlivened by an occasional outside lecturer, seminars were introduced, an Economics Society was established, and visits were arranged to nearby factories and works. But what set our group apart from most of the others was that this was a programme highly charged with political interest.

Up to now I had been politically inert, accepting without thought or much interest my father's political orientation, which was conventionally conservative, verging on 'reactionary' (a new word for me, and used mainly by left-wingers as a term of abuse). He applauded the students who, like my Uncle Alasdair, had driven trams during the General Strike, and would refer disparagingly to 'Ikey Moses' and 'Jew boys'. He even said he disliked Catholics on account of their religion. This was ironic, considering he showed very little sign of religious belief himself.

I remember coming back from church one Sunday to be greeted by Father with "And did you see the Holy Ghost popping out of a bottle?"

He was a sceptic, and his politics, too, were a matter of habit rather than conviction. My parents read the *Daily Telegraph* and had simply become accustomed to the climate of its opinions. The Labour victory in the general election of July 1945 had no doubt been a tremendous surprise to the readers of the *Daily Telegraph*. Many of my fellow students had contributed to make it happen.

Ted Cocksedge, who was to become my closest friend, was a staunch Labour supporter. Pale, round-faced, of medium height and heavily built, he was a clever, quietly serious student of solid character, who lived with his widowed mother above a shoe shop in Walthamstow, which she either owned or just managed. Ted was the 'steady' member of a trio which kept together, striking sparks off each other, throughout our time at Walthamstow Tech. The other member, in addition to myself, was Bernard Landsman, a short, thickset, pugnacious Jew, quick-talking and with a devastatingly effective gift for sarcasm. He was even more left wing than Ted – not a communist, but definitely a fellow-traveller.

We three often attended political meetings in London. I remember a series of lectures given by men who were at that time famous opponents of the atom bomb, such as P. M. S. Blackett (who was to win the Nobel prize for physics), Bertrand Russell (a household name in those days), and Professor J. D. Bernal of Birkbeck College, London (known to all and sundry, including his own family, as the Sage).

Bernal, as it happened, lived at the Old Rectory in Combs and would sometimes come over at harvest time to give a hand to Uncle George. As a good communist, he no doubt felt it incumbent upon himself to join 'the workers' when he had the leisure to do so.

We were fiercely supportive of these speakers, who were insisting on the peril to humanity of nuclear weapons even at a time when Russia had not itself exploded one (though it was to do so in 1949). It was almost a point of honour, at these talks, for one of us to pop up and ask what we considered to be acutely penetrating questions. We would then go off to a quiet pub or café for a pint of beer or cup of coffee until eventually compelled to go out into the night to catch a late Tube train or bus home.

At a meeting on post-war Germany, R. H. S. Crossman, an aggressive, clever Labour politician (and minister) was arguing that the Allied armies of occupation must remain there indefinitely. I nervously asked whether it was realistic to envisage an indefinite occupation of Germany.

Crossman, who was a very arrogant man, replied dismissively, "I certainly hope no *socialist* government would countenance the withdrawal of British troops from Germany."

It struck me as a curious reply: what had socialism to do with it? But that was the context within which politics were discussed then. History was the struggle of 'classes': the proletariat against the capitalists. Capitalism *inevitably* led to a fascist state (such as Germany, Italy and Spain), and was thus the mortal enemy of socialism. All this was meat and drink to us; and although I could not stomach the crudities of communist language and propaganda, I recognised what gave them some credibility: governments of the industrial countries had abjectly failed to arrest the economic decline and depression of the 1930s other than through right-wing totalitarian military dictatorships. And we all now knew where that had led us.

The issues that caused endless argument were nationalisation (for example, of the Bank of England, coal mines, electricity, steel, etc.), the health service (which my father initially opposed, as did most doctors), and the Cold War, then in its early stages. I had a reputation in the family for being left wing, or 'red', as David would have said. I certainly refused to accept our home newspaper, the

Daily Telegraph, as a satisfactory source of news, and therefore decided to order the *Manchester Guardian* for myself. This was a newspaper which was in those days still bathed in the reputation of its revered former editor, C. P. Scott; and indeed it was a very good paper – all six pages of it (newsprint still being rationed). It was a 'Liberal' organ, very different from the pinkish *Guardian* that it has now evolved into, beloved of social workers and bolshy teachers. So it was probably the nature of my studies (and to some extent my associates) that inclined my family to think my views more outlandish than was really the case. Political theory and economic history were bound to stir up ideas and cut across conventional bourgeois values. Yet even to use that useful word 'bourgeois' was to be smirched as 'leftist'. In our family one just didn't say that – apart, of course, from Molly and George. I remember how horrified my Uncle George had been when, from the army, I went to help him on his farm and he discovered I had never heard of Karl Marx.

"What! Never heard of Karl Marx? Alan, your education has been sadly neglected."

Jack's Farm, in the parish of Combs, near Stowmarket, was, like Burridge Heath, not much different from what it had been 200 years ago; and, again like Burridge Heath, it was tucked away in the depths of the countryside, its fields nestling comfortably between thick long-standing hedges. It was a charming place, its fields lying on both sides of the winding access lane: an old thatched house with yellow daub walls and a jumble of black wooden barns, beyond which was the stackyard bordered on one side by huge ancient elms, where rooks nested and geese waddled about, honking and hissing at any invaders of their space. Opposite the house, at a bend in the lane, was a duck pond overhung with the branches of willow trees and overgrown bushes, and in the darker reaches of the pond moorhens scurried about. Here Molly kept Muscovy and Aylesbury ducks, and the cows would pause for a drink on their way out from the 'milking parlour'. It was a mixed farm – part dairy, part arable, with about fifteen cows and heifers, each with her own name and recognised personality, whom George addressed in various terms alternately of intimacy, affection, exasperation and fury. The fields too, varying in size from twelve acres down to about two (eighty-four acres in all), had names that had endured through the centuries: Wasp's Meadow, Far Wurzel, Little Spinney, etc. Sometimes George kept a few pigs, and of course there were hens, ducks and geese all over the place. Molly's garden was a riot of flowers and weeds at the front of the house, and a riot of nettles at the back. In the old orchard to one side she kept a couple of beehives.

I got to know the farm well, and spent much of my vacation periods there. Between 1945 and 1950 Uncle George had two to six weeks' tokenly paid, or totally *un*paid, work from me every year – usually during the harvest, but at one time or another including all the seasons. By the end I could turn my hand to virtually anything except opening a first furrow. George took that responsibility himself, but I was allowed to plough once he had got a couple of nice straight lines of turned soil drawn out across the field for me to follow. Sitting on the sturdy little Fergusson tractor, fighting to keep its front wheel in the last furrow, the moaning sound of the engine shutting out all else, I rejoiced in my productive solitude – alone under the sky save for the birds which flocked behind my plough.

George was also helped on the farm (for a more realistic wage, no doubt) by its previous owner, Wilfred Knock, who lived in a cottage nearby. Wilfred was a lean, pink-faced, cantankerous old sod, but whose habitual pessimism was mitigated by a puckish sense of humour.

"Naow, yew can't dew that," he'd say in his Suffolk whine.

"Oh, why can't I do it, Wilfred?"

Wilfred would pause, cast vainly in his mind for a reason, and resort finally to something like "Cos yew in' owld enough."

That, with a twinkle in his eye, was supposed to be funny and annoying at the same time.

Nobody ever saw Wilfred without his hat – certainly he never took it off indoors. He was both a blessing and a bane to my uncle. Having farmed there with his brother all his life, he knew the farm intimately, from the wet patches in a particular field to a defective hatch bolt in the hayloft. He was both a fund of experience and a channel of continuity – extremely useful, but his advice was not always welcome. The trouble was Wilfred knew *everything*. George had only sound practicality, supported by his reading of the latest books and a background of partly relevant experience from sheep farming in Australia and keeping hens in Burridge Heath. But it was now *his* farm, after all. He and Wilfred were bound to clash. The surprise was in how well, nevertheless, they managed to get on with each other. That they did was due to George's ineluctable dependence on Wilfred, and Wilfred's inability to stay away from his old farm. I knew how he felt: even from the few weeks and months that I used to stay with Molly and George (pitching my tent in the orchard in good weather) I came to love the place. Its Molly-ménage, help-yourself, easy-going life, with hard work in the open air and no social demands, suited me down to the ground.

Molly and George naturally reinforced the politically left-leaning influences on me, but they, Ted and Bernard were counterbalanced by my friendship with Adrian Arnold, another fellow student, and with my second cousin Elizabeth Jamieson. Adrian began his studies at Walthamstow Tech, but managed later to secure a place at Cambridge, partly perhaps because of his proficiency at games. I think he took to me originally because he thought I would make a suitable friend for one of his sisters. His family lived at Bournemouth, where his father was the Conservative Party agent – which must surely have been one of the cushiest jobs in politics! As it happened, I saw rather more of a second sister, who was a (young) matron in a small London nursing home. She became, ultimately, rather fonder of me than I was prepared to be of her; and in some confusion, and dismay that a simple friendship was becoming complicated, I backed away.

Elizabeth (Lizzie) was the daughter of Bill Jamieson, a cousin of my father's, who had come down to London to live with us while she did a year (or was it two?) at the Royal College of Art. She was already an accomplished artist, and had been teaching at the Glasgow School of Art, like her husband-to-be, Ted Odling. At the time, Lizzie's relationship with Ted was passing through a turbulent phase, and she was seriously languishing – pining almost – for a love that seemed then destined not to be. Yet, with her dark features, lithe figure and pawky Scottish humour, Lizzie was, when not in the doldrums, a cheery little soul we were all happy to have with us. Her artistic nature, albeit sometimes a bit over the top (as when, for example, she was ecstatically enthusing over shades of grey-purple – or was it a delightful mauvish hue? – in a perfectly ordinary road surface), and her chirpy conversation brought a breath of fresh air into our lives at Plashet Road. Mother and Father were very fond of her, and came almost to treat her as the daughter they never had. Lizzie's own father, like Aunt Sis's husband, had left his wife and only daughter soon after his marriage, he too making a new life in Australia. The reason for taking such a radical step seems to have been his wife's reluctance to leave her own family and embark wholeheartedly on married life: her two sisters were constantly in tow, so Bill may have wondered whether he had not in fact married three women rather than one – except that in this case the possible benefits of polygamy were not on offer.

Bill was also a man of an intellectually rigorous disposition, who would apparently be driven to distraction by his wife saying things like "Turn off the porridge, please, Bill."

"How many times do I have to say it?" her husband would reply through gritted teeth, "You *take* off the porridge; you *turn* off the GAS!"

In those days one could not get a divorce on grounds of incompatibility, so the thing to do was to put as much distance between the two of you as possible; and Australia served very well in that respect. However, unlike Bert Wisely (Aunt Sis's husband), who died there, Bill Jamieson came back after his own wife's death; and there, in Glasgow, he met his daughter Lizzie as if for the first time. It was an affecting reunion, the more so as Lizzie had been brought up to think of her father as an ogre and discovered him far from that. It was sad that they had such a short time together before Bill, too, died.

Lizzie took me in hand on art appreciation, walking me round many of London's galleries, large and small. I eventually became quite passionately fond of a number of modern artists – Paul Nash, Graham Sutherland and John Piper in particular – and was intrigued by the geometrical shapes and colour of such as Ben Nicholson and Victor Passmore. The French Impressionists I came gradually to appreciate, but never really got to grips with Picasso (only bits of him) or, to be honest, Matisse, and certainly not Paul Klee. I ended up profoundly impressed by Cezanne and his classical forerunner Nicolas Poussin. Precision and line seemed to grab me most. I could go overboard for Botticelli, but couldn't say the same for Rubens. Strangely, Lizzie was dismissive of my own efforts at painting, and made no attempt to encourage me; but it was she who overcame my philistine attitude to classical music – through the Promenade Concerts. She and I travelled up on the Underground to Kensington for every one of a current series, usually standing in the middle of the auditorium, but sometimes sitting high up on a balcony, looking down on the orchestra and tiers of eager promenaders as from an Olympian height. Sometimes we met up with a fellow student of Lizzie's at the RCA, Maureen Stafford (then Johnson) – a stunningly beautiful girl – and we would go back to Maureen's bedsitter for coffee and biscuits and exciting discussions about any subjects (no holds barred) before trailing back through the dreary suburbs home again.

I went to the theatre then more often than I ever have since. It was much more accessible to impoverished students than it is now. The cheapest seats in a London theatre would be about half a crown or at most three shillings (between twelve and fifteen pence of today's money). That was for the gods, where you would either be standing at the back of the upper circle or sitting on very hard seats or benches up there. I remember standing through about five hours of Bernard Shaw's *Man and Superman*, with John Clements speaking most of the time in the title role. (Quite a feat – does anyone remember him now?) It was mostly straight plays then; I don't think we ever went to a musical or 'show', such as those which now seem to dominate the West End theatre. I remember seeing *The Lady's Not for Burning* by Christopher Fry on its first run – famous now, perhaps, for Mrs Thatcher's alteration of the last word. The play was very much in vogue then with the critics, but I found it somewhat baffling. Opera, too, presented difficulties to the earnest seeker of aesthetic enlightenment, although one of Gian-Carlo Menotti's (title forgotten) about the dreadful predicament of a girl caught up in the toils of bureaucracy and petty officialdom made a strong impression on me. After post-war disagreements between the

Western powers and Soviet Russia, the Cold War was becoming a dreary set piece in our daily newspapers, and Menotti's evocation of the bleak inhumanity of totalitarian state power was inspiring because, sitting in the audience, one could not but identify with a helpless individual battling fruitlessly against the system.

I don't want to bore you with politics, but this wouldn't be an accurate account of my life as a student if it didn't touch on the controversy of capitalism versus socialism. This argument has now been decisively resolved in favour of capitalism (to be replaced, perhaps, by environmentalism versus globalisation), but at the time it was a hot issue which dominated the discussions of our little faculty, provoking furious disagreement between the rival parties; and it was partly to get a closer look at communism in action that Ted and I decided to go on a 'working expedition' to Yugoslavia in the summer vacation of our first year at the Tech. The plan was that we should work for two weeks on the Belgrade–Zagreb highway (which was then under construction), followed by a week's holiday on the Dalmatian coast as guests of the Yugoslav Government. Marshal Tito had recently broken away from the alliance of East European states – a courageous thing to have done when Stalin was Russia's leader, but an indication of Yugoslavia's geographical advantages and thus relative security from punitive attack (such as Hungary and Czechoslovakia later actually did suffer).

The British Brigade was led by Joe Ball, one of our fellow students, a small, dark, misleadingly diffident member of the Communist Party. He was a typical apparatchik, with nothing to recommend him in personality or intellect; yet, by dint of perseverance, dedication and guile, he had managed to worm himself on to any committee or position of authority that could serve to advance the influence or authority of 'the Party'. (He ultimately became president of the Students' Union.) In addition to the British Brigade, there was a French brigade, a Belgian brigade, a Norwegian brigade . . . Nearly every Western European country sent its brigade. And, after breakfasts of bitter coffee and black bread with a blob of jam, we all marched out to work under the banners of our respective national flags. Yugoslavia may have been a renegade communist country, but it still was a *communist* country.

Everybody got terribly sunburned out on that wide, straight earthen tract flanked by fields of tall yellow maize, and carved through the landscape by the same kind of manual labour as built the railways in nineteenth-century Britain – two or three hundred of us were doing what a couple of bulldozers could have done in half the time. We lived in a hutted camp out there in the Serbian countryside, and there was nowhere to go in the evenings; so we stayed in and received propaganda lectures instead from a succession of Tito's men, pointing out ad nauseam the justice of Yugoslavia's cause. Joe was having kittens lest any of us should challenge some of this guff. His position was curiously anomalous: he was a fervent supporter of Soviet communism and regarded Yugoslavia's apostasy as deplorable disloyalty to 'the cause'; yet, far from being openly critical, he adopted a totally opposite stance. Being naturally devious, hypocrisy caused him not the slightest embarrassment. He was almost certainly engaged in spying activity on behalf of the Party at home. As for myself, although bored to distraction by the niceties of party-line disputation, one had to admire the single-mindedness of these zealots.

An afternoon visit to Belgrade persuaded me that it was the ugliest city I had yet seen, full of nasty featureless concrete-block buildings; there was no decent architecture, and hardly a tree or blade of grass. With very little that was palatable in the restaurants and nothing in the shops, the place had an air of soullessness and dusty dejection that contrasted oddly with the doctrinaire enthusiasm of our camp. Perhaps we saw the wrong bits of the town.

Another Sunday we were transported in trucks to one of the local villages, where in an old orchard on trestle tables we were treated to a good plain meal with as much white wine as we could drink – which was more than I should have drunk. And during our carousal with the villagers, with no minders present, we received an insight into the collectivisation fears of the small farmers. Of course, they supported it – 'a very good system' . . . but not appropriate for *their* situation. To see them in that orchard, with their modest ramshackle buildings, and the odd cow or horse, with chickens, ducks or geese pecking away or waddling about, it was impossible not to fear, in sympathy, that a collective straightjacket would be destroying a way of life that went back through the centuries. Yet now, more than seventy years later, I have to recognise that those centuries-old traditions were riven with hatreds, fears and bitter memories, which Tito did at least, by his unifying system, manage for a time to suppress.

The Dalmatian coast was idyllic. We dived off rocks into sea that was clear as glass, and one day sailed in an old barge to a tiny island – a craggy hilltop emerging from the sea about three miles from the mainland, with a little village surmounted by a church and bell tower clinging to the rocks. We ate our lunch and drank wine under an ancient fig tree at an inn. The sun glinted on the sea and its heat bounced back from the courtyard stones . . . Heaven!

I travelled home independently, via Italy, soaking myself in the picture galleries and churches. In Rome I stayed at the very reasonable YMCA hostel; in Florence I shared a double bed – quite innocently, I hasten to add – with another British student and an army of fleas, all of us seeking cheap accommodation; in Bologna I had an unpleasant landlady; and in Milan, having outwitted two plausible fraudsters who tried to part me from my money, I then blew most of it on a really splendid meal at one of the smartest restaurants. You have to hand it to the Italians: a comparable English establishment would have thrown me out on sight. I walked into this swell joint with my rucksack and a tear from top to bottom at the back of my shirt. The waiter didn't turn a hair. Pausing only to ascertain that I was indeed wanting to eat there (rather than seeking work in the kitchen), with a flourish of napkins he prepared to pull back a chair for me.

"*Buon giorno, Signore! Vuole mangiare?*"

That meal cost me nearly a third of my holiday money for three weeks. Whether it was the quality of the food or the price of it that stays uppermost in the memory, I'm not very sure.

Normally, when not working at Jack's Farm, the vacations would find me walking and camping somewhere in Britain, usually by myself, hitch-hiking – uneventful, but peaceful and relaxing after the term's exertions. Two expeditions, though, with David as companion, were a little more exciting. Hamish had recently taken up canoeing as a sport in which he could participate on level terms with anyone else. Although his work in London (at the Employers' Liability Insurance Society, on the Thames Embankment near Charing Cross) did not allow him to join us on this occasion, he lent us his two canoes for a passage down the Wye from Builth Wells to Hereford. This involved negotiating in places a series of rapids, one or two of them quite tricky even for experienced canoeists (which we were not). The wise thing to do was to carry the boats round difficult stretches; and with my experience of sailing in Loch Gilp as a warning you might have thought I would choose discretion over valour. But fraternal rivalry scorns caution, so whoever was in front pressed on into swirling waters. By the time he realised that was a silly thing to do, it was too late to get out of them and the other had perforce to follow. By sheer good luck we bucketed over several rapids without mishap and, having survived a particularly hair-raising chute between massive boulders, I was congratulating myself on my skill while waiting for David to come through. My elation gradually subsided and turned to alarm, however, when I realised that David had *not* come through. There was no sign of him. From self-congratulation I now cursed my foolhardiness. It was impossible to paddle back upstream and I was making for the side, intending to walk back, when I heard a plaintive call.

"Alan! *Alan!*"

And there was a very forlorn David, dripping wet, standing on the opposite bank. The sight of his bedraggled figure, apparently unharmed, was a tremendous relief. He had indeed capsized and for a few seconds had been underwater, trapped in the cockpit of his canoe, in peril of drowning or hitting his head on a rock – which would have had the same result. Well, we managed to retrieve his canoe – a bit battered, but not too badly damaged – and pitched our tent for the night. It was a small adventure which, in retrospect, may perhaps have taught us a useful lesson not to be stupidly reckless. We completed the trip next day, but left canoeing to Hamish after that.

The following summer we (David and I) were joined by my cousin Ian (Uncle Alasdair's son) on a walk from Pitlochry, cross-country towards Aberdeen. Ian was a hardy outdoor individual who in the war had been commissioned in the Argyll and Sutherland Highlanders – one of those annoying all-weather enthusiasts with a great contempt for anyone not equally robust. And it *was* pretty atrocious weather as we tramped the heather, Ian glorying in it, I doggedly determined to enjoy the beauty of the scenery (when it could be seen through the mist and rain), and David, as usual with his own agenda, keen to reach a road where he could hitch-hike to meet a 'chum' in Aberdeen.

On the second or third night it was already beginning to get dark as, very late and tired, we descended towards what we thought would be the River Dee. Unable to find a suitable spot on which to pitch our tents, owing to the roughness of the terrain, we slung a couple of groundsheets over two large boulders and wedged ourselves down between them for the night, too exhausted to do much more. During the whole of that night the rain pelted down. Our groundsheets dripped, and part of the boulder gap became a watercourse. We stoically had to put up with a thorough soaking until daybreak, when the rain stopped and we could crawl out of our 'shelter' to take stock of where we were.

"First, what we need is a good mug of brose," said Ian, rather enjoying the sight of his companions' damp and dishevelled appearance. (He, of course, merely looked as if he had just emerged from an invigorating shower.)

So we boiled up a pan of water, half filled our mugs with oatmeal, put in a dob of butter and a pinch of salt, then poured on the boiling water and stirred it all up. Excellent and, indeed, as Ian had said, just what we needed to warm us up! I can recommend it.

Further down the hill, as luck would have it, we could see a fine ornate footbridge over a burn – just the thing, we thought, on which to dry our sodden clothes and bedding. Within ten minutes we had made a fire and, with our blankets, socks, shirts and underwear festooning the bridge, we settled down with relish to a second breakfast of sizzling (albeit slightly burned) bacon and sausages. Ah, what joy it was to be out in God's countryside, breathing in the fresh, clean air of the hills! Did ever bacon taste so good? Were sausage ever—? But there was a sudden change in the script. Just as we were tucking in, the night's despondency completely banished in the aroma of sausages, bacon and mountain air, we espied three large gamekeepers, in plus-fours and hairy socks, tramping up the hill in our direction. Their manner was unfriendly.

There was no "Good morning. Sorry you've had a bad night – would you like to warm yourselves down at the house?"

No, it was "Ye're on private property. Ye've got five minutes to be *oot*!"

The feeling of being unwelcome got through even to Ian. We were in fact encamped on His Majesty's Balmoral Estate (George VI was still on the throne); and indeed, on our way 'oot' we passed within a couple of hundred yards of the castle. I am surprised we were not actually escorted out – we could have walked right up to the front door. But no, having delivered their stern rebuke and given us our marching orders, the three gamekeepers resumed their patrol, apparently confident that, as loyal subjects of the King, we would duly make ourselves scarce – which we did, of course. They wouldn't be so trusting nowadays. We probably wouldn't even be able to get there now, let alone be chucked off.

My last expedition, just before qualifying, was to take myself off for a few days' walking in the national park in South Wales – alone – to switch off and clear my head in preparation for my final exams. Having a relatively poor memory for facts, I wanted to have a fresh, alert mind, rather than clutter it up with tedious last-minute cramming. As I returned to London in the train, duly invigorated to face the prospect of a week in the university examination halls, the newspapers were full of sensational news about the prospect of war in Korea.

I ended up with a lower second honours degree, which didn't please me very much. I had hoped for an upper, and think I probably would have managed that if I had been an internal student exposed to better teaching.

13 – ANDOVER

A degree in economics offers a range of possible careers, but, unfortunately, little qualification for any one in particular. Having got mine, I was still not at all clear what I wanted to do. I was definite only that I did not want to go into commerce – the idea of joining a company appalled me. At the back of my mind was a snobbish conceit that selling things was demeaning; what was important was to perform a service that was of some use to one's fellow men. This was more than the highfalutin idea of an immature young man with little experience of the world. We had been brought up to believe in 'service' – you did not live only for yourself. On both sides of our family (Uncle George being a notable exception) the chosen professions for two or three generations back had been in the Church, medicine, engineering and academia. I had no feeling for the Church (and at that time I was weak in spiritual conviction), no great enthusiasm for medicine or engineering – both of which I had briefly entertained as desirable possibilities – and not a good enough degree for academic life. Journalism fell by the wayside – I am not quite sure why. Looking back, I faintly regret that I didn't give it a go. The investigative and foreign correspondent sides of that much maligned profession are appealing, and I did want to go abroad. Anyway, by a process of elimination I was led in the direction of the Colonial Service; but it was Mother, scouring the London University careers list, who discovered a post of 'cooperative officer' in Uganda advertised by the Colonial Office.

The Colonial Office in those days* did not have the prestige of the Foreign Office, yet it did have a kind of raffish glamour; and the Colonial Service had about it an exciting aura of famous men: Cecil Rhodes, Richard Burton, Sir Stamford Raffles, the Brookes of Sarawak, etc. Such names conjured up in the mind deeds of adventure and exploration in Africa and the Far East: trading posts and small British garrisons in the outposts of empire, gunboats and dhows, gold mines, tea plantations, opium and spices. Uganda, where John Hanning Speke had discovered the source of the Nile, definitely sounded promising. I put in my application.

While waiting for this to be processed, a period of some months, involving several interviews with craggy, suntanned officials in the gloomy Colonial Office building in Great Smith Street – and while the result was necessarily unknown to me, I sent out applications to a number of prep schools with the idea of filling in time by doing a spot of teaching. I drew a blank with all except one. The headmaster (and owner) of West Holme School at Andover, in Hampshire, phoned suggesting I come for an interview. Mr Cruikshank was a tall, brown, thin-faced man with a pleasant personality, who struck me, while the interview progressed, as being far keener to employ me than he thought I might be to be taken on. In a comfortable little sitting room at the school (which was a fairly ordinary suburban house) he spent some time describing the amenities of the place, buses, train services, etc. Then his wife came in – a blond, fairly young, vivacious (and curvaceous) woman, all smiles. The conversation came round to drawing, about which they had very little to say except that none of their boys was any good at it, and Mr Curley (whose place I was to take) had no idea either. It was at this point, as I see from the diary I kept at the time (and from which I mainly quote in this chapter), I began to assert myself to such effect that I was offered the job there and then at a salary of £6 a week – which I considered very reasonable, and accepted with alacrity.

---

* The Colonial Office, of course, no longer exists. It has been replaced by the Department for Overseas Development, most of which has been banished to East Kilbride.

14 January 1951
I am to take Form 3, but, as the headmaster put it, 'If you get bored or want a change, just come and see me, or one of the other masters, and we'll swap round for a bit.' He leaves, he says, his masters very much alone: 'So long as you're getting on with your work, I don't care how you do it.' As I have had no experience, I pressed him to say a little bit about his own methods. . . . He was rather vague. . . . My evident anxiety to do things just as he wished them done surprised him. 'You know, you do take us rather seriously,' he said. 'If you feel a little rusty about Algebra and Geometry, just give them a miss for a couple of weeks. Give the class General Knowledge instead – or anything you feel like. You'll soon get the hang of it.'

There were two other masters at the school: Mr Woolley, the science master, who, burly and grizzled, looked more like a plumber, was in charge of Form 4; and Mr Fletcher, a young boy with wide, friendly eyes, was the junior master in charge of Form 1. Mr Cruikshank took Form 2.

18 January
Mr Woolley is a nice, silly chap. 'If you have any difficulties, Mr Hall, just come and see me.' He and I walk up and down the little path round the lawn, and he tells me all about the school, his family life . . . and soil culture ('I've made a very thorough study of Agriculture – I should think I've read . . . oh . . .'). He talks in a very confidential way, occasionally emphasising a point by giving me a vigorous dig in the ribs. . . . He has little piggy eyes, and they twinkle with sudden fire (for they are usually very dull, ruminating). He has very strong views about most things (like most people who do not think deeply) and gives me them all with sometimes irritating assurance. But I like him too.

And I do Mr Fletcher. He is the junior master, a young boy, not very well educated (that I can see) but reasonably intelligent. Perhaps [I say that] because he agrees with everything I say (I really am disgracefully superior sitting here in judgement on everyone, but I don't suppose I'm any different from others; only I write it down). I hope he won't keep it up; it will be so awfully dull after a little while. He is very self-deprecatory and rather shy.

Mr Cruikshank had already made arrangements with a landlady who would look after the new master, and he took me round to make the introduction. I was to be charged £2 a week for board and lodging, on the understanding that I would be away for the weekends and that lunch would be had at the school.

> *21 January*
> Mrs Goddard is a kind old thing but gossips almost unbearably. She and her husband have no children and I get the impression she lavished all her affection on her dogs. Night after night she tells me about 'Tinker', how he was killed, what she did after that and how fond she is of dogs. She is, too, poor thing (I doubt if she can feel much affection for her husband, a very quiet, almost dispirited man). . . .

Reading this in retrospect, many years later, I cringe with embarrassment for the crassly opinionative judgements of my youth, the brashness of which I seemed myself to have been partly aware of – which may, perhaps, be advanced in mitigation.

> I live as one of the family; she treats me very well, though I am not nearly so comfortable as I was at home. Mr G. is out most of the day and evening. He began by being very quiet, almost grumpy. He would answer in monosyllables, as though he couldn't care less about anything. After a little encouragement he started coming out of his shell. He now talks a great deal to me (hardly ever to his wife) about his factory and football. He is Secretary of the local branch of his Union. I tried to get some interesting information from him, but his conversation seldom goes beyond trivial details. Both he and his wife are good, kind people but I do wish I didn't have to live in the same room as they do. I am quite at the mercy of their conversation. . . . If Fletcher introduces me to (of all things) the Conservative Club I shall spend some time at that.
>
> *27 January*
> Things are not going to be so easy as I had thought. The class is inclined to be noisy; their work is very backward; they try to avoid doing work. All this will take time to get right. But I am not yet cynical. I have an idea now of what I am up against. . . . One thing is certain: if teaching is to have any impression on a boy he must have his interest awakened. His energies – and he is full of them – must be canalised into profitable channels, not dammed up by a harsh discipline which merely makes him rebellious.

My diary is interspersed with long, serious cogitations on language, philosophy, the meaning of art and the international political situation – I must have something of my great-grandfather Jamieson in me. But I will spare the reader of these memoirs.

3 February
And now I am back home again. Even though I am earning my own living now I still cannot think of myself as being 'on my own'. . . . At the back of my mind always I know there is a place for me here. It is comfortable but uncomfortable at the same time. I dislike being a burden on others – the feeling of obligation is frustrating. Foolish ideas about trying to repay the 'debt' sometimes muddle about in my mind. Independence is a very precious thing. Sometimes, because I want it so much, I feel I must be selfish. . . . Part of the reason is pride – a foolish thing unless born of self-respect – but chiefly it is a craving for freedom, for a position where I can completely control my own life, where I shall be unfettered from the inhibitions and habits that love and affection demand. Perhaps I am chasing a myth.

5 February
On Monday mornings I have to get up at a quarter to six, so that I can catch a train that gets me to Andover at nine-thirty. . . . On Sunday mornings I usually sleep until half past nine; yet, on Monday, as soon as Mother taps on the door, or even a second or two before, I become instantly wide awake with all my faculties clear. And I do not begin to feel at all sleepy until I have been on the train for half an hour or so.

7 February
Mr Woolley, the senior master, is an active member of the Conservative Party; I think he is the Secretary of his local branch and has some business in the party affairs of his constituency. When he is not talking about his physical condition or his daily journey to and from school he discusses politics in the diffident manner he uses to water – down his obvious bigotry. I expect that when he gets to know me better and I do him (for my own diffidence discourages dogmatism) he will drop this sweet reasonableness and bang his drum as hard as he can. Mrs Cruikshank told me the other day that he was 'dying to know what my *politics* were'.

She added, with her agonising smile: 'Don't tell him, just to please us – just to please us.'

It is probably typical of her. I have heard vague things about

Mrs C. – nothing very favourable – but she is always very pleasant to me. She and Mr Woolley have a feud: it may exist only in Mr W.'s imagination (for he seems to have some kind of persecution complex).

'Did you hear that?' he might say, when Mr or Mrs C. has just left the room. 'That was meant for me; a gentle dig, you might say. Did you notice it, Mr Fletcher?' And he would go on for several minutes, minutely picking out all possible shades of meaning from what he took to be a wounding innuendo.

To go back to Mrs C.'s remark, it is improbable that I would be able to tell Mr W. what my politics were even were he to ask me; certainly they do not fit comfortably inside the politics of any one of the parties. To say that illustrates the gulf that separates W. and me. He thinks there is a fundamental opposition between Labour and Conservative; to him, the man who stands between does not understand the issues.

21 February

My life is rather monotonous now. I live in Andover five days of the week and go home each weekend. And every one of the five days has a dull familiarity. The same time each morning, I get up; I go to the school at nine, say good morning to a few boys in the garden and, after hanging up my coat, take my books and morning paper into the sitting room. If I am early no-one else is there and I can sit down and read the headlines. But it is never very long before I hear the front door open, someone scraping his feet on the mat, hanging up a coat in the hall: in comes Mr Woolley, rubbing his hands energetically.

'Good morning, Mr Hall,' he says very cheerfully.

And I reply, 'Good morning, Mr Woolley,' with similar vivacity.

'My goodness, the roads are bad this morning! I had to get off my bike more than once before negotiating some of the more, er . . .' He gropes for a word.

'Icy?'

I am ignored. . . .

'Tricky parts.' He takes out his pipe and wipes his lips before inserting it in his mouth. 'I rather suspected it, you know,' he goes on, as though he had given much wise thought to the matter (he speaks very indistinctly round his pipe stem). 'I can usually judge with a fair degree of accuracy what kind of weather the fates have in store for us the following morning.'

'On the previous night, you mean?' I ask intelligently.

'A *fair* degree of accuracy – I don't say for a moment that I'm always right; in the nature of things, things being as they are, I can't set up as being a human metero . . . metiero . . . weather forecasting . . . er . . .'

He leers round at me, and I add, 'Machine.'

He stands in the middle of the carpet and works his feet into it as though into specially fitted slots. He wastes many matches trying to light his pipe satisfactorily . . . and puffs furiously until he forgets it.

Mr Fletcher comes in soon and we all exchange enormously bright good mornings, but it doesn't disturb Mr W.'s conversation: 'My runner beans. I had hoped to get them in before this, but the weather being so bad and my health not being so good as it normally is . . .' Here he is in a dilemma whether or not to talk about his health – he cannot often resist doing it.

Mr Cruikshank may come in before the bell goes, but he does only if he has something to say. ('I wonder if you would mind. . . . Mrs Whatnot phoned up last night. . . . Apparently. . . . You would? Oh, that's grand. . . . Yes, yes, oh yes, I do agree. . . . Well, if you would. . . . Thank you very much.'

Then the bell goes.

I walk out into the garden, round the side of the house to my classroom, which is a wooden hut, much too small for twenty-two boys. Outside it about seven boys are changing their shoes. (That is one of the things the headmaster really is particular about); a few others lounge about, doing nothing. I have stopped asking them why they are not inside: they all have wonderful excuses. I just hustle them in. Inside the classroom, the boys are all over the place, some clustered round a comic, some arguing about foreign stamps, perhaps two of them rolling about on the floor locked in each other's grip, or one swinging from the cross sections of the roof (which is not very high – about eight feet). I walk in and stare about until they are all standing up quietly.

'Good morning.'

'Morning, Sir.'

'Sit down. Stop talking.'

Discipline is not very good yet, especially among the older boys, who have had experience of Mr Curley. A few cluster round me and ask their questions all together, which means that, in order to be heard, they have to shout as loud as they can, gesticulating energetically. Usually it takes little effort to disperse them, achieve a precarious silence, and bring them to their feet for prayers. I enunciate a collect clearly and loudly, and they respond with 'Amen.' Then we gallop through the Lord's Prayer.

Teaching here is full of difficulties. Only four boys have desks that they can put their books in; the others must keep books in satchels or pile them up on the tables they work at. None of them has any text book; everything must be dictated or written up on the board.... Few boys have an atlas; many have no pencils even. They are all cramped together. Efficient work is therefore almost impossible. It is rather discouraging, but I do what I can.

'Get out your English books.'

'Please Sir, mine's full up.'

'Please Sir, I haven't got a pencil.'

'Use a pen, then. You should have got a new book yesterday; use a piece of paper.'

'I haven't got one, Sir.'

'Can anyone lend Greene a piece of paper? Here, use this. DON'T TALK, the rest of you. We shall go on with the analysis we began—'

'Sir, will you tell Clark to give me back my pencil?'

'I haven't got one, Sir.'

'You should have one, Clark; and anyway, use a pen.'

'I've run out of ink, Sir.'

'Then fill it.'

'There's no ink here, Sir.'

'Very well, use a pencil.... Yes, lend it to him, Fenning. You should all have done the five sentences I gave you last week.... If you weren't here, Sim, then obviously you can't have done it. Those who *were* here... For your benefit, Allum, I shall explain it again.... Put that marble AWAY!'

And so it goes on. The room is very stuffy; two oil stoves burn away, giving off a stale, oily smell....

After morning classes I go up to Mr Woolley's Form room and preside over the lunch of a miscellaneous collection of boys [those who do not go home for lunch]; some have sandwiches and some the school meal. The tilt of the desks makes eating from a plate a difficult business – especially if there is much gravy. After lunch, I say Grace and go down to whatever duty I am put down for: football, patrolling the grounds, or simply sitting in the sitting room, talking to the man who should be patrolling the grounds. Afternoon classes end at a quarter to four. If I am not giving Tozer tuition I go back to my lodgings, and either go out to the pictures, or stay in and read or write (if I am able to give my attention to it); then supper and bed. I never read in bed – too cold.

26 February 1951
I have just been correcting a batch of my boys' essays; some of them are quite delightful. . . . The boys had to write an essay about a fire – any composition, so long as a fire is part of it. None of them attempted anything descriptive; it was all factual stuff, usually a narrative of events. One essay was entitled: 'The Case of the Swiss Wristwatch', but it had nothing to do with a Swiss wristwatch; it just, he said, 'sounds good'. Other boys of imagination turned their fire into something very sinister: one had a boy who was kidnapped; the police arrived just in time to prevent him being roasted alive on a pile of burning rubber tyres (he was bound and gagged, of course). Exactly why the poor devil should be so warmly treated I could not find out: I got the impression that any question about it would be quite beside the point. Another essay on similar lines was even more inconsequential; I shall paraphrase it. Bill was a fireman who was called out to a fire at Something-or-other Manor. While he was 'rummaging about in the hedges' [I had learned not to question this seemingly astonishing action of a fireman who should have been putting out a fire] he found a cigarette lighter with the initials 'JB' on it. Later on, after the fire was put out, a frizzled body was found in the house. Bill suspected foul play; so did the police. All they needed was proof. Bill produced his lighter; that was all they needed. Confronted with this damning piece of evidence, the Murderer confessed. The number of bodies that were found in fire-gutted houses was astonishing. None of these corpses was allowed to have been merely burned to death; that would be far too prosaic. . . . All murderers, or attempted murderers, were caught, and most of them duly sentenced to death or some other specific punishment.

One boy set his story in Fairyland; one or two described Guy Fawkes mishaps that they had actually witnessed ('. . . and a policeman came round and asked Daddy how Mr Synge's hut had been burned down and we told him and Daddy had to pay Mr Synge for another hut'). The best essay described a party in a cottage that was surprised by a thunderstorm ('. . . and the rain came down in bucketfuls and the sky was black, and grey with the clouds that were there'). There was tragedy too, but it was brushed aside with youthful buoyancy ('. . . and they were all burned to death. The man [husband of the incinerated family] was very sad, but they put the fire out alright.').

5 March
Elizabeth and I went to the Albert Hall – to a promenade concert – on Saturday night. Most of it I enjoyed very much; but a new concerto (I think it was) by Murril rather dragged – at least, I found it a little tedious. . . . My approach to painting is more intellectual than emotional; to music it is the reverse. I can feel more stimulated by music when it is being played, but it does not leave a lasting impression; art does. During the interval we went out onto the stairs and looked from a high window onto a lamp-lit street below. People were scuttling about, dark forms, casting long, shifting shadows; occasionally a bus or car sped swiftly along, noiseless, for we could hear nothing through our closed window. The hard corner of a building jutted blackly against the diffusion of lights, and in its looming shade the angles and lines of interesting architecture could be dimly made out. Beyond the building and the pale glare of street lamps a murky greenness suggested the edge of Hyde Park; the rest was formless gloom in which anything could be imagined. I remember all that much more vividly than any of the music; and the recollection is more satisfying.

13 March
On Saturday I went to the Old Vic to see *Henry V*. The theatre [newly refurbished] is charming: red and pale grey; not very large, but beautifully clean, neat and compact. The only part I did not like was the pillars, but since they were necessary, they were as pleasant as they could be. The stage is set in such a way, in a series of steps up from the amphitheatre, that the intimacy between audience and players is strengthened; I think this series of steps is called the proscenium [approximately right]. The play is done with very simple scenery (if it can be called that): a few draped curtains, heraldic shields, three army baggage carts and perhaps a backcloth: all this fortified by skilful use of lighting. But nothing was done that might have taken away from the beauty of the words in the play. These were in fact very carefully emphasised by the complete absence of movement of those who were not speaking: the normal petrification of soldiers and courtiers made them almost part of the setting. No movement or action was ever allowed to distract from what was being said. I would have appreciated this all the more if I had known the play better.

19 March
I spent Monday afternoon and evening with Ted; I do enjoy going over there. He is one of the few friends of mine whose interests are much the same as mine. Down here I live so much inside myself. I have found no-one I can talk to and really enjoy it. I sometimes argue politics with Mr Woolley, but he is not very bright, and very prejudiced. Since he finds me seldom in agreement with him he has begun patronising me: 'We are all young once, Mr Hall. I like to see a youngster favouring the Left.'

20 March
I am sitting sideways on a rather hard kitchen chair, writing at the table in the kitchen (or living room). It has a scarred leather top on it – dark, and stained with rings and blobs – and on this top are a pile of *Manchester Guardian*s, a book by Proust, and one about Landscape in Art by Kenneth Clark, and there is a vivid yellow ruler that I forgot to take upstairs to my room when I had finished writing up my reports. Beside me, in one wall, is a large, old-fashioned kitchen stove, not used for cooking, but occasionally to warm the room: a shovel-full of coal and some sticks are lying on top of it now. But we are using the gas fire and it is softly hissing away, making the room abominably stuffy (I shall open a window. . . . I have). A tall scuttle of coal stands in the hearth on one side; beside it, a pair of Mr Goddard's shoes. On the other side is an ugly, twisted bit of wood, culminating in an ash-tray at the top, around which are hung poker, brush and tongs. Two arm-chairs draped with odd bits of clothing (a skirt and some blue material), a sideboard, a desk and another hard chair – all tawdry, unvarnished or hideously varnished stuff – complete the furniture. Except for the pouffe – 'dumty', Mrs Goddard calls it; that is behind me. The wallpaper is a dismal brown. A large clock ticks slowly on the wall opposite me; another, with a faster tick, stands on the mantelpiece: both are chimers but, thank goodness, only one of them chimes the quarters. I have forgotten the gramophone: that stands in another corner, a big walnut cabinet with ridiculously thin little legs; it is used for putting odds and ends in: ration books, thimbles, library books.

Except for the ticking of the clocks and the smooth hissing of the gas, it is very quiet; quiet and warm. Outside I can hear the trains shunting about and letting off steam. Mr G. is upstairs above me; occasionally I hear his bed creak (he was on night shift last night). Mrs G. is out; she does not often go out, but tonight she has, and I am alone. . . .

The ceiling is low and cracked, yellow-coloured; the room is small and drab – poor things, they know nothing better – or rather, I have done nothing that deserves better. How silly! I am getting maudlin. I should like to have a sledge hammer and knock a hole in the fireplace.

5 April
I am going to see Ted and Bernard, and a cousin of Bernard's. We are going to see *Mad Woman of Chaillot* at St James'. Mother and Father came home from seeing it last Thursday, and their opinions about it were most equivocal: they had not really enjoyed it but it was a very clever play; I would enjoy it. It was a very mysterious report.

Elizabeth went up to Scotland the day before yesterday. . . . Poor girl, she was not looking forward to it very much. I feel very sorry for her. And yet, at the same time, I feel I am becoming more unsympathetic about her predicament: she does nothing to help herself; merely lives in a stuffy little introverted world, unenthusiastic about anything, interested in practically nothing, narrow-minded and self-centred. She used to go out to shows with me, or concerts (there must be nothing 'low-brow' or frivolous about her entertainment) but now she will clutch at anything which excuses her from upsetting the dreary routine of the day. . . . Perhaps one day I shall have a talk with her; but I do not suppose I shall have any success: she is as narrow as one can be, and most unreceptive to advice.

16 April
I am going to have an interview with the Colonial Secretary's Adviser on Cooperation on Friday. I wrote an angry letter about two weeks ago, asking why my application was taking so long to be considered; this must be the result of it. This afternoon I shall spend in the library, reading up as much as I can about cooperative societies.

Adrian spent a couple of days with us last week. He has just come out of hospital after breaking his leg at football, and was still on crutches with his leg in plaster. That did not prevent him from having two fairly strenuous days. On Tuesday we met two Dutch girls (whom he had met at Nice). . . . We gave them lunch and took them off to Hyde Park . . . the park looked green and pleasant in patchy sunshine. We took out a boat and rowed about the Serpentine and, when a shower came upon us, sheltered under a bridge and ate sandwiches. We had told the girls about the speakers at Hyde Park Corner, so we went across to hear them. But only one man, inoffensive, not very eloquent, was there, trying to sell (or give away) Testaments. After listening to him for a few moments we crossed the road and went into a large and rather garish hotel (the Cumberland, I think) which had bookstalls in the foyer and large armchairs; the lighting was ostentatious and efficient; it was all very clean and modern, full of people and uniformed pages hurrying about. It was really rather like a luxurious station waiting room (complete with loud-speaker). Anyway, it looked very magnificent and was quite admirable for having a wash and brush-up. The girls were most impressed. Then we trundled them off to a picture and ended up in a pub. They saw quite a bit of London on their first day. Their delight at riding on the top of a bus was charming . . . but we were not such good guides as we were expected to be.

1 May
I had my interview a week ago last Friday; it went off quite well. I say that, but I have no idea what the result will be. One is so keyed-up and apprehensive before it that merely being put at ease gives a feeling of achievement. The men on the Board were quite charming, and I soon settled down. When I think of the intelligent questions I answered and asked, I think what a fine fellow I must have appeared; but then I think of the silly things I did say and the clever things I did not say. Really, I don't know what to think.

9 May
The Festival of Britain has attracted a great deal of attention: most criticisms have been favourable; in fact much of the comment has been most enthusiastic. The whole thing fills me with pleasure. . . . It shifts the emphasis away from [post-war] gloomy thoughts and brings to everyone a glimpse of what we can do and what we normally do, puts things in perspective.

My application for a post in Uganda must have dropped through a hole in the Colonial Office bureaucracy, because I was eventually accepted for a similar job in Tanganyika (now Tanzania). I noted in my diary, some days after receiving the good news, 'I am delighted, and very busy. I leave the school at the end of this week.'

Shortly afterwards I made a trip up to Islay with Mother and Father, to stay with my Uncle Alasdair and Aunt Jean. Father and I went fishing on a lonely loch, from a small boat, in wet and windy weather. Back in the Smiths' house, at Port Ellen, a small incident, not recorded in my diary, sticks in my mind: how annoyed Mother was with me for insisting on listening through to the very end of Beethoven's Fifth Symphony while everybody else (who had treated it simply as background music to their conversation) had gone off to play clock golf. Mother stayed behind with me, grimly drumming her fingers, furious at my lack of sociability, while I obstinately waited for each succeeding record to plop down on the turntable.

I mention that trivial little scene, not simply because it has stayed with me, but because it seems to show me (and you, the reader) the young man I was seventy years ago, as also does the diary from which I have extensively quoted in this chapter – parts of which show me as crassly arrogant and opinionated. Are all young people like that? (For that matter, do we become any better as we get older – or do we just learn to be more circumspect?)

The final entry in my diary describes visits to the Festival of Britain. This brilliant idea, inspired and brought to achievement by Herbert Morrison, the Labour Home Secretary, mirrored the famous 1851 Crystal Palace exhibition, and was intended to banish the gloom of post-war drabness; for Britain had remained, throughout the six years of Labour government, a dingy, exhausted country. It had been impoverished by the tremendous war effort. Rationing had continued for more than five years after the end of it, supplies had been so tight. The job of reconstruction, of reabsorbing the hundreds of thousands of demobilised servicemen (like myself) was enormously demanding. The Festival of Britain, on London's South Bank, was therefore a flourish to cheer us all up, to demonstrate the exciting possibilities of scientific progress and industrial renewal; and, in the Battersea Festival Gardens, its funfair gay with painted canvas, sideshows and roundabouts, we were able to shake off at last the wartime mentality that had become almost a way of life. In its refreshing optimism, the festival's call to the nation precisely reflected my own mood. The symbolism, as I made ready to embark on my new life, was apt.

14 – TANGANYIKA

In 1951 there was still something romantic about the colonies. Perhaps West Africa was no longer 'the White Man's Grave', but East Africa still conjured up pictures in the mind – of Stanley meeting Livingstone at Ujiji, of Speke discovering the source of the Nile, and Burton's dramatic denunciation of him at the Royal Geographic Society in London. 'Going out' to Africa still meant something of an expedition, calling for special preparation and fitting-out. Indeed, there were in London two old-established firms of 'tropical outfitters', whose purpose and pleasure it was to provide for every conceivable need of young men posted to the hotter parts of Britain's far-flung empire. As I searched out the premises of Messrs Griffiths MacAlister in a dingy side street near Piccadilly Circus, I felt that I was treading ground that the great explorers, too, had trod. The eyes of Messrs Griffiths MacAlister's assistant lit up as I entered their unpretentious shop.

"Ah," they seemed to say, "this isn't someone looking for a few spare candles for his water filter. This one's here for the full treatment."

Having quickly established that he was right in that assumption, and that I had little idea what I might need, he produced, with a practiced inclination of the head and a helpful smile, a list as long as your arm, headed 'Essential Clothing and Equipment for Persons Travelling to Tropical Countries', which he politely suggested might be helpful to me in deciding what to order. My eyes skimmed down the list: '6 prs shorts (khaki), 10 cotton shirts (white), 12 prs socks, 2 mess jackets . . . 6 tubes toothpaste, 3 tins Andrews Liver Salts,

1 camp bed, 1 mosquito net, 1 camp chair, 1 camp basin/bath . . . 1 map case . . .' Hang on a minute: *one map case?* Was that really necessary?

The assistant stroked his chin, pondered, and replied with the air of one who has been putting years of experience to work: "Well, I think we could perhaps dispense with the map case, sir."

I sailed from the Albert Dock (only about three miles from where we lived) on the *Dunottar Castle*, one of a line that then plied regularly between Britain and the Cape via the Mediterranean, the Suez Canal and East Africa. Air passage was still an adventurous and unusual mode of travel, and making these long, slow journeys out by sea was one of the delights of the Colonial Service (especially as travel time was counted as 'duty' – even when travelling on, or back from, leave). With the exception of Genoa (which has a romantic enough history of its own), the ports we stopped at were like a roll call of the British Empire: Gibraltar, Port Said, Suez, Port Sudan, Aden, Mombasa . . . I shared a cabin with three other young men, whom I have totally forgotten, but I spent time with two pretty South African girls, twins, who unfortunately had too many other admirers for me to make headway. One of them complimented me on the neatness of my fingernails, but that was as far as it went. Both could speak Xhosa, complete with 'clicks' – which was quite a party trick – but were scornfully illiberal in their attitude to 'bleck' African development.

Shipboard acquaintances and a new slant on political argument were, however, no more than ripples on the great swell of new experience which now attracted, intrigued and delighted every fibre of my being. It is difficult, though, to convey in a few generalities of description the sharpness of detail that quickened my senses in each new port, and indeed on the ship itself: the narrow, bustling streets of Gibraltar (where the ship stood off in the straits, to disgorge us precariously down gangways on to pitching launches to be ferried ashore in a flurry of spray and diesel smoke); the little boats of the Port Said hawkers beneath the cliff-side of the *Dunottar Castle* (lines were thrown so that passengers, leaning over the rails, could haul up goods for inspection – "Just to look, Mrs McGregor, just to look" – with a little bag for cash, if 'Mrs McGregor' wanted to keep the leather belt or embroidered rug, or perhaps even a camel seat, if Mr McGregor was willing to give a hand). I was amazed at the stately progress of enormous ships in the Suez Canal, and how, at certain crossing points, there was the incredible sight of an ocean liner sailing majestically through the desert, or so it seemed. And there was the sun. The sun had followed us all the way – glorious August sunshine as we made our way up the Thames Estuary, becoming warmer in the Mediterranean – a daily invitation to swim in the ship's small pool, or to seek a quiet corner to recline in an extended deckchair with a book and a *pint* of orange juice (a great luxury). Almost suddenly, in the Red Sea warmth became oppressive heat. Then, instead of perspiring in the airless confinement of rather smelly cabins, most of us sought respite by sleeping on deck at night. This tropical gauntlet nevertheless served as a sort of inoculation against the degrees of heat that we were to experience almost continuously from then onwards, as our ship vibrated, hummed and thumped its course steadily through open waters, with seagulls flying alongside and in our wake. Sometimes we were accompanied by a school of porpoises, sometimes by flying fish; and just occasionally there would be a glimpse of land to confirm that for most of the time we were hugging a coastline.

I was scheduled to disembark at Dar es Salaam (haven of peace) and my luggage had been labelled and stowed accordingly, but at Mombasa a message reached me to say I was to disembark there and proceed by train to Moshi. The personnel people at the Colonial Office had not realised that the headquarters of my department was at Moshi, in the north of Tanganyika, and not at the capital. Moshi was about 250 miles from the coast – a mere day's journey. So it was from a quite comfortable sleeper of the East African Railways that, once we had crossed the border, I had my first sight of the country I was to live and work in for the next twelve years.

At more than 360,000 square miles (including part of the great lakes of Victoria, Tanzania and Nyasa), Tanganyika* is a large country – bigger than France and Germany combined – and crawling along those 250 miles (the train splitting at Voi, with the

*I use throughout the names as they were at the time. Tanganyika is now, of course, Tanzania.

main part going on to Nairobi, and my smaller bit puffing round Mount Kilimanjaro to Moshi) even the top north-eastern corner of it that we traversed, seemed big. Once we had left the tropical coastal belt (with its uniquely memorable 'baked-potato' and decaying-vegetation smell), it was just miles and miles of mostly open grassland, dotted with the occasional flat-topped acacia, or groups of stubby baobab, 'the trees that God planted upside down'.

All that I had known about East Africa could have been written on the back of one of the handsome postage stamps illustrated with pictures of a snow-capped Kilimanjaro, giraffes and the head of King George VI, which were used throughout Kenya, Uganda and Tanganyika, and which I had assiduously included in my stamp collection at King's Leigh. Tanganyika had a history of penetration by the Arabs for almost 500 years before Vasco da Gama arrived at Kilwa, south of Dar es Salaam, in 1502, 'with a very large fleet'. For 200 years the Arabs and the Portuguese tussled it out for dominance of the coast, until eventually the Portuguese settled for the strip south of Cape Delgado (from which they were to colonise Mozambique), leaving power over the northern part of the coast – and effective influence over the tribes of the interior – in the hands of the Sultan of Zanzibar.

The Arabs, therefore, were 'exploring' and trading (mainly slaves and ivory) in East Africa long before Europeans other than the Portguese came on the scene. But it was the reports of explorers and missionaries, such as Burton, Speke and Livingstone, which drew wider attention to the opportunities for trade – and which ultimately led to a 'scramble for Africa' in the last two decades of the nineteenth century, when most of the Western European powers, by one means or another, staked out and appropriated huge chunks of territory for their respective empires. Indeed, by a process of skullduggery, sharp practice and diplomatic arm-twisting the Germans – with the British and French looking on – managed to extract from the Sultan of Zanzibar his reluctant acquiescence to a German 'sphere of influence' over what is now Tanzania. In 1890 the territory was ceded absolutely to Germany; but the Germans, who ruled it with extreme harshness, were to hold it for little more than twenty-five years. After their defeat in the 1914–18 war (which included military defeat in East Africa) the territory was put under British trusteeship by the League of Nations – precursor to the United Nations. That was its status in 1951. It was not a colony, like Kenya; it was a trust territory.

My train clattered on through this vast landscape, sometimes stopping at wayside halts so that we could walk along the track to the restaurant car – and later, at another stop, back to our carriage. Meals, as on the ship and in most East African hotels, were announced by an attendant walking up and down the track, playing on a small xylophone a variation of 'Come to the Cookhouse Door, Boys'. After about fifteen hours – interrupted by much shunting about at Voi during the middle of the night – we finally hissed slowly into Moshi Station. The platform at once became alive with descending passengers and struggling porters. One or two Europeans stood out in the melee, scruffily dressed in bush jackets and shorts. A tall, cleaner-looking man, seated on a shooting stick, was scanning the carriages – the only 'official' sort of person in sight. It proved to be Bill Wenban-Smith, the Acting Commissioner for Cooperative Development.

It was characteristic of the Colonial Service that senior officers upcountry took a close and particular interest in their junior compatriate staff, personally meeting them off planes or buses (or trains) and supervising their arrangements for accommodation. It was a kindness that was reciprocated when they, in turn, visited you at your duty station and you would be expected to put them up in your own house. It made for pleasantly informal relationships and a very good working understanding. Wenban-Smith shook hands, enquired whether I'd had a good trip, and proceeded at once to have my luggage and freight – which, I observed with relief and some astonishment, had accompanied me intact – put on to a dusty pickup outside the station. He then drove me in his own car 200 yards down a dirt road to a rather tatty-looking, originally white building with a sign outside stating 'Piccadilly Hotel'. Here Wenban-Smith dropped me, saying he expected I'd like to have a bit of a rest, and that he would call for me the following morning. Having introduced me to the hotel manager, a thin, unkempt-looking Englishman known as Scotty, he then departed in a cloud of dust, leaving his newly arrived subordinate to cope by himself with the sudden materialisation of what had been, two days previously, only a vague, romantic idea of 'Tanganyika' into what was now the smell and feel of a real destination.

Upcountry hotels in East Africa at that time had a style and character unmistakably their own. Apart from the railway hotels in some of the larger towns, such as Dodoma, Iringa and Mbeya, most of them were owner-managed. The heart and soul of these usually ramshackle and often none-too-clean establishments was the bar – a place where you could expect to find *someone* at least drinking at any hour of the day and almost any hour of the night. At 'lunchtime' – beginning around ten thirty and continuing until sometime after three in the afternoon, but having little to do with an actual meal – and in the evenings following closely thereafter, the bar was a place of great conviviality and noise, presided over by the proprietor. He did this partly to keep a beady eye on the bar boy, and partly because he enjoyed the company and had nothing else to do (all the serious work of running the hotel being left to the 'boys', with daily bollockings to keep them up to the proprietor's idea of scratch – in practice not too demanding, though invariably distant from the boys' idea of it). The accepted method of accounting was by chitty, on which you wrote down what drinks you had or stood other people. This no-cash system undoubtedly helped to foster East Africa's reputation for hard drinking – leading quite a few men to dissolution and ruin.

Bedrooms were as often as not (mercifully) separate from the main building, sometimes in grass-thatched rondavels. Containing perhaps a bed, a chair and a battered wardrobe, they would usually have a concrete-floored annex with a drain, where washing and showering was done. Bedrooms were hardly ever mosquito-proofed. Routinely, therefore, every evening, the room boys would let down the mosquito nets above each bed and *piga dawa* (literally 'beat the medicine', i.e. pump a 'Flit-gun') all round the room. If the boy forgot to close the windows, the effect of the spray rapidly dissipated; if not, the smell of insecticide lingered throughout the night.

In the morning you were awakened about six thirty by a boy

bringing tea on a tin tray. You would probably notice then that the sheets were stained, the cup chipped, and the boy's kanzu (a long-sleeved calico – Indian cotton – gown reaching to the ankles) torn. The tea had the taste I associate with Carnation tinned milk. The water was boiled over the wood fire in an outhouse kitchen, where the cook slept for much of the day.

Tea drunk, you would poke your head out of your room and bawl, "*Boi! Lete maji.*"

Swahili is a subtle language. *Lete maji* is the polite way of saying "(Please) bring water." If you simply shout, "*Leta maji*," it's an order without any respect for the person addressed.

On the way to the dining room (it is best to say nothing about the lavatory) you would quite likely see the owner having a row with one of the boys. Your presence would make no difference to the altercation, and the boy's face, when he came eventually to serve you, would betray no evidence of it. Disputes with servants were, regrettably, part of a normal day, especially of wives (whose standards were more exacting than their husbands') and the lower orders of expatriate; but in the colonial service such disputes were deprecated and considered to show an inability to relate properly to the local people – which was indeed often the case.

At the Cooperative Department office I was introduced by Wenban-Smith to three fellow Cooperative Officers, with whom I was to spend about a month's briefing: Leslie Chapman, the local man, middle-aged, inarticulate, pleasant (with a considerably younger German wife and new baby), who was supposed to give us the briefing, and two new men, like me – Andy Walker and Bill Clegg – who were to receive it. In practice, Leslie was too busy with his own work to give us much of his time, and the other two seemed quite sure that they already knew everything that it was necessary for them to know. As for myself, 'taking things seriously', as Mr Cruikshank would have said, I was irritated by their willingness to spend the days in discursive conversation about literally anything – chit-chat that might as well have been over a drink in a bar. Both already had experience of Cooperation with a capital C (which probably explained their blasé know-it-all attitude), so I was able to tap their brains about this, for me, novel type of socio-economic organisation. In spite of their propensity to drift away from the subject, they did nevertheless teach me the elements of standard accounting practice, and an idea of Cooperative principles, albeit while simultaneously providing an insight into the rival merits of Rangers and Celtic (both Andy, a former commando, and Bill were Scots).

Everybody knows that the first cooperative society was started in the middle of the nineteenth century by the Rochdale Pioneers, as a means of protecting the poor against exploitation by employers and their own thriftlessness. Indeed, its association, in British minds, with the working class, socialism, and shops that always seem one step behind the competition, has given Co-ops a persistently downmarket cachet. My brother David's nostrils would flare at the mention of 'cooperatives', and I am amused by the reflection that, were he to have mentioned it (which he probably didn't) he would have found my profession a severe embarrassment in the wardroom of his ship. Although we had a Co-op within fifty yards of our house at Plashet Road, Mother never set foot inside it. It was just one of those things people were unashamedly snobbish about – even among Europeans in East Africa, where *ushirika* (cooperation) was a tradition of the people.

What is the difference between a cooperative society and a joint-stock company? In the general conduct of business there is no difference: both are organisations established with a specific trading objective. The cooperative societies in Tanganyika were almost all set up to help farmers sell their crops. In Songea, where I was to be posted, the two main cash crops were tobacco and coffee. Here in Moshi – or, more accurately, on the slopes of Mount Kilimanjaro – the Chagga tribe also grew coffee. Like many hill tribes, they were a progressive people; and they were fortunate in having the assistance of a remarkable Englishman. A. L. B. Bennett joined the Colonial Service from the air force (with a DFC) as a labour officer, and in this capacity he got involved in the business of coffee marketing, which not only changed the district dramatically, but had an influence throughout Africa. From a free-for-all system under which the growers had individually sold small quantities of badly processed coffee beans to local traders at rock-bottom prices, he built up, over a number of years, about twenty-five separate marketing cooperatives. Scattered over the lower slopes of the mountain (which is a pretty huge area) these rather basic outfits had the simple task of assembling the coffee, separating it into a few standard grades of quality, and weighing it accurately. It doesn't sound very exciting, but it revolutionised the Chagga farmers' economy: under the old regime traders and farmers cheated each other with abandon; under Bennett's system a fair price was paid for *accurately weighe*d fair-quality commodities. Low-quality commodities got a low price; higher-quality commodities a higher price. For the first time farmers could see that it paid to take pains over matters of cultivation and (quite complicated) on-farm processing; there was also an incentive to produce more.

As it happened, the time of my arrival in East Africa coincided with the start of the Korean War, when the price of many commodities went sky-high. In Tanganyika this was a tremendously encouraging boost to the organisation of farmers' cooperatives, and to the production of coffee in particular. The traders – overwhelmingly Asian – were associated in farmers' minds with sharp practice and low prices, the cooperatives with a fair deal and higher prices. And there was also the great advantage that the cooperatives paid twice: first, what was called an 'advance' payment; and secondly, after the produce had been sold and all expenses and necessary appropriations (cause of much disputation at AGMs!) met, a final payment in which all the remaining money was shared round in proportion to the crop of each farmer member.

That was the general picture – the media presentation, so to speak, reasonably accurate but leaving out the blemishes. We shall come to the problems, drawbacks and headaches later, after I have described my arrival in Songea district. First I had to learn how things *ought* to be done, and at that time there was no better place to learn than Moshi. I was, in effect, on a pilgrimage to the shrine of A. L. B. Bennett, who had brought into being the famous KNCU (Kilimanjaro Native Cooperative Union), the union of those twenty-five or so primary cooperatives, with an overall membership exceeding 20,000, producing each year about 5,000 tons of coffee.

Andy, Bill and I made several visits to Bennett in his then

unpretentious office. (In accordance with Parkinson's law, the KNCU was in the process of building itself a large and impressive new headquarters building). He was a small, engagingly shy, roly-poly man of about fifty, with a round bald head and twinkling eyes. He spoke in a quiet, clerically modulated, self-deprecatory voice, as if conscious of his role as the Tanganyika cooperative guru.

"There is nothing magic about our success; we simply ensure correct weights and fair prices."

Officially he was executive officer of the Moshi Coffee Board, a position which gave his advisory function the steel of government authority – a very convenient arrangement, which was copied in other parts of the territory, including Songea (where I eventually occupied a similar position). Bennett lived up in the foothills with his ancient mother and, reputedly, three African wives (although this may be an underestimate).

My month in Moshi was passed quite agreeably with my two fellow novitiates, both of whom were accompanied by their wives and, in Bill Clegg's case, by a small son about three years old. Bill Wenban-Smith, an administrative officer who did everything by the book, invited us all to lunch – including the little boy, who, to his mother's intense embarrassment, played up appallingly, shrieking and drumming his feet under the table. The Wenban-Smiths throughout all this *kelele*, in the extraordinary British way of politely ignoring social gaffes, continued with the conversation as if the boy did not exist. Intended perhaps to show that *they* were not put out, the effect was actually the reverse of that intention so far as the Cleggs were concerned. I felt sorry for Molly Clegg. The Chapmans were more sympathetic hosts. We ate many lunches at their house, and from both of them gathered more useful information than we had ever received by way of official briefing about the sort of life we were now embarking on.

On 24 October, briefing (such as it was) completed, and accompanied still by my two tin trunks and three crates, I boarded a 'railways' bus for Njombe, a two-day journey on the corrugated, red murram Great North Road down the centre of the territory to Iringa, then branching south-east into the hill country of the Southern Highlands above Lake Nyasa. Njombe was as far as the railway services were prepared to go, even by bus. Beyond that I was counting on TeeTeeCo, the local bus company, whose full title, the Tanganyika Transport Company Limited, rather overstated its geographical importance. Road conditions permitting, TeeTeeCo ran a bus service between Njombe and Songea. Although no more than 160 miles, the road was normally bad to impassable and the journey involved negotiating an escarpment between the two districts. It was necessary, therefore, to spend a second night at the Njombe hotel before attempting the journey on.

The next day, ready to leave at eight as scheduled, I waited for the bus to call for me. At about 6,000 feet, Njombe is beautifully situated in rolling hill country – grassland with few trees except for those cultivated in the valley bottoms. The air is fresh and clear, briskly cold in the morning sunshine. Cocks were still crowing as I stood on the steps of the two-roomed Indian-owned hotel, and the sound of voices easily carried from one hillside to another. How peaceful it was . . . but no sign of the bus! I walked back up the road to where I was told it would have been parked overnight, and found a small crowd of intending passengers gazing intently at a pair of feet extending from beneath a cattle truck. This proved to be, in fact, the bus, and the feet belonged to its driver, working on something that had apparently gone wrong. The clerk in TeeTeeCo's white (originally) daub office hut explained to me that the engine was 'broken', which sounded rather serious, but that it should be mended 'shortly'. The Swahili for shortly, *bado*, is the commonest word in the language and may also mean 'not yet'; so you can take your pick whether it's likely to be five minutes or next week. It proved to be about seven hours, so it was not until after four in the afternoon that we finally got going, with me in front beside the driver, my loads on the roof, and everybody else with their children, chickens, baskets and small bundles squashed into the back.

This last stage of my journey, mostly through *miombo* bush, in darkness, was uneventful but memorable. For more than ten hours I was cooped up in the cab of that jolting vehicle, with the driver (who must have had an extra springy seat) bouncing about beside me at times so violently that I wondered how he'd have managed without the steering wheel to hang on to. The beams of our headlights dimly illuminated endless trees and a canopy of branches. Now and again the lights swung alarmingly through space as we swivelled round a hairpin bend. At 4,000 feet, Songea is 2,000 feet lower than Njombe, most of the descent being at the escarpment, where the road was in places literally perilous. It was just as well I could not properly see how the land fell away on my side of the bus.

We stopped once or twice at wayside halts, where animated conversations ensued as people got on or off, and loads were transferred with much shouted advice between ground and roof, the 'turney-boy' standing up there rather helplessly as five or six different sets of instructions were yelled at him simultaneously. The turney-boy was an employee without whom no bus or truck over three tons could legally use the roads. His primary and essential function was, whenever the vehicle came to a halt, to leap out and place a chock under the rear wheels, lest on a slope the brakes should fail, or the driver miss his gear change. His other duty was to crank the engine with a starting handle, as virtually no bus or lorry had a self-starter – hence the name turney-boy. In practice he was used as the driver's dogsbody, and being a turney-boy was the unofficially recognised way an ambitious youth learned to drive. My presence in the front probably frustrated the opportunity for him to have a go on this particular trip.

Owing to my still small knowledge of Swahili, I was not able to have much conversation with the driver; nor did I have much idea where he should drop me off. All I had by way of direction was the copy of a memo from Wenban-Smith addressed to the district commissioner:

A. S. M. HALL, COOPERATIVE OFFICER

The above officer is expected to arrive in Songea on the 26th October and has been instructed to report to you.

2. It will be his duty to assist Major Stephens in both his capacities, ie. Executive Officer, Songea Native Tobacco Board, and Manager, Ngoni-Matengo Cooperative Marketing Union, Ltd., and eventually to take over from him when he goes on leave. . . . It is hoped, however, that when he has had sufficient acquaintance with local conditions, he will be given as much opportunity as

possible of guiding the primary societies in cooperative principles and practice, and eradicating the shortcomings to which attention was recently drawn by the auditors. . . .

W. Wenban-Smith
Commissioner for Cooperative Development

The best I could do, therefore, when at about two o'clock in the morning we finally reached Songea, was to indicate that I wanted the house of Bwana Stephens. Fortunately, the driver knew both Bwana Stephens and where he lived; so, still with our complement of African passengers, we drove on for a mile or so, then off the road and up a winding track to an open space where I could just make out the shape of a bungalow-type house. I had been a bit nervous about arriving in the middle of the night, and had half formed in my mind the notion of quietly dossing down on the Stephens' veranda until morning. However, even supposing I could have arrived and unloaded my luggage quietly – which was unlikely – the driver seemed set on waking everybody within a radius of half a mile: he revved the engine, honked the horn and, getting down from his cab, shouted out, "*Hodi! Hodi!*" (the East African equivalent of knocking on your door) at the top of his voice. I was horrified, but it certainly resolved my unspoken quandary.

A querulous female voice spoke sharply from the house, in 'kitchen' Swahili, "What d'you *fanya* all that *kelele* for?" And then, in an altered voice: "Is that Mr Hall?" It was Mrs Stephens, in an instant remarkably good-tempered, standing on the threshold in a dressing gown. "Come in and meet Steve. He's drunk as a newt, the old sod. We were expecting you hours ago."

I thankfully overtipped the driver, checked my luggage had been offloaded and followed Mrs Stephens into what was obviously their bedroom. A recumbent form under a mosquito net was snoring loudly.

"Steve, you old drunk! Wake up! It's Mr Hall." Then, turning to me: "It's no good – he's out for the count – completely blotto. We've all been celebrating Churchill's victory. The Conservatives have won the general election. You probably haven't heard, Churchill's back as prime minister."

15 – SONGEA

In a country with several remote districts, Songea in 1951 had the reputation of being especially remote. The road which I had travelled from Njombe, over an escarpment that was littered with the wrecks of trucks and buses that disastrously had failed to make the grade, was closed for six months every year during the rainy season. The 400-mile road from Lindi on the east coast, although light-heartedly classified as 'all-weather', was in practice, along one or other of its sections, effectively impassable for periods of days, weeks or even months at a time. Only the most resolute of drivers, with excruciating disregard for maltreatment of somebody else's vehicle, would be likely to get through. The road south to Mbamba Bay on Lake Nyasa was similarly hazardous as a trunk road, chiefly on account of the escarpment above the lake.

From November until April, therefore, Songea was virtually isolated from the rest of the country. An East African Airways Dakota called in once a week on its way from Dar es Salaam and Lindi to Njombe (sometimes), then Mbeya, Iringa, and back to Dar es Salaam. If the airfield was too wet, though, the plane did not land. I was fortunate to have got through before the rains set in.

In spite of my late arrival, there were no concessions to my fatigue. It seemed that I had barely closed my eyes when a smart-looking boy with a red cummerbund (so that his kanzu looked less like a nightie) and the customary fez came in with tea and, without asking, began pulling up my mosquito net.

"*Habari ya safari, bwana?*" ("How was your journey?") he said, as if my being there were the most natural thing in the world and this was just another day, as habitual for me as it was for him.

"*Mzuri sana,*" I replied. ("Very good.")

The answer to every customary greeting (such as "How are you?" or "How are things at home?") is always "*Mzuri.*" If you were asked how your grandmother was who had died that morning, the appropriate answer would be "Fine, but unfortunately she's just died."

I found my superior-to-be, Major 'Steve' Stephens, sitting limply at the breakfast table, looking if anything rather more hung-over than I myself felt, though for a different reason. He was a shortish middle-aged man with a red face, baggy eyes and a moustache midway between handlebar and walrus; this latter was his most distinctive feature. He greeted me affably and shouted to alert the houseboy that I was ready for breakfast, he being already in the middle of his own. Over the meal we both took the opportunity, while chatting conventionally, to size each other up. Steve was a big fish in the Songea pond, and he was clearly interested to know what sort of creature had plopped in beside him. His voice had a light drawling military tone, evocative of the officers' mess rather than the parade ground. I could see at once from his friendliness, and from his apparent assumption that we shared the same values, that – provided I wasn't going to rock the boat – we could probably get along together very well. Yet, as he 'filled me in' over the toast and marmalade, I began to feel in my bones that, for all his cordiality, there was a cultural divide between us which might in time prove to be a battle line. Steve had a Kenya 'settler' background, and had recently retired from his regular commission in the KAR (King's African Rifles) – which meant that his outlook on Africa and African development was fundamentally different from my own. He 'understood' Africa; I was a naive greenhorn. For the time being I was prepared to accept that this was true.

After breakfast Steve drove me down to meet the district commissioner, and for the first time I was able actually to see something of Songea (the township gave its name to the district). Steve's house was situated on a ridge above the township. On the other side of the road, further along the ridge, were three more isolated houses, one red-brick, two white stucco, lining the fairway of a nine-hole golf course; and beyond that, at a distance of two or three miles, the undulating crags of the Matagoro Hills – known locally as 'mountains'. Most of the remaining government houses, all with corrugated-iron roofs (only Steve's had red-brick tiles) were scattered about further down between cassava shambas* and sun-bleached scrubby grassland; and beyond these was the township proper, the approach to which was dignified, on each side of the road, by mature mango trees. The first indications of the actual township were a few government offices, of which the only significant buildings were the white-walled Boma† and its neighbouring open-walled courthouse, where any passer-by could lean over and listen to the proceedings. These two buildings and a rather scruffy corrugated-iron police station were fronted by a bare-earth parade ground with the Union Jack flying from an impressively tall flagpole. The road skirted the parade ground and continued down the hill, past the market square and its huddle of Asian *dukas* (small shops), and on into Mfaranyaki, the African village of about 700 souls. The township was given character by the mango trees that had been planted, probably in German times, along the three main roads into the town; the centre was an oasis of shade. Apart from the tobacco factory – which I had yet to see – this was Songea, administrative centre of a district of more than 16,000 square miles.

Denis Hill met us on the veranda outside his office. He was a big, beefy former rugby player whose conversation was conducted in surges of amusement leading up to gusts of cackling laughter.

"Oh, you missed a wonderful party last night. . . . [Jocose exchange of banter with Steve.] Do you play hockey? What? We'll soon change that. [Great guffaws.] Put him down for your side next Friday, Steve." This was followed by more laughter.

Denis and Steve were clearly thick as thieves. I found it all rather bewildering – it was more like joining a club than reporting for duty. Later I came to recognise Denis Hill's levity as typical of the underplayed style of leadership that characterised British colonial administration – relaxed, humane, informal, but with a genuinely serious concern for the people under its jurisdiction. Denis was

---

* Peasant farmers' plots or gardens.
† The District Commissioner's administrative building.

responsible for an African population of 170,000 scattered over an area more than twice the size of Wales.

Songea was mainly inhabited by two branches of the Zulu Wangoni, whose chiefs had their respective barazas at Gumbiro (thirty miles up the Njombe road – I had passed it in the night) and Lumetcha (about twelve miles down the Mbamba Bay road). The Wangoni leadership had been annihilated by the Germans in repressing the 1905–7 Majimaji Rebellion, and from being a proud military tribe they were now, half a century later, an aimlessly demoralised people with little agricultural tradition and, because of the tsetse fly, little opportunity for cattle rearing. Yet they had to cultivate to live. It was a task which, apart from forest-clearing and new cultivation, they were content to leave largely to their womenfolk, the men preferring to hunt or just socialise, with much drinking of home-brewed beer. They had the reputation of being boastful layabouts, for ever invoking their former martial glories, not deigning to improve their lot by the lowly occupation of hard work.

As one old man told me, "Our work is the ngoma." (Literally the drum, or dance.)

The other important Songea people were the Wamatengo. Driven up into the highlands above Lake Nyasa by the Wangoni in their prime, the 'inferior' Wamatengo had adapted themselves successfully to their mostly treeless, hilly terrain, and introduced there the much praised (by British administrators) Ngoro 'pit' system of cultivation: without the use of terraces they could cultivate incredibly steep slopes and suffer no soil erosion. There were no tsetse flies in the highlands; so with the possibility of keeping livestock, and good use of water by means of furrows, the Wamatengo were to the manner born excellent farmers. Most of their homesteads (there were few villages as such – more, areas of population settlement, so to speak) were marked from a distance by tall clumps of blue wattle (eucalyptus), planted for building poles and firewood. These little plantations, and the ordered pattern of cultivation on open, rolling countryside, gave the Matengo Highlands a pleasantly 'settled' character which contrasted strongly with the featureless miombo bush country in the larger northern and eastern parts of the district, where the

Wangoni slashed and burned for shifting cultivation.

Below the Matengo Escarpment, on the eastern shores of Lake Nyasa, was a miscellaneous group of peoples, mostly Protestant Christians related more to the people of Nyasaland than to the tribes of Songea district proper. Having been converted by English or Scottish missionaries, they exhibited a distinctly British influence, recognisably different from the Teutonic Catholicism of Ngoniland. However, they were few, and, apart from the cultivation of paddy (rice) and some fishing, they played no significant part in the economy of the district, from which they were physically cut off during the rains.

The European population of Songea was predominantly German, Austrian or Swiss Catholic missionaries of the Benedictine Order, whose bishop's seat was at Peramiho, a large and impressive establishment about fifteen miles from Songea township, with many – possibly twenty – dependent mission stations throughout the district. Nearly all these outstations were relatively long-established (that is, since before 1914, while Germany was the colonial power) and their substantial brick buildings (cloisters, belfries and mature walled gardens) presented an appearance of almost feudal authority – rather more so, in fact, than the British administration itself. The resident priests and lay workers (sometimes no more than one of each) were wholly taken up with their local flock, but would nearly always extend jovial hospitality (they lived well) to government officers calling in on safari. One wondered sometimes whether the transfer of Tanganyika from German colony to British trusteeship rankled with them. I had the impression that with some of them it did; but their mission was with the African population, and for all that they saw of the British there was little cause for personal resentment. British missionary influence was confined to the lake shore, where the Universities' Mission to Central Africa (UMCA) had a station at Liuli, and a small Anglican community in Songea township.

There were no 'settlers', as such, in Songea. Government officials and their families comprised most of the remaining Europeans – about forty adults in all. The only 'freelance' Europeans were Albert Shreckenhoeffer, an Austrian former Benedictine brother running a small building contractor's business; 'Oppie' Oplustil, a Polish jack of all trades; and a legendary character known as Dynamite Dan, living down by the Rovuma river on the border with Mozambique, who was reputed to shoot at low-flying aircraft and visiting administrative officers (few) on sight.

Asians – the merchants and traders of East Africa – were even fewer than the European population, and more concentrated in Songea township, where there were about twenty *duka*s (shops). They had perhaps another ten at Mbinga (on the edge of the Matengo Highlands) and two or three at Nyamtumbo, near the eastern border of the district on the road to Lindi. Apart from my dealings with the two (rival) transport companies – TeeTeeCo and Ali Mohamed Osman – and Songea Store, our local provider of everything from toothpaste to tinned sardines, I was to have little professional contact with the Asians. Like the Benedictine missionaries, they knew the district well. During the produce season they were out in every corner of it, no matter how remote, buying up maize, pulses, oilseeds, sorghum, etc., collecting the debts owed to them, and making available their traditional merchandise – virtually everything an African family might require, from bicycles and radios to food supplies (fresh, dried or canned), kitchen utensils, hoes, insecticide, corrugated-iron sheets . . . You name it, they had it.

Of course, this knowledge of Songea was not acquired wholly on my first day – and not all that was confidently imparted to me during my early listening period proved later to be wholly reliable. After that brief and rather jocular introduction to the district commissioner, we got back into Steve's powerful green Chevrolet pickup and drove to the tobacco factory that was to be the main focus of my professional activity for the next ten years. It proved to be a complete surprise: a long, sleek, brand-new building, standing in a vast clearing as if planted there by a giant child. It had indeed just been completed – designed by Sir Alexander Gibb & Partners to replace the old factory that had served the Ngoni Matengo Union for the past fifteen or twenty years. Astonishingly in that remote upcountry station, it was state-of-the-art technology for handling tobacco leaf – an ambitious gamble on future development.

A bull-necked man in a khaki shirt was supervising the unloading of tobacco from a lorry, shouting at the labourers in a jokey, bullying tone: "Come on, you lazy buggers – don't just stand there! *Lift* the bloody thing. You've got two arms, haven't you?"

It was the factory manager, 'Chummy' Lockwood, formerly of South Africa and Southern Rhodesia (now Zimbabwe) – as was evident as soon as he opened his mouth to speak.

Steve introduced me with a faint suggestion of amusement: "This is our new Cooperative Officer," as if to say this young twerp has come to teach your grandmother to suck eggs.

Chummy also seemed to find something funny in my arrival, and made a remark something like "Let's hope he can chase those cooperative buggers in the field to do their bloody grading properly."

We left him, and Steve led me through a store piled high with dark-brown cured leaf which had been brought in from the field.

"Look at this stuff!" he said scornfully. "Hopelessly mixed up! They think that just by calling it 'grade one' they're going to get more money. They're just cheating *themselves*."

We walked on into the grading room – a large hall where lines of ragged workers seated on the floor (men and women segregated) were regrading the leaf into 'sales' grades. With all the dust and noise, and an overwhelming smell of tobacco and human sweat, it was an amazingly primitive scene, which I found quite incongruous in the lofty architecture of that spanking-new building. The thought did not occur to me then – but it did later, when we were worrying about how to cover the costs of this boldly conceived investment: they could almost have done the same job equally well on the floor of a big mud hut. The next room was a similar snake pit of workers and piles of tobacco on the floor, as more than 100 women and children used their nimble fingers to strip out the midrib from the large tobacco leaves, and then tie them in 'hands' for processing.

Amid all the factory hubbub Steve was drawling away about 'field grades', 'bulking', 'stripping', 'moisture content', etc., and I was only taking part of it in. Beyond us were 'drying chambers', and then 'steam chambers' and, beyond them again, two large hydraulic presses where ten-foot columns of leaf were squeezed into bales of little more than two feet square. Somewhere a heavy diesel generator emitted a steady echoing rumble. Men were shouting; steam hissed. The heat under that enormous corrugated-iron roof was suffocating.

We emerged finally at the far end of the factory, where bales were being loaded on to lorries for transportation to the coast. This, in a place of sudden calm, was the culmination. Within the space of twenty minutes I had seen the whole process; and, for all the 'plantation' style of labour utilisation, it was an impressive introduction to the Songea tobacco industry. I was indeed very impressed. What I did not then know was that the factory process was the least of our problems: our challenge was not in the technical know-how of the factory, but out in the field with Chummy's 'cooperative buggers', the farmers. Another thing I did not know then was that the factory had been overwhelmed by an unprecedentedly large crop, and that a significant proportion of the leaf had been – and was continuing to be – 'burned in the bulk'. (Like a compost heap, tobacco with too much moisture in it will heat up, with disastrous consequences for the size of payments due to the growers.) Those chickens would come home to roost in a few months' time. Steve must have had a good idea of the trouble in store, but he gave no hint of anxiety as he showed me round and then drove me over to his office, which was about a mile away at the site of the 'old' factory.

Steve's office (which was later to be mine) was a modest three-roomed red-brick building with a thatched roof (much cooler than corrugated iron) situated in a mature grove of eucalyptus trees. Strictly speaking, it was the office of the Ngoni Matengo Cooperative Marketing Union Ltd (Ngomat), of which he was the supervising manager. He was also executive officer of the Songea Native Tobacco Board (Sontob), which had no office of its own. As a result, Steve's two functions – manager of the Union and executive officer of the Board – became inextricably mixed together, particularly in his own mind. Yet the distinction between them, from the point of view of African advancement, was important, as will become evident from the discontent that was to ensue. At the Union office I was introduced to Nelson Nkangama, the secretary of the Union. Nelson was a tall, pleasant, unassuming Protestant, originally from Nyasaland (note how we classified people by race and creed). He was, in effect, Steve's right-hand man in the Union.

In the afternoon Steve left me with his wife, Mary – a pretty, rather scatterbrained woman with a squealing little laugh and a kind heart – for an informal introduction to Songea's social life. This began with a walk across the golf course – "Do you play golf? What? Well, you'll be learning here" – to the Lockwoods' house, which was the last one along the ridge. Alice Lockwood, who was as unmistakably South African as her husband, lay in bed recovering from a bout of malaria, her nose and a pair of spectacles poking above the sheets. As if the sudden appearance of a strange man in her bedroom was the most natural thing in the world, she and Mary twittered away like a couple of birds, making arch references to my bachelor status and how well I was likely to be entertained.

"Everybody takes pity on the poor bachelors – they get invited to *all* the curry lunches."

My first day ended in the bar of the Angoni Arms hotel – otherwise known as the Agony Arms – just off the main Lindi road and quite near the Stephens' house. It was a small daub-walled building with a grass roof and only three rooms: a bar in the middle, behind that the proprietor's bedroom-cum-store, and beyond the bar the only in-house guest bedroom. There were a couple more bedrooms in an outside hut. Before being a hotel, in the days when Songea had a small, permanent garrison, this had been the KAR company office. Appropriately enough, the hotel tenant, Major 'Pop' Harris, had himself been posted there during the course of his army career. Of the same seniority in rank as Steve, Pop was at least fifteen years older and a good deal stouter. With a white moustache and white flowing mane of hair on a splendid head, he looked remarkably like the First World War prime minister, David Lloyd George.

Growling and muttering behind the bar, his apparent surliness magnified by deafness, he barked at his customers with – to those who did not know him – disconcerting ferocity: "What? You'll have to speak up. I can't *hear* if you mumble."

As everybody did sooner or later, I came to realise that Pop's bark was worse than his bite. He had a wife who lived somewhere like Clacton-on-Sea, from whom he was separated, if not legally, at least permanently by distance, as he had no intention of returning ever to Britain, and she, apparently, none of leaving it. Pop's pub was the hub of Songea's social life.

You may ask yourself what I mean by 'Songea's social life'. Alas, it has to be admitted that, off duty, government officials and their families (especially their families) socialised largely with each other; the Hassanali Lada Dinanis and Nelson Nkangamas and their respective wives did not form part of our social circle, nor we of theirs. It was a paradox. The Colonial Service was passionately pro-African and fiercely against any kind of colour bar, yet, with their wives on the scene, it was an elite which 'mixed' only as a form of ritual cordiality on recognised occasions like the Queen's birthday, or the district commissioner's Christmas drinks party-for-everyone (as distinct from his party-for-*us*). Race is a difficult subject, and arguments about it are more often really about culture (as I came to realise more fully when I later took up service with the United Nations). At any rate, I accepted the situation as it was quite happily, because it was on *their* ground, rather than ours, that I was to come fully into contact with the African population. The same applied for most of my colleagues. As for the Asians, their wives' preference for seclusion ensured that social contact, when it occurred, was confined to the men. Michael Heredia, the Goan grocer, and his brother-in-law, Mr De Souza, both joined us in our Friday hockey matches (and put most of us to shame with their prowess); and Mr Amin, the owner of TeeTeeCo, held an annual party for the *Wazungu* (Europeans) – excluding missionaries, of course – at which his wife, in a back room, cooked with famous expertise spiced food and sugary sweetmeats. But these were exceptional occasions.

I found that I had been allocated quarters in the 'Chummery' (bachelors' household), cohabiting with two district officers, Keith Mather and a New Zealander whose name was something like Stig Anderson. It was a spacious white bungalow, partly buried in great clusters of red bougainvillea and, at a distance, mango trees interspersed with the lovely and more delicate jacaranda. Keith and Stig, being already in residence, had naturally bagged the best rooms; I had to make do with a thatched adjacent hut. But the arrangement was convenient to all three of us: we each had our own space, and shared the communal facilities. Stig, being the senior of us, was responsible for ordering our food and deciding what we should eat; Keith, a short Mancunian with a neatly clipped beard, was supposed to supervise the other aspects of housekeeping. In practice, each of us had a personal boy, and the three of them shared duties between them. This meant that Stig's boy ruled the kitchen, Keith's took responsibility whenever there was a blitz on the rooms we shared in common, and mine had a fairly easy time.

I was fortunate in Rashidi, a short, shy, quiet man who had been quite well trained by his previous memsahib. He had been recommended to me by one of the wives as 'dependable' – which was accurate enough, in that he could be depended on to do what he thought would please me, and to look after himself into the bargain. He proved to be a competent servant in all respects – as cook, houseboy, and on safari – and stayed with me until I got married five years later, when to my great sorrow he got his marching orders (memsahibs almost always got in the way of a happy relationship with one's cook).

The Chummery was something like living in a club. Conversation was conducted mainly at meals, which were served with some ceremony, with one of the boys always waiting at table. In the evenings we played tennis on a hard court 100 yards from the house, or went to the pub (or did both) or read books or weeks-old newspapers in the hard armchairs of our common sitting room, the silence unbroken save for the hiss of tilley lamps and the whirring noise of insects outside. As often as not one or other of us would be away on safari, where most of our work was done; and at weekends there would be the curry lunches, the regular hockey match and, yes, golf. I invested in five clubs and six balls. That was the Sunday-morning activity which served instead of church.

Keith I remember chiefly for his taste in books, supplies of which he regularly received from Heffers in Cambridge (strange how such details remain in the mind): *Dust in the Lion's Paw* (he was a fan of Freya Stark), volumes of Steven Runciman's *History of the Crusades*, and the *Decameron* of Boccaccio. He was one of those readers who like to share their enjoyment of books by reading out passages that happen to amuse or strike their fancy, regardless of whether anyone else wants to listen. All three of us had similar tastes – although Keith's verged on the self-consciously esoteric – but we never became particularly friendly. Stig was shortly to marry and be posted to another station, and I subsequently moved into the Stephens' house when they went on leave. But I think the main reason people did not often form close friendships (Steve and Denis were an exception) – apart from the fact that they rarely stayed on the same station for longer than one tour (thirty months) – was that, where sociability was so narrowly confined, it tended to mean that you were friendly with *everybody*. This was actually one of the great strengths of the Colonial Service: esprit de corps was excellent. The fifteen officers or so stationed at Songea (agricultural officers, vet, doctor, schoolmasters, forestry officer, Public Works Department, etc.) were a band of brothers, each in his own department responsible for a field of activity different from the others'. We all worked closely together when necessary and each of us was firmly convinced of the civilising thrust of our professions. And I do believe, for all its complacency and tendency towards paternalism, the British Colonial Service was a genuinely humane force for good. I felt this sense of mission from the beginning in Songea – a typically British sense of a 'civilising' mission, which expressed itself not in any overt self-righteousness, but – perhaps misleadingly – by a 'style' which was a throwback to an earlier age of imperial confidence and, yes, which might indeed (but mistakenly) nowadays be thought effete. The man from Griffiths MacAlister had got it just about right in his list of 'essential requirements', right down to the white mess jackets and yards of black silk cummerbund that we donned on formal occasions – no less essential for being seldom needed and faintly ridiculous in that upcountry setting. To be without them when occasion demanded would have put one beyond the pale.

But the real Africa was not in the few black-tie occasions when we solemnly forgathered and drank the health of Her Majesty the Queen. It was when I began going out in the district on safari that I found myself in thinly populated bush country that can hardly have altered from the time of the early explorers, Arab or European. Because of the lack of roads to many of the places we had to visit, there was often no alternative to going on foot; and as, typically,

I would be away for a week or two, it was necessary to travel with porters, to carry not only my own 'essential' requirements of cook box, food, folding table, chair, bath, camp bed, bedding, clothing, etc., and possibly a tent, but also the more modest quota of personal effects of those who travelled with me – including the porters themselves, who kept up their spirits by singing, much as soldiers on the march:

> "Oh, we are the porters who carry the food
> Of the porters who carry the porters' food."

As the almost animal shouting, groaning, gurgling and whistling sounds were in their own language, Kingoni, that little verse may not actually have been in the Songea repertoire, though it was said to be.

Getting together a sufficient number of porters was always a struggle. You would arrive at a village of perhaps eight huts to find one old man dozing in the shade, a few scrawny chickens scratching about in the dust, and an emaciated dog engrossed in biting its fleas. Some distance away, two women would be alternately pounding maize with log-like pestles. Your arrival would provoke the appearance of a small boy from behind a hut, who would stare at you, standing on one leg, picking his nose. Chiefs and headmen were obliged to provide porters for government officials on safari, but it was an unpopular obligation. Able-bodied men tended to make themselves scarce when wanted, and the village headman (if he could be found) would almost invariably deny having received advance warning of our requirements. One could easily waste half a day waiting for the necessary complement to be mustered. But this was Africa, and I soon learned that time was of no consequence.

It was when walking that one stood the best chance of seeing game. Although not to be compared with the game parks of Northern Tanganyika, Songea had many of the typical species, including various types of gazelle and buck. There were buffalo, lions, crocodiles and elephants in certain parts, and of course plenty of hyenas and baboons, which were a great pest to farmers. A big talking point when I arrived in Songea – it had made news throughout the territory – was a pair of man-eating lions that had been ravaging villages in the Gumbiro area for several months previously. The game warden from Nachingwea had eventually been called in to track them down, and did succeed in shooting both of them; by that time, unfortunately, they had attacked and killed about twenty of the local people. This story thrilled me when I heard it.

'Gosh!' I thought. ('Wow!' had not then been coined.) 'This really is Africa!'

Well, as it happened, it was to Gumbiro that I was first sent out in an empty tobacco lorry, with one inspector and Rashidi, to see for myself how the tobacco was handled in the field. We were to walk back. Both Denis and Steve, who didn't do much (or in Steve's case *any*) of it themselves, believed walking safaris were good training for young officials. In my case, this was probably true. Gumbiro proved to be a dismal clearing surrounded by four or five grass-thatched huts with mud walls, and a small collection of sun-dried brick buildings, only one of which was wholly built, with a rusty corrugated-iron (*bati*) roof and partly surrounded by an old bamboo stockade. Beside it, dirty and unswept, was a crumbling courthouse. This was the baraza of Nkosi Zulu, one of the two Ngoni paramount chiefs. The place had an air of desolation and neglect – not a soul to be seen, just a few cooking pots and the usual scrawny chickens scratching about in a litter of maize husks, to suggest human habitation. Having expected to see a bustling rural tobacco market, this was disappointing. Where was everybody?

The inspector with me – a thickset bulldog-faced young man named Peter Moyo, led me through the trees to another clearing with a mud building similar to the baraza, but if anything even more dilapidated, its thatch partly slipping off to leave gaping holes in the roof. This, apparently, was the Gumbiro Cooperative Marketing Society Ltd.

The driver of our truck was shouting "*Hodi! Mlonda! Yuko wapi, mlonda?*" ("Where's the watchman?")

From a nearby hut a woman appeared who said she was the watchman's wife and that her husband was ill. Where, then, was the committee man who was supposed to be supervising the loading of the tobacco? Where was the secretary?

The woman jerked her chin to indicate the direction they might be found, but as much as to say, "Drinking, as usual."

It was not a very encouraging introduction to 'the field'. I didn't know then that the Gumbiro people were considered to be among the most degenerate, dissolute and shiftless in the district, and that the red-eyed committee man, when eventually he was summoned from his cups, was a fair representative.

I spent about twenty-four hours at Gumbiro: the best part of a morning waiting for the committee man 'in charge' to turn up; another couple of hours while he went off looking for the secretary; and half an hour looking at his filthy, dog-eared books and checking the cash in his safe. Trying to learn from the partly inebriated committee man – with Peter Moyo interpreting – how tobacco was cultivated, cured and handled by the society was pretty hopeless. The growing season was long over, curing finished and, anyway, they – Peter included – found it incomprehensible that I did not know it all already. All I was able to see were a few wretched little heaps of tobacco leaf lying in the dust of their *gulio* before (after more delay rounding up labour) it was loaded on to the truck. The main thing I learned was that time didn't matter very much. In the evening, while I was sitting in my new 'Roorkie' chair in the bamboo rest house that was the best Gumbiro had to offer, the secretary eventually turned up – with a gift of eggs. It was my first experience of African hospitality, and, after my unfavourable first impressions, humbling. In Swahili the word for stranger, *mgeni*, is the same as for guest.

Next day, the Chief, Nkosi Zulu, came to pay his respects (this always happened when government officers arrived anywhere: the local chief presented himself) and, after an exchange of civilities, Peter informed him that we would require so many porters – probably about ten, hoping for at least six. He was a dapper little man with a shiny bald head, smartly dressed in a suit and tie.

As he was the paramount chief, providing porters was no problem at all: he simply instructed the local headman, "Provide porters for this bwana," wished us a good safari, and left us while we waited for them.

And waited.

I got fed up with this after some hours and rashly decided it would be a good move for me to go on ahead, leaving Rashidi and the inspector to follow on with the porters when enough of them had eventually been roped in. It was thirty miles back to Songea on a road that we had travelled by truck only a couple of days previously. I walked on by myself.

It was *miombo* bush, thickety, scrub-like forest, and I stuck to the road. Although it was the 'main' road, there was absolutely no traffic – no people even – just the narrow, red dusty track, its ruts and tyre marks comforting reminders that I was not totally lost. And there was hardly any sound – it is mostly at night that Africa makes itself heard – only the padding footfalls of my excellent new veldschoen. The sun beat down, and I fell into a sort of trance in which I daydreamed as I plodded along – a dream in which I gradually became conscious of a noise other than my own footsteps. At some distance, but then definitely getting nearer, a powerful elemental groaning noise seemed to fill the spaces between the trees with sound. There was no doubt about it. It was a lion. Nervously I walked on, hoping to put more distance between us; but the grumbling, grunting rumble instead got closer, until I was convinced the animal was behind an enormous anthill about 150 yards to my right. I quickly shinned up a tree, climbing as high as I could, painfully aware of my total isolation. The terrifying noise persisted for some minutes, while I clung to my perch wondering whether I'd been scented and if lions climb trees. It was the most frightening experience I can remember. I stayed up the tree for at least twenty minutes, until the intermittent bass roaring eventually receded into the distance and, more importantly, away from the direction I was going. I wondered what the porters coming on behind (assuming they were) would make of it. It had not occurred to me that a hunting lion wouldn't have been making all that noise. Walking on, I met two men with a bicycle loaded with a sack of maize or beans, timidly apprehensive of moving further up the road.

"Did you hear the lion?" one asked. My Swahili was up to that.

"Oh, yes," I replied airily, "it's moved off that way."

The men looked at me as if I had been under the special protection of the Almighty, not knowing – though they might have guessed – that, to be on the safe side of Providence, I had been quaking up a tree.

16 – UPHEAVAL AT SONTOB

I was to remain almost nine years at Songea – that's three tours, including two six-month periods of home leave. It was an exceptional stint at one duty station, and it spanned most of the period leading up to Tanganyika's independence in 1961. The usual procedure in the Colonial Service was for a district officer's responsibilities to be taken over for a full tour by whoever relieved him when he went on leave; on return, he would be posted somewhere else. But dark-fired tobacco was not a typical crop; so, in view of the experience I was to acquire in that extremely unhealthy commodity, I was, untypically, twice sent back after home leave to my old district. However, it was my first tour that was to be the most dramatic – not to say traumatic – not just for me, but for everybody else connected with Songea's tobacco industry.

Apart from its brand-new tobacco factory, the Songea that I was introduced to by Steve can have been little different from its 'darkest Africa' state in the 1930s. Although the post-war Labour government of Clement Attlee was mandated to set all British dependencies on the road to independence – to 'break up the British Empire', as Winston Churchill bitterly condemned it – there was in Songea not the slightest indication that any steps were being taken in that direction. The people still revered and looked to their chiefs for authority, and could do nothing without it. Indeed, the Swahili word *ushupavu*, which conveys the idea of independence, can also mean insubordination. And it was not just in big things, like building a house, say, or choosing a plot to cultivate, but the smallest deviation from customary practice – going on a special journey perhaps, or buying a bicycle – would require *ruhusa* (permission). The idea of democracy was not merely foreign; it was incomprehensible, even to the chiefs themselves. In Songea they were utterly subservient to the district commissioner. Denis Hill, as the senior representative of the British administration, was held in almost godlike respect, akin perhaps to the awe with which lowly peasants in medieval Europe would look upon their feudal lord. Tanganyika might very well be starting on the road to independence, but it was clearly a very long road, and not one that we were travelling with any great speed.

Indeed, the government's complacent attitude to this leisurely pace of 'progress' is well illustrated by its official comment when a United Nations Visiting Mission in 1954 audaciously recommended that Tanganyika's self-government should be achieved within a timescale of 'twenty years'*. As a condescending civil-service put-down, midway between amusement and outrage, it is vintage Colonial Office Sir Humphrey Appleby:

> [The UN mission] caused some commotion, owing to the attitude of some of its members who appeared to overemphasise their private theories at the expense of public policy and practicality. . . .
>
> The contretemps will, however, have had its value if it results in better appreciation of the fact that Tanganyika, while ready to consider informed advice, is administered solely by H.M. Government in the interests of her population, and that the ultimate aim of this administration . . . is self-government when internal development makes this appropriate. [Sotto voce: 'Put that in your pipe and smoke it!']

The implication of this pompous rebuke was that self-government for the people of Tanganyika would not be for a very long time, and that in the meantime these foolish people should go away and mind their own business.

Sir Humphrey's sentiments were entirely in accord with those of Steve and the other European staff of the Songea Native Tobacco Board, who did not remotely anticipate independence within their lifetime. Personally, although interested, I was not concerned with political matters – that was the district commissioner's department

* In fact it was achieved in 1961, seven years later.

– but my official responsibility was to put beef into the running of Songea's cooperative marketing societies. This meant turning them, from being inert shells administered by the Board merely as field stations for tobacco buying, into properly functioning commercial organisations run by the farmers themselves – or, more precisely, run by staff appointed by managing committees elected by farmer members of the cooperatives. This transition, and the many problems associated with it, occupied the whole of my time from 1951 to 1959. I have written an account of it elsewhere* and will not bore you with technical details here. Nevertheless, the human aspects are worth telling, and my story would be incomplete without them. Our working lives in Songea occupied much more than 'working hours' and were inextricably mixed up with our social life, such as it was.

The Colonial Service was strictly hierarchical: district officers reported to senior officers at provincial level, and provincial officers reported to *their* senior officers at headquarters in Dar es Salaam (I was, I think, unique in reporting directly to Dar es Salaam). Whenever anyone from Lindi (provincial headquarters) was to arrive, there would be a great smartening up of the ranks and cuffing of junior clerical ears for not having done what should have been done long before this.

There would be cries of "Amos [or Benjamin, or Samuel, or whoever], sometimes I despair! How many times have I told you to . . . ?"

Wives would be mobilised, hospitality laid on, the district commissioner alerted. And, of course, it was all great fun, and never so much as for a meeting of the Songea Native Tobacco Board, when the Great Ones arrived not only from Lindi but also from Dar es Salaam.

The prime mover and shaker was Robin Malcolm, Commissioner for Cooperative Development (the man Wenban-Smith had been standing in for), scion of a Scottish lairdship, whose deceptively languid appearance was confusingly at odds with his stiff military-

* *Tanganyika: Recollections of the Songa Tobacco Industry – 1951– 1959*, a memoir by A. S. M. Hall, deposited with the Colonial Service Archives, Bodleian Library, Oxford.

style moustache and an acute intelligence which missed nothing. One of the funniest men I have known, Robin Malcolm's cultivated style of world-weary wit and irony nevertheless concealed a fundamental seriousness. Many years later, my brother David met him in Hong Kong and judged him to be effete and dissolute; he could not have been more mistaken. Malcolm was a district officer who had become convinced that Tanganyika's peasant farmers could never progress beyond subsistence cultivation unless they increased their bargaining power vis-à-vis the traders, and that cooperative societies were a way not only to strengthen their hand in the market but to educate them in matters of trade and commerce. In a surprisingly imaginative appointment, Malcolm was nominated Tanganyika's first Commissioner for Cooperative Development. It was a popular appointment too – in the department he was spoken of with admiration amounting almost to reverence.

He flew down for a Board meeting, shortly before Steve was due to go on leave, and made a point of seeing me alone. It was not the first time we had met, as he had been on my 'selection board' in London. Unusually for headquarters people on safari, he wore a white linen suit and an old school or college tie – indeed, much as he had been dressed in Great Smith Street at my Colonial Office interview. He chain-smoked cigarettes and spoke in a soft, drawling voice, offhandedly, yet sizing me up – perhaps to see whether his first assessment of me (whatever it was) had been accurate. He quickly moved away from pleasantries though, and it was a shock to hear him speak of Steve as if the Board's executive officer were an obstacle to progress.

"These characters were wished on us by Andy Pike in a fit of AUTHORITY," he said. "Unfortunately, Andy knows as much about the tobacco business as a bar of soap, and he hasn't yet decided to wish them away."

In the Union's sun-baked brick building with its grass-thatched roof, in a dusty red-earth clearing, partly shaded by the small plantation of blue-wattle trees, I sat in on the Board meeting. There were about nine of us squeezed round a trestle table pulled up against Steve's desk. In addition to Robin, Denis and Steve, there was Andy Pike, provincial commissioner (Denis Hill's chief, based at Lindi, 450 miles away on the coast), son and brother of Anglican bishops, straight as a die; James Brett, the provincial agricultural officer, also based at Lindi, a grizzled, seasoned official who quite approved of Steve's military style of management (*he*, Brett, was not going to rock the boat); and three chiefs. They were Nkosi Zulu, a bald-pated little man (the one who had met me at Gumbiro), incongruously more like a court clerk than head of the once feared martial Wangoni; Nkosi Laurent, large, fat, sweating and ill at ease in a tight-fitting suit and tie (apart from Robin Malcolm, the Europeans were all, as usual, in shorts); and Akida Wabu Musa, turbaned and in flowing robes, the only Muslim, shrewd, relaxed and humorous. None of *them* was going to rock the boat.

It was customary for proceedings to be conducted in English, even though all the 'official' members spoke Swahili well and none of the African members spoke English at all. However, since much of the agenda would have been discussed informally beforehand by the officials, a thrashing-out of the more difficult questions had often already taken place over the district commissioner's breakfast table or the previous evening in Pop's pub. The practice at Board meetings, therefore, was for discussion to proceed fairly briskly between the officials and, at suitable points – either when a decision had been virtually reached, or when the uncomprehending spectators were beginning to look glum – the chairman (Andy Pike) would summarise in Swahili and invite comments or opinions from the African members. The chiefs' contributions were mainly from the viewpoint of the tobacco growers, and, as such, were valuable. But in every other respect the chiefs were, in my experience, excessively compliant, tending almost without exception to accept the weight of professional opinion as endorsed, or modified, by the administration.

'Professional opinion' at Board meetings was represented by three people: the executive officer (Steve), who was secretary but not himself a member of the Board; the provincial agricultural officer (Brett); and the registrar of cooperative societies (Robin Malcolm with his 'legal' hat on). Of these, of course, only Steve was on the spot: Brett was based 450 miles away and Robin

Malcolm another 350 miles further up the coast in Dar es Salaam. So, in practice, apart from these six-monthly visitations Steve and his good friend Denis more or less steered policy and ran the show by themselves without exciting much cause for interference from their superiors. There had been a fair consensus all round on what needed to be done through the agency or authority of the Board. That was until the 1950 tobacco crop 'spoilage' finally manifested itself in disastrously low payments to the growers – their consequently vociferous complaint – and the registrar's decision to throw a spanner in the Sontob works.

Steve administered the Board's affairs in much the same way, I imagine, as he had run his company office in the KAR: meticulously and with authority. The Board's twelve or so field instructors were even termed *waskari wa bodi* (Board soldiers), not inappropriately since their role was less to teach than to enforce correct tobacco cultivation. Between the field instructors and the executive officer in ranking were the factory manager, Chummy Lockwood, and two recently recruited field officers – one from Northern Rhodesia (Zambia) and one from the ill-fated Groundnut Scheme at Nachingwea: Steve's sergeant major and platoon commanders, so to speak.

Steve was there 'to make the show work'. He had little or no enthusiasm for cooperatives: he shared common prejudices about them ('socialistic' flim-flam – 'hopelessly unrealistic' to expect ignorant peasants to run a business) even though, as a good military man, he accepted the situation as it was and attempted to make the best of it. So my arrival, with specific instructions to 'promote cooperative development', was regarded by the senior Board staff much as the Tory Party looked on Clause 28 of the Education Act 'for the Promotion of Homosexuality in Schools'. That is to say unfavourably, to put it mildly. My terms of reference were not necessarily disruptive of the prevailing order, but they were – if I was to do my job properly – almost bound to ruffle a few fine feathers. Steve had been appointed manager of the Union (Ngomat) by Robin Malcolm at a time when 'making the show work' was the primary objective; but his 'educative' role – in essence working himself out of a job – had been taken with a pinch of salt: in more than one sense, he had no time for it. Nevertheless, however honoured in the breach, the intention was that, ultimately, the manager (Steve), in handling the assembly, processing and sale of the tobacco crop, should be fully responsible to the Union committee, and that the executive officer of the Board (same man) should cease to have a hands-on function, and retire to a purely monitoring role. You need a picture of the Union committee to grasp what all this was likely to mean.

Africans respect age as embodying wisdom, so the ten committee men (always men) were typically voted from venerable and ancient members of the tribes. Although each of them was likely to be the chairman of his own society, there was nothing much to distinguish most of them from ordinary working farmers: their dress was typically a brown or white kanzu with a European-style jacket – usually rather shabby – and turban-like headgear, a battered hat or a fez. One or two wore shoes, but most did not, and their feet bore evidence of a long, dusty walk from their native village into the township. For some this would have been two or three days' journey, but if they were lucky they'd get a lift in a passing truck. Most could read and write only with difficulty; but for all their modest education they were men of standing in their own community, usually having substantial (up to two acres, or even more) tobacco shambas of their own. Nevertheless, it was easy to take the view that these were indeed ignorant peasants who could be patronised and jollied along to agree with whatever the *bwana mkubwa* thought best. In the 1950s there was an almost universal belief, exemplified by the government's official comment quoted earlier, that 'Africa' was not ready for self-government; and by the same token, proceeding from official good intentions down through Denis and Steve's sceptical pragmatism to Chummy Lockwood's unvarnished bigotry, the tobacco farmers were 'not ready' to manage their own business: they 'did not have the capacity' to make decisions based on a rational analysis of facts, they were 'irresponsible', they 'did not persevere', they were 'lazy'. In short, sadly (big sigh) the gap between African and European culture was 'too wide' to be easily bridged.

Even for greenhorns like myself, programmed to expect that

everything was possible, it was difficult not to agree that Africans lived in a different world, and quite charitably could be viewed as 'much closer to nature'. For example, my shamba boy, Walila, had instructions to water the garden every evening during the dry season. The local people weren't accustomed to doing that; they cultivated with the seasons. Their philosophy was 'You plant the seed; God brings the rain.' Walila must have thought all this piddling about with a watering can was quite futile. But he did it because he was paid (a very small sum) to do it. He would even continue after the rains had started. I would look out of the window, the rain pouring down in torrents, and there would be Walila stoically watering the sodden ground. I remember also another occasion, when I happened to notice my washing hanging out in the rain. Instead of shouting for the boy, I rushed out myself and started pulling the clothes off the line, only to be interrupted by a shout from Rashidi, who saw me from the cookhouse.

"No, no, bwana, they're not dry yet!"

The idea that clothes could be dried other than in God's good time seemed to him to be positively unnatural. To the natives (using the word in its strict sense) the European penchant for taking shortcuts, always trying to be one step ahead of the natural order of things, was too clever by half – a quirk, nevertheless, which they were prepared to humour, although not always seeing the point. To the Europeans, on the other hand, this laid-back disposition could be – and usually was – seen as indolence (forgetting how hard Africans could work when necessary).

"The blighters have no idea of time! They don't start thinking about cultivation until it's almost too late. They talk about food shortages (snort), but they don't bloody well plant in time."

So said the Chummy Lockwoods and, with some slight modification of language, the Mary Stephenses. Yet in some respects they had a sentimental fondness for Africans – that is to say Africans who knew their place and who conformed with an unthreatening stereotype, because, if you thought about it, Africans who aspired to positions of authority *were* threatening. They threatened Chummy's job for a start – not that he could easily be replaced, but because he represented, by his attitude, an obstacle to the legitimacy even of African advancement. He was unpopular, and that made him vulnerable. He was unpopular with self-important committee men who 'supervised' the movement of tobacco (i.e. rode in the truck beside the driver) from primary societies in the field to the factory; they had been elected to a position of dignity, but were treated by Chummy as common labourers. He was unpopular especially with the educated young men who occupied clerical posts and who bitterly resented his contempt for 'jumped-up' black men. It was people rather than policies who were to change all this.

Paul Wren, the district commissioner who followed Denis Hill, was a new broom uncompromised by personal friendship with Steve. I was in his office at the boma one day (district commissioners, although not directly in charge of departmental officers, liked to keep tabs on what was going on and, where possible, give a gentle steer). Paul was a round-faced tubby man, of less than average height, who more than compensated for his lack of stature by owning a magnificent open-topped vintage Rolls-Royce. It was just about the most unsuitable vehicle you could imagine for Songea roads, yet he drove this enormous car with its 'spokeless' wheels and forest of knobbed levers on the steering column as if it were a Land Rover, evoking admiration wherever he went, a veritable plenipotentiary of Her Majesty the Queen. (Paul also had a most stunningly beautiful wife, but that is by the way.) He told me about a young man, just out of secondary school, who sounded promising, and it was agreed between us that I would take him on the Union staff as a management trainee (Steve had not yet returned from leave). The young man's name was Hironymus (Hiro) Msefya.

So Hiro and I would go out on safari together. He was a stocky lad of about sixteen, with a vigorous yet unassuming personality, still hardly more than a schoolboy, but speaking good English. And together (my Swahili was still fairly rudimentary, though it later became fluent), in meeting after meeting, we hammered home the message to growers that the *chama* (society) was *their chama*. If they wanted good prices for their tobacco, *they* had to see that low-quality leaf was graded out; *they* had to get on to rethatching the leaking roof of their tobacco store. If *they* did not take the initiative *themselves* they would lose out in damaged leaf and low prices. "Yet this crusading message, which was meat and drink to my inspectors, and to Hiro sweet as honey, was judged uselessly circumlocutory by Chummy and the two field officers. For them, if the bloody roof was leaking you called for the chairman, tore him off a strip, and told him to get on to it sharp! There was no fiddle-faddle nonsense of explaining the consequences of not having thought of it for themselves. Hiro's introduction as a trainee had been decidedly unwelcome, and on one occasion Chummy's verbal abuse of him was so unpleasant that that the poor boy came to me in tears.

This state of affairs, or 'stand-off', occurred while Steve was on leave, not because I had stirred up trouble but because change was inherent in the decision to post me to Songea. Although suspected of being socialistically inclined (communism and cooperation both beginning with c), I had in fact no political motivation. I was simply following my terms of reference. To be precise (I have just looked this up), the cooperative societies' legislation, which as a civil servant I was bound by, stated, 'The control of the affairs of a registered society shall be vested in the general meeting' which elects a committee which 'shall exercise all the powers necessary for the full and proper administration of the society'.

In Songea these powers were not being exercised. The committee of the Union was virtually ignored. It did not occur to Steve that he was in any way subordinate to it; nor did it occur to the committee that they had any authority to direct the Union's business. This state of affairs – of the Board, via its executive officer, virtually running the growers' business with only the most perfunctory consultation – was what I had been briefed in Moshi had to change. There were four reasons why, over the next two years or so, the situation did change.

First, the growers were outraged at the low prices for the 1950 crop and suspected they were being cheated by the *Wazungu*.

Secondly, expenditure on the new factory had been vastly over budget, and costs associated with raising the crop to its peak in that year – such as recruitment of additional expatriate staff – continued to expand even after subsequent production began to decline. As a result, overhead costs bore ever more onerously on growers. The Songea Native Tobacco Board was becoming more 'visible' just as criticism of it grew ever more vocal. The European Board staff alone enjoyed conspicuous privileges (such as a free Union-built house, free use of Board or Union vehicles, and free firewood by the lorry load from the factory stock), all of which served to exacerbate criticism of Board costs and gave it an unpleasantly racial tone: "*Hawa wazungu wanakuwa wakikula faida yetu yote.*" ("These Europeans consume all our profit.")

Thirdly, as I have explained above, the educative role of my inspectors and myself had a profound effect in shaking previous misconceptions in growers' minds about the structure and control of the industry. We didn't seek (at least I didn't; I'm not so sure about the inspectors) to undermine the authority of the manager/executive officer, but there is no doubt our departmental 'line' did call into question the authoritarian attitude of Board staff.

And finally, the crunch came because government – in the form of Robin Malcolm, supported this time by Andy Pike and Paul Wren – decided that an arrangement which had served the industry well in the past had passed its sell-by date: it was no longer a force for progress, but a brake on it. It had to be changed.

It is difficult to convey to a present-day reader the atmosphere at that time, but looking back now, at a distance of almost exactly seventy years, I see very clearly that the turmoil of events in Songea was typical of the 'wind of change' blowing through Africa that Harold Macmillan spoke of in a famous speech a few years after the dust of it was settling in our remote upcountry district. The Board's radical decision to sack all the European staff save one ('Dilly' Dillingham, the field officer from Nachingwea) was a dreadful shock, not only to those who lost their jobs, and to their families, but to the whole close-knit community of expatriates on the station. For me, who was now ex-officio secretary of the Board, it was especially wretched. No matter how much I might have disagreed with my colleagues' professional attitude, we had been friendly with each other; they had introduced me kindly to my new life and I had experienced the warmth of their hospitality.

Now they had lost their jobs. And yet, in spite of my sympathy for them, I could not feel other than that the decision to remove them had been right. Although I had no part in it, feelings on the station had been polarised, and there was for some months – even after Steve and the others had departed – covert animosity towards me in some quarters. But with the passage of time, and the normal rotation of staff after leave, bitter feelings of 'unfairness' abated, and a new order gradually emerged – with problems enough of its own.

My first tour of duty in East Africa, therefore, was definitely an experience of being thrown in at the deep end; or, to change the metaphor, I had found myself a foot soldier – or second lieutenant perhaps – in a crisis that developed into a drama and ended in a palace revolution. And there were more skirmishes to come.

But first, early in 1954, I was due some home leave. Robin Malcolm, who lived in a charming old German bungalow shaded by acacia trees in the centre of Dar es Salaam, put me up for a couple of days while I waited for my BOAC Comet flight connection. During this time he tried to rub off some of my upcountry rough edges, insisting that I drink pink gins at the Dar es Salaam Club and eschew my preference for beer. Nevertheless, I have an uncomfortably guilty memory of myself uninhibitedly wolfing the cashew nuts and olives which he generously provided to accompany our drinks in the evening. In spite of the heavy responsibilities I was assuming so early in my career, there was a lot I still had to learn.

17 – LETTERS FROM SONGEA

In 1954 one was still permitted to choose either an air or sea passage when taking or returning from home leave. So, having elected to get home as quickly as possible, by air, I then naturally opted to return by a slow boat to Dar es Salaam – this time by the *Kenya Castle*. By an extraordinary coincidence, the girl sitting opposite me at table in the dining saloon* was going out to Songea to marry one of our district officers, Bill Hay; and as I was definitely the only other person on the ship destined for that out-of-the-way place, we – her name was Sheila – formed a friendship during the voyage. Beside me, however, at the same table, was another girl, who proved to be even more interesting – partly because she was something of an enigma: she did not join in the social drinking that was such an enjoyable way of passing the time on board. If, when we were at sea, I saw her other than at mealtimes, it was usually to find her quietly reading in a deckchair, tucked away in some obscure corner behind a lifeboat; and she religiously attended the shipboard church services, which few others did. Yet at the same time this unusual girl did not strike me as being straight-laced. Her demeanour at meals (for which she would appear directly from her cabin, demurely disdaining the preprandial conviviality that Sheila and I enjoyed in the bar) was one of chatty pleasantness to all and sundry, but with no particular attention to *me*. Her laughter, which was frequent, was delightful – the most beautiful expression of genuine amusement

---

* Places were allocated by the chief steward according to some arcane order of seniority or social standing. God knows how he divined that, but he knew how to put the right people on the Captain's table.

that I'd ever heard. Her name was Beryl Veronica Mungavin – Beryl to her family and Veronica to the world, as I was later to discover.

During the ship's leisurely course through the Mediterranean, Suez Canal, Red Sea, etc., sharing brief excursions ashore when it tied up at the ports that I could claim to have 'been to before', and having realised, of course, that Sheila was 'off limits', I became more friendly with Veronica. I learned that she had been born in India, came to Britain immediately after the war and trained as a stenographer. After serving for a period as secretary to the manager of a displaced-persons camp in Scotland, she developed a yen for travel (or got fed up with the weather in Beith-Dalry) and joined the army, ending up as PA to Sir Geoffrey Bourne, high commissioner and commander in chief, Malaya – not that she made much of this: it just emerged. Now she was destined for the secretariat in Dar es Salaam, and I, by the time some weeks later we finally arrived there and parted at the dockside, felt sufficiently attracted to search her out at her preliminary billet in Mgulani Camp. I remember using the pretext of returning to her a packet of cigarettes that she had left behind on disembarkation, and recall the note of pleasure in her voice when she heard me calling her name outside her tent – probably no more than glad to hear a familiar voice after being plunged abruptly among strangers (her first night had been disturbed by a man from the neighbouring tent being sick outside hers), but it gave me (at the time, probably false) encouragement.

There was naturally very little time to develop our relationship further, but we began corresponding by letter shortly after I had returned to Songea – a correspondence that was to endure for two years before eventually we married. We both kept the letters that we received from each other. I have been reading through them and find, as one would perhaps expect, that for the most part they are disappointingly humdrum, even when they developed (after a few snatched exchange visits to Dar es Salaam and Songea respectively) into what might be called love letters (or parts of them at least). Perhaps only poets can do justice to intensity of feeling; the efforts of lesser mortals may possibly be touching to a third party when read at a distance in time. To their writer (speaking for myself) they are gauche and clumsy. Nevertheless, there is in my letters an immediacy of description which accurately conveys an idea of the sort of life I was leading at the time. The following are extracts from some of them.

8 July 1954

I'm at the Beach Hotel in Lindi (popularly known as the 'Dysentry Arms'). Except for two miserable Marmite sandwiches and three chocolate biscuits stuck together with the heat, I haven't had any thing to eat since breakfast, and now it's nearly five o'clock. . . . I ask where I can go to have a wash and the boy rushes off to bring a bowl of water into the lounge! . . . I suppose there's no bathroom. . . . The hotel manager is a funny chap with a very large head. I've been here half an hour and he has spent the whole time yelling, absolutely yelling, at the top of his voice, into the telephone. Tonight I am sharing a room with two other chaps: they have the inside berths; I'm out on the veranda. I suppose they call this the Beach Hotel because, if the worse comes to the worst, they put the guests out on the beach.

11 July

Back in Songea. . . . Sheila was on the plane, looking all keyed up with excitement and nervous, poor girl. . . . Half Songea had turned up at the airfield to meet her. . . . Colin Horley [my relief] had come along, half expecting me. (Rather foolishly, I hadn't sent a telegram.) He is completely worn out and was delighted to see me – or seemed to be anyway.

The wedding was a big success. A very short service and a prolonged reception with apparently limitless quantities of champagne. I tried very hard to get tight on it but it must be impossible. Fortunately, beer had been laid on for the barbarians. . . . Everything went well except that there was some difficulty in cutting the cake, and the Doctor (who proposed the bride and bridegroom's health) had obviously forgotten Sheila's name. They went off in one of the Boma lorries, Bill driving, and a great pile of safari gear, boys and messengers on the back, and miscellaneous household goods trailing behind, tied on with rope.

17 July

I'm going on safari on Wednesday, and shall probably be out, on and off, most of the time for the next two or three months. I have been playing golf this evening – very badly; one gets out of practice very easily. . . . The night is terribly quiet; you can hear the insects with their incessant whirring in the grass, and the occasional dog barks. It was very quiet, but now the moon is coming up. . . . There is something about Africa at night that makes one feel awfully small and lonely – not unpleasantly lonely – just alone; and the sky is enormous, with a luminous quality about it.

23 July

Last night there was a dance at the hotel (now legally a 'Country Club', the advantage of which being that the licence is much cheaper, and we are all supposed to be members, paying fat subscriptions. So far, Pop Harris hasn't managed to persuade anyone to join). Songea dances are quite simple: all you need are an empty room, a gramophone, records, and a bar – and some people. The chap who's nearest winds up the machine and puts on what he likes. The dance stops when nobody wants any more.

The roads are just as bad [as they were when I went on leave] and much more dusty. We have a chap here called Rousham Roberts, who looks after the roads, and his chief occupation is to rush up and down these 'main' roads in a vehicle made for that kind of thing, looking for a patch where the going is fairly good. When he finds one (and it's not altogether easy) he immediately summons a hundred and fifty thousand labourers who throw thousands of tons of mud (in the wet season) or dust (in the dry) . . . on to the road; if there are any tall trees in the vicinity, these must be felled right across the track. The object of this exercise is known only to Rousham and to God. . . . Chama (cooperative) roads are just as bad, but in a different way. . . . When an African wants to go from one place to another he goes by the shortest route – i.e. as the crow flies, except that he sticks to the ground. You will therefore find footpaths going across all kinds of country: over mountains, rivers, swamps and goodness knows what. Now, when it's a question of getting a three ton load from place A to place B, all you have to do is to widen the footpath by chopping down nearby trees and cutting the grass. (A concession is sometimes made to vehicular traffic by building an occasional bridge – 'occasional' because it occasionally bears the weight.) In the dry season, with a strong engine and a couple of spare springs aboard, it's not too bad; in the wet it can be quite fun!

I went to see how the marketing was getting on. This is the first year the Africans have done the thing by themselves. First market OK. Next day another not so OK. In fact we had to suspend collection for two hours while a lot of angry feelings were expressed. A complete waste of time except that the blokes felt a lot better when it was all over.

1 August

I'm at the Marine Hotel, Mtwara. . . . You know about Mtwara [groundnut port] I suppose: the Hope of the Southern Province! Really it is most impressive, and quite a tribute to the faith and far-sightedness of the Government [famous last words!]. We are sending our export tobacco through Mtwara this year. . . . I got a lift from an Indian who happened to be going to Lindi [also on the coast, north of Mtwara]. We got two punctures on the way to Mtama (the railhead) one of which . . . (after we had used the spare tyre) meant a wait for four hours until a lorry came along the other way, from whom we borrowed a repair kit. We didn't stop that night at all, but bashed on to Mtama, which we reached at 11 the next day – very tired and very hungry. . . . By good fortune the daily train to Mtwara was due to leave in an hour's time. So I decided to go by that, rather than continue via Lindi. . . . The journey from Mtama to Mtwara (about 60 miles) takes 7½ hours. There was plenty of opportunity to sleep, but I couldn't. The noise from adjoining carriages and at the various points we stopped at was something terrible. The S.P. Railway is still a pretty new thing and an object of considerable interest to everyone who lives within five miles of it. At one point of the journey we had stopped at an isolated, filthy old village for a couple of African women to get aboard. . . . The guard waved his flag and we moved off. Suddenly a couple of men hove in view from one of the huts, staggering under the weight of a bag of posho (meal), accompanied by a crowd of frantically gesticulating Africans. The guard, a man of some perception, realised the two bibs [women] had left their food behind and he tried to stop the train; but his view of the engine-driver was impeded by the crowded row of black faces protruding all along the line of the carriages, yelling encouragement to the blokes with the bag. The guard nearly went mad: 'Get out of the way, you goats, sheep, dogs, cattle, you – get your heads in!' Of course, the heads only craned out further to see what all the fuss was about. . . . The wretched man was nearly in tears, screaming at the top of his voice, leaning out of his van as far as he dared, shaking his flag in a positive fury of imprecation. But all to no purpose. . . . The unfortunate bibs left without their posho.

15 August

Got back from Lindi OK. . . . Awful journey, simply terrible. . . . Colin left yesterday morning. He had resolved to be off by 8 o'clock, and fortunately for his resolution he woke up at 3 in the morning with his liver out of order; and as he couldn't go to sleep again he got up and <u>did</u> in fact manage to get away by half past eight. So I have now moved from the rest camp to my own house, and spent the whole of yesterday afternoon re-arranging the furniture, putting up my pictures, dusting the books, and generally getting the place in decent order.

I went to a sundowner at the M.O.'s (medical officer) the day before yesterday. Silly things, sundowners. You stand around making conversation, toying with your drink which it's no use finishing quickly, because nobody notices when it's empty. You miss your dinner, and just when you're getting into a party mood (having decided meanwhile that you've just got to help yourself, which is OK because your host is still not noticing) it's time to go. The only thing to be said for it is that, provided you are sufficiently dilatory in attending to your guests' thirsts, it's a fairly cheap way of entertaining a large number of people. I shall always remember a particular sundowner here which Steve (my predecessor on the Board) gave to various odd bods who happened to be around looking at tobacco. Steve forgot the golden rule. He was, in short, generous with his drinks. All the important people left at the appropriate time, but the locals had the bit firmly between their teeth, commandeered a gramophone, rolled back the carpet, and didn't depart until about one o'clock in the morning. Steve's wife was furious, but Steve himself aided and abetted. . . . The Governor, when he was down here, had the thing absolutely taped. He simply got the band to play 'God save the Queen'. [Sir Edward Twining, a large and impressive character, who was Governor for most of my time in Tanganyika, would, prefiguring Boris Yeltsin, often conduct the band himself.] He then took up his position at the exit. We went.

16 August

Litola [about thirty miles along the Lindi road from Songea] – There's nothing much here except a fairly large tobacco marketing society – where I'm staying for the night. Well situated though, on a long, high ridge; on the north side is a wide plain with miles and miles of *pori* (bush) and another parallel line of mountains on the far side of it. To the south is more bush. From the air the area looks deserted, but in fact people live and cultivate shambas (plots) all over it. The Wangoni . . . are very much afraid of witchcraft and are afraid to live too near their fellows. You never see a 'village'. All the houses are dotted about, with as much space between one house (or household) and the next as can be managed.

You'd probably enjoy this life. It's not at all uncomfortable really. You carry everything with you – everything down to table napkins, and a mat to put your feet on when you get out of bed in the morning. . . .

Met up with Bill and Sheila at Lipumba, still very much newly-weds. Whether or not they were pleased to see me I really can't say. I plonked myself down with them in the rest-house anyway. Sheila seems quite well adapted to safari life and is already quite blasé about it all. We went for a walk in the evening and Bill explained what all the birds were that we saw. . . . I took a gun but didn't see anything. Fortunately, my cook Rashidi went out, by himself and got three guinea fowl and two green pigeons – with two shots! Not bad. So the pot is well stocked for a day or two.

19 August

Mbinga . . . it's 65 miles from Songea to the west, in the Umatengo area. This point is fairly high, and in the highlands to the north (where I'm going the day after tomorrow) it goes up to nearly seven thousand feet. The people round here, the Wamatengo, are noted for their farming. Compared with the Wangoni, they are a very hard-working lot, especially in the higher areas where coffee is grown. Coffee is fetching fantastic prices these days and the Wamatengo are certainly cashing in on it. There is a general air of prosperity . . . lots of bicycles, gramophones, good brick houses; the people are better dressed – and very much more quarrelsome than the neighbouring tribes. Very difficult people to deal with; awful liars. You can never really know what they want. I'm sure they lie just for the fun of it. But they are redeemed by their energy and intelligence.

I went out to see the new coffee store this morning. A really fine bit of work, done entirely by themselves. I gave them the plan, and they got a bit of advice about mixing cement and so on from the local Building Inspector. . . . It is quite another story <u>how</u> they got on with it: the bickering about the place to build it; a fearful dispute over water; battles with the transporter; and, finally, the whole work nearly came to a standstill because the chief mason denied that he had contracted to build the gable ends. . . . The Wamatengo are a wonderful people.

I have forgotten the name of the building inspector, a short, chirpy Cockney newly out from the UK – let's call him Fred (it was something like that). An enduring memory is of Fred coming out to inspect the foundations of this building, with the coffee union committee standing in a huddle, looking with awe at *Bwana Fundi* (literally Mr Skilled Craftsman) squinting through his spectacles along the lines of marker string on the ground. After some minutes of squinting, Fred straightened himself up, sucked his teeth ominously, and carefully removed his spectacles, which he then handed without a word to the chairman, motioning for him to have a look for himself. Thereupon the chairman placed Fred's spectacles on his own nose and looked intently through them, pronounced himself satisfied, and gravely handed them back to Fred. Throughout this pantomime nobody laughed; nor was there so much as a smile.

20 August

It's so cold this morning that I have discarded shorts for long trousers and, as well as that, a heavy pullover and jacket. Tropics indeed!

Oh, what a troublesome meeting. Talk, talk, talk, talk, talk, roundabout all over the place, and rarely to the point, over and over the same ground. But I'm sure the chaps enjoy it no end. I would too – it's certainly good for my Swahili – but at the same time bandying about argument and counter-argument, there are the bones of the thing being covered over and obscured. You have to have a very great deal of patience. I suppose it will be much the same thing tomorrow.

28 August

Songea has been full of visitors. There is a big court case on here and the place is choc-a-bloc with lawyers, magistrates, witnesses and what not – to say nothing of commercial people and the odd bod down on a bit of local leave. We had, for once, a very good turnout for hockey on Friday. And afterwards in the pub it was quite a boisterous evening.

4 September

I promised to play tennis this evening. I must rush. . . . Now I'm back. The bathwater is cold and my cook is drunk. Fortunately, I'm going out to dinner tonight. . . . We had a meeting of the Songea Club the other night. Sheila and I have been elected to the Entertainments committee. We are expected to put on a play at Christmas.

2 October

Housework . . . I leave everything to Rashidi. I give him 45 shillings [£2.25] a week, and let him get on with it. If he makes anything out of it, that's his good luck; and if I don't get enough to eat, or if the house is scruffy, that's his <u>bad</u> luck.

I got my usual birthday letter from Father the other day, the first paragraph of which is the same every year: 'How well I remember the day you were born, etc. etc.'

17 October

I'm at Nangero (81 miles out) – in my tent. It's dark now, and all I can see is the circle of light thrown out by my Tilly lamp, grass, the trunks of two trees, and, over to the right, the camp fire and a burble of voices. Supper's being cooked. It's all very peaceful.

19 October

I got up before 6 and went out with a chap who said he knew where some guinea fowl were. We walked for miles but didn't see a thing. But on the way from Nangero to here (Mchomolo) we passed a nearly dried-up lake – it was mostly grass and weeds, with lots of tall, bushy reeds; in the middle was a small patch of water, with a solitary little black duck sitting on it. We stopped, and I darted about in a ridiculous doubled-up position from clump to clump of grass, cautiously peering up every now and again to see if the duck was still there: he was; he never moved. I got within thirty yards and wondered if I should try a shot. No, better make sure. So I slowly sploshed my way nearer [thinking of supper, not sportsmanship] . . . and he disappeared! Vanished. He must have dived. I waited for about five minutes to see if he'd surface, but he never did. And that is the sum total of my huntin' to date.

Mchomolo is an awful place, all sand and dismal *mahogo* [casava] shambas; also fairly thickly inhabited. Why anybody should want to live here I don't know. There's a rather noisy ngoma going on about a couple of miles away, and the sound carries very clearly across the valley.

21 October

Do you know the secret of success for a Departmental officer in an up-country station? This: you <u>ignore</u> your department so far as possible. Leave a clerk in charge of the office with instructions that all mail is to be acknowledged on the official post-card (which simply says 'Your such and such received and is being dealt with'); all letters are thereupon filed in a chaotic filing system. From time to time you make out a report of such tremendous length and complexity that nobody dares criticise it [if, indeed, it would have been read at all] . . . and after a little while you find you have acquired the reputation of being the only person who understands your job and things are so much better if you are left to yourself. . . . Fortunately for me, my head of department doesn't like bumf either. (He leaves that kind of thing to people like Colin Horley . . . now in Dar.)

22 October

Mkongo . . . not a very interesting part of the world, but very quiet. It's typical *miombo* bush . . . nothing but trees, stunted and nondescript. This is the time of year for bush fires; and at night time you can see great red glows all round. The grass gets all burned up but the trees have some resistance – or else the fire goes through them so quickly that they don't have time to catch alight.

If you were here, I would take you, after tea, to a lake near here that I know. It's probably dried up by now, but the country is rather hillier and open, and you can see where you are. In the bush you just can't see a thing for trees and grass. . . . It's my boy Rashidi that has the real hunter's instinct – I haven't. I like to walk around with a gun and, if I see something, have a pot at it; but he sets about it in a much more business-like way, and will spend hours waiting at a place where he expects something to come along; or else travel miles to . . . where he has heard has game. . . . He is pretty well versed in tracking, and interpreting different sounds he hears; he knows the habits of what he is after. . . . For all their (what is to us) laziness, Africans are very much more observant than we are – in their natural surroundings, that is.

23 October

All our speed has brought nothing but a blank two days ahead. We arrived at Ligera to find the Secretary away in Songea. He has the keys and we can consequently do nothing; so we get a weekend off after all. . . . Ligera is the last R.C. Mission in this neck of the woods. Further south they do not go. . . . The local chief has just popped in to say hullo; he has a letter from the Agricultural Officer which he was unable to read. Considering it was probably the fifteenth carbon copy, hardly surprising . . . a most abstruse screed about various demonstration plots that were to be laid out. I am sure the old boy was little better informed when I had read the letter out to him. But he pronounced himself satisfied. (He'd probably already decided that he wouldn't comply with the instructions – on the grounds that he couldn't read them!)

24 October

It's a real Sunday morning, rather warm but a pleasant breeze. Everything's very quiet and I haven't been bothered by anybody; am sitting slothfully in my chair reading Fisher [History of Europe]. . . It's time we had some food and made a move.

Lusewa

Well, we've arrived [down near the Rovuma river, bordering on Mozambique] 7 hours for 40 odd miles. The Lusewa safari nearly always brings troubles (The first time I ever came here I spent a night in the truck). This time it was a bridge that had been burned down. Fortunately the river bed was dry, so we made a small detour through the bush, and bounced horribly into the bottom – and there we stuck. . . . One of my chaps went back to the nearest houses on a bicycle (We were fortunately carrying one). . . . He eventually came back with four chaps and one hoe. . . . It was very hot. After several attempts, with everybody pushing, the engine screaming at a horribly high pitch, and a ghastly smell of burning rubber, the truck bouncing and slithering most alarmingly, we eventually got it up the other side, loaded up again, suitably rewarded the four good Samaritans, and moved off in good order.

The next thing was a bush buck. These creatures will stand and stare at a car with its engine running, but the moment they see somebody on foot, they're off like a flash. So I passed it; then stopped for Rashidi to get out with his gun; and reversed with him on the far side, until we came opposite the bush buck which was still standing there. Rashidi took a shot from 25 yards, but even that range is too great for a shot-gun using SSG, and though his aim was good, he only stung the animal, and it was off and away. . . . The next thing was a bunch, group, covey (whatever it's called) of guinea fowl. We followed them, but no success.

At Lusewa we put up the tent, and in it I am now ensconsed very comfortably. I have had a bath, eaten some cold *kanga* [guinea fowl], drunk ten cups of tea, and will now read a couple of pages of Mr Fisher and go to bed. It's a wonderful life.

25 October

Very pleasant people at Lusewa, but extremely lazy. Their society [cooperative] is quite bankrupt because they don't grow enough to sell through it. This year they are being forced to grow tobacco. . . . The chaps themselves admit that this is the only way; if you encourage them to grow tobacco by exhortation and visions of wealth, they will do nothing; but if you compel them to grow it, they will – with perfectly good grace. . . . It's been terribly hot today, really unpleasant, and I've had ants crawling up my legs all day. Also I've been bitten by a tsetse fly and my left foot is like an obese German sausage.

There's a funny old chief here called Kwisombe, a doddering old ass but of the old school. He rarely goes on safari now, but when he does he goes on a litter. Whenever he comes down to see me I groan inwardly. He . . . comes to cadge cigarettes, but pretends he has just come for a talk. His Swahili is very poor and usually we have to have an interpreter. Today he was telling me that one European, in the dim and distant past, had given him a bottle of gin, and how he sat over it for three days by himself until it was finished. I told him it was very bad for him. 'Oh no,' he said very seriously, 'very good for me . . . a little water and ve-ery little gin, and hup! Then a little water and ve-ery little gin, and hup!' This went on for three days and was very good for him.

26 October

I have quite a cargo of children on this trip: six of them, most of them going back to school in Songea, one going to hospital. They are a cheery crowd, like a collection of little sparrows. Rashidi puts them to work to fetch water and firewood and peel the potatoes – that sort of thing: they love it.

27 October

Just having breakfast, or rather, waiting for the other half of it to come along. It's a lovely morning: bright sun, cool, blue sky, no clouds at all. Birds whistling away. But it's early yet. It'll be stinking hot in no time. . . . Here's the rest of breakfast, 3 fried eggs cooked to a firm, india-rubber consistency. After about seven days all the perishable stuff is finished, and you're reduced to eating stuff that keeps, or what you can scrounge or shoot. I avoid tins as far as possible, because I can't be bothered to keep track of them and the boys go through them like nobody's business.

29 October

[Back in Songea] The Chief Secretary is down here now. . . . There was the usual sundowner for him yesterday evening. The same old thing. The usual bevy of Europeans making the usual strenuous conversation; the usual bevy of Indians trying to look at home and feel at ease; the usual bevy of African chiefs and people of clerical importance, trying to drink as much as possible in the shortest possible time; the usual sprinkling of R.C. missionaries – fat, jolly fellows, drinking hardly anything but having a whale of a time; and the usual wretched little group of African wives, dressed up to the eyebrows, standing miserably in a corner, drinkless and speechless. I felt awfully sorry for them, but I confess I was afraid to go and talk to them. Oh, sundowners! They are supposed to be a merry get-together of all the races – one great big happy Colonial relationship. But in fact they do more than almost anything else to make people conscious of their race and status. . . . I sometimes wonder if we are not trying to do too much too quickly, forgetting the enormous weight of tradition and years behind our different cultures.

5 November

I climbed to the top of a high hill above Mnyanganyanga [in Umatengo] this evening. The sun was pleasantly warm and a fresh wind was blowing up from the valley. From the summit you get a really magnificent view of the surrounding country: the great expanse of two parallel valleys on either side and, as far as you can see, smooth, rolling hills, with the sun playing on their crests and throwing the folds and depressions into deepest shadow. It was almost like a toy panorama, with tiny houses surrounded by coppices and shambas, and the ribbons of road winding their way round the hills, disappearing round the edge of one and reappearing up the side of another. . . The Wamatengo have a network of the most impossible roads, mostly built by the coffee societies.

I had a man to man talk with Rashidi this morning – about food. He said, in so many words, that he was doing his best, and should not be held responsible for the variegated tastes of my stomach: he thought marriage was the best solution. But I am not so sure he would like that much. Most boys prefer working for bachelors: they don't get fussed so much – to say nothing of not <u>doing</u> so much. Rashidi may be an exception. He said that his late memsab wept bitter tears when finally she had to part with him – damned liar.

15 November

The bloke who kindly gave me a lift to Mtama (when I was going to Mtwara, remember? we had a puncture and sat on the roadside for 4 hours) sent in a bill a month later for 100 shillings '1st-class fare to Mtama'. I wrote him a stinker saying I thought he had been <u>helping</u> me but apparently he was helping himself. He sent me a credit note for 100 shillings.

2 December

I went out to the Matengos the other day and got caught in a tremendous rain storm; the truck was skidding about no end. Then coming back, there was another storm and my beastly windscreen wiper wouldn't work. It was dark too, and very awkward. I had a very large African wife squashed between me and Rashidi . . . and she was fairly sitting on the gears and wouldn't budge an inch when I wanted to change gear. So I found I was changing <u>her</u> at the same time. . . . It looks as if the rains are on.

6 December

There's a steady drenching downpour of rain going on outside and all kinds of froggy creakings and croakings in the grass. . . . One of the UMCA padres has just looked in. A decent chap but rather depressed by the general apathy of people about the church (He said he'd heard I was a 'pillar' of it!)

17 December

What am I going to do over Christmas? Well, we have quite a formidable programme arranged. Rose [wife of the agricultural officer] is the prime mover, though I was chairman of the station meeting that worked out the general details, with Rose sitting close by telling me exactly what to say. . . . I'm going to have two Xmas dinners, one at lunch and one at night (Bachelors come off well in that respect). Then there's carol singing round the houses of the station, a barbecue, <u>three</u> dances (within two weeks), children's party, church service (which is also an 'event'), a scavenger hunt, special golf, hockey and tennis matches, tournaments and goodness knows what. . . . We shall all be very glad to stagger off on safari when it's all over – in <u>different</u> directions.

18 – FIGHTING ON TWO FRONTS

Most of the Songea tobacco was sold through a broker in Liverpool. Getting the crop graded, processed, baled and shipped out through Lindi was a highly complex operation under difficult conditions. Communications with the coast were normally by telegram, via the airfield, where a young Scottish telegraphist lived with his wife in lonely isolation. There was a phone line from the boma which could be used in an emergency, but to use it for normal business was out of the question, not only because it was just the one line but also because it was liable at any time to be 'down'. Even when you did get a connection (you twirled a handle to ring through to an operator who always seemed to be conducting a conversation with somebody else at the same time as he tried, often unsuccessfully, to put you through) reception was terrible.

The marketing organisation that had been set up by government – Board, Union, etc. – had been very much a hands-on operation. Now, here we were, after nearly a quarter of a century of government calling the tune, suddenly standing aside – or appearing to do so – and saying in effect, "Right, lads – now it's up to you." The Union (Ngomat) was eager to assume control, but totally unqualified to exercise it. Nelson Nkangama, the secretary, had been well educated up to secondary-school level; he spoke good English and was considered completely loyal to the system as it was – or, now, as it had been. A pleasant, unassuming young man, he had no pretensions to take over Steve's job as manager, although the Union committee, warming to the exercise of their duties, liked to refer to him as *mwangalizi wetu* (our manager). Still, this was a courtesy title: he was not appointed manager, and did not behave like one. In effect, I did the job, and the unspoken intention (of my department, not the Union) was that I, or my successor, would over a period of years train up the staff until eventually someone with the appropriate qualifications would 'emerge', so to speak, who could actually take over as manager.

Of course, it didn't take the committee long before it began to click that Nelson, however much they might call him *mwangalizi wetu*, wasn't the real thing. Demands for the Union to be embellished with the dignity of a proper manager began, about six months after the reorganisation, to centre on a particular individual, one Luxford Mbawala. I had not previously met him, but his name had sometimes surfaced, in general conversation among expatriates, as a 'political troublemaker'. Some five years or so previously Luxford had served briefly as a cooperative inspector employed by the Union, but he had either been dismissed, or somehow been eased out, because he was thought to be stirring up feelings against the *Wazungu* – chiefly against those in charge of the tobacco industry. He had then left the district and was currently serving somewhere as a school teacher.

We at first resisted the pressure for Luxford to be appointed manager, not so much because of his reputation as a political agitator, but because he was manifestly not qualified to do the job. Although he spoke English quite well his formal education had not proceeded (as was still quite common) beyond the primary stage, and his knowledge of tobacco was sketchy. On the other hand, he had a commanding personality; he was Mgoni; and he was the man who some years previously had been attacking the European management of the Union, whose unsuitability the government had now implicitly acknowledged.

It was about this time, I think, that Robin Malcolm retired and was succeeded by Sandy Dyer, a gritty Scot of military bearing.

"Who is this bozo?" he wanted to know. "Well, I don't suppose he can make a bigger balls of the job than the other lot."

He then cheerfully, if unwisely, but perhaps inevitably, agreed that we had to allow this Luxford Mbawala to come on board, and then give him enough rope to hang himself – if possible without his doing too much damage in the process.

Luxford duly appeared, and installed himself in the manager's office, Nelson hovering confusedly in attendance. He was a thickset, heavily jowelled man with dark, staring eyes.

He greeted me with careful cordiality – "You are my teacher; I am your pupil" – and then roared with laughter.

It was a moderately good start, and I was equally careful in my responses. It was my job to show him how the business worked, what were the critical factors, and what we were trying to achieve in the field, in the factory and in the world market. He listened attentively, with a kind of resigned patience, at the same time sizing me up. I was determined not to fall foul of him needlessly, and I think he had much the same attitude towards me. He made it plain that he wanted to get out into the field as soon as possible, to speak to the people.

"They are discouraged, Mr Hall. They are *crying*. For so many years all their efforts have been eaten up by those Board people."

Before long, Luxford was organising safaris throughout the district, accompanied by Hiro Msefya and a small retinue of committee members, field instructors and messengers.

His message was "The *Wazungu* have gone. Now you have one of your own people in charge. Grow tobacco! You can now be sure that ALL the profit from those fabulous European markets will return to you in full measure, instead of being siphoned off into the pockets of the *Wazungu*. I, Luxford Mbawala, shall see to it."

The enthusiasm was tremendous. The word spread to the furthest and most remote parts: "Luxford is here. The Europeans have gone." It was as if the Messiah had arrived.

While Luxford progressed throughout the district, holding court wherever he arrived, raising hopes and expectations among the people, the Union's business was unobtrusively overseen in the field by George Brookbank, in the factory by Dilly Dillingham, and in the office by me. Doggedly assisted by Nelson Nkangama and De Souza (whose first name I never discovered; he was always Mr De Souza), we aimed to keep the business going much as before Luxford's advent among us. Nevertheless, he was a constant irritation, and would return from time to time to hold meetings in his office, and to summon staff from their work, for interrogation or instruction, which as often as not cut across what was already being done. He would hire staff without consultation, alter the pay of individuals, and dispense patronage like a medieval prince. Far from acting as a 'pupil', he gloried in the outward exercise of power, but paid little attention to the routine business of the Union he was supposedly managing.

This went on for about a year – a period of much aggravation and worry for me, who had to go along with this charade while trying at the same time to ensure that nothing went seriously wrong. Eventually, however, Luxford overreached himself. Typically perhaps, it was a very minor matter that led to his downfall: the vice-president of the Union, an old Mmatengo with a voice like a quacking duck, felt himself to have been insulted by Luxford: the manager, who was supposed to be answerable to the committee, was making a habit of ignoring them; he, the vice-president, had not been consulted about a particular staff appointment. He had been ignored. He had been insulted. It was too much! Trivial as this was (the old man probably had one of his own relatives lined up for the job), it was the culmination of a series of indignities. Too many individuals had been favoured at the expense of others. The Union committee, with much hesitation and trembling, but emboldened by anger at having their toes constantly trodden on by an overweening subordinate, told him he 'could go'. Although Sandy Dyer, as registrar of cooperative societies, could himself have sacked Luxford – for any one of a number of reasons – it was important that the committee should themselves get a grip of their responsibilities and act accordingly, unprompted. With customary African politeness, they now invited him to look for other employment.

Paul Wren, who had been a great support to me, was succeeded as district commissioner by one George Baker, a different character altogether. Baker had been a sort of aide-de-camp to the provincial commissioner at Mtwara, and he carried with him an aura of one who has been accustomed to move in exalted circles. This impression of being *du haut monde*, so to speak, was further bolstered by his arrival at our dusty upcountry station in a beautiful pale-blue Mercedes. Paul's ancient Rolls-Royce had been impressively eccentric; Baker's Mercedes was a deadly serious display of one-upmanship. He was a tanned, beefy, aggressive-looking man, with a jutting chin, beak-like nose, and a grinding voice, not loud but monotonously insistent. From the start he made it plain that he thought Songea needed shaking up; and it was my misfortune that he brought with him a strong prejudice against cooperatives, and active hostility towards Ngomat in particular. Luxford Mbawala's displays of bombast and managerial incompetence (widely known), although now in the past, were dredged up as evidence to support Baker's preconceptions; and it was not long before I, too, was included in the new district commissioner's demonology. I discovered much later that Baker seriously believed me to be a 'security risk', that I was a 'communist' and a dangerously subversive influence in the district. All this, apparently, had been confidentially reported, over a period of months, to the provincial commissioner, who duly passed on his mounting concern to my own chief in Dar es Salaam. Fortunately, Sandy Dyer gave it short shrift.

This *fitina* (a very common Swahili word, meaning discord, feud, mischief, or simply misunderstanding, depending on how you feel about it) went on for about two years. I bore it stoically. With all the constraints and daily frustrations, I was confident in my own grip on what needed to be done in the Songea tobacco industry. I already knew where the weak points lay, and they were not capable of facile solution. In any event, it was not a uniformly depressing outlook: I was also responsible for the Matengo coffee union, which was manifestly thriving on high world coffee prices.

Luxford and Baker were in different ways thorns in my side, yet I was fortunate that, in their respective roles, they followed each other and were not aggravating me both at the same time. In a way, they kept me on my toes – as I had to be. Most of my colleagues took a jaundiced view of cooperatives, which were seen, at best, as pretty dicey set-ups: the business could have been handled, so they thought, much more efficiently if the Union and its affiliated societies had all been just swept away, and a single company put in to do the job without all the nonsense of elections, delegation and consultation that we had to go through before anything could be done. This was true enough, but it missed the point: our job (mine in this case) was to teach Africans to run the business for themselves – not to do it for them.

19 – APPROACHING MARRIAGE

While my working life continued its bumpy course, I maintained a voluminous correspondence with Beryl, almost all of which we have failed to destroy. The following excerpts from letters, some of them from my parents, give a general idea of the lead-up to our eventual marriage.

9 March 1955

It was simply wonderful staying with you, and now I can hardly wait until you come here. I asked George and Rose what the Songea people would think of you going on safari with me. They said what the hell does it matter? It was up to you. . . . So it's up to you. I don't think very much of taking somebody else with us for the sake of appearances: he'd only feel he was in the way – and he jolly well would be! . . . Don't forget to start dosing yourself at least two weeks before you come down here. This a bad place for malaria and kindred diseases.

17 March

Should you write to Rose? [American wife of George Brookbank, the agricultural officer.] Well, you may as well, to say you've heard they'll put you up; very kind, and shall you bring a tooth brush, or can you use George's . . . that sort of thing. I'm fixing a safari from the Tuesday following Easter . . . that'll mean two weekends in Songea itself and 11 days on safari, but . . . one rarely gets back on the day you aim to. . . . There'll be six of us altogether: you, me, Rashidi, Franz (messenger), driver, and an inspector.

In this way Beryl was duly initiated to life 'upcountry'. Before she returned to Dar es Salaam I proposed to her. Having regard to the relatively short time we had known each other – intermittently at that, and in large measure courtesy of the postal service – Beryl wisely took time to mull over the idea. I meantime went off on a trip to Nyasaland, and it was some weeks before I returned to find not only the eagerly anticipated 'Yes', but an accumulation of letters looking forward to the actual event – that is to say, our marriage. (A wife-to-be, however cautiously evasive beforehand, once committed does not allow the grass to grow under her feet.) I replied ecstatically, suggesting we get married 'as soon as we can: May next year, if possible, but if not, then June'. In a mad rush of generosity I enclosed a cheque for £25, which I assumed would be more than enough to cover the cost of an engagement ring. Unfortunately, by this time, the engagement ring had already been bought – for a sum considerably more than what, in my ignorance, I had thought was already a mark of princely liberality. I was, in the following order, outraged, aghast, surprised, bemused, rueful, conscience-stricken, mortified.

16 May

> I really did blush for my wretched £25 and wished so hard that I could have recalled it. It's just that I hadn't the beginning of a notion how much these things cost. . . . I'm only now beginning to recover my self-possession and see the funny side of it.

A small thing, it was in a way as if I had suddenly been introduced to myself: not thrifty, but mean – and perhaps a bit of a curmudgeon.

8 June

> Today is the official celebration of the Queen's birthday, with a parade at the Boma. We all turned up in our best suits; the police contingent went through their paces, and the Peramiho band played loud and martial music. Paul made a long speech. The whole show rather depressed me. What effect could all this rather second-rate

showmanship have on that crowd of gaping Africans (who had to be prodded to stand up for the National Anthem)? . . . It all seemed so out of touch with reality – though Paul's speech was not at all bad, if you miss out the platitudes. But I felt ill-tempered at the end of it, and so didn't go to 'drinks at the district commissioner's' afterwards. (Everybody I meet now will be saying 'What happened to you?)

I expect the worries and frustrations with Ngoni-Matengo were getting me down, but the outlook was shortly to change dramatically:

22 June

Monday really was a red-letter day. . . . Luxford has been sacked. I'm simply delighted. That man has been on my back for the past year. He was brought here largely because the blokes thought he was a miracle-worker. In fact he was just a political agitator . . . a continual trouble-maker, and now we are rid of him. The Union is a different place already. On top of that came a letter from Noakes (European agent for selling tobacco) saying he hoped to get better prices this year. I'd been badgering him strongly. We're going to send a trial consignment to the Limbe auctions in Nyasaland – to keep the existing markets on their toes. And I managed to settle a very difficult *shauri* [problem] that had been causing trouble for several years, about grading. And finally there was good news from Kotakota about the new paddy agreement. So we're set fair for a bit (touch wood).

17 July

I've just had my hair cut. The Ag. Gov. (or the Officer Administering the Government, as he prefers to be called) is coming here today, complete with wife, ADC', pte. sec., 6 cars and 14 servants. The Hoi polloi (that's me and everybody else) don't see anything of him until tomorrow when we all turn out dressed in accordance with General Order No. such and such, paragraph (d) (ii) 1 – ie. shorts, shirts and socks (and shoes for those who feel more comfortable with them on – that part of it is apparently optional). . . . Rashidi has just brought in tea, with gorgonzola sandwiches as usual; he never gives me anything else these days since I told him I liked it.

Saturday ... Goodness me, you're looking up in the world, Miss Mungavin – PS to the AG (which I suppose is personal secretary to the Attorney General).... Now we'll be seeing your name in starry lights in the *Gazette*.

My brother Hamish has just come back after five years in Australia. Mother and Father seem to have found a tremendous difference in him and hadn't quite got used to it when last I heard.

15 August

About the furniture. I have half-made a bargain with Roy Davis [forester, best-man-to-be] to swap two of the Vernon chairs for his sofa, and my dining table for his smaller, round one. The point is, it's almost impossible to get any furniture in Songea. It means making it specially and they never have any money. But once we have a sofa it'll be easier to get another chair if we need one. . . . This is definitely not Dar es Salaam.

I am in the middle of Duff Cooper's autobiography. He was one of those fabulous people, born right, went to the right school, Eton, Oxford, army, diplomatic service, member of parliament, ambassador to France; knew all the right people, belonged to all the right clubs, plenty of money, intelligent, cultured, good linguist, poet, – the lot. A civilised man and of a kind (the old school) that is fast disappearing. We are the poorer for it. These people fill me with awe; in their way they are perfect . . . they fit into a background that is, one might say, just as much of them as they are of it – the quintessence of aristocracy. . . . But what am I writing about this for? I don't know.

I include the foregoing naively gushing eulogy mainly as a commentary on myself at the time, and to nail a common belief that, in my younger days, I was a 'red-hot socialist'.

27 October

I saw Padre Rice-Jones the other day. He's just come back from leave. I told him he'd have a wedding in July, July 6th. He wrote it down in his little book and said he'd let me have a form to fill in.

9 November

[In the pub this evening] Pop Harris was in a simply foul mood and was attacking and slandering everybody. Bill was a brainless ------ fool (which is one thing he isn't), Roy a whited sepulchre; and as for me, I just can't repeat it. I don't think I've ever been insulted like it before, except that I wasn't insulted. The poor old chap is very embittered about lots of things and it all came out in a rush.

The wretched furrow has dried up again and all my beautiful lettuces and peas are parched. I can't plant out anything either and there's a seed-bed full of things ready to go in.

Rashidi is back at work now. I just couldn't bear the cooking of that old rogue, Salum, any more – filthy old man: dirty finger-marks, tea too strong, irons shirts the wrong way, puts dirty old kettles on the beautiful new paint . . . Yesterday they both went off till 5.30 and I was kept waiting for tea (Of course, typically East African, it didn't occur to me to make it myself). I gave them a ticking-off, but was sorry to find them both waiting up for me at 11 o'clock last night. They probably think I'm cantankerous. I slang them for not being in the kitchen and then I slang them for being in the kitchen.

The dentist has been down here this week. . . . Most dentists are well-practised in the art of the monologue, but this chap not at all. He wasn't content with 'Ughs' and 'Ghrruus'. He whipped all his instruments and fingers out of your mouth, gave you a couple of seconds for a short, snappy reply, and then whipped them all back in again. Very decent of him, but a bit embarassing if you can't think of a short, snappy reply. You just sit there, literally, with your mouth open.

11 November

I've come to a decision that if the Union hasn't started to pay its way and start looking successful before we go on leave I shall write and ask to stay here. I should like to see the thing firmly on its feet before moving on somewhere else. . . . After all, I've been here 4 years now and know more about this tobacco organisation than anybody else, and know that, given time, we can make a success of it. There are many worse stations than Songea, and few better.

12 January 1956

Paul Wren is going on leave in February now, and apparently we <u>are</u> getting George Baker in his place. G. Baker is a man with a reputation. A very keen and efficient type who likes to have his district team toeing the line. It'll be interesting to see what he really is like.

24 January

Sandy Dyer . . . is coming on Monday. . . . He doesn't seem to be really interested in Songea; hasn't been here for more than 18 months. I'll have to start putting Songea on the map. The trouble is that Songea in his (and most other people's) mind means Ngoni-Matengo, which was a pet toy of everybody's, given to the 'fighting Wangoni' more than 20 years ago to compensate for their loss of pillaging and plundering activities. It's a bit bashed and battered about now, and nobody – particularly the Wangoni, who are not even interested in themselves – is much interested in it. In the meantime, a quite sturdy coffee business is being built up, which, within the past five years, has equalled and now surpassed Ngoni-Matengo. Some day somebody will wake up to the fact. I put up a plan for attempting to resuscitate Ngoni-Matengo. The Wangoni think it's marvellous and will undoubtedly make a hash somewhere. Sandy Dyer says Congratulations, I entirely agree, and promptly forgets all about it; and Paul is going on leave and doesn't care about anything at all anyway.

28 January

For the first time in about ten days we've had a few hours sunshine. I'd begun to think the rains would never stop. As it is, the Lindi road is out of action and is likely to remain impassable for about two months at least. One big bridge is down and I don't suppose they'll be able to repair it while the water's up. So Songea is cut off on all sides by road: north, west and east – and south for that matter. The price of things like paraffin, beer, and tinned stuff is likely to soar. The plane was delayed again, and had to spend the night on the airfield. There were 17 school-boys and girls on it, and they had to be boarded out for the night among people on the station. . . . Funny little creatures, they didn't care a bit.

17 February

I've just come back from playing a most strenuous game of hockey.... George Baker was there; he arrived by today's plane; seems full of beans. He's faintly 'hearty', definitely tough. He practically brought me to my knees with his handshake. Quite unnecessary. A firm grip's all very well, but a chap that takes everybody he meets as a 'try-your-strength' machine gives me a pain, in more ways than one.

29 February

Mkongo... Rashidi is out hunting. It's nearly 8 o'clock, blast him. He'd better bring something back. I went for a stroll this evening. I love the bush at dusk. Everything is so still and quiet; one has the feeling of untouched creation, vast, dark, primeval: and so it is, practically. Tonight the sky seemed huge, and each quarter of a different quality.... The night sky is so altogether mysterious and fascinating; the world is lost in darkness and, freed of it, your mind can lose itself in eternity.

49 Plashet Road
London E13
19 March

My dear Alan ...

We had letters from all our boys last week – David after a 5 week interval – full of the joys of life. I think he must keep a diary, as his letter reads like the entries from one. Not much of the monastic life with him now! Dinner parties with the Dutch deputy consul, and minor celebrities. The appropriate wines with each course. Cointreau ... with grapefruit, which was a new one on me! Dinner by candle-light – jet black china – 160-piece set. Sherry with the soup – hock with lobster, Saint Emillion & roast mutton – strawberries & champagne – dessert & port, liqueurs & coffee – & at the end he says, His whisky was very good & his cigars excellent! It is a wonder to me how he could tell what it was like after all that food and wine – and where he managed to squeeze in whisky.

Hamish sounded in much better fettle.... He has moved up one rung – by being invited to the clients' cocktail party.... This is the first time Ham has been invited to the Clients' 'do'. They are the big business & wealthy bods of Adelaide. . . .

We had a visit from our parish priest on Thursday. I felt rather terrible. He has been here for 18 months and I had never seen him – & didn't even know his name! He seemed very shy of us & was difficult to entertain. Father said he wasn't so bad when I left the room to get some tea. . . . He finds his church rather empty & on parting expressed the hope that he would see us along! Forlorn hope I fear. . . .

Our fondest love,
Mother

In spite of what she writes in that letter, Mother was a religious woman; but having been not merely brought up in the Church of Scotland, but wholly immersed in its practice and conventions for the first twenty years of her life, she found the liturgy of the Church of England stilted, and perhaps almost pharisaical in its set-piece worship.

16 April

The Union committee yesterday authorised the dismissal of thirty members of the staff. . . . We're really stripped for action now. It's make or bust, and the chances are even.

22 April

There was the most awful rumpus at the Board meeting yesterday. Baker behaved in the most irresponsible manner you could imagine and George Brookbank weakly followed in his steps. In the end it was only myself that was urging that Dilly should not be allowed to go. But, as it happened, it didn't matter either way. Dilly sent his resignation in to me the same morning. And I'm sure . . . that Baker put him up to it. . . . I was very angry – and so was he. Well, I shall run that factory myself and Baker can do what he likes. He says it's 'out of the question', and so emphatically that his only possible motive can be that he wishes such an awful nonsense to occur that he'll get sufficient weight to argue that the Chama should be closed down. He is utterly prejudiced and takes no interest in what is being done to pull the Chama up. And the gossip flying around is nobody's business (or should I say it's everybody's?). . . . It shouldn't be necessary to clash with the DC: Government is supposed to be of one mind. Yet here is this bloody hypocrite saying that if the Chama shews evidence that it's shaping up to its problems he'll 'support it to the hilt'.

28 April

The old man has woken up with a vengeance . . . and one thing Sandy Dyer is sensitive about is interference with his Department. George Baker's got in his hair and it's all hands on deck! Action stations! . . . A telegram came this morning: 'Hall your ---- standfast AAA action being taken AAA do not budge from stand you have taken AAA send immediately copies of . . . etc. etc.' The only 'action being taken' of any use now is a private directive to Baker to lay off the Chama.

49 Plashet Road
26. iv. '56

My dear Alan . . .

It won't be long now, my lad. You'd better make the most of the few weeks left to you as a person who may do, for the most part, just what he will. Your mother and I, of course, feel a little out of things, but for my part I am quite glad you are getting married away from home. When I think of the long, boring – for the most part – speeches at Ian's wedding, I'm quite sure you are doing the correct thing. . . . The cine camera is an excellent idea, and I think a recording would also be fun. I have several patients who own these recorders. Amazing! What they want them for beats me. People in what Granny would call 'the working classes' have most things they desire nowadays – money seems no object. I expect the 'quiet wedding' will turn out to be no quieter than the average event in these wild places. . . . I expect you'll have a fearful time. I'll never forget the wedding of a staid and proper parson up in Banchory. He arrived at our Manse on the evening before the marriage, begging asylum from the horde of young 'friends and parishioners' who wanted to tar and feather him or do some equally unpleasant pre-marriage rite on his terrified body. I trust you'll escape those rather unpleasant escapades. Who will be your best man? David, who as usual is on top of the world, entertaining and being entertained by all but Royalty itself, would dearly have loved to fill this post and manage everything for you. And he'd do it jolly well too. . . .

    Your affec. Father

May 1956

Sheila came round the other day to start the ball rolling towards the wedding. I confess I felt a bit of a clod. I've made no initiative at all . . . but I did shoot her down on the bacon and egg stunt. That may be all very well for a seven forty-five wedding in the Rocky Mountains, but at 10 o'clock in East Africa – on a working day! No (quite apart from the fact that wedding cake, bacon and egg, and champagne would undoubtedly do grave damage . . . to my already precarious equilibrium). . . . The reception itself will be at Rose's house, because their garden is better. . . .

Sandy Dyer wrote to say that he would probably be coming down by the 'Mombasa' [coastal freighter] and would require me to meet him at Mtwara on <u>7 July</u>! But he said he had an idea that I was getting married. . . . So I wrote back very promptly saying we were getting married on 6th July [and] we were only taking 'a weekend honeymoon'.

49 Plashet Road
11th May

My dear Alan . . .

Ham is still in a hotel [in Adelaide] & all his clothes & baggage which went out from home is in store. Apparently his landlady turned him out. I don't know how it all came about, as he says that he still goes to her for a meal at the weekend & she isn't at all repentant for throwing him out. . . .

We had the usual tales of woe from Uncle George. Things are so bad that he put the farm in the hands of agents for a week and then retracted. He has got rid of all his help & is trying to manage alone – & at the same time says that he wants to increase his herd. I am afraid that poor George is missing out somewhere. It is a pity he has to work so hard at his age. . . .

    Our fondest love,
        Mother

12 May

After a long wait, Sandy Dyer's 'letters' turned up as one letter, saying that 'as the battle was likely to be pretty hot and furious' he had, 'on 2nd thoughts decided to keep me well in the background'. And I think that may be interpreted as meaning he is meeting with stronger resistance in Dar than he had bargained for. . . .

No, I've never played Scrabble. It sounds a most unsuitable game to play on one's honeymoon, something between squabble and scrap. What is it, a card game?

16 May

I'm just waiting for the Mbinga AGM to get under way. They're making a fearful noise. . . . The Wamatengo intonation, singsong-whining, loud, explosive, not unlike a Suffolk farm-hand talking about pigs, can be infinitely irritating. So can the Wamatengo. . . . Very early this morning I got up and had a look outside the tent. The dawn was just beginning to break and everything was painted in one dark and silvery colour with only a gleam of light over the hills, just enough to throw up the shapes of trees and the valley mist and the tall grass all laden with dew . . . and cold, my goodness it was cold!

Yes, you buy the book on 'a sane sex-life'. I know practically nothing technically (and certainly nothing techniquely) about sex, and there's a good deal more to it than letting nature have her head. But I'd rather you read it and (if it's any good) send it on to me by post. . . . It's just as well that nature should be educated.

49 Plashet Road
30th May, 1956

My dear Alan . . .

Thank you for your birthday wishes. . . . Retirement? Five years to go – Father will be 60 next month. Life is very full for me these days – with the fine weather I see all the dust & dirt, and I am waging war on it. . . . Ian is still with us. I am afraid he annoys me quite often. His attitude to women is one of Master & slave. He doesn't like having to help me with the washing up. . . . Poor David [in Hong Kong] is still in hospital. He sounds quite happy. . . . Hamish is very silent these days. He wrote to me for my birthday, but we haven't heard since then. I think he hasn't settled down properly this time. . . . I wish he wasn't so far away & without regular leave.

 Our fondest love,
  Mother

7 June

I must warn you that Nelson Nkangama (the Union Secretary) wants to collect a few of his friends together and serenade us when we come back from our honeymoon. . . . He said, 'English songs, and only those of my friends who have sweet voices will be allowed to sing.' I told him their own songs would be better. . . . I was rather touched. Rashidi also intends to celebrate, and is diplomatically angling to enquire how much I am prepared for his celebration to cost me.

12 June

There is one chap we've missed out of the invitations to the wedding, but I don't know his name and I've never even been introduced to him. He has recently been taken on at Kitai [the single foreign estate in Songea district, about sixty miles out of the township, off the Mbamba Bay road, growing flue-cured tobacco and pineapples on the banks of the Rovuma]. I shall let the Hughes know that their invitation is to be construed as one for the whole Kitai ménage. . . . George Baker has, I believe, made arrangements to be on safari on 6th July, which is just fine – it would otherwise probably be faintly embarrassing for him to try to be nice; for me too. I haven't spoken to him for about 2 months.

26 June

I wonder when next it will be that I write you a letter. I hope not for a long time ahead. I feel like writing about chapters closing and new chapters opening, but shall resist the temptation. . . . I have to go to Masasi tomorrow [about 300 miles east]. . . . I'll be in Songea on Sunday evening, all being well – and it had better be well, for my own sake! . . . Do you feel on the threshold? I don't. I just want you to hurry up and come, so that we can start living.

49 Plashet Road
28.vi.'56

My dear Alan

It's a very good thing that this wedding business is not a recurring event in our family. It entails far too much letter-writing for my liking & things like 'stinkers to Mappin & Webb', reminders to Hamish that 'Alan gets married on 6th July, & have you written to him yet?' It's all very trying & time-consuming. . . . (Mother always brings the boys' letters up to me in bed. Result, I'm late for surgery, if I don't cut a bit out of my chin.)

I believe Mother is in the dining room, concocting a 'letter to her eldest son on the eve . . .' so I'll not need to write v. much. You know that we shall have you – and Veronica, whom we do not yet know – much in our hearts in the coming days. . . . Mother is a bit weepy about it all, which is perfectly natural, but I think she has quite the right feelings about her boys & has realised for some time that you have all grown up now.

Give Veronica my special love. After all, she'll be my first daughter-in-law & she'll have a very special welcome when you bring her home. Bless you both.

Your affec. Father

P.S. I've just had the Wolesley retuned . . . and it's like a new car.

20 – MARRIAGE, JEREMY AND OXFORD

Our wedding was celebrated in the little UMCA church, at the quieter end of the dusty, bare-earth market square of Songea township. The church was at the time undergoing some much needed repairs to its cracking mud walls and rusty corrugated-iron roof; and we had to walk up a plank bridging a muddy trench to get inside. It was rather dark because there were no windows, such light as there was coming from a gap along the eaves. To give some proper dignity to the occasion, we had borrowed a black Standard Vanguard from Alimohamed Osman (who some months previously, wishing to improve his chances of getting the transport contract, had unmistakably suggested to me that, if his bid was successful, a brand-new one could be mine to keep!). Apart from George Baker's Mercedes, it was the only decent vehicle on the station.

Beryl wore a simple three-quarter-length white wedding dress, and was led up the aisle (having negotiated the plank outside) by Bill Hay, bald head gleaming, who had met her for the first time the previous day. The service was memorable for Padre Rice-Jones' Freudian slip at a crucial moment – 'Those whom God hath joined asunder . . .' – quickly corrected. The unaccompanied singing was loud and lusty; this was, after all, the second station wedding in eighteen months and the congregation had had plenty of Friday-evening singing practice in Pop's pub. One of the guests, dressed in a leopard-spotted frock, retreating backwards after the service to get a better camera shot, fell into a water-filled crater. This caused great amusement and got the reception off on a happy note.

Three days later, having been seen off at the airfield by virtually the whole station – pelted with confetti all the way to our seats in the plane, children running up and down the gangway – we returned from our fleeting honeymoon at the Southern Highlands Club and started married life proper in my little thatched 'gingerbread' house that looked out over the Matagoro Hills. Beryl adapted well to the unaccustomed privations of upcountry life, without electricity or running water, and to the challenge of coping with ready-made friends. As often as not she would accompany me out on safari.

Partly as compensation for our necessarily brief honeymoon, we had decided, for our first leave together, to travel home by sea; and after several weeks' tedious negotiations through the minefields of 'standing orders' (which had difficulty in accommodating staff wishing to travel home on a *French* ship by such a roundabout route) eventually obtained approval to arrange berths on the Messageries Maritimes' *Jean Laborde*, sailing for Marseilles via Madagascar, Réunion and the Cape. The trip proved to be everything we hoped: as the only British aboard, it almost felt as if we had the ship to ourselves. Our fellow passengers were all French colonials returning home on leave. They played cards incessantly and their children stayed up till all hours, until finally they fell asleep in their chairs. Mealtimes, with flasks of wine routinely on the table, were an exquisite pleasure after thirty months of Rashidi's cuisine – the French take such an interest in their food. We were intrigued to see how meticulously they wiped their plates clean with bread – a reassuringly bourgeois touch to their otherwise slightly intimidating culinary reputation. It was on the *Jean Laborde* that I first learned to appreciate the pleasure of eating artichoke, leaf by leaf, dipped in a mixture of seasoned olive oil and lemon juice.

The facilities on deck, however, were not so impressive. There was a usually fruitless early-morning scramble for the ship's few rickety deckchairs; so, at the first opportunity ashore, we bought ourselves two good folding chairs for our own exclusive use.

Freight seemed to be more important than passengers. Diégo-Suarez, on the northern tip of Madagascar, was a typical port of call: on berthing there, the ship heaved up against the harbour's old wooden piles with such a creaking and splintering of timber we thought the ramshackle quay was going to collapse (surely it couldn't survive that kind of treatment *every* time?). While the derricks got busy with cargo we had time to disembark and wander along the dusty main street, critically comparing the French colonial scene with our own (such as at Lindi or Dar es Salaam). It had a desolate, run-down appearance, and we sniffed disparagingly at the dilapidated wooden buildings, peeling paint and unkempt verandas. The 'exotic' island of Réunion was little better. We spent two days there, taking on a vast quantity of sugar: a constant stream of sweating, half-naked porters, each bowed under his load, filed up gangplanks and, sack by sack, manually filled up the holds. This went on hour after hour – a fascinating scene, like something from a Joseph Conrad novel. We could almost have been back in the nineteenth century – and indeed the slow, heavy rolling of the ship, when fully loaded and we were traversing back westwards across the Indian Ocean, did have a rather alarming old-fashioned feel of being close to the dangers of the deep.

Durban, with its wide streets and bright, busy shops, was another world. You could well forget you were in Africa, there were so few blacks; and those we did see, loping along in shabby clothes, looked as if they were merely passing through, going somewhere else. I saw one African man hovering near the cash desk of a bookshop, nervously out of place while he waited for all possible white customers to be served. A middle-aged woman pounced and seized him by the shoulders.

"Stand there, boy," she commanded.

About a foot and a half taller than she was, he meekly shifted to where she put him, without the smallest sign of resentment. Nor was the woman more than mildly irritated: it was as if she had moved a piece of furniture that was in the way. And I was reminded of that little scene some years later, when I was travelling to Lesotho. Its African director of agriculture met me at Johannesburg Airport – outside, at the exit gate. As a 'black' he was not permitted inside, he told me matter-of-factly. The extraordinary *submission* of Africans to apartheid perhaps goes some way to explain their remarkable magnanimity to whites after the end of it.

At Marseilles we collected the first new car I'd ever owned: a Peugeot 304, which had a deservedly good bar-room reputation for standing up to rough country driving. In a small, bare restaurant by the old harbour we had mussels with lots of garlic; and the following evening, at the hotel, bouillabaisse. I did not enjoy either very much and, the next morning, took my revenge on the French by ordering bacon and eggs for breakfast.

The conditions for touring Europe at that time – the spring of 1957 – were infinitely better than they are now, and we had an idyllic, slow journey along the Grandes Corniches of the south of France into Italy – Cannes, Genoa, Pisa, Florence, Rome. Now notorious for traffic jams and aggressive drivers, even in Rome the traffic was light. I remember that we stopped and parked in the Piazza Venezia (the Trafalgar Square of Rome) while we went to look for a suitable pensione. Who could possibly imagine doing that today? We had the delightful feeling, like travellers in the nineteenth century, of absorbing with all our senses an experience of the Grand Tour. We found a pensione off the Via del Corso, with a slanting view through a gap between the ancient stucco walls of cheek-by-jowl buildings – all shades of sun-bleached colour (brown, orange, yellow) – to a glimpse of the ruined arches, ancient stones and columns of the Roman forum.

During the few days that we had allowed ourselves – bearing in mind that we both had families at home agog to see whom the other had married – we wandered in the sunshine through the historic parts of the city. We climbed up the steps of the Campidoglio, gaped at the ceiling of the Sistine Chapel, marvelled at the stupendous proportions of St Peter's, and conscientiously took in as many other churches, museums, galleries and monuments as the guidebook recommended en route.

Our last night on the continent, at Boulogne, brought us a

reminder of the romance of Africa. We walked that evening along the ramparts where, almost exactly 100 years previously, Richard Burton, orientalist, East African explorer, translator of *The Arabian Nights* and *The Perfumed Garden / Kama Sutra*, met – or at least first set eyes on – his future wife, Elizabeth Arundel. Burton, with John Hanning Speke, who discovered the source of the Nile, was one of the first European explorers of Tanganyika, and his character and exploits fascinated both of us – especially Beryl.

Our first home leave together, when we respectively introduced our newly espoused partner to family and friends, was also, in a sense, a voyage of discovery. We had arranged to rent a house in the country, near Mayfield in Sussex: the gatehouse to a much bigger one that had belonged to a Harley Street doctor but was now owned by his daughter. As she wasn't living there at the time, we had the extensive gardens to ourselves, which was delightful. Mother and Father came over almost immediately – probably on a Saturday – and stayed the night: a terrifying experience for a new wife! All I can remember of the visit is of me asking Beryl whether she had put salt in the water for the poached eggs, and getting a hissed blast of suppressed fury (Mother and Father happily waiting for their breakfast in the next room) in response. I had early learned to stop praising my mother's cooking, so I should have appreciated the sensitivity of the occasion. And the fact that this little incident has remained in my mind suggests that another lesson was learned: relations with in-laws can be tricky.

Then it was my turn: up to Scotland to meet the Mungavins. The family was of Irish descent, but since the beginning of the nineteenth century had lived and worked in India. However, with the advent of independence, shortly after the war, Beryl's father, George Leslie Mungavin, had decided that as he had reached the age of retirement it was now time finally to leave. Six of his seven children – four of whom were already married – also determined to leave India; only Jack, doing well in the Pakistan Navy, opted to remain. Athel, the eldest, whom I never met, eventually took his family off to Australia. The others, more or less independently, but coalescing so to speak in the environs of Glasgow, settled in Scotland. George Mungavin and Beryl's mother, Nora (Mrs M. to me), were at the stage of preparing to follow when he suffered a heart attack, which he did not survive. It was an event not only grievous for the family, but, being wholly unexpected, it must have been traumatic. None of them, in saying goodbye to their father, can have imagined they were never to see him again. And yet, perhaps in the end it was fitting that, after four generations, the last Mungavin in the service of the Raj should also finally be laid to rest in India.

My recollected impression of that first visit to my new relations-in-law is of complete bewilderment. Not only were George and Nora Mungavin blessed with many children, but these in turn were similarly blessed. While not all were then born, Beryl's brothers and sisters would ultimately have, between them, twenty-four children. Sorting out brothers from husbands, and sisters from wives (to say nothing of the occasional brother and/or sister of the respective wives and husbands), and trying to remember the names of the children – and who belonged to whom – was for me an exercise which, over time, I would eventually begin to master until, alas, my own advancing years and the family's continuing proliferation has again reduced me to the former condition of bewilderment.

Our first visit, up north, was to Annbank, a mining village of Ayrshire – or rather, an ex-mining village, since the pit was now closed – where Phyllis, Beryl's younger sister, had married George Fitzsimmons. George's father had come over from Ireland to work as a miner; he had since died, and George and Phyllis – with one, or possibly two, babies at that time – were temporarily living with George's uncle, also a former miner, while waiting to get a house of their own. They were all living higgledy-piggledy on top of each other: it must have been a challenging experience for Phyllis, still a young girl, from a totally different background marrying into that close-knit community. But she had done it as if to the manner born, turning Catholic into the bargain – and not merely 'turning', but embracing it wholeheartedly.

"Protestants don't know how to worship," she informed her family, to their indignation and amusement.

Mrs M. arrived. I can still remember Beryl's little squeal of joy: "Mummy!" as she threw herself into her mother's arms. It was an affecting reunion. I, an unaccustomed appendage, waited to be introduced.

One's wife's parents normally expect to meet their daughter's *inamorato before* they actually get married – if not, nowadays, to seek their approval, at least to be able to run a shrewd and careful eye over what they trust will not prove to be a disastrous choice. The eye that sizes one up *after* the event is, therefore, bound to be somewhat baffled, not to say intimidatingly intense. Mrs M. a reserved and, to me, somewhat inscrutable lady with an air of quiet confidence and self-sufficiency, received me in a friendly manner but without enthusiasm.

On that first visit up north, in addition to Mrs M. and Phyllis, I met for the first time (in Glasgow) brother Patrick, his wife Deborah and six children; sister Laura, her husband, Frank ("Spelt with an *I*," it was said among the Mungavins; former sergeant major, now home DIY expert on everything), and their five children. Of the other three brothers, Athel, in Australia, I was never to meet; Jack was in Pakistan; and Gerald, Beryl's youngest brother, was studying for the priesthood (in Edinburgh, I think).

We returned in July for my third and final tour in Songea, to find that Baker had been succeeded by Jock Scott, and the atmosphere had markedly improved. A round-faced, rubicund Scot with an irreverent sense of humour, Jock brought with him a new spirit of leadership. In place of a Gauleiter we now had a man who knew how to get the best out of a team. However, my responsibilities had in the meantime expanded to cover the whole of the Southern Province, and there were still battles to fight on behalf of the cooperatives – in most of which I was strongly supported by my chief in Dar es Salaam, though occasionally with some slight equivocation. The following letter from Sandy Dyer gives some flavour of the laconic formality that characterised official correspondence between us:

> Dar es Salaam
> 4 September, 1957

Dear Hall

    Please refer to the letter of 1st August from the Southern Province Chamber of Commerce and Agriculture in reply to your 9/235 of which I do not have a copy. I have no doubt in my own mind from my brief experience with this Chamber that your expression 'sanctimonious humbug' correctly describes the activities in question, and could properly have been used orally in your office to a delegate of the Chamber. At the same time I support the Chamber when they claim that it is an unsuitable expression to be used in correspondence and I must request you to refrain from the use of such unparliamentary expressions in your future correspondence.

    Yours sincerely
    A. M. Dyer

On the strength of a rumour that had somehow taken hold on the station while we were away, that a baby was expected, we were allocated a larger house, up on the ridge, conveniently sited near the second tee of the golf course, and approached down a shady avenue of mango trees parallel to the fairway. Jock was a bit crestfallen to discover the rumour false, but left us where we were. Our family did grow nevertheless. We ordered a batch of fifty Rhode Island Red and Light Sussex day-old chicks from Iringa, and reared them to maturity with scarcely one loss. To these were added about ten Muscovy ducks and, later, a pig. Eventually we were supplying eggs to families at the secondary school. Situated near the top of the furrow, where the flow was much more reliable (good for the ducks, too), we now had a good vegetable garden. We also had two dogs: Beryl's faithful Splash, and another very beautiful cocker spaniel that we bought as a puppy while we were on local leave in Nyasaland (Malawi).

    That Nyasaland trip is memorable for the cool, peaceful, almost intoxicatingly resin-scented forest on the plateau above Zomba, where we walked along a trout stream that might well have been in the Highlands of Scotland; it is memorable also for the 'civil disorder' that was supposed to be taking place during our visit.

While it was common to hear Africans talk of 'the struggle for independence', in Tanganyika, apart from noisy political meetings there was in fact very little 'struggling'. But Nyasaland did hit the world's headlines about a week before our arrival there: riots broke out, cars were being stoned, and Banda* himself was taken into custody. Hearing all this on the radio, we had nervously contemplated putting off the trip; and, apprehensively watching our nearly new Peugeot being inexpertly winched aboard the battered old lake steamer MV *Ilala* at Mbamba Bay, we almost wished we had. Yet all we saw as evidence of the riots and commotion was the presence in unusual numbers of representatives of the international media, morosely drinking in the hotel bars of Blantyre. Having been expensively assigned by their news editors to this part of the world, they had to continue filing copy, and this no doubt kept the thing going for a bit. So far as we were concerned, there was no hostility at all; people waved out to us as we drove along, much as they always did in Africa.

In 1960, at the end of my third tour in Songea, I was sent, thanks to a recommendation from Sandy Dyer, on a year's postgraduate study to Oxford. I was enrolled in Trinity College as an undergraduate student, since Oxford does not recognise degrees from other universities. American graduates were especially riled at the indignity of having to wear a short gown for tutorials, but that did not bother me: I was thrilled to be part of this ancient university. At the little ceremony when freshmen were introduced, in batches of about six, to the president of the college, I was surprised (though should not have been) to find that the others with me were at least fifteen years younger than I was. All, as was evident from the introductions, were from public schools, and every one had a father who was a company director. I wonder whether this strange ritual, of requiring new students to state their school and father's profession when introducing themselves, is still part of the system?

I attended the first meeting of the JCR (junior common room), where a main subject of debate was whether women should be

---

* Dr Hastings Banda, a GP in Britain for many years, had returned to his native country and was leading the political movement for independence.

allowed, as guests, in the dining hall. Remarks such as "Surely, Mr Chairman, it is not being suggested that we can *have* women in the dining hall?" characterised the tone of the discussion. My centre of gravity at Oxford, however, was not my college: I lived out, with a wife and, later, a baby son; and my studies were followed largely, though not wholly, at the Agricultural Economics Research Institute (AERI).

We were fortunate in finding a small two-up two-down house – 2 Cambridge Terrace – at the end of a short alley opposite Christ Church. Although a mean little place with tiny rooms and no heating other than two fireplaces downstairs, it was right in the centre of town and, with a small undemanding garden, suited us admirably. The research institute, occupying a largish house in South Parks Road near the Bodleian Library was little more than ten minutes' walk away; and it was there, in its lecture theatre and library, that much of my time was spent.

The director and presiding genius was Colin Clark, an avuncular figure with a mop of white hair and, unusually for an Australian, considerable charm. Unusually too, for an academic, he thought it worth listing in *Who's Who?* 'polishing furniture' among his recreations. He was covertly unpopular with many of the staff – dons more interested in research than teaching – some of whom made no secret of their opinion that he used the institute largely as a base for cultivating his own international reputation. And he was indeed an economist of world renown, author of a then famous work, *The Conditions of Economic Progress* (the most unreadable book I have ever attempted), some of whose prognostications, buttressed by a formidable array of statistics, had been remarkably accurate. Nevertheless, the institute was concerned not so much with global economics as with such esoteric yet mundane agricultural subjects as the 'corn-hog ratio', 'cobweb theorems', marketing boards, and factors underlying the price of milk 'at the farm gate'.

My tutor, Dr Beckett, a small man with a Lancashire accent, clipped moustache and fuzzy haircut, specialised in cooperatives. Although he, too, had a reputation of sorts and was the author of books in his field, he did not strike me as more than industrious –

that is to say a man who got where he was by sheer hard work rather than brilliance (much as Joe Ball had impressed me). Beckett, too, was a communist, though his politics did not obtrude on our work. It was Beckett who encouraged me to follow the full postgraduate diploma course in agricultural economics, rather than pursue a leisurely course of studies leading nowhere in particular – as I could have done. The Colonial Service actually deprecated the pursuit of 'pieces of paper', and their intention in sending us to Oxford was simply to 'add a bit of polish' to our education. Nevertheless, so far as I was concerned, they should not have been disappointed: I used my year to maximum advantage. For concentrated intellectual and cultural (and emotional) experience it was a period of my life that proved to be positively exhilarating.

My social life – in so far as I had one independently of my family – centred on the Colonial Service Club, which had an agreeable, homely atmosphere under the genial presidency of a former Tanganyika provincial commissioner named Rowe. His job was to keep a fatherly eye on the Colonial Service students – about eighty of us altogether in various colleges. I did have a 'moral tutor' at Trinity, the chaplain; but the only time I ever saw him in his official capacity was when invited to drink sherry 'at home'. I didn't get any moral tutoring.

As it happened, Beryl and I had been working out problems for ourselves. We had discovered, taking an opportunity for fertility checks while docked at Mombasa on return from our first home leave together, that I was completely sterile. It was a shock, and I was initially devastated by this inadequacy on my part. Yet Beryl took it amazingly well – better than I did – and, fortified by her understanding and support, and her unquestioning acceptance that such was the will of God, I eventually came to terms with it, privately reasoning that having mumps in adolescence probably had something to do with it. At any rate, as we had been determined from the beginning to have a family, we firmly resolved during the following tour that this was now destined to be through adoption. Having the best part of a year at home was providential.

The process of adoption is itself a form of gestation: there is no physical pain or discomfort, but the anxieties, longueurs and complications are equally, if not more, acute – and no less mysterious. In our case the whole procedure lasted rather more than nine months, during which period, as in natural childbirth, we never knew definitely whether our wish for a child really would, miraculously, be answered. Communications from the Children's Society were interspersed with visits from kindly but earnest lady officials from the local authority, delicately probing to ascertain our suitability as prospective parents: our own form of antenatal clinic. Yet although the prospect of Jeremy's hoped-for arrival was constantly in our minds, it was too poignant a subject – tempting fate, perhaps – to mention it in my diary until the day when, finally and definitely, we learned that we would indeed have a son. The following extracts describe his eventual arrival, and how we combined bringing up a newborn baby with my life as a mature student.

1 January 1961
New Year's Eve spent with David and Elizabeth at their house on the Isle of Wight. They were very kind and thoughtful. Mother & Father and Hamish also there. D and E have made a wonderful job of their home – everything very 'tasteful', clean and generally attractive. But I am becoming a bit suspicious of 'gracious living'; there is something a bit unreal about it. . . . Back (1st class for the first time in my life) [So much for my contempt for gracious living!] in the evening to spend the night at Plashet Road.

2 January
B and I returned to Oxford. B did not like the Monet [reproduction] that I had ordered; she will in time. We had a pretty basic row in the evening and made up magnificently afterwards.

3 January
I had determined to start work today but hardly got down to it. David Murray [a New Zealand fellow student] called. He seems to have been conscientiously visiting agricultural cooperatives all over the country. . . . The Laos 'crisis' astonishes me. I cannot imagine why America puts itself in a position where the politics of such tin-pot states can endanger world peace. At any rate, their policy of supporting anti-communist governments seems old-fashioned in modern Asia.

4 January
We are to go and see Jeremy tomorrow: great excitement.

Gomez, one of the Diploma students, came in for a drink (I had thought he was from Egypt but he fortunately revealed in conversation that he was from Colombia before I could make a faux pas). A very conceited fellow, but interesting enough for a short while. It is extraordinary how little we know about South America. Gomez confirmed my opinion that that place is a bomb with a slow fuse. America is very badly placed to handle things when they blow up there.

5 January
Jeremy is with us: poor little chap, so small and helpless – but so good. A long and tiring journey, latterly in pouring rain. But we got him home safe and sound. We are both delighted with him. So far he is pretty non-committal about us.

6 January
A very busy day monopolised by Jeremy. B is extremely tired and has gone off to bed. Feeding time in 8 minutes. He is by me now, beside the fire, making small noises. I shall take him up to B when I have written this and read a bit from the Bible. Nothing makes sense without true religion. B brought me back to it, but I am still appallingly weak in faith.

As children we had been brought up by Mother to kneel and say our prayers every evening before getting into bed: "God bless Mummy and Daddy; God bless David and Hamish; and make me a good boy. Amen." There was more to it than that. I think uncles and aunties and all my cousins were also blessed, and thanks given for all good things in the day, but it is chiefly the bit about making me a good boy that has stayed in my mind – and oddly enough it is the same sentiment that inspires my prayers today: I don't make a habit of breast-beating, but do constantly catch myself out in selfishness, thoughtlessness, greed and hypocrisy. Bertrand Russell, a great hero of students during the mid twentieth century, used to get very impatient with the Church's banging on about sin, and man's fallen state. But how many of us, knowing the miserable condition of so many in the world, lose any sleep about it – yet profess ourselves 'concerned'? And indeed, out of childhood, and beyond the unthinking conformity of school churchgoing, to say nothing of army church parades, I had easily dropped religion in favour of more exciting, and more easily credible, beliefs. My field of studies at Walthamstow had led directly to politics and, like many of my age, I saw reason and political action as the road to salvation in this world; and as for the next, that was for the fairies.

Beryl, coming from a family strong in orthodox Christian belief, had no religious hang-ups; her faith was, and remained, pure, simple and unquestioning – much as my mother's, although Mother was latterly not much of a churchgoer, chiefly because she found the Church of England uncongenial. She had been prepared to put up with it for the sake of her children, but for herself could do without it. In Songea I too had found it easy to do without it. Now the balanced stimulation of so many influences at Oxford reinvigorated my sense of a spiritual dimension to our lives: an inexplicable serenity in a world of sin (don't laugh; think about it).

8 January
Got up very early to meet Krisha Oplustil [daughter of the Polish contractor at Songea] at London Airport. Hired a car and arrived in very good time. Had breakfast at the airport. B will be glad of Krisha's company. . . . Jeremy had his first outing in the pram, through Christ Church meadow, and slept all the time.

12 January
Hamish arrived for a few days. I find his company invigorating and amusing. He is very downright and opinionative, but no humbug.

Reason tells us no more than the implications of what we already know. The 'subconscious mind' is a misleading concept. The reality is 'mind'. That part of it we reason about [and with] or consciously acknowledge, and also that part we do not consciously acknowledge, are together one thing, not two. A child's mind in this sense is the purest.

14 January
Took Ham for lunch at the Oxford Union – an excellent lunch for 2/6 [12½ pence], which is astonishingly cheap. . . . Term begins today, but not much sign of activity anywhere.

15 January
A very busy day. Mother and Father came for lunch and to collect Ham. No sooner had they gone than up rolled Ian [Gow] and family. A tall, thin boy came to look at the roof. . . . It is extraordinary how well and easily Jeremy has fitted in. B manages him splendidly and makes an excellent mother. I find being a father profoundly satisfying.

16 January
A busy day. This term I am going to be even more occupied than last. Had lunch at the Club. Saw the old faces again – a lot of heartiness in the bar, but I like quieter companionship. . . . I am again going to professor Frankel's lectures at Rhodes. I have a great respect for his views, as he has his feet so firmly on the ground of reality – perhaps too much so.

S. Herbert Frankel was a South African personal economic advisor to the Minister of Finance in Field Marshal Smuts' wartime cabinet. Very right wing, a Thatcherite long before Thatcher, he was profoundly opposed to apartheid, not so much on humanitarian grounds as because he considered it to be an economically inefficient system. He held a weekly seminar at Nuffield College, attended mostly by dons (a good indication of its interest), which I also attended. Touchingly, Frankel actually seemed pleased to see undergraduates there. He had little time for the United Nations and none at all for government 'aid' initiatives, but nevertheless believed that wise colonial administrators with a sympathetic understanding of the peoples under their charge could best help them to prosper in the modern world. The British system of 'indirect rule' (i.e. governing through the native chiefs) was, in his view, a good one.

Another Nuffield fellow at whose feet I sat was Margery Perham, biographer of Lord Lugard (the colonial administrator who originated the principle of indirect rule), a motherly lady who presided over her weekly seminar like the headmistress of a school, insisting that we wear a gown and requiring written work to be produced at every session. Not that I had any objection – far from it. I found the opportunity of learning from people at the leading edge of thinking about development in Africa to be immensely stimulating. However, my own special field of interest and study was agricultural marketing boards – a favourite tool of British colonial administration – so it was ironic, and a bit disappointing, to find that Frankel and many of the AERI staff looked on them with a somewhat jaundiced eye. I was already familiar with the strong, not to say virulent, criticism of the West African marketing boards by P. T. Bauer of Cambridge, but now found that *all* marketing boards were being judged against the iron laws of the free market – and pronounced defective as instruments of policy. Politicians, to say nothing of civil servants, seemed to be ten or fifteen years behind the academics in their thinking. Here was the Colonial Office enthusiastically promoting and supporting marketing boards (the word 'quango' had not yet been invented) in virtually all the British dependent territories, and according to most of my Oxford mentors they had generally got it wrong!

27 January
Now that Jeremy has arrived, I eat my lunch out from Monday to Friday: it eases the day for B, and I do more work. . . . We had a letter from Sandy Dyer this week explaining that I shall be urgently required back in Tanganyika after this course. So I have cancelled my sea passage and booked one by air. I should rather have welcomed a sea voyage, but it can't be helped. We are going to Mbeya – which is wonderful – provided they don't change their mind! . . . Jeremy behaving very well. He seems very contented and gives us much joy.

We had a fairly regular routine. During the day, and often in the evening, I left my little family and more or less single-mindedly pursued my studies; there was time even for occasional visits to the theatre or attendance at union debates. Jeremy meanwhile spent most of his time in our little walled back garden, even in the coldest weather, cosily swaddled and protected from the elements. The old lady next door tut-tutted to see him out in the snow, with just his little face poking out under the pram hood and awning, but he was perfectly warm and happy. At the weekend my responsibilities at home took first place. Not having a car, we were more or less confined to the city, but we enjoyed walking out with the pram in the parks and down by the river.

Just as my final term was about to begin, we received an unwelcome letter saying that our landlord (whom we had thought safely stationed in Hong Kong) was returning home and wanted his house back. Under the terms of the lease we had no option but to decamp to the club, which luckily happened to have a free bed-sitting room. For me it made little difference, but Beryl found the lack of privacy and enforced sociability of club life rather trying. Still, it was only for ten weeks and the opportunity of getting a reliable babysitter when needed was some compensation. I particularly remember the Trinity commem. ball, when Beryl was the *only* female wearing a long dress. Oxford-like, we almost felt distinguished to be out-of-touch colonials – being somewhat tiddly helped, too.

After the exams, Colin Clark hired a barge and invited the whole body of staff and students for an afternoon cruise up the river. Few of them had previously done any entertaining, and it was interesting to see eggheads in unbuttoned mood. Clark himself, in a striped pyjama-like shirt, sat prominently in the stern, playing popular tunes like 'Daisy Bell' and 'My Old Man Said Follow the Van' with gusto on a small squeeze-box accordion.

Shortly afterwards we returned to Plashet Road, where I was phoned by David Murray with the amazing news that I had passed my diploma exams 'with distinction'.

On 28 July I flew to Dar es Salaam by BOAC Comet (the very first passenger jet aircraft – later taken out of service after two disastrous crashes) leaving Beryl and Jeremy to follow at a more leisurely pace, by sea, on the *Warwick Castle*.

21 – UHURU

Mbeya was the provincial town of the Southern Highlands, about thirty miles from the border with Northern Rhodesia (now Zambia), and on the main north–south route between Nairobi and the Cape. At an altitude of roughly 6,000 feet the climate was much cooler than Songea's; the mornings were delightfully crisp and the air bracing – ideal for 'settlement'. And, with 500 Europeans and about 800 Asians in addition to the less prominent, but of course much more numerous, African population mostly tucked away in their own suburban village, the township had a distinctly colonial character, and a – for me – slightly disconcerting Home Counties feel about it. Eucalyptus groves softened the outskirts and prepared the visitor for an attractively 'civilised' urban area, overlooked to the north by a steep range of hills. The first thing I noticed was the pleasantly green golf course, around which the town – or at least the modern part of it – had been built.

We had looked forward to a change of duty station, yet it was a pang to leave Songea. I had lived there, with three periods of home leave, for nearly ten years – longer than I had ever stayed anywhere. Its remoteness, simplicity and intimate links with the local people entirely suited my temperament. For all its lack of domestic amenities, a climate that could be unpleasantly hot, and a more than even chance of getting malaria (I had had three bouts), Songea was Africa, and our lives there were bound up with the lives of Africans. Here in Mbeya, with its shops, commercial agencies, 'European' boarding school, provincial and district government offices and a prosperous club at the centre of its social life, the vitality of Africa was to an extent smothered, pushed back at a safe distance beyond the stands of bluegum trees. Here Donald Troup, the provincial commissioner, and his provincial team (of which I was to be a member) set the tone, and Ivor Bayldon, MLC, spoke up for the white farmers.

With a tanned, leathery skin and a bristly moustache, looking as if he might have come up the Limpopo with Cecil Rhodes, Bayldon was a leading businessman and farmer, who was also a prominent member of the legislative council in Dar es Salaam. As chief spokesman for Tanganyika's relatively small number of settlers, he featured regularly in the *Tanganyika Standard*, promoting their interests and commenting trenchantly on government decisions and policies. Compared with some of the wild, reactionary white farmers in Kenya, who would likely have preferred to be dealing with Lord Delamere, he was moderate. For reasonable men there was little alternative: by this time the tide of events was moving strongly towards independence, and Tanganyika's settlers, however much they would have liked to, could not hold it back. They were striving now simply to maintain as much influence in government as could be negotiated against the clamour of irresistible counter-demands from the Africans. Meanwhile, Mrs Bayldon led the (European) wives in good works and chivvied her gardeners.

Compared with the spaciousness of our house in Songea, with its spectacular views to distant hills from our wide golden-shower-bedecked veranda, the compact little suburban dwelling we were now allocated was a bit of a let-down. It was sited at the blunt end of a long wedge-shaped garden bisected by a good water furrow planted, along part of it, with agapanthus and thick clumps of untidy cannas. On one side of the garden, lining a dusty side road, was a correspondingly dusty macrocarpa hedge; the other side was bounded by trees – mostly wattle – and scrub. The front of the house, partly obscuring the windows, was a mass of crimson bougainvillea. The usual way of cutting grass in East Africa was for a boy to swing away at it with a *nyengu* (a sharpened leaf of a car spring bent up at one end) but this garden hadn't seen a *nyengu* for a long time: it was a riot of unkempt spider grass and weeds.

When not out on his walks – i.e. being pushed in his buggy –

Jeremy spent much of his time in this garden. This being Mbeya, I was able to buy a lawnmower from one of the Indian *dukas* (£6), and it was amazing what a difference a 'haircut' made to the jungle we had inherited. We rigged up a makeshift swing by suspending an old car tyre from one of the trees, and Jeremy got as much fun out of that as any boy would on a proper swing. Our excellent servant Kassim (who had superseded my dear old reprobate Rashidi, finally fired by the memsahib) had followed us from Songea, and his wife, Biaisha, now became Jeremy's ayah. She was a large chubby-faced woman, and she devotedly trailed after him in the garden to make sure he did not fall into the furrow or otherwise come to harm. Their five-year-old son, known as Kaka (meaning elder brother), also took a good-natured interest in him. Children have no colour prejudice, but Kaka took his cue from Biaisha and treated our two-year-old son with great respect.

Although my responsibilities in Songea had latterly stretched 400 miles eastward to Masasi, Nachingwea and the Makonde Plateau, they were, in terms of workload, essentially a one-district job. Now I was 'provincial', in a province of 45,000 square miles – only slightly less in area than England. My office for this exalted post was a rented shop on the main road, behind whose plate-glass window I baked in the midday sun, and was an object of mild curiosity to passers-by in the street. Fortunately, most of my time was spent travelling: from the rolling hill country of Njombe at the eastern end of the province to the sparsely populated bush of Chunya in the west.

In Chunya, a remote district, once the scene of a brief gold rush, there was a brave attempt by fishermen on Lake Rukwa to sell their catch cooperatively. It was a long-established occupation, with traditional ways of preserving this highly perishable merchandise: the fish (tilapia) were splayed open like kippers, and dried in the sun, then packed into flat reed baskets for transport in battered old lorries for sale in the Copper Belt of Northern Rhodesia (Zambia). In former days they had supplied the Lupa goldfield and neighbouring districts; but the gold had petered out and, in 1949, the lake had disastrously dried up. It was not until 1952, with the return of the water and, miraculously, the fish, that fishing was resumed.

It was a strangely stirring sight, after driving for miles through dreary, unpopulated *miombo* bush, and becoming conscious of a subtle change in the smell of the air which grew stronger as one approached, to come suddenly upon the lake and the unexpected human activity along its shores. Lake Rukwa is elementally one of God's gifts to the local people. But the sale of fish was firmly in the hands of a few traders, and the fishermen were complaining of getting a bad deal – hence the request to government that we help them set up a cooperative to handle the marketing. The biggest problem was in maintaining the loyalty of their own members, who were easily tempted away by the traders offering short-term higher prices.

Also in the Chunya district was a group of happy-go-lucky diggers scratching away and panning for gold in the abandoned workings of the old European-worked mines. They, too, wanted to transact their business through a cooperative. This was at a time when the price of gold was fixed by America at $36 an ounce – a ridiculously low figure, even in those days. There was something rather sad, and deeply ironic, in the fact that these poverty-stricken African miners should be adhering so meticulously to the dictates of the London bullion market, when they could have done so much better for themselves on the Indian black market. Of course it could be that the cooperative was merely a cover to legitimise the workings. If so, I was a dupe – but in retrospect a willing one.

At the other end of the province, in Njombe district, pyrethrum was a new crop – new at least to African farmers. It had recently become profitable as an 'environmentally friendly' insecticide in place of DDT (now long since banned, but then still widely in use). The upland hills of Njombe were delightful – I used to think of them as God's golf course – swooping, undulating grassland, with occasional small settlements in the valleys. One of my most vivid memories is of driving round the brow of a hill in a thunderstorm and seeing below me a patchwork of pyrethrum shambas – scattered fields of long-stemmed white daisy-like flowers – with shafts of sunlight picking out extraordinary contrasts of light and shade in an otherwise dark, wet landscape against a battered orange sky.

But Njombe, too, was sparsely populated country, and we would travel on sometimes impassably muddy, but normally bumpy and dusty, trails, long distances between halts, without seeing a single soul. On the plateau above Lake Nyasa (now Lake Malawi) – a vast treeless savannah-like plain – there were no people living there at all when I first saw it. To reach it we climbed, with the Land Rover permanently engaged in high-ratio four-wheel drive, grinding up a mountain track of about thirty terrifying hairpin bends. But once on top it was like being on the roof of the world: whichever way you looked it was grassland meeting sky. A botanist's paradise, it was totally unspoilt; yet, a million miles away in Dar es Salaam, proposals for 'developing' the area loomed, and were fiercely debated between various government departments (with conservationists, naturally, on the losing side). It was so peacefully idyllic up there that it was tempting to sleep in the open, but you were advised not to if you didn't want your face eaten off by hyenas. Fortunately, if you drove on far enough, you eventually – if you didn't lose the way – reached an old German boma standing in lonely isolation, surrounded by a stone wall at least eight feet thick, evidence of its age attested by the mature trees growing out of its crumbling masonry. This place, once an outlying post of German colonial administration, but now a rarely used rest house, had a magical, almost Wagnerian quality about it, as if the spirits of Teutonic imperial ambition still resided there, untouched and undisturbed by the passage of time. It was tended by a single ancient *mlonda*, who, appropriately but nevertheless incredibly, proved to be the last German district officer's cook. Visiting officials (about one in two months) stirred him to a frenzy of punctilious hospitality. He would espy our Land Rover from afar and, as we drove through the gates, there he would be in the courtyard, standing to attention with his hand quivering at the salute. In the evening, after he had attended to our requirements, he would tell us tales of the Wadachi (Germans) in tones of simple admiration.

Although I always carried a 'cook-box' (one of Messrs Griffiths MacAlister's sturdy black tin trunks) in the Land Rover, and was more or less self-supporting, it was traditional to be offered hospitality: a place to sleep (in many out-of-the-way places there would be no rest house) and usually an offering of eggs or goat's milk, and possibly a live chicken. I was constantly reminded by these spontaneous, natural acts of welcome, that the Swahili word for stranger or foreigner, *mgeni*, means also guest. One's 'retinue' did especially well, feasting and carousing into the small hours (since our arrival was likely to be quite an event) while *bwana mheshimiwa* beside his purring tilley lamp and its attendant flying creatures was set at an appropriately aloof distance in a small mud-walled room like a cell, wishing he'd thought to bring the tent.

Between the geographical extremes of Chunya and Njombe, my chief area of activity was in Tukuyu district – rich, fertile, hilly country at the head of Lake Nyasa – where coffee was the main crop. Arabica coffee was a nice, clean, orderly product, not traditionally grown by African farmers, but recently introduced in response to high world commodity prices occasioned periodically by frosts in Brazil and, latterly, by the Korean War. African peasant cultivation tended to be a battle with nature in which the odds were always stacked against them: it made little sense to be meticulous when fate played so large a part in the outcome. Nevertheless, shifting cultivation, however slapdash and inefficient as a system, still involved an immense investment of time and energy: in effect, farming by reclamation every few years! The bush had to be cleared, trees cut down and burned, the land then hoed between the debris, and planted when the rains were expected – so much effort, so much left to chance.

Now, however, with a new and profitable crop like coffee, it was possible for the government to introduce improved standards of cultivation without facing the charge of teaching their grandmother to suck eggs. This time the government would be allowed to know best. Plots with properly spaced-out planting holes had to be inspected by the local authority (village headman or chief) before permission was given even to plant; and the planting material had to come from an authorised source – not any old cutting from a neighbour's shamba. I had served my apprenticeship with coffee in the Matengo Highlands, where production had increased tenfold in as many years. Indeed, it was I who was credited with having brought high prices to the district (unlike the former government officials, who 'kept too much for themselves'). My job was to ensure that, so far as possible, the true price of a product was presented clearly to the farmers so that, without any need for browbeating and haranguing – though we did plenty of that too – they produced what the market wanted and got rewarded accordingly. In Rungwe this meant not merely growing and processing good-quality coffee for sale, but making sure that good prices were not swallowed up by inefficient or corrupt marketing.

A properly pruned arabica coffee tree does not grow much higher than five feet. Spaced about nine feet apart – sometimes more if interplanted with banana – the average shamba would be about a quarter of an acre, planted out in orderly rows. Compared with maize, sesame or cassava, it is a demanding crop, calling for year-round attention in respect of weed control, pruning, spraying against insects and, after harvesting, a sequence of processing that can make the difference between a good- and bad-quality bean. The coffee 'cherry' has to be removed by 'pulping' it in a kind of mangle with lots of water, and the resulting 'parchment' coffee is then laid out to dry in a controlled manner on wire-mesh trays.

I mention some of the detail not so much to introduce the reader to coffee production as to illustrate how improved farming was able to draw Africans away from primitive, shifting cultivation, and bring them into contact with the disciplines of a modern cash economy. The problems in this transition were less technical than psychological. If you are accustomed to working with the grain of nature, so to speak, accepting drought, disease and famine as *shauri ya Mungu* (God's business), then trying to ward off these calamities may seem fruitless – presuming to thwart the will of the Almighty even. What many Europeans in Africa saw as a predisposition to idleness was really much more likely to be an expression of African scepticism that man's (or, more specifically, *their own*) personal effort could overcome the dismal experience of centuries.

African respect for 'hierarchy' was also a brake on development. It was difficult for an individual who did not already have a recognised social or political standing to get ahead of his fellows economically. Individualism was thought to be presumptuous – unneighbourly almost. Jumped-up people are not popular in any society. Besides, hard work was all very well, but the good money that you made from it would certainly have to be shared with your needy relations.

In this respect cooperative societies (*vyama vya ushirika*, a precise translation, meaning exactly the same thing in Swahili) were ideal vehicles for lifting the prosperity of a community: they accorded with traditional social practice, they provided technical services, and they served as a forum for discussion and making decisions. They were also a good introduction to democratic practice.

It was often alleged that cooperatives were run by crooks, and that poor farmers were cheated by dishonest secretaries and committee men. In practice, although there were occasions when a secretary did dip his hand in the till, or try to fiddle the books, the routine checks and audits that we conducted were on the whole sufficiently close to deter or catch up with rogue officials. And, of course, they watched each other. One secretary had the effective idea of pasting a notice on the inside of his safe reading, '*Anakutazama Mungu.*' ('God is watching you.') Allegations of corruption, like those of laziness, rested on a misconception of African nature: tribal society was essentially law-abiding. It was the introduction by Europeans of new laws, new ways of doing things, that cut across established moral values, and blurred the edges of good and bad, right and wrong.

In West Africa, shortly after independence, government was commonly known as 'the money machine'. Corruption was a somewhat meaninglessly pejorative term – it was what any sane person did when he got his hands on the power to make money, whether as a customs clerk, a junior postmaster or even (or perhaps especially) as a minister of the government. In Nairobi and Kampala housebreaking and violent crime were to become endemic; in Tanganyika the cooperative system was ultimately to fail. Yet while we were in Songea crime – apart from the occasional murder and grievous bodily harm – was virtually unknown. The courts were mainly concerned with civil litigation (a social pastime). When we went on safari our houses were left unlocked.

In 1961 Tanganyika achieved *uhuru* (independence from British rule). At a midnight ceremony outside the provincial office at Mbeya the Union Jack was slowly lowered (a ceremony repeated at every station throughout the country) and at the same time the green, yellow and black flag of the new state was slowly raised.

It was a moving occasion: a sea of heads, with faces illuminated round the flagstaff, but the majority of the vast crowd only dimly visible in the darkness beyond a pool of light where dignitaries were gathered to celebrate the occasion with speeches and prayers for all denominations. There was a roar of triumph as the new flag reached the top of the flagpole – the moment that symbolised the transfer of authority to African government, and the birth of Tanganyika as a nation state. I had mixed feelings, of course; but we were all, I think, carried away by the spirit of great joy and, yes, liberation. The country had been under colonial and trusteeship administration for more than seventy years – a lifetime of subjection shading into resigned deference, shading into discontent and impatience. Now, without much of a struggle, they were free.

We awoke the next morning, Independence Day, to find the celebrations getting into their stride. The streets had been decorated with flags and foliage, festooning shopfronts, telegraph poles and trees – indeed anything to which banana leaves and bunting could be tied. Young men were whooping round the town in Land Rovers or open-topped lorries. Women, crammed together in separate vehicles, sang songs and ullulated triumphantly as they swished past. Down in the African part of the town the pounding of drums sounded unmistakably where the serious drinking and dancing were going on.

Well, it was all to be 'African' now. Not that there had ever been a colour bar: the separation of the races and maintenance of privilege had been much more subtly arranged than that. But now the government houses that were home to us Europeans would gradually acquire African tenants, and the neat gardens of Mbeya here and there would begin to take on an 'upcountry' appearance. The bar of the Railway Hotel would dominate its trade even more than in the past. The boma would be taken over by political appointees. Only the club, that impregnable bastion of the British abroad, resisted for a time the march of events. Of course, it was opened to all races, but few Africans were interested in playing golf or tennis, and hardly any wished to socialise with the *Wazungu* on their home ground. But the club occupied such a prime position in the town and, as a watering hole for foreigners, was so obviously anachronistic that I would be surprised to hear that it survived for long.

And indeed, for the British, who had done their best for Tanganyika by way of civilised and humane government, but little to prepare the people for democracy, it was the beginning of a weary packing of bags. First to go were the very senior officials – pre-eminently the governor himself, whose place was taken by Julius Nyerere as prime minister and ultimately as president.

I had met Nyerere only once, about three years previously, when, as leader of TANU (Tanganyika African National Union), he visited Songea to drum up – or, more accurately, orchestrate – support for the party. TANU, demanding independence NOW, was about as popular with government officials as votes for women in a golf club. Nyerere had arrived unannounced to visit the factory, accompanied by a disreputable-looking gang of toughs (probably his bodyguard), who debouched from the back of a battered Land Rover. He himself, slightly built and carrying an ivory-topped cane, could hardly have been more different from his companions. He was to prove an exceptional leader – a man of great charm, a fluent and witty speaker, he had a genuine vision for the future of his country, not simply a lust for power. Unfortunately, his record suggests that he was also economically naive, and that he was personally responsible for leading Tanganyika down several ruinous sidetracks to national penury.

In the first heady days of independence it was soon becoming evident that standards were (perhaps naturally, considering the lack of preparation) going to slip. Leading TANU officials were appointed to senior posts. In Mbeya, our beefy, jovial provincial commissioner departed and was replaced by a small man with a neat moustache and a very strong conviction that he was going to be an instrument of change. The changes, however, were at first mainly of style. Africans in positions of importance – rapidly growing in number – were accorded exaggerated respect. *Mheshimiwa* (honoured sir) replaced *bwana* (sir, or Mr) as a form of address for the new elite. Their use of official cars and other government facilities often went beyond what was considered proper. (We conveniently overlooked our own, albeit relatively modest, 'social' use of government vehicles upcountry.) Their behaviour was sometimes arrogant, and occasionally outrageous.

Our ayah, Biaisha, was seduced (in effect probably raped) by the new deputy provincial commissioner, a notorious womaniser, within days of his appointment. A furious and deeply offended Kassim locked his wife out of their quarters behind our house, believing her to blame. Beryl, equally outraged, took Biaisha's part and went off immediately to the police station. Absolutely nothing came of her complaint: the police sergeant's attitude towards a memsahib trying to interest him in something to do with one of her servants became positively hostile when he learned who was involved. It was clear he would not dare to pursue the matter, and he had a convenient let-out as Biaisha was equally afraid.

Professionally I was still very busy. In addition to my normal duties I was secretary of the Rungwe Coffee Board in Tukuyu, a board member of the Kyela Rice Mill at the head of Lake Nyasa, and chairman of an official inquiry into the feasibility of setting up a coffee-curing works in Southern Tanganyika (there was at that time only one for the whole country, in Moshi). But I had a sense of things slipping away: decisions were being taken on insubstantial grounds; the government was chasing hares and demanding the allocation of staff and resources to pet projects which ignored ongoing commitments; it appeared to attach little importance to boring but vital matters of inspection, audit and control, without which the cooperatives could so easily fall apart – and ultimately did.

The former secretary of the Rungwe Union, J. S. Kasambala, was now the Minister of Cooperatives and Agricultural Marketing. I had barely known him as he had, to his ultimate benefit, been much occupied with politics in the days leading up to independence; but presuming on our brief acquaintance, and wanting to release myself from duties which I felt increasingly unable to perform as they should be, I proposed for myself a somewhat ambitious project to investigate food-crop marketing throughout the country. The cooperatives had up till then dealt almost entirely with cash crops, such as coffee, cotton and tobacco (the Kyela rice was an exception); but there had been constant pressure for them to branch into food crops, such as maize, pulses and oilseeds. These on the whole lower-value products were overwhelmingly grown for self-subsistence, of course, but large quantities were often pledged in advance of harvest as security for loans advanced by Asian traders. Farmers selling on these terms did so at considerable disadvantage, and typically thought themselves ripped off. The risk, in fact, was more that they would sell too much of their crop and leave little enough food for themselves. And so dependent were they upon rainfall that periods of drought often led to pockets of serious hunger throughout the country – and a consequent need for famine relief.

The colonial administration's first line of defence against that ever present danger had been to order the chiefs to enforce compulsory planting of 'reserve' crops, such as cassava (a root crop that could remain in the ground for several years until it might be needed in time of emergency – it was not a popular food). But, in the socialistic fashion of the times, the new government's inclination was to 'control' food supplies, partly through the instrument of the cooperatives. Going with the grain, I thought it was reasonable that they should start off by knowing the facts and thinking them through.

I submitted my proposal through my new boss in Dar es Salaam, Maharagi Juma, who ten years previously had been Robin Malcolm's clerk (and who, coincidentally, was an elder brother of the man who had interfered with our ayah). Maharagi was a squat figure with thick glasses and a thin moustache, in appearance rather like an African Tojo – a sterling character, but nevertheless an NCO who had now suddenly found himself in the Colonel's boots. He had little formal education, but many years of practical experience: he was fully aware of the problems he was likely to face if cooperatives were instructed to 'take over' the business of food-crop marketing. He must have given his blessing, because shortly afterwards (one was becoming used to decisions being taken by the government flying by the seat of its pants) I was instructed to hand over to my assistant and transfer immediately to Dar es Salaam.

It was a final fling. I had already, in September 1962, given notice of my intention to resign with effect from June the following year.

Mbeya was the last place in Africa that we left with a tug of emotion and regret, the last place we had put down roots in the same soil as had nourished (or starved) its own people for centuries. As Europeans we had led our private lives – in so far as each of us had one – separate from the people; but, as with their own chiefs, our concerns had been wholly with the people's well-being. Our day-to-day activities had been ninety-nine per cent with Africans, only intermittently with fellow compatriots or other foreigners (when our conversation would be almost exclusively Africa-oriented). We had grown to love the Africans' generosity, spontaneity, humour and zest for life – however impoverished. And notwithstanding their determination for self-government, as self-respecting human beings on the same plane of existence as their colonial masters, there was a bond between them both which no amount of political rhetoric could wholly obscure. I find I have kept two letters which convey something of the genuine affection between colonial officers (and their wives) and the ordinary civil servants with whom they worked from day to day.

The first is from Timothy Sankey, cooperative inspector in Tukuyu (who, with reference to the first paragraph, I think probably joined us for a meal after we had both returned late to Mbeya from safari).

12.5.62

Dear Mrs Hall

I am so sorry for not writing you a letter since your very kind generosity been offered. It will be a for ever remembrance-story indeed to dine with you.

I hope you also know that what you did was a kind of goodwill respected me your servant, as one of your most house servant who shall never never forget you & my Masters. Thank Bwana Hall *pia* [also].

I hope you are well and are not shaken by fear of young generation voices & insults. Leave/Live at peace & enjoy do not care what people say. But I know all British are Christians do follow Christ who sent you.

Peace be with you & in the house & all your possessions be blessed.

Your loving servant
Timothy M. Sankey

The second is from Samuel Ikaridebe, my clerk in Mbeya.

10th April, 1963

Dear Mr Allan

Thank you very much for your two dear letters sent to me some time past. One of the two letters made me wonder when I discovered that you changed the address, and I couldn't judge what was the position. Up to this moment I do not know whether you are on leave in England or not.

My aim in fact was to post something that should get you in Dar es Salaam and such a thing would be just for remembrance between you Mr Hall and I. To speak the trueth your departure made me very very sorry indeed, especially when leaving Mbeya for Dar es Salaam the reason was that: – No farewell took place between you and I; but to the other hand that was my mistake because I left Mbeya for Tukuyu during the day. More-over I didn't know whether that was a departing day. I didn't expect that you could leave Mbeya with nothing from me or with nothing from you, but unfortunately it happened so.

Will you please kindly tell me what thing do you like best from Mbeya that can be sent in post to you, it must be a thing which is not found in England; then I will send it to you as a small present.

For your information I am pleased to let you know that I was promoted to Clerical Officer with effect from 1/12/62.

During your presence to Mbeya office you in fact kept me very busy indeed that I worked so hard and at last liked the job, I am now finding myself quite expert in office procedure. The more drafts you gave me the more speed I gained, until I typed fifty words per minute which with no doubt is the only speed that enabled me to the present rank.

I do not dispair as you explained in your first letter, I am trying my best to work the best until I find my bright future.

May God be with you wherever you will go and please remember me.

Pass my warm greeting to Mama.
Thanking you,
Yours very sincerely
   Samuel (S. S. Ikaridebe)

As befitted a newly arrived officer with only three months of his contract to run, we were allocated what was probably one of the least desirable government residences in Dar es Salaam – in fact it was hardly in Dar es Salaam at all, a small house situated out on the old airport. There is nothing quite so dreary as a disused airfield five miles out of town. We had only one neighbour – a customs official who spent most of his spare time buffing up a new Fiat, of which he was excessively proud. Otherwise we were totally alone among the crumbling concrete foundations of buildings now demolished, in a vast expanse of yellow grass and the remains of tarmac runways.

That desolate airfield – which Beryl endured more than I did (though, fortunately, she had friends in town) – sadly set the tone for our departure from Tanganyika, a country we had come to love, but which now was assuming a character different from what we had known. For an upcountry man like me, Dar es Salaam held few attractions beyond the beach at Oyster Bay. It was the end of an era. Two weeks before our final departure – unsung by any farewell party – I carelessly backed my car over Beryl's faithful old spaniel, Splash, peacefully sleeping in its shade. I dug a hole and we buried him there beneath a jacaranda tree, the one defiant spot of beauty in an otherwise featureless waste.

My last three months in Tanganyika – until March, when we took leave pending retirement – were spent mainly on tour in the Eastern, Lake, Western and Southern Highlands regions, poking into oven-hot grain stores at the back of Asian *dukas*, drinking hospitably offered cold beer with members of the owner's family, while a bearded Sikh, or perhaps a bald-headed Hindu comfortably attired in his pyjamas rattled off explanations at the incredible rate of articulation which only people from the subcontinent seem able to achieve.

I drank warm beer in bars with committee men and staff from local cooperatives, talking of gunny bags and godowns to background music from radios turned up at ear-shattering volume. I learned everything I needed to know about up trains, down trains, bogies, syndicates and 'rings', and in the end became more than ever convinced that the only people who understood the food-crop markets were indeed the Asian traders – any reform which aimed to bypass them completely was almost bound to fail. That was not a conclusion the government would be happy to share.

My final report – which owed almost as much to my year at Oxford as to that last countrywide safari – was an exercise in diplomacy.

22 – CHANGING DIRECTION

We arrived back in London, Beryl, little Jeremy and I, in the spring of 1963, and made our temporary base at Walnut Tree Farmhouse at Bacton, in Suffolk, where my parents had settled on Father's retirement. For years my mother had dreamed and spoken of a house in the country with roses round the door. Now, with the help of Molly and George (whose Jack's Farm was only a few miles off, on the other side of Stowmarket), they had found it and, after much hassle, worry and expense, had finally got it into a state which transformed it from what had been an almost derelict abode for Starkadders into a charming and comfortable home. At the end of a country lane about half a mile from the village, it had only one (equally old) house opposite, at that time unoccupied; and all around them were hedgerows and fields. With its old barn, outhouses, orchard and pond, it was idyllically peaceful.

As for us, we had no house of our own. I had no job, but we were optimistic about our prospects for both. In common with all colonial civil servants retiring early, I was awarded compensation for 'loss of career' – about £12,000. This was a large sum in those days – much more than enough to buy a decent house (we never knew what it was to have a mortgage). As for a job, I had three irons in the fire. Our first priority, though, was to find somewhere to live: even if, as proved to be the case, we were again to go abroad, we were determined to have a place of our own in Britain. The prospect of having home leaves with young children (we had already decided that, if at all possible, Jeremy should have a sister), perching here and there between family and rented accommodation, was not attractive. So, putting our 'lumpers' into a house seemed to be a good investment*.

For a mixture of reasons we confined our house-hunting to the southern Home Counties: our parents were living more or less in that area, there was a chance that I might find myself working in London, and, most importantly for us at the time, the Church of England Children's Society was also based there. We started off in Hamish's natty little Triumph Herald (borrowed, with his permission presumably, while he was still abroad in Kuwait or Ghana), and, travelling unbusinesslikely en famille, scoured the estate agents of Tunbridge Wells, Sevenoaks, Lewes and Haywards Heath. My recollection is of doing this in pouring rain, viewing a succession of unsuitable houses whose enticing descriptions in the agents' brochures proved to be disappointingly misleading. Jeremy whiled away his boredom by indelibly decorating the back of the driver's seat with his coloured chalks (to Hamish's later displeasure).

After a week or two of this unsuccessful foraying out from Bacton, we at length settled, more or less in desperation, on a characterless bungalow named Standish, beside a field near Ightham where little girls in jodhpurs and hard hats practised jumping their ponies, and from which the owner – no doubt illegally – conducted his business of car bodywork repairs. Yet we were saved from the consequences of this uninspired decision by the man's own reluctance – he was apparently under financial pressure – to conclude the deal. While he havered and prevaricated, I took Beryl and Jeremy up to Scotland to stay with her sister Phyllis in Ayrshire, and then began a hunt of my own to find temporary accommodation to tide us over. It was while doing this that I came across the house that was, in the event, to become our family home, and in which we were to live, intermittently, for the next twenty-five years.

Sunny Crest (rather too twee a name, and later renamed by us as Cone Hill) was the sort of house at which sensible people would look, sigh regretfully, and then turn back to the real world. About four miles out of Sevenoaks and splendidly situated on the green sands ridge beyond the woods of Seal Chart, the house had

---

* And so it proved. The house we bought for £6,500 was sold eventually for £223,000.

no means of access from the country road below, other than by a winding series of steps made from old railway sleepers, leading up the steep hillside for about 150 yards – fine for mountain goats, but quite impracticable as a family home. Mr French, the Sevenoaks agent, a cunning old fox of deceptive charm, sent me there with one of his staff, ostensibly as a prospective short-term tenant, although he knew the place was for sale.

The entrance, on a blind bend, through a gap in a high privet hedge clipped by passing vehicles, gave on to a small clearing shaded by a huge triple-boled oak and occupied by three dilapidated wooden or asbestos-sheeted garages, festooned with ivy. Behind them, nettles, docks and briar struggled for supremacy. From these the railway-sleeper pathway led up the hill in a curving ascent between a number of large oak trees, a slender copse of sweet chestnut, and a tangle of good but neglected rhododendrons. It had been raining and the ground was wet with dripping branches. The blossoms ranged from deep red to pink, and yellow to purest white; and down in the small valley below we could see an enchanting drift of bluebells against a pale thicket of tall bamboo. Birds sang and the scents of the wood filled the air, fresh, clean and – from a bank of leggy yellow azaleas – intoxicatingly sweet.

I puffed up the steps behind French's assistant, brushing past wet foliage on the steeply ascending path by a macrocarpa hedge on my left, and glimpsed, at a distance, beyond a mass of overgrown heathers on my right, a large Italian urn on a massive pedestal standing alone in the middle of a roughly cut terraced lawn.

I thought, 'This is simply heavenly!'

We climbed up further to where the path led on to a second lawn, slightly better kept – and there was the house. My first impression of it, taken in somewhat absently (struck more by its situation), was of a substantially built but faintly sinister bungalow with pea-green paintwork, dirty white cement-rendered walls, and a rather odd shape. Its exaggeratedly large bow windows looked like Mickey Mouse ears on either side of latticed smaller windows and a double front door, the stained-glass panels of which featured peacocks in full plumage. Above Mickey Mouse's forehead, so to speak, was a balcony fronted by a wooden guard rail in the shape of a pea-green rising sun, radiating asymmetrically, and correctly, from the east side of it. The appearance of the building had a kind of art-deco, E. Phillips Oppenheimer quality about it: the sort of house, in the south of France perhaps, where you could imagine a grisly murder as having been committed – fairly recently.

 Inside, the rooms were what you might expect in a house shaped like a mouse's head: some of the rooms had curved walls and, apart from a central corridor, not one of them paralleled another. All the doors, including the peacock-decorated front door, were sliding rather than hinged, which meant that the interior walls were unusually thick. There was only one word to describe Sunny Crest: weird. Yet, standing inside those large bow windows – each more like a small conservatory – looking out on to the garden and the trees surrounding it, and beyond them across strawberry fields and orchards to the Weald of Kent and Tonbridge, my thoughts had little to do with the house. I was enchanted with its setting.

 We ended up, therefore, not renting, but buying it. With two and a half acres of mainly woodland, £6,500 seemed very reasonable, and for another £200 we acquired most of its old Paduan furniture, which the owner would have found it laborious to remove. A few days later we were in residence, with time now to reflect on what we had done, almost on the spur of the moment, *all'improvviso*. We were not disappointed. The drawbacks – the 150-yard climb, the suicidal exit on to the road below, and an antiquated solid-fuel central-heating system (for part of the house only) – were as nothing. We were young, it was spring, and we were starting a new life. Whatever the future might hold for us, we had no qualms. It was an adventure.

 About a week after our moving in, Mother and Father came over to see our new home.

 They were carefully non-committal, but, as I afterwards learned from my father, Mother said to him, on leaving, "What on earth possessed them to buy a place like that?"

 Granny Mungavin also came for a weekend, and had rather more reason to make disparaging comments (though she did not – at least not in my hearing): her help was enlisted to manhandle a refrigerator up the steps through the wood. After that, we bought a strong sack truck for heaving heavy objects up from the road level below.

Gasping grannies notwithstanding, we were still highly delighted with Sunny Crest (Cone Hill-to-be). It was a strong, well-built house, and we knew its history through three consecutive owners since its construction in 1936. The first, named Reece, with a business of two or three small grocery shops (in the manner of the first Mr Sainsbury), had specifically designed and built it as a secluded place for his retirement. His wife had epilepsy, which apparently was why the doors had to be sliding, in case she fell against one and it couldn't be opened. At least, that was what we were told by Mr Woodgate, our friendly but very nosey neighbour at the bottom of the hill, who seemed to know more about the owners of Sunny Crest than they might have been happy to be the subject of neighbourly gossip. The Reeces were followed by a wine merchant named Rossi, who was presumably one of the less professionally active members of that family, since he was said to spend all his time on the golf course. A large, demonstratively amiable man, he came to see us – or rather the house – some years later, accompanied by a dignified but bored Italian lady who was not his wife, and pronounced himself 'enchanted' with our improvements. I imagine it was *his* furniture we had taken over from the man who followed him, an insurance inspector who mostly worked abroad (much like Hamish, I imagine) and whose only mark left on the place was fair wear and tear.

As for the fourth owner, what could *I* be said to be? A one-time schoolmaster who had most recently been helping Africans to run cooperative societies in coffee, tobacco, gold-mining and dried fish. It was hardly the sort of experience an employer in Britain would be clamouring for. Nevertheless, there were opportunities for people with 'Western skills' in what used to be called 'backward' or, less offensively, 'underdeveloped' or, latterly, 'developing' countries. I had been scouting possibilities while still in Tanganyika. The most promising were with FAO (Food and Agriculture Organisation of the United Nations): it paid well and had posts throughout the world. I had seen a position advertised for a 'Marketing Expert' in Nigeria and, assuming (correctly) that the word 'Expert' had no serious meaning, applied for it. At the same time, scouring the ODA (the UK Overseas Development Administration) listings, I saw they were looking for an 'Agricultural Economist to study the land-use systems and agricultural practice of the Malaysian Aborigines'; so I put in for that, too. Although not so well paid, professionally it looked the more interesting.

Weeks went by without any news at all – I had yet to learn that this was exasperatingly typical of international appointments. Then, in response to a patiently restrained enquiry from me to ask FAO what, if anything, was happening, they simply replied that the Nigerian post was 'now filled'; did I wish to be considered for 'a similar one in Mauritius'?

'Well,' I thought, 'thanks very much for letting me know.'

But Mauritius? I knew little more than that it was an island in the Indian Ocean; but that was enough. I replied by return of post that, YES, I was interested.

It did not occur to me at the time, but my recruitment for this job was a complete gamble – on both sides. Without any kind of an interview, relying entirely on my answers to questions on a fairly elaborate application form, giving references (which I now know were most unlikely to have been taken up), FAO apparently satisfied itself that I could fill a post I had not applied for, and was now merely waiting for the government of Mauritius, on no better evidence of suitability, to accept my nomination. It was a very rum way to select staff, but, as I was to discover when I was myself later assigned to FAO headquarters in Rome, it was typical of the way UN agencies operated. The ODA recruitment procedures were not a great deal more impressive.

While all this was going on I happened one day, while walking up the Haymarket in London, to bump into a man who worked for the EIU (Economist Intelligence Unit). I had last met him in Mbeya, where he'd been on a mission, and had liked him enough to invite him over for supper. I told him what I was doing, or rather not doing, and he insisted I meet one of his more senior colleagues with a view to considering whether a career with the EIU might suit me – and them. They still occupied their old building in St James's – more like a gentleman's club than an office. I met John

Pinder, who writes also for the *Financial Times* – or used to – but all I remember of the conversation is his description of himself riding a camel in West Africa.

In the event, I was accepted for both Malaysia and Mauritius; and, forced to choose, I opted for Mauritius. Looking back, I occasionally speculate on how my life might have been different had I gone for either of the other two openings. Those Malaysian aborigines would have been an interesting challenge.

The summer of 1963 had been fruitful not only in getting me a new job and finding us what was to be our family home; it was also the beginning of a long gestation in the arrival of Hilary. As we were bound for Mauritius, it was inevitable that the process of our adoption of a daughter would be extended over the whole period of our stay there – corresponding perhaps to the usual procedure of 'trying', and in that respect not so different from the hopeful anticipation of any other family, except that in our case we had the advantage of being able to express to the powers that be a preference for the sex of our hoped-for baby. Her eventual arrival was not to be until our return to Cone Hill at the beginning of 1965.

The author's father shortly before his marriage.

The author's mother shortly before her marriage.

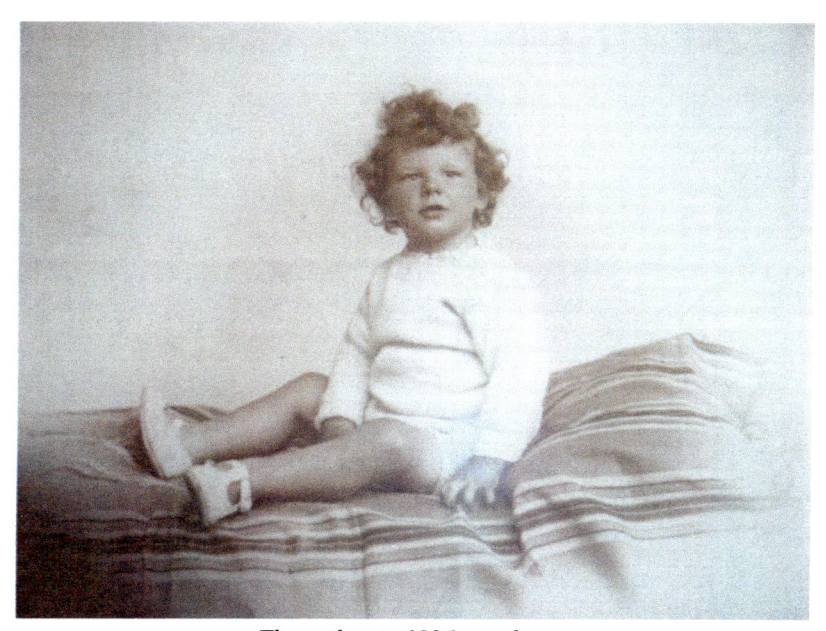
The author in 1926, aged one.

The author about to join the Colonial Service.

Beryl Mungavin, personal assistant to important men.

Alan and Beryl on safari in Songea, before their marriage.

Beryl with Jeremy in Mauritius.

Hilary, aged two, and Jeremy, aged six, neither looking very happy with the embrace; yet the Roman photographer was so impressed with this photograph that he blew it up ten times the size and put it in his shop window as an advertisement.

Hilary, the author, Jeremy and Scally at Bracciano.

Seated left to right: Nikfarjan, the author and Haddad at a village meeting in Iran.

Hilary in France – an oil painting by the author.

Three generations at Leigh. Left to right, front row: Hamish, Richard, Katherine, Eleanor. Back row: Jeremy, Jon, Beryl, author Hilary and David.

Alan and Hilary, about to set off for a pensioners' reunion.

23 – MAURITIUS

The island of Mauritius is volcanic in origin and covers an area of approximately 720 square miles. The land rises from the coast to a central plateau . . . and [is] bounded on the north, west, and south by mountains. . . . It is almost surrounded by coral reef and its associated lagoons. . . . [There is] a formidable mixture of races, religions, and languages . . . with a population density approaching 900 per square mile. . . . The rate of increase of the Mauritian population has become one of the highest in the world. Recent calculations suggest that, if fertility rates remain at their present high level . . . the population of the island will rise from its present 600,000 to no less than 3,000,000 by the end of the century. This is a truly terrifying prospect. [From *The Economic and Social Structure of Mauritius*, by J. E. Mead and others, Port Louis, 1960.]

Apart from my knowing vaguely that it was an island in the Indian Ocean somewhere to the east of Madagascar, the name Mauritius recalled to my mind little more than its famous triangular postage stamps (goggled at as reproductions in Stanley Gibbons' catalogue by us boys at King's Leigh School, the originals being much too valuable to feature in our own stamp collections) and its equally famous reputation as the land of the dodo. These three elements were nevertheless enough to conjure up for me a romantic picture which proved, in the event, to be remarkably felicitous. I have never been in a country where geography and history bear so heavily on the character and atmosphere of a place.

Until about the fifteenth century, Mauritius was uninhabited except for its wildlife. The Portuguese seem to have been the first to discover it, but were not sufficiently interested – in what was, after all, just a forested volcanic outcrop – to do much more than note its existence and then move on to more interesting places further east, like Goa and Macao. Then along came the Dutch, who took a close look at the primeval forests, discovered valuable stands of teak that had evolved undisturbed over aeons of time, and in much shorter order proceeded to rip it all out. Having done that, and killed off much of the wildlife – including the dodo, an apparently succulent fowl – the Dutch, too, lost interest, deciding that Java was a much more profitable place to settle. And perhaps they didn't want to tangle with the French, who had meanwhile craftily observed that the island would be a convenient staging post on the journey out to their 'possessions', as they were called, in India.

Anyway, the Dutch left; the French arrived and, being French, made themselves comfortable by bringing out wives from France and slaves from Africa. Quite often, naturally enough, the female slaves served as wives too – or rather, in place of wives – but chiefly the slaves were brought over to work on the sugar estates that were being developed in the spaces opened up by the depredations of the departed Dutch. In fact, sugar cane proved to be a crop so ideally suited to the land and climate that, over the next century and a half, it expanded to cover almost all of the cultivable parts of Mauritius.

From the air, coming in to land at Mahebourg Airport near the south-eastern shore, arriving passengers get an accurate impression of the whole island: roughly pear-shaped, it is only about fifty miles from north to south, and thirty-five from east to west. Black mountainous crags rise up from a carpet of brilliant green neatly patterned by irrigation furrows and the ordered lines of sugar cane; and, surrounding the green, the shoreline and white-flecked reefs are circumscribed in turn by the vast blue expanse of the Indian Ocean. For me, arriving alone (Beryl and Jeremy followed a few days later), this exotic panorama was no sooner sighted and registered with excitement than it narrowed to the landing strip, and we were down with a bump amid clouds of dust.

In 1963 the Mahebourg terminal building was a modest concrete structure which on most days would be virtually deserted (tourism not yet having taken off as an important part of the Mauritian economy); but on Mondays (the day the plane arrived) it attracted from every part of the island, and from every community in it, the numerous friends and relations of each and every arriving and departing passenger, all tumultuously jostling together in the single departure-cum-arrivals hall, and on a dangerously overcrowded viewing-cum-waving platform on the flat roof above it.

You would hardly realise, from the babble of French and Creole being spoken, that Mauritius was actually under British administration, and had indeed been a Crown Colony for more than 150 years – since 1810, in fact, when, fed up with the French harrying of our shipping during the Napoleonic Wars, a British force of 8,000 men had most unfairly taken control of the island from the utterly outnumbered French, but nevertheless kindly allowed their merchants and planters to remain undisturbed in possession of their commercial resources and estates. So, apart from having a British governor and a handful of senior British civil servants, life for the Mauritians had continued much as before. The only serious inconvenience for the French was when the abolition of slavery compelled the estates to seek indentured labour from India; the freed slaves mostly scorned, even for pay, the work they had formerly been forced to do under the whip. I was not able to judge it at the time, but the crowd of Mauritians attracted by the one weekly plane would probably have represented a fair cross-section of the population: mostly Indian, many Creole (mixed race), several European (mostly French) and some Chinese.

I was met on the tarmac with some formality by two officials in suit and tie: a chubby-faced, sleek young Indian who introduced himself as 'Mr Purmessur, principal assistant secretary of the Ministry of Agriculture', and an older, rather uncomfortable-looking gentleman, Dr Staub, a deputy director of agriculture in the veterinary service. The latter, a Frenchman with whom I was to have very little to do during the whole of my time in Mauritius, seemed to have been detailed off as part of the 'official reception' and was not too pleased about it. Purmessur on the other hand, a civil servant of the (Raj-tutored) Indian school, was to be for the next eighteen months the main – and often exasperating

– channel through whom I had to work with the government. While it may surprise you that a junior UN officer such as myself should be received by such a relatively distinguished welcoming party, that was the form in those days. UN 'experts', so-called, had – especially in a small country – a cachet which, deserved or undeserved, gave them access to the highest levels of government. I was now operating on a new plane: a slightly bigger fish in a small pond, it seemed.

My job was to help the government set up an agricultural marketing board. Too much of the Mauritian economy depended on the sugar crop; so the idea was to provide a secure outlet for the production of *other* crops. Roughly this meant assisting with the drafting of enabling legislation, giving advice on recruitment of staff, and doing a lot of legwork in the field, trying to understand where and how potatoes, onions, milk, tea, etc., were produced and sold – mainly by small farmers. This may sound pretty straightforward, but I soon discovered that nothing in Mauritius was straightforward. The 'small pond' was in truth a veritable jungle of double-dealing, backbiting and political intrigue – all promoted or conducted with courtesy, apparent friendliness, occasional flashes of honesty and much genuine kindness.

However, this depth of understanding was still ahead of me. My first surprise was to discover how varied the climate could be from one part of the island to another. From the tropical heat of Mahebourg we drove about twenty miles up to the cool peak of the island at Curepipe. Here I was installed at the Park Hotel, where a week later I was joined by Beryl and Jeremy. Two very full weeks had intervened since I had left them behind at Cone Hill for my briefing at FAO headquarters in Rome, and, after so much that had been new and unfamiliar, it was a joy to see the two of them (Jeremy was then not yet three years old) appearing at the top of the steps from the plane! We were a family again.

The Park Hotel was to be our home for the next week or two. It was a grey, wooden, French-colonial-style building in park-like grounds ornamented with tall palm trees, bougainvillea, hibiscus and camellia. Curepipe is famous for its camellias: the climate, cool and misty when not actually raining, is ideal for them, and they flourish in abundance throughout the open spaces and neat gardens of this very French little town. Jeremy took to the spacious surroundings of the hotel as if he were the owner of it. In its vast dining room, pillared veranda with cane chairs and large potted plants, and chalet-like rooms in the garden (one of which was ours), he was entirely at home, chatting away with aplomb to the hotel servants, other guests and the hotel cat. He made an especial friend of the head waiter (which my father would have approved of, 'Always give a good tip on arrival to the head porter' being one of his maxims). Jeremy would walk in ahead of us to breakfast in the morning with grand seigneurial dignity, and gravely shake his friend by the hand before climbing up to his chair at the table. This punctilious observance of French early morning greetings – albeit, on their part, not extending to shaking hands with the servants – caused some amusement, and he became quite a favourite with staff and guests alike.

Meanwhile, my arrival in Mauritius featured prominently in the local press, and a rather scruffy young man from the local radio station, an Englishman – the administration liked to keep the key jobs British – appeared one evening to arrange for a broadcast interview to explain to the public at large who I was and what I had come to do in Mauritius. This was duly recorded a few days later and put out almost immediately. Listening to it, I thought it came over rather well; but as it must have been mostly waffle about marketing boards in general, leaning on my experience in East Africa and what I had soaked up at Oxford, perhaps I was just pleasantly surprised to have survived and to have sounded (to me at least) as if I knew my stuff. It was nevertheless fortunate that the director of agriculture, ffrench-Mullen (another Brit for another key job), was on leave at the time, since he would certainly (as I realised when we later met) have insisted on vetting the questions and suggesting answers to accord with his own very decided opinions.

The relationship between British colonial officials and UN civil servants (especially when they too were British) tended to be one of restrained hostility. Professional relations were 'correct', but were sometimes soured by a feeling that while they, the British

Colonial Service, had borne the heat and burden of the day, we, the UN 'experts' (with a curl of the lip), had parachuted in, so to speak, and, on the basis of knowing 'sweet FA' about the facts on the ground, were now proposing to tell them how to do their job. And it was additionally galling that we were better paid.

My immediate counterpart was Raymond Rochecouste, a charming Creole undersecretary at the Ministry of Agriculture. He was my right-hand man and main source of information, and it was he who put me in touch with Guy Desjardins, a French car salesman in Port Louis whose father-in-law had a house to let in Curepipe – next door to his own, as it happened. Desjardins was a foxy-looking man with a disconcertingly persistent (though no doubt unconscious) habit of fondling his testicles throughout the course of any conversation with him. Actually, we were to have rather less to do with him than with his parents-in-law, who lived in a small house in the garden behind the bungalow that we did finally agree to rent – for an amount that Raymond advised was 'reasonable'. In this instance the level of rent was actually less important to me than to the government, which had – quite unusually, and to its later regret – agreed to pay the cost of my accommodation in Mauritius.

Living in rented furnished accommodation was an occupational fact of life for international civil servants (in the Colonial Service we lived in houses provided by the government, for which we paid ten per cent of our salary) and, depending on the country of post, it could vary from opulent splendour to almost disgustingly squalid. The same rent in US dollars might in one country secure for you a palatial villa with swimming pool, and in another leave you feeling lucky to get a two-bedroom flat over a butcher's shop with a steam laundry next door. In this case, Mr Masson's two-bedroom concrete bungalow in a quiet side street of Curepipe, with a tidy little lawn, four palm trees, and low iron railings to the front, was perfectly acceptable. The furnishings were very French: round tables, antimacassars and flowing muslin drapes between the sitting room and the dining room – bourgeois seraglio, perhaps, if you had to characterise the style. A parquet floor throughout was pleasantly austere, but rather chilly-feeling in cold weather.

Jeremy's freedom-to-roam happiness in society at the Park Hotel came to an unwelcome (to him) end when we moved in beside the Massons – the old parents behind us, the Desjardins next door – and arrangements were made for him to attend the nursery school Jeanne d'Arc. This was most conveniently situated just one house away, on the other side of the Desjardins, and looked after about fifteen little boys and girls. Very young children have no difficulty operating in a foreign language, knowledge of their own, after all, being itself rudimentary; and Jeremy was a very sociable little boy, so he soon enough got into the swing of this new experience. He would come home in his little blue-chequered smock and proudly sing us his rendering of '*Frère Jacques*' or '*Sur le Pont d'Avignon*' with some garbling of the words, but an impeccable French accent.

My office – a single room with nothing more at first than a couple of tables and chairs for Raymond and me – was at Réduit, near the Department of Agriculture, where ffrench-Mullen and various other agriculturally specialised people had their separate empires (veterinary, forestry, agricultural college, etc.) in little clumps of mostly wooden buildings with red corrugated-iron roofs, dotted about pleasantly among the shrubs and trees, a compound with neatly tended grass giving the appearance more of a country club than government offices. Réduit was some ten miles or so down from Curepipe, but my office there was little more than a perch from which Raymond and I would sally forth to look at slaughterhouses, vegetable markets, fields of onions, tea plantations, etc., and to have many earnest conversations, discussions and arguments – most interestingly with the farmers and traders, most frustratingly with government officials and politicians. These latter discussions were mostly in Port Louis, the capital, on the west coast, where the secretariat, prime minister's office and most of the ministries were grouped in the central square. On three sides were the modestly imposing classical French-colonial-style two-storey government buildings, their otherwise dour appearance relieved by wrought-iron balustrades and zinc finials; on the open side was the quay, with fishing boats (mainly Japanese) tied up or riding at anchor in the harbour. A statue of Queen Victoria dominated the centre of the square.

The only other UN official in Mauritius was an agricultural extension* specialist – a tall, fair-haired Dutchman, who came up and introduced himself, on my first appearance at Réduit, as Ernst Van Heurn. He, too, was new to Mauritius, having arrived with his wife, Trudy, and two children just a week or two before me; and, being similarly out on a limb, so to speak – relating closely to the government, but not being part of the civil service – our two families quickly became friends. Beryl also became early on roped in by French ladies doing good works: she joined the Curepipe section of the Red Cross and, later, was induced to join a committee engaged in setting up a new Mauritius Cheshire Home. Eventually, by a familiar process of coffee-morning prearrangement and backstage buck-passing, she found herself acting as secretary and general factotum to the committee.

Our lives, therefore, settled down into new routines in an entirely different environment. My diary for the first half of 1964 (the only time I ever managed to maintain one for so long a period) probably gives a sharper picture than I could attempt to draw now, looking back more than fifty years later; but, as a background to it, I must just sketch out the politics of life as it was for Mauritians at that time.

The man on whose authority I depended for almost everything I did was the Minister of Agriculture, Mr Boolell, a Hindu politician in the classical tradition, pleasant, devious and completely untrustworthy. I probably spent five times longer waiting in his annex to see him than I actually did in his presence. He always knew in advance what I was going to say to him, and indeed the substantive discussion on it would already have taken place between him and Purmessur, the principal assistant secretary, and a decision (if only to stall) would already have been taken. The meeting with me, therefore, would typically be something of a charade, or bout of wary fencing if what I was recommending differed from what

---

* Agricultural extension is a term more used in America than it seems to be in Britain. Roughly, it means the promotion of agricultural 'best practice' among farmers: for example, passing on the results of work done on agricultural research stations, such as use of particular insecticides, seeds, etc.; or recommendations about planting distance, say, or the pruning of fruit trees.

he actually intended to do. What *that* was would usually become apparent only as a fait accompli, since to state a decision firmly would, by the minister's convoluted reasoning, have reduced his room for manoeuvre.

"Ah, Mr Hall, why have I not seen you for such a long time?" he would say, knowing full well that I had been pestering Purmessur for an audience with him for the past fortnight. "You know my door is always open."

"Yes," I would say under my breath, "but not to me, you rogue."

Boolell was a leading member of the governing Labour Party, in the thick of sectarian intrigue, and known to be in cahoots with the prime minister, Mr Ramgoolam. And Ramgoolam, a shrewd and genuinely wise old bird, who with his squat figure and thick horn-rimmed glasses looked remarkably like Aristotle Onassis, was the real power and guiding spirit of the country. For although the last vestiges of British rule were still represented by an old-style governor (in the person of Sir John Rennie, ensconced in lonely splendour at the gubernatorial mansion), most of the day-to-day powers were exercised by an elected government, and Mauritius was well on the way to full independence. In anticipation of this, during the whole period of our time there the country was in a turmoil of seething political activity.

Public life was dominated by the rivalry of two major parties: the Labour Party, largely supported by the Indian sugar-estate workers (numerically the biggest part of the population), and the opposition, mainly Creole, Partie Mauricien. Unfortunately, race underlay the patterns of society, and race dictated the way politics was conducted. If you were Indian you could rely on the steamroller of rural numbers to win members of the legislative council (parliament) and perhaps gain backstairs influence where it might be useful to your family. The Creoles, less numerous but longer established, were, compared with the industrious Indian workers, sometimes caricatured as good-humoured layabouts, descendants of slaves who preferred to lie dozing under a palm tree with a fishing line tied to a toe, rather than do an honest day's work. Although there was an element of truth in this, the Roman Catholic Church was a strong influence among them and, educationally, had over the years probably given many of them a head start over the illiterate Tamil labourers brought over from Southern India. For whatever reason – perhaps because the British seemed to like them better – the Creoles held most of the middle-ranking government posts. Certainly they were very much part of the government machinery. Nevertheless, the Labour Party was now in power and determinedly gathering to itself the fruits of patronage.

The somewhat aloof French, on the other hand, contented themselves with holding the really important levers of economic power – in the sugar estates – confident that their wealth and influence were more than sufficient to ensure that French interests, and the prosperity of the island, were well taken care of by a benign plutocracy underlying the flummery of politics. As for the Chinese four per cent of the population, they were inscrutably into everything – trade, manufacturing, government service, sugar-estate ownership even – but usually kept a low profile.

What made the interracial jostling rather frightening was the threatened population explosion – a combination of Indian fecundity and Creole promiscuity, as off-duty talk at the bar of the (mainly British) Vacois Club might have put it. But from whatever angle the problem was approached, it was a prospect that was very definitely exercising the minds of all Mauritians. Not only were living standards (already low) threatened, but there seemed to be a serious ultimate risk of civil strife. There had already been rioting in one or two towns, and many of the houses of the poor in the countryside had recently been destroyed or devastated by cyclones of unprecedented force. As it happened, we too were to experience a cyclone.

24 – MAURITIUS DIARY, 1964

1 January
Heralded by a fusillade of firecrackers that lasted all night and continued throughout the day. How do such poor people afford this extravagance? B, J and I took a lunch basket to the sea side at St. Felix. We found a nice quiet little bay surrounded by a coral reef and spread ourselves beneath the shade of a conveniently situated tree on the beach. Lovely sun, beautiful calm sea. J played in the rock pools and I goggled underwater: fascinating rocks and weeds and lovely blue coral; some nasty fat slugs and snakes (harmless) and clams too. On our departure we saw a notice: 'It is dangerous to bathe here'.

2 January
Spent the morning polishing my study, Aggy [maid] not being well: a satisfying occupation – occasionally. In the afternoon we dropped J with Helen [ayah] in the Botanical Gardens and went for a walk in the forest reserve area near Piton du Milieu – poor, stunted growth: the 1960 cyclone has terribly ravaged the island. But it is refreshing to get away from the crowded little centres of population (they don't somehow deserve the name of town) and the monotonous expanse of sugar cane.

Read over the 80 odd pages of my attempt at an exposition on agricultural planning in u/d [underdeveloped] countries: it has some acute points but rambles. I shall go back to it though.

3 January
Took Mr and Mrs Van den Ameele (FAO Marketing at Madagascar) to Chartreuse tea factory. Bad day, as it followed the holiday, and no machinery working. His English and my French are equally bad, but we managed. B and I go to the Park

Hotel for a drink with them this evening.

Mother and Father's Xmas parcel arrived today. *"When We Were Very Young"* for J. How it took me back. I shall enjoy reading it to him.

4 January
Very sore back from Wednesday's expedition. B puts a mixture of cold water and vinegar on it morning and evening, which puts me in suppressed(!) hysterics at every dab. This is a remedy recommended by old M. Masson next door. If it's doing any good I must conclude that, without it, I'd have been in a really bad way.

6 January
Trying to get some action from the Ministry to get this Board going. They talk of extending my assignment but make poor use of the time I <u>am</u> here. So many days pass without any progress at all.

7 January
The Creole for 'I have gone' is '*Mo fin aller*'. They don't distinguish between the definite article and the noun itself. Consequently 'Dog' is '*Lechien*', and a literal translation of 'a dog' would be 'a thedog'. I am making no attempt to learn the language, as it is no use elsewhere and would tend to corrupt my French; but the etymology of some of the words is interesting: a snail is '*courpas*'(doesn't run).

9 January
A phone call from a man who has office accommodation [for the Board] and wanted to speak to Raymond. People like using the back door in this country.

10 January
The noise of a football match appears to be the same the world over. We live next to a stadium [actually it was on the other side of the road, a little way off] and the roars and cheers might just as well come from West Ham.

11 January
A cocktail party at Lim Fat's. He had invited a number of people from various orders of society so skilfully that one was not conscious at all of racial differences. As pleasant an evening as these things can be. Got back rather late.

13 January
A good day. Saw the Minister and got most of the questions that have been holding me up settled. He says he has no objection to my having 6 months in Jan. 1965. Let's hope he sticks to it.

Heard from Jenner [our part-time gardener at Cone Hill] and the Woodgates. All progressing reasonably satisfactorily at Cone Hill. Jenner asking about plants for the rockery is reassuring.

Raymond says (à propos Cyprus and Zanzibar) that this country will see bloodshed after independence too. I fear the ingredients do indeed exist.

The reference to '6 months in Jan.' was, of course, in anticipation that our request to adopt another baby would be duly approved, and that a daughter would somehow miraculously be waiting for delivery on our return to England. We understood (not quite accurately) that adoptive parents were required to reside in the United Kingdom for at least the first six months after the adoption. However, in January 1964 we were still uncertain of the outcome.

17 January
A cyclone warning class two is in force: there are some quite violent gusts of wind and a sleety rain. The Curepipe shopkeepers are putting up their shutters and there is a general hammering noise of people taking precautions. I shall remember to close up all windows before going to bed. The cyclone is 220 miles off the island but there is a 50% chance of high winds tomorrow. The early-warning system is excellent and bulletins are broadcast regularly throughout the day.

18 January
Cyclone Daniel is 120 miles NNW of Mauritius and is at present stationary. A class three warning is in force and it is not known which way the next move of the beast will be. Hardly anyone on the streets since midday. High, gusty winds and driving rain. M. Desjardins next door (who had his house blown down by [cyclone] Carol) has been securely boarded up and sitting with his electric lights on since morning. G. Masson called this morning to advise secure locking up of doors and windows (anxious about his house – it's leaking).

19 January

Danielle (apparently she's feminine) started moving south at six miles an hour this evening, and the wind has increased to a tremendous gale with the rain lashing down in great wind-blown clouds. The leaks in the roof are more pronounced, and we have moved Jeremy in with us.

The Director of the Vacois observatory was interviewed on the wireless about the prospect in store for us, and spoke about the cyclone as if he were God.

20 January

We got hardly any sleep last night, and were eventually driven to put the beds in the kitchen and study, which were the only dry rooms, the rest literally swimming in water. The power and force of the wind was tremendous, we thought the windows were going to burst in at any moment. Jeremy thought it all great fun and did not appear to notice the tremendous noise outside. The garden is wet and bedraggled, all the dahlias blown out by their roots and the small fir trees bashed on their sides.

21 January

Damage is less than was feared; although the wind force was high, many of the weaker houses and trees had been destroyed by the severe cyclones of 1960 and 1961. Since then people have become more cyclone-conscious and had strengthened their defences. Still, there were several thousand people driven from their homes, and in comparison with their plight our own discomfort is nothing.

22 January

A lovely, sunny day, excellent for drying out wet houses and clothing.

23 January

The SVO [senior veterinary officer] is annoyed with me – probably to do with Beef – and practically blew me off the end of the telephone this morning: too busy to see me; so is Gassin [the SVO's number two]. Sooja is an extreme example of a colonial civil servant who has built up a little private empire (this one is literally surrounded by wire; and you have to undergo a kind of interrogation at the gate before being allowed to enter); he even flies his own flag at all vet stations. It's amusing in a way that he should be an Indian. A great talker, thinks and acts big – mainly bullshit.

24 January
Looked over several places that might do for offices [for the Board], but so far as the Ministry is concerned (which for the time being, unfortunately, is wholly) the landlord's face seems more important than his property.

25 January
Jeremy gave us a nice little concert this evening before going to bed: he is most amusing when not showing off.

26 January
B and I went to Communion this morning for the first time in several weeks: getting rather slack. The church shouldn't make a difference but I'm afraid it does. We wouldn't miss at St Lawrence's at home.

I have written to Randall [lawyer] asking him to contact Budd [actually his name was Rose] to see if he will sell us a bit of the forest land behind Cone Hill to give us access to the road.

Jack [Beryl's brother] wrote the other day to say the place was looking as pretty as ever and no signs of damp in the house. Cobb [the estate agent] seems optimistic about getting a tenant. Hope he does. Ifs worrying having the place empty for so long.

27 January
Had a go at mowing the lawn this evening and got in a great sweat: one gets unaccustomed to manual labour. But on the whole I'm very fit.

Old Masson passed over his telephone bill to us for payment – said it was ours. The old devil. B also suspects him of pocketing 5 rupees that he said we should pay his son-in-law for mending the mower (it was a most unusual request to make). Bob Russell [registrar of Cooperative Societies, designate manager of the Board] says all Mauritians are crooks; and those we have encountered are often dishonest. Guy Masson openly told me he was hoping to keep the rent I pay him secret from the Income Tax authorities.

28 January
Today is the festival of Cavadee (signifying what I'm ashamed not to know). We drove down through Medine sugar estate on the west coast (this being, of course, in Mauritius, a public holiday) to have a look at the sea. They had tumbled heaps of rubbish down onto the rocks. On the way back we passed one of the ceremonies. Crowds of people – mostly spectators – on either side of a river. Many flower decorations and coloured costumes. An old man with a

flexible stick was waving it with great energy, putting into a trance, slavering and skewered through their tongues, several men, one after the other: the jerking was repulsive (accompanied by a frenzied little drumbeat and a tinkling bell) but once they had calmed down I was impressed by their relaxed, innocent expression; and how clean they were. Indians' hair is usually lank and greasy: to see it soft and fluffy above those childlike expressions was rather moving.

1 February
Jeremy has been invited to Sophia Desjardins' birthday party next Saturday. The card said 'Travesty is of rigour', which, as an indication for Jeremy to get into fancy dress, we thought rather appropriate. Poor little Sophia always seems to be in the company of her nurse, a grim old bird.

6 February
The British Council is an excellent institution – for the British abroad anyway. Here the branch does not appear to be awfully active (a few film shows and art exhibitions) but it has a good library and reading room. We use it regularly (although I have several of my own books unread yet). The weekly papers and *Times* and *Telegraph* come in by airmail; and there is a wide selection of familiar magazines. It must be admitted that we do feel somewhat beleaguered in Mauritius.

7 February
Met the Director of the Central Statistical Office today (he had been on leave): Mr Honoré – a charming and enthusiastic man, genuinely helpful and interested. Why do people think of statisticians as cold fish? Those that I have met have been men of singular goodness and humility. There is undoubtedly something in the mathematical discipline that inspires a practical feeling for truth and straight-dealing, and also, I think, personal humility.

8 February
This morning Raymond and I went to see Roche Bois slaughterhouse. I had not been looking forward to it and was consequently relieved to find that slaughter had not yet begun. Dr Lionnet was there and conducted us over the place, explaining everything with lucidity and intelligence. He is doing a good job and is gradually effecting many improvements; that he is succeeding in getting the cooperation of both Municipality and butchers is a credit to his powers of diplomacy.

9 February
Bishop Rogers took the service this morning: a very English churchman: booming voice, sort of Radio Doctor, no-nonsense accent. Ripping through some passages at great speed, then suddenly pulling himself up to enunciate with studied emphasis and clarity a sentence of particular significance. (Jeremy is now standing in my wastepaper basket, asking innumerable questions, one of which is: 'You like your wastepaper basket very much?')

10 February
Since the beginning of last week I have a new French instructor. Alwyn Ekstrom has left for England (may, like so many of the Creoles, emigrate for good. Hopes to join the RAF) and on his last evening brought along Gaston Laurent, rather cleverer than Alwyn but not, I think, such a solid character. Both of them have the tendency to assume that their superior knowledge of the French language leads them also to know more about grammar, punctuation, good composition – and at times the English language too. But they are both decent and conscientious boys who take their duties seriously.

11 February
Another public holiday. For the past few days members of a Hindu sect having some original links in Madras have been walking to a central lake at Grand Bassin, in small groups and processions, clad for the most part in the rather bluish whites that Indians sport on occasion, and carrying delicately constructed bowers and temples of red and white decoration: within these elaborate ornaments, some of them very large, are vessels (mainly glass bottles) for the holy water that they get from the lake, and then bring solemnly home for the feast today.

12 February
B met a woman in the Curepipe market whom she had known slightly when they were both stenographers in Dar es Salaam. Her maiden name of May has now blossomed into Broadhead-Williams, which amused B very much. Apparently she has been here for three years. We are not in touch with the English community, which appears to centre on the Gymkhana club at Vacois. We shall not join it, as we don't like colonial clubs of the latter-day empire. Perhaps it is unsociable, but our experience is that they are tedious and futile and horribly hearty; never serious, and opinion basically cynical.

13 February
Today is the Chinese New Year and – naturally, in Mauritius, which has 4% of its population Chinese – a public holiday.

The Medical Service announces that if the moon will have been sighted on Friday evening, vaccinations will take place the previous morning! The Prophet himself might have a little difficulty in working that out.

14 February
This evening I went to hear Colin Leys lecture on the Idea of a University and its place in the development of Culture. He is a refreshingly natural and unaffected speaker, with a quality of adventurous intellectual honesty that is much in accord with my own disposition. [Yes, I know, there are chunks of the smug young prig in this diary, but let's plump for the 'honesty' bit, and leave them in.] He believes that a university should be geared to the development of a country (breaking the vicious circle of no education; no development; no money for education). It is a bracing idea, but I rather think he has succumbed to the African (emotionally held) view that Development is a matter of physical inputs: Brains (manufactured by education system) plus Capital equals Progress.

15 February
The moon was spotted and a public holiday announced at 10 o'clock yesterday evening. Ramadan presents a particular difficulty in modern society, as one never knows until the last moment which of two possible days will be celebrated as Idd el Fitr. In the desert this doesn't matter, but I imagine it makes business houses a bit testy.

This evening we go to the Rochecouste's *campement* [house or hut by the sea] at Roche Bois. . . . A very pleasant day, swimming and playing Scrabble on the beach until dark. J fell asleep on the way back and we didn't wake him on arriving back home.

16 February
A typical Mauritius Sunday. B went to church; J and I breakfasted at 8.30; whereafter letter-writing for me, and J to his swing (he can manage to amuse himself by himself well enough early in the day). After B had returned and breakfasted we all drove down to the Rosehill vegetable fair; then home by a roundabout route. Did my weekend French exercise. Lunch; read *Economist* for two hours (B and J resting). Then Tea, talk and drift till 4 when Helen came to look after J. We took them to the Bot. Gdns., then went to

the forest reserve for a walk. Then home, with J (supper and bed) and the evening reading and listening to the wireless.

17 February
I have practically given up smoking my pipe. It coats my tongue and four pipes in working hours gives me a headache. Perhaps the tobacco is old. B, too, has given up cigarettes, but is happy to take the odd opportunity for a smoke.

We did not finally give up smoking until about two years later, in Rome – purely for health reasons, since tobacco there was for us duty-free.

19 February
The momentum of my job is running down and I feel rather flat about it. The inertia of this government is galling. I tell myself this is simply a doldrum and that in a week or two things will begin to pick up again. I hope so. I hate inactivity – or rather, aimless work (for it is impossible for me to be idle).

21 February
I took some snapshots of Jeremy on three different occasions last week. On each day he exhibits a different aspect of his character. Just now he is passing through a disobedient and aggressive phase, and is consequently running up against authority. He is such a determined little boy that we have to be very careful not to make this a contest of wills.

22 February
We followed a man to Roche Bois this afternoon, to look at his *campement* (we think of taking one for about 6 weeks in July/August, as Curepipe is so cold then, and wet) but the bungalow was ugly and utterly lacked privacy or graceful neighbours; B thinks the lack of a fridge rules it out anyway. Two other people have approached us – but <u>only</u> two, in spite of two advertisements in the press. Let's hope that one of them is suitable.

24 February
Guy Masson s son, who has been living by himself in the house at La Baraque now that his parents have gone to Europe, has swollen glands and is apparently in a bad way. His grandfather phoned for the doctor to call, but the man refused, saying he had no time! That strikes me as astounding. We know of two doctors here, who

own large, vulgar houses, ostentatiously embellished with statuary, stone jars on pedestals, and chained drives. It must be a paying game this doctoring.

25 February
Cyclone Giselle – warning class two this afternoon quite out of the blue (at least to us: the locals say they recognised the indications from yesterday). The car was having a 3000 mile service at Rogers in P/L, so B and I walked to the market for a few provisions (mainly for the old Massons) and got soaking wet. Later, the car turned up, and I took the man who brought it home. He seemed surprised that I should do so and asked how long I had been in Mauritius. By 7 pm it was class III. Later, God's mouthpiece, Mr Davies [the observatory director], is to speak.

28 February
Giselle dithered about and rather confused the meteorological office, which eventually got tired of changing warning signals; and when the weather was worst I think there was no warning at all. But on the whole we have not been much troubled by this cyclone; and Cyclone Frances, which preceded it, hardly affected Mauritius at all.

1 March
We all went to church this morning. Helen sat in the pew behind and took J out at the beginning of the sermon. Rees-Hughes [vicar] has the habit of mentioning names of British worthies (usually bishops or generals or some obscure writer) that most of his congregation can never possibly have heard of. We now wait for sentences beginning '. . . As ----- said, . . .' This afternoon we drove to the south coast and took tea. J had a fine time splashing about in the pools, and B gathered some pretty shells. Rock pools are endlessly fascinating and beautiful.

3 March
The interesting question of whether Sooja is going to lower his extraordinary barricade of secrecy and permit me to talk with one of his specialists on poultry still is unresolved. I have been fairly persistent and am hoping for the gates to open fairly soon. But if not there will probably be some unpleasantness. The situation is quite extraordinary. How a Departmental head can successfully insulate himself from his Ministry to the extent of refusing a request for information (for that is what it amounts to) is beyond comprehension. It could surely only happen in Mauritius.

4 March
We get our groceries from Sik Yuen store. They have so many Chinese assistants (seemingly all members of the Sik Yuen family) that you never have to wait to be served. The old man presides over the cash box. His daughters look pretty tough – chubby, bespectacled and cheerful.

5 March
Orson [gardener] works in the garden in the pouring rain – never takes shelter. He is a quiet, good worker, but not very strong. He has to <u>pull</u> the lawn-mower – which strikes me as being rather more effort than the more normal way, of pushing it.

6 March
On our return from the botanical gardens in the evening with Jeremy and Helen we often stop at a little tin, lean-to shack at the side of a Chinese corner-shop. An old Indian woman squats there making gâteaux piments. B always insists that ours be fresh, boiling hot, so that they will not have had time to become infected by the somewhat unsavoury conditions. Sometimes, but less frequently (since one cannot be at all sure of <u>his</u> wares being safe) we buy dhal pourri from an old man who stations himself opposite the London Store, by the traffic lights. He has them in a box, and smears on a very hot lentil sauce, folds them in quarters, and slaps them into a grubby piece of newspaper. They are tasty but probably injure the stomach. I have never been able to understand how curry can be a staple food. Perhaps it isn't so injurious after all.

8 March
Mauritius is to have a coalition government – in the circumstances of a racially divided society politically aligned on racial lines, this is clearly a desirable situation. Not many people appear to think it will last, though. And when you consider that the allocation of portfolios had to be refereed by the [British] Secretary of State, it does not augur well for government-formation after Independence. The only hope for this society is, in the long run, a United Nations police force.

How wrong that judgement was! But, at the time, such was the degree of animosity between the two main races that few rated their chances of living harmoniously together after the departure of the British. As it eventually turned out, the Indian, Creole and Chinese populations looked into the abyss and sanely concluded that there was no alternative but to 'live and let live'. Perhaps the Israelis and Palestinians will, in *their* small part of the world, ultimately come to a similar recognition of inevitability, if their grandchildren are to have a future worth living.

10 March
My taxi driver, Ramjane, always seems to be tired. Sometimes I think he will fall asleep at the wheel. Most drivers . . . make minute adjustments to correct the steering as they go along. Not so Ramjane: a fractional turn of the wheel will remain uncorrected: we zoom along, inclining ever so slightly but resolutely off course . . . until suddenly, lounging exhausted in his seat, Ramjane will swing the car back on course with a vicious jerk. He has about three differently pitched horns and uses them all with great frequency. Like almost all Mauritian drivers, he has no regard at all for dogs, and practically none for pedestrians. The extraordinary thing is that the pedestrians appear to have no regard for the cars. All (including the dogs) are astonishingly bold, and face death unflinchingly twenty times a day.

12 March
A two hours long argument with ffrench-Mullen and Graff, on G's proposed milk scheme. G was angry and frustrated; and I think he has every right to be: the govt. have been dilatory, and when finally they accepted his plan (which I had criticised a long time ago) he naturally regarded the matter as settled. It was most distasteful for me, throwing a spanner in the works at this stage, but I am quite sure the plan is unworkable as it stands, and it is better to have the matter out now than later when things have gone too far.

The saga of the Mauritius Milk Marketing Scheme exemplified everything that typically could go wrong with a well-intended foreign-aid project to 'modernise the economy' of a developing country. The scheme's ultimate failure, which occurred after we had left the island, was predictable.

Most of the rural labourers who worked on the sugar estates supplemented their meagre incomes by keeping a cow. They had no land for pasture, so the cow was kept in a shed beside their house, and the wives would go out every day scavenging the roadsides to gather fodder which they would carry back on their heads, sometimes having to walk miles for it. Even when cane tops were available it was a task that could take up a fair part of their day, depending on the season. To see these women scuttling along, hips wobbling, straight-backed under a massive bundle of fodder, you would think, 'What awful drudgery for so little return!' Yet devotion to the needs of their cow, to a Hindu a sacred duty, was not measured simply in terms of the little money they got from bicycle milkmen, who made a daily tour of the cowsheds. Each bicycle milkman had his regular suppliers and a regular door-to-door milk round of housewives in the towns – a very simple, straightforward system.

'It may be simple and straightforward,' said the Department of Agriculture, 'but it is also most unhygienic and could be done much better if all the milk was channelled through the modern dairy which an enterprising businessman has already built and equipped, but which at present is vastly under-utilised.' And Mr Graff, the Israeli manager of the dairy, had a plan: instead of having a thousand bicycle milkmen (with difficult-to-clean tanks welded on to their bikes) collecting milk from 18,000 cow keepers, there should be twenty-five collecting centres, to which the cow keepers could deliver their milk directly. From these centres bulk tankers would deliver the milk to the dairy for pasteurisation and delivery in cartons to consumers. At a stroke, with a little extra investment (the 'white elephant' dairy was already in place), Mauritius would have a good modern hygienic dairy industry. Unfortunately, it would also have 1,000 unemployed bicycle milkmen whose unhygienic equipment would be declared illegal. And there was the little matter of convincing the cow keepers that it would be a good idea for them to walk up to five miles morning and evening with their wretched three or four litres of milk, instead of having it collected directly from their cowshed. And, to top it all, the pasteurised milk ('much better for you') would cost the housewife more.

The minister, thinking no doubt of his rural electorate and the votes that might be lost, could see the drawbacks but liked to be associated with 'progress'. It was a dilemma, but one which allowed him to say one thing to me and another to ffrench-Mullen. Mr Graff, on the other hand – a typical Israeli technician accustomed to the smooth-working systems of a kibbutz, where everyone knew what he had to do, and did it – had no such doubts. He was fanatically attached to every smallest detail of his 'plan', and brushed aside every objection. I was no longer in Mauritius when the scheme, against my advice, was finally put in motion . . . and quickly ran into the sand. Nearly everybody except the manager of the dairy was upset by the new system – and in one way or another, like good Mauritians, worked round it: the dairy industry almost overnight turned into a black market.

As Clare Pineo (the American who succeeded me) told me later: "You sure looked into the crystal ball there!"

However, at the time of my two hours of argument with ffrench-Mullen and Graff (and there were to be others, including acrimonious board meetings) all that was in the future.

13 March
Eventually got my way with Sooja and managed to have a talk with [his subordinate] Gassin – broken up, though, after an hour or so by Sooja poking his head through the window to suggest that Gassin was too busy to give me any more time. At the second intervention the conversation perforce ended. I don't think I have ever met a Colonial civil servant who carried their occupational failing of personal autocracy to such maniacal lengths as Sooja.

15 March
Jeremy gave us a little concert this evening with great gusto. He loves to occupy the centre of everyone's attention. On these occasions he gets it. He began by reciting some of his nursery rhymes. 'Sing a song of sixpence' he knows without any mistake, and many other, shorter ones such as 'Little Jack Horner' (ending 'Oh! You good boy!') and 'Bah, bah, black sheep'. But he has difficulty with 'Simple Simon' ('Said the pie man to the Simple Simon . . . to the Simple Simon to the pie man'). His dancing is unaffected and very amusing.

16 March
Gaston has begun to give me French poems to learn (I had been getting a little restless with all the written work, which smacked too much of many fruitless years of school learning). I am surprised to find how quickly I am able to commit them to memory. At school, learning by heart was always an awfully tedious chore. Or perhaps it is simply that Jean de la Fontaine is easier than Shakespeare.

17 March
Rather disturbed about Father's health. Mother's letters usually end on a hopeful note. But the previous week always seems to have been rather grim.

Today was the opening of the new session of the Legislative Assembly (no longer 'Legco'). No riotous crowds this time. All passed off quietly. The Governor's few sentences about the marketing board were as I had drafted them; but how easily he could have landed us in embarrassment had Purmessur not casually happened to show me what he had drafted. Or would anybody have noticed?

18 March
Thieving servants are so irritating. B had a plain talk with Lizzie [maid] and Helen, but I think they are incorrigible. They think us so rich that the little things they take from us cannot possibly be of any great consequence. Nor are they, really. But having such a principled objection to theft is something that is probably alien here. These girls are pleasant enough, and I very much doubt whether their general characters accord with what one would in England expect of petty thieves. The trouble is one doesn't know where they draw the line.

19 March
We are now subscribing to the following magazines, etc.

1. Daily –   *Le Cernéen*
2. Weekly –   *M[anchester] Guardian Weekly*
3.   *Country Life*
4.   *The Economist*
5. Monthly – *Geographical Magazin*e
6.   *Rural Econom*y
7.   *Kent Life*
8.   *Housewife*
9.   *Parent*s
10.   *Encounter*
11.   *Homes and Gardens*
12.   *Good Housekeeping*
    (waiting for) *Farm Economist*

Homesick? (27 March) It does seem rather a lot, doesn't it?

21 March
Jeremy says that he wants to be a Chinaman when he grows up.

A rather grim cocktail party given by the manager of the Cooperative Bank, in honour of the Southern Rhodesian Registrar of Cooperative Societies, who is over here studying the Credit societies. Mostly Indians present. Awfully hot to begin with.

22 March
Whoever wins the British general election the result is not going to be terribly exciting. Neither Wilson nor Hume [sic] strike one as measuring up to the times. W appears to be an opportunist, lacking genuine humanity[!]. H carries complacency to the point of fatuity; he seems to be dangerously insulated from feeling reality[!!]. In the long run it would probably be best, though, for him to win, since nothing less is likely to shake the opposition into providing an adequate alternative to the present dreary leadership.

24 March
The question of what building the Board is to occupy has at last been settled. It is so difficult to achieve anything when the PAS, Bob Russell and myself all occupy different offices, and only I, without any executive responsibility, am working full time on this job. Still no [members of the] Board appointed. I really do not understand how dilatoriness can go so far.

25 March
During a walk through the woods to a place near a tea plantation that we had been to only once before – about two months ago – Jeremy suddenly said that he wanted to see 'the crab's house'. For a few moments we could not understand this request, until B then remembered that on our earlier visit here we had shown Jeremy a spider in the middle of his web. The purity of children's memories is enviable.

26 March
Jeremy's school holidays begin today. He came back, beaming, to say that it was 'all closed up'. Nonetheless, he will find time lagging heavily on his hands. Most evenings Helen looks after him in the Botanical Gardens (where we take him by car – and then go off for a walk, calling back for him later). There he meets lots of other children also out with their nannies.

27 March
I have not been to church for the past three – or perhaps four – Sundays. It's too easy to fall out of the habit. The actual church one worships in should not make all that difference – but with me it does: a grim, more than half-empty church, an unsympathetic clergyman, and the veritable stampede for the Communion rail here: they put one off. But they should not. Goodness me, they should not.

30 March
Went to our beach at Belle Mare; a dull day, squalling rain and wind. Still, we put on our bathing costumes and collected shells. Jeremy got fed up with wearing his and walked about without any clothing at all – until he got too cold and finally donned Mummy's.

31 March
The Van Heurns' and Rochecoustes' for dinner. A pleasant evening. Raymond told the story of an old farmer who wanted to be buried in a green suit. Happily, he died at the same time as a neighbour who <u>did</u> have a green suit; and so they simply exchanged – heads.

1 April
Weather getting cooler now. It has been most unpleasantly hot at Réduit for the past couple of months. Jeremy is now on holiday from school. The Woodgates report that they have fallen out with Jenner. Annoying. But apparently Cone Hill has a tenant – Scots people. Nothing about it from Cobb though.

Our neighbours down on the road below had always taken a close and more than friendly interest in Cone Hill and its owners and tenants. Having lived there in Stone Street for longer than any of the shifting occupants of our house, they had an almost proprietorial concern for the place, and from their vantage point by the garages at the bottom of the path up through the woods they observed with beady eyes all the comings and goings to and from the house. David Woodgate would take a delight in being the first to tell us things that normally one would expect to find out for oneself.

3 April
Mother reports that Swill Tub Cottage [their neighbouring property at Bacton] is being restored. Lots of workmen at work. It will be good for them to have neighbours. We hope they like them. Hamish

is due to come home on leave on the 9th. That's good too. Father is making progress but still very weak.

4 April

B and I walked rather farther than we intended this evening, and having left J in the park with Helen, had to run back to the car. Fortunately, they had started to walk home – J quite unconcerned. He had lost his ball (A bigger boy had kicked it onto the roof of the bandstand) but came back with a tin Japanese toy motorbike that someone had forgotten. He has agreed to return it tomorrow.

5 April

Took lunch to Belle Mare: a big one. All but J feeling rather sluggish. We eventually took to the sea and [then] walked along the beach on our shell-collecting expedition. An overcast day which latterly turned to rain.

At about 9.30 (B was in bed) we heard awful screams from Desjardin's house, as though someone was being murdered. This was immediately followed by a lot of normally pitched conversation. Goodness knows what they were doing.

9 April

At 9 in the evening, B and I to the theatre – '*A Man for All Seasons*' by R. Bolt. Ambitious for a local company, but they did well. Perhaps it was the hard seats, a half-hour power failure, and the late start that made the second half drag out to a symphony of creaking chairs. Whatever it was, More here did not strike me at all as a man for all seasons, but rather <u>tediously</u> honourable – which was presumably the reverse of what was intended to be brought out.

13 April

An enormous post today. The boat (which always brings several numbers of the weekly magazines and one or two monthlies) coincided with the aeroplane.

14 April

Some of the old wooden French houses are splendid and full of character. Mostly grey and white, with tall, wood tile [shingle] roofs, heavy shutters over the windows or thrown back against the walls. Spacious verandas; sun-blinds or reeded mats; little dormer windows along the roof. Sometimes flanking semi-turrets. Decorated guttering, and below it, to the rear of the veranda, a vast expanse of small-paned glass [windows]. Here and there potted plants, basket chairs, sculpted urns; perhaps a balustrade with stone steps, and two sculpted lions.

18 April
The French in Mauritius are a race apart. One comes in contact with a few. They are confident and usually charming and intelligent, speaking excellent English. They have a tradition of aloofness. Of all the people in Mauritius they are the ones I find most interesting: an aristocracy that does not appear to have become effete with inbreeding. But that may be a superficial impression. Certainly the younger generation of the commercial French look rather degenerate.

20 April
Father is now on the mend, we are glad to hear, and is getting out and pottering. It's difficult to get used to the thought of M and F being old. When I was a boy I used to think how nice it would be to be a man, grown-up, confident, knowledgeable. Yet I still feel myself to be just the same boy as I ever was. The 'savoir faire' of other men I just cannot share. Although lack of society is an undoubted deficiency, the rootless coming together that we kind of people suffer as society, is mostly corrupting[!?].

23 April
A Muslim public holiday – something to do with God staying the hand of Abraham as he was about to sacrifice his son.
    A book I am reading (about Mauritius) called '*Island of the Swan*' is hardly recognisable. On the whole an amateur effort, some of it in bad taste. He describes Curepipe as being grey, green and blue – no colour. Very accurate. Add: brown, wet, dank; wrought-iron gates; bamboo hedges.

6 May
After the Triveni [Indian cultural and social club] talk [which I gave] yesterday B and I again went down the hill – this time to the Agricultural College, where Ernst was showing some Dutch films in honour of Queen Juliana's birthday. Very many people who had been invited failed to turn up – which was especially rude, as E and Trudy had laid on an abundance of tea and cakes. E was very patriotic and made two little speeches: I thought for a moment he was going to give a solo of the Dutch national anthem, but he didn't.

7 May
This evening we had the Lim Fats, Claude Delaître and Miss Baumann over for dinner. Lim Fat and Delaître were both entertaining and we enjoyed the occasion. Miss Baumann (over from Tanganyika) says the November mutinies were more than simply dissatisfaction over pay.

Some years later, we heard from George Beddoes, an accountant in Dar es Salaam, who subsequently joined my project in Iran. He gave us his eyewitness account of how the British, four years after independence, came back to the rescue of the new Tanganyika Government. Nyerere (the President, who had fled from the capital) sent an urgent SOS to London, and by great good fortune a Royal Navy aircraft carrier (I believe it was – anyway, a big, impressive vessel) happened to be in the vicinity. While the mutineering soldiery were using their military muscle in the city, this massive ship, bristling with guns, helicopters and other menacing technology, appeared from nowhere and took up station in the harbour, white ensign flying, and fired a single shell into the guardhouse of the barracks. That was all it took. The soldiers rushed out with their hands up. End of mutiny.

8 May
Packed all my books and papers into a taxi and moved office to Port Louis. The new Board premises (new to the Board, that is; they are an old French building in the centre of the town, yet oddly with a clear view of the hills) are very suitable and have been decorated quite adequately. Most of the excellent new furniture was still piled up in the Boardroom and the place was festooned with telephone cables being installed.

Cocktail party at the ffrench-Mullens' in the evening.

9 May
We have succeeded in getting a satisfactory *campement* for the cold season. B saw a place she liked and persuaded me (much against my will) to discover the owner and find out if he was willing to let it. At length I tracked him down, and he was willing. 'That is how one does things in Mauritius,' says B. But it strikes me as being something of a fluke.

14 May
Met the Board Chairman, Moutrie [an Englishman], a tall, oldish man – perfectly pleasant but not pretending to know much about his new job. After a general chat with the Minister, I took him over to see the Board offices, and fed him with bumf. Too soon to form much of an opinion about him.

15 May
Purmessur is a tricky little fellow, for ever intriguing. I am getting rather exasperated with his oblique conversations that he summons me over for much too frequently. I shall make a point of dealing with him as little as possible. Joynatsingh [who took over from Bernard Rochecouste as my official counterpart] is also plotting for his own advancement and is quite definitely the Minister's 'man', but at least he is pleasant, cooperative and, at present, efficient.

I was sorry to have lost Bernard, but it was clear that the minister wanted someone much closer to *him* to keep an eye on me.

16 May
They say that May is the best month in Mauritius. It has been damp and depressing until today, which is really lovely. Now that I am working in Port Louis, Saturday is a free day (so far anyway). I have been mending J's kite. (He tore it five minutes after getting it, and we have not so far had an opportunity of flying it.) But this afternoon – provided the weather holds – should be ideal. B is out at a meeting of the Cheshire Homes.

27 May
To the Van Heurns' this evening. The Yip Tongs – both unquenchable talkers (How they manage together at home I don't know) – were there. Ernst showed some of his films and we brought along some of our Tanganyika reels, which made us nostalgic for Songea and the wide open spaces of Africa.

29 May
There is something awfully sad about Mauritius. Perhaps in days gone by it really was an idyllic island. It is difficult to fathom the Indians, but the French and Creoles often strike me as oppressed with nostalgia for the past – for a time when life was slower-moving, more gracious; when privilege and grand-seigneurity were not simply tolerable but the very fabric of an ordered and simple life;

when there was room and work enough for all, and every man knew his own place.

You catch glimpses of this former existence in some of the old houses and gardens, many of them now passed over to the new order: badly maintained, crumbling, overgrown, desolate – or perhaps desecrated by the litter and rubbish of a more banal world. (Writing this, one becomes almost a Mauritian. This mood, though, can become maudlin and tedious.)

10 June
B is rather busy with work for the Cheshire Homes. It gives one an insight into the workings of charitable organisations – though I trust this one is not typical of most. An enormous committee of important people seem to spend most of their time squabbling with each other. The ostensible cause of their activity are six wretched crippled boys who have been dragged from a government home where they were perfectly happy, and more or less forcibly installed in the new 'Home' at Tamarin. B has been dragged in as dogsbody and does the work of the Secretary. I hope she will be able to free herself when the present flag day's spree is over, as really these people seem to be rather discreditable in their motives.

13 June
In the afternoon we went to the races – an aged institution in Mauritius, reeking of privilege and condescension.
The evening: first, the Governor's reception in honour of the Queen's birthday. There must have been at least a thousand guests crammed into quite inadequate space. One had positively to yell to be heard. It struck me as an awful waste of money. Then B and I went to a Chinese restaurant in Rosehill and had a splendid meal.

19 June
A rather late Board meeting to consider the milk marketing program. A lot of confused thinking and nonsense spoken. The Chairman very dozy. We finally broke up on passing a quite meaningless resolution rather than face the issue.

20 June
J and I drove to Moka and climbed about the slopes above the gorge. He has no fear, but hangs onto me like a dead weight. Then he sat on a succession of tree-stumps which became, respectively, an elephant, horse, giraffe and camel. B stayed at home in rather bad humour. She is hating Mauritius and not always making the

best of it. For better or for worse we are here for another six months and should use the time positively.

1 July
To the seaside at Pointe aux Sables. We have hired a wooden *campement* from a young man called Robert who lives at Moka. Rather primitive conditions, but light and airy, and plenty of sun.

7 July
Daily routine:
   7 am. – Get up, make B's cup of tea; wash and shave.
   7.30 – Take wireless out to garden overlooking the sea. Do exercises while listening to the news in French. (This is what I call my valuable 10 minutes: keeping fit, improving my French, keeping up with the news at the same time.) There are usually a few fishermen in their boats a few yards off shore; sometimes a big steamer standing outside the harbour, waiting for the pilot.
   8.00 – breakfast.
   8.45 – taxi to office.
   12.30 – remove two large sandwiches and one apple from the little lunch basket, and have lunch at desk.
   4.00 – taxi back to *campement*.
   5.00 – walk with B along the sea shore (J being out with nanny), just sauntering, picking up the occasional shell.
   Back by 6. Read to J having his supper.
   7.00 – Supper.
   7.30 – Do some French.
   8.00 – Read till bed time at about 9.30–10. Bath in a bucket every other night. (It takes 4 kettles.)

18 July
I'm getting rather depressed about the Board. They have absolutely no idea what they are about. We just buy up produce and sell it off and things will somehow or other adjust themselves! The trouble is that the 'build-up' of this Board had been going on for several years and a lot of confused aspirations are now taken as a matter of fact: you just press the button. Also most of the Board give no time at all to studying the issues. Partly, no doubt, it's my own failure to make myself clear.

30 July
Had our medical examination for the second adoption. The preliminary vetting is rather trying.

After that last entry in July my diary more or less dries up, which is a pity because the tone of it had become for several days rather flat and occasionally pessimistic. Yet in many ways our life in Mauritius was idyllic and, looking back on my official reports at the time, it is clear that, in spite of daily frustrations, a great deal was accomplished in little more than one year: legislation had been drafted and passed into law, the board appointed, good offices located and equipped, its staff recruited from scratch and now in course of training . . .

We were about to receive news from the outer world which would change, in two very different ways, the whole course of our lives as a family.

25 – HILARY AND A GRANNY SHE NEVER KNEW

What we call the beginning is often the end
And to make an end is to make a beginning.
The end is where we start from.

T. S. Eliot

Almost providentially, as we were making arrangements in hopeful anticipation of the possible arrival of a new baby, I received the following letter from my chief at headquarters:

Rome
31 July, 1964

CONFIDENTIAL

Dear Mr Hall

    A new post is to be established in the Marketing Branch. . . . The incumbent would work with the Branch in Rome undertaking short field assignments to prepare projects, and carry out investigations etc. as required.

    I am writing to you informally to enquire if you would be interested in such a position. . . . There will be open competition for this post. . . . Without any commitment we would like to be sure that you are aware of this and shall send you a copy of the announcement when it is ready.

    Yours sincerely,
        J. C. Abbott, Chief, Marketing Branch

This was quite unexpected, and most encouraging. Although my post in Mauritius was to be extended – and in the normal course of events we would expect to continue there – Beryl and I had already realised that it would be impracticable for me to combine the adoption requirements in the UK with a job on an island in the Indian Ocean. A Rome posting – if it came off – would suit us perfectly. Another consideration was that my mother was in poor health, and our being so far away was a worry.

And then, almost exactly a month later, our weekly mail produced a letter from the Church of England Children's Society to say that our application had been 'favourably considered' by the adoption committee. After so many months of jumping through hoops, answering questions, waiting and hoping, this was, you might say, for us the moment of Hilary's conception: still only a thought, but the very definite idea of a child in prospect. We were elated. From that moment onwards, although it was not definite that either a baby daughter or Rome job would eventually materialise, we blithely excluded from our thinking any possibility but that they would.

My decision to break loose from Mauritius was made easier when, about the same time, the man who had been appointed manager of the board, Bob Russell, returned from leave and in effect took over from me much of the day-to-day administrative work which, in the absence of a manager, I'd had to do myself. I had met him some years previously when we were both on a Colonial Office refresher course in Moshi. At that time he was serving in Northern Rhodesia (Zambia) and before that had been an army officer. Bob was an unusual character: rather abrasively 'right wing', yet (until this new appointment) finding himself, as registrar, promoting cooperative societies – the sort of thing which, in his much preferred military persona, he would consider to be an almost contemptibly left-wing activity. However, now free of any cooperative 'taint', Major Russell was able to be himself; and for my last four or five months in Mauritius I shared the otherwise deserted boardroom with this burly ginger-haired ex-soldier. I will never forget Bob Russell, and his name will always evoke in me a stab of guilt: the memory of a painful lesson about life, and how we as individuals relate to other people.

In spite of his briskly, almost aggressively military manner and a habit of making what we would now call 'politically incorrect' observations about 'black bastards', etc., I managed to get on fairly well with Bob. For all his sometimes outrageous conversation he was an entertaining and amusing talker. But we had two quite different personalities. He was an extrovert; I was the opposite, and hated the pushing of 'personality' to impress other people. I still do. This need not have led to a breakdown of relations (I am quite capable of hypocrisy in the interests of harmony). But it did. It happened that Bob (who was living bachelor-style, his wife having remained in England) invited Beryl and me to come over to his flat one evening for dinner. Beryl, who hardly knew Bob but had decided he was not the sort of person she did want to know, was determined not to get herself into a false position.

"Just tell him the truth," she said. "'Say thank you very much, but we really don't have anything in common."

I forget how I put it, but that, in essence, is what I told him. The effect on him was appalling, and I regretted them as soon as the words were out of my mouth. It was as if I had suddenly whipped away a layer of outward confidence to reveal in him a quite surprising vulnerability.

Bob said nothing for a few moments, and then, looking away, "Well, if that's how . . ."

And he didn't say another word to me for at least two weeks. Not a word. When not out and about, we continued to sit at our separate desks in the same large room, silently engaged in work that concerned us both, but each communicating only with the staff, he utterly ignoring me and I perforce ignoring him. Eventually, of course, the daily round of other people coming in to speak with both of us led to some kind of indirect conversation which, as the days passed, evolved into a frigid formality of communication between us. But that wretched little episode lay like a pall over the last few weeks of my work in Mauritius. It had been so unnecessary: a stupidly insensitive snub for which I blame only myself (Beryl was not in a position to see more than her own side; I was). A white lie would have been so much better.

The arrival of Clare Pineo, who took over from me as FAO

marketing advisor, was a relief in more ways than one. Clare was a charming man and, for an American, quite unusually modest, almost to the point of being deferential to the opinions of others. Older than me, he was what Americans would call 'a country boy', a simple God-fearing soul who genuinely devoted himself to doing good in the world. With his William Hague cranium, spaniel's eyes, naivety and sweet smile, he was the kind of person easy to mock affectionately behind his back; yet his humility and integrity were a rebuke to cynicism.

We arrived back in England, via Rome, on 9 January 1965 – two days after Hilary's birth, although at the time we were ignorant of her almost simultaneous arrival into the world. Nevertheless, all the careful preliminary enquiries and procedures to finally establish (or re-establish) our suitability as prospective parents had by then been completed and, did we but know it, we were within days of an addition to the family.

Indeed, we had barely settled into Cone Hill, noting with some relief that the tenant had done less damage to the place than feared (merely failing to pay his last laundry and phone bills), when we received a letter to say that a small daughter had been 'found' for us and that we should go to see her at the place, date and time specified; and if we liked each other *we could take her home with us*. If? If indeed! There was never any question with us of 'choosing', or even of 'deciding' – no more than a mother has a choice in what sort of child she bears. These things are in the lap of the gods, and we were content to leave them there. From the moment we opened and read that letter, Hilary (her name already decided) *was* our daughter.

The day arrived and we were all excited – including Jeremy, who had been looking forward with great interest and curiosity to having a sister. Unfortunately, I didn't allow for the amount of traffic on the A25 (there was no M25 in those days) and we arrived at the address we'd been given in Farnborough more than an hour late, to be welcomed with somewhat frosty smiles by two ladies who did not try very hard to conceal their exasperation at our apparently casual approach to this momentous occasion. (In fact we had been in agonies of frustration and embarrassment owing to the impossibility of overtaking the lines of slow-moving cars and lorries, and dreading the possible consequences of missing our appointment.) The tiny Hilary, swaddled up in preparation for a decidedly chilly journey, was impervious to our apologies, barely opening an eye as she was held up for our admiring appraisal. There was a bit of chat about her last meal, inoculations, sleeping habits, etc. A few questions – Beryl was already a fully fledged mother and knew what to ask – and in no time at all we were all four of us back in the car and on our way home, our feelings a mixture of pride, relief and joy; but Jeremy was doing most of the talking.

We had wondered, naturally, how he would take to having a sister, and had been reassured by how enthusiastic he was about the idea; and for the first few days he fussed about this actual materialisation of it with as much care and anxious solicitude as if he were the mother himself.

He would gaze into her little utterly impassive face, cooing questions, like "Want more milk?" or "Go sleep now?" until, eventually tiring of a one-sided conversation, he would suggest other ways of provoking a more animated sign of happiness from this unresponsive baby, such as "P'raps she wants to go for a walk, Mummy?" adding hastily, "In the pram, cos she can't walk yet, can she, Mummy?"

In many ways Jeremy was a very mature boy for his age. And when he later began to see that there were possibilities of a downside to Hilary's arrival, his uneasiness was betrayed not by bad behaviour but by a diffidently diplomatic response to the question "Do you like your new little sister, Jeremy?"

"Yes [pause], shall we take her back now, Mummy?"

Once any uncertainty about that, in Jeremy's mind, had been swiftly removed he quickly adapted to the role of elder brother. Actually, although Jeremy was more than keen to think up ways of amusing his sister, 'walking' with Hilary at Cone Hill was in practice confined to perambulating backwards and forwards on the lawn; the path down to the road was much too steep, and the narrow country road with blind bends too dangerous for mothers with prams.

Ironically, a moment of actual danger for baby Hilary occurred when, left out in her pram on the lawn one day, the brake somehow became disengaged. We had a springer spaniel named Trigger, who we think leaped up on to the pram (at any rate, he was an excitable dog who did that sort of thing, and we decided that he should take the blame) – and the pram with its precious occupant began rolling at increasing speed down the hill in the direction of a sunken bed of roses, which it might well have overshot and careered down on to the second lawn, further down the hill, if it didn't hit a tree before that! Catastrophe was averted by providentially quick thinking by our gardener, Palermo, who happened to be working up on the flat-roof balcony area above the front door. He saw what was happening and, literally leaping off the roof to the ground, hared after the runaway pram, and just managed to grab hold of it before it toppled into the rose bed.

It was quite coincidental that we should have a part-time gardener whose home town was Rome. Gino Palermo had been living in Sevenoaks for some years and may well have been a prisoner of war before that (he never made clear how he came to this country). Unusually for an Italian, who as a people tend to pine for their native land when abroad, he seemed very content to make his life in England. He was in appearance typically Italian – dark, wiry-haired, short but very strong. His wife came in for a time to help Beryl in the house; but it was Palermo we relied on, over several years, to look after the garden and generally keep an eye on the place (which normally had a tenant in residence while we were away). In that function he was much more helpfully reliable than the inquisitive David Woodgate or our official managing agent in Sevenoaks, who took ten per cent of the rent for responding, at our expense and without question, to the slightest complaint about 'things that need doing' from the tenant.

All that was still ahead of us. At the time of our return from Mauritius and the arrival of Hilary there was still a big question mark over my professional future: how was I going to feed my family? I had deliberately refused an extension to my contract in Mauritius, and the few days I had spent in Rome debriefing had done nothing to leave me any wiser about what I might be doing next.

I had, of course, duly put in an official application for the post at headquarters that John Abbott had written about, but he had been away from Rome when I passed through, and his deputy, Hans Mittendorf (who probably had a candidate of his own in mind), had been the reverse of encouraging – at least in that respect.

It was typical of FAO at that time for staff effectively to be recruited and appointed in post by the person who was to be their immediate boss: whatever the administrative bureaucracy involved (and there was a lot of it), in practice it was an 'old-boy' system. If the top man liked you, you were in. So, in spite of having potential assignments in Mexico and Colombia, 'for which I think you will be very suitable', shoved enticingly in front of me by Hans, I was clinging to a gut feeling that Abbott would not have written to me as he did if I had not been his preferred candidate. So I doggedly told Hans I wanted to await the outcome for Rome before anything else. Although that left everything up in the air, there was in the meantime plenty to do at home. After all, we had hardly spent any time in (what was now) Cone Hill since buying it on the eve of our departure for Mauritius. We threw ourselves into the task of improving and planning the refurbishment of its quaint facilities. Out went the solid-fuel stove in the kitchen (and the daily chore of feeding it with anthracite and coke); out went the Edwardian sinks and their attendant convoluted plumbing (but we kept the excellent very long pea-green bath). The conservatory got a new Perspex roof and quarry-tile floor; the (most useful) outhouses off the back passage were virtually rebuilt.

Yet when, finally, I heard I'd got the position that had been dangling in front of me for nearly a year, my delight (and relief) at being able to go off and start the new job in Rome was tempered by growing anxiety about my mother. She had been in and out of hospital without anyone being able to discover what was wrong with her. In spite of a history of cancer, her doctors had still not found any evidence of it – worrying for me, but much more so for her. She was not just in pain, but was being told it was 'all in the mind'. She wrote to me in Rome (Beryl and the children had to stay on for at least the statutory six months after Hilary's adoption). Mother was by nature self-denying to a fault, ever concerned with the welfare of others, so it was alarming to read her own report on herself expressed so bleakly:

> Walnut Tree Farmhouse
> Saturday 22nd May '66
>
> My dear Alan
> I really must try & stir myself & send you a few lines. Many thanks for all your letters. I wrote half a letter to Ham the other day & Father finished it off – apart from that this is my first attempt at a letter since I last saw you here. I have had no energy, no initiative & life has been one constant nightmare. Father would tell you that he brought me home from Ipswich last Friday, & the hospital verdict there was exactly the same as St. Thomas' – My pain was all derived from sheer physical weakness thro' my inability to eat. I am having twice weekly injections – some hormone stuff which is supposed to help my appetite. It is a bit too early to say, but I <u>am</u> trying very hard to overcome it. . . .

Typically of Mother, the rest of her letter continued for another two pages giving bits and pieces of family news, venting exasperation with

> Jack [their farmworker gardener] is a terrible fellow. He goes flaying around with that sickle of his, & he decapitates anything & everything within his range. He has absolutely no feeling for flowers at all, whole shrubs go west. He does the kitchen garden & hedging & ditching, & one has to count one's blessings & not say too much. . . . We were sorry to hear that Veronica [Beryl] has lost her Mrs Gibson [home help]. We had a nice long letter from her last week & she said that someone Paddy is coming to stay with her. You <u>will</u> be glad when you have the family united again. . . . The swallows are back again nesting in the S.R. [sitting room] chimney. We had to start fires again & they cleared off . . . & now they have returned again! Little devils – they make <u>such</u> a mess. . . .

One of the heartbreaking things about cancer is the way in which hope against hope alternates with crushing disappointment when a fleeting improvement, eagerly observed from day to day, is ultimately not sustained. The last letter Mother wrote to me, only a few weeks before she died, was more like her old self:

Walnut Tree Farmhouse
8th June 1965

My dear Alan

It seems much longer than a week since you returned to Rome. It was very nice seeing you again & thank you very much for the flowers. They were in good condition – fresh – & have lasted the full week.

I am pleased to report that I am going on all right. Dr Lawton has put me on to some more new tablets & my general health is certainly improving. I take my food better & have less discomfort afterwards & I also feel that my whole outlook on life is improving. For a time I had no interest in anything – I lived in a kind of vacuum – & it worried me, but now I <u>can</u> read the paper & I am hoping everything else will fall into line. I did a bit of weeding in the garden last week, but the weather still isn't good. It has been cold, with a N.E wind.

Father has been doing good work. He has cut all the orchard grass again & raked it. Now he has to start planting the annuals in the borders. He put in some salvias last week – they are very showy against the buildings when in full bloom. We have had a splendid gentle rain all night, & again this morning. And I just wish that all the young plants were in. A perfect growing day for them.

We heard from Ham [in West Africa] at the end of the week. He doesn't know when he is to get leave, but he is hoping to stop off at Rome to visit you and hopes you will be in your flat by then. You won't be moving in until sometime in August, I should imagine.

I see from today's '*Guardian*' that Uncle George's successor at Jack's Farm, a recently-made Peer of the Realm, is hitting out at irresponsible action in the Unions. We were just thinking how fortunate you were that you hadn't to travel this last weekend.

There really isn't anything to tell you. Father has gone to Bury to get some fish & have his hair cut I think & I am just waiting for him to come back. I heard from Aunty Jean [her brother Alasdair's wife] last week & she sounds as though she is getting on quite nicely.

Did you manage to see the man about the drive? I hope they will soon commence the work & that it will be completed & all the other works before you all vacate Cone Hill for Rome.

I also hope your new agents will be more alert & will find a suitable tenant for you. The old firm sounded rather doddery.

I shall leave a space for Father in case he has something he wants to say. With fondest love,
Mother

The last page of this letter is completed by my father:

> My dear Alan,
> 　M. has given you all the news, or nearly all. She doesn't mention the difficulty she has in walking through pain in her left hip. I had a look at her last night. . . . She hasn't been able to lie on her R side for months, but never complained of her hip & seemed to walk easily enough until about a week ago. So let us hope it may be just a bit of rheumatism. Don't mention it when you write. I'll put Lawton onto it when he comes. The pain is only severe in weight-bearing. Were it due to something sinister, I'd expect it to be boring away all the time. She sleeps well on the whole. . . . We were so pleased to see you & feel you're not too far away in Rome. . . .
> 　　Love.
> 　　F.

Even Father, who had intimate personal and professional knowledge of Mother's condition, was still persuading himself to trust her Ipswich doctors when they said they could see no evidence of cancer . . . until, inevitably, not many days after that letter was written, one of them did.

I do not remember whether I was summoned back from Rome, or whether I came back for Hilary's christening. I returned and was standing at Mother's bedside, and mentioned Hilary's name. She had heard it before; and whatever her opinion of it as a suitable name for a granddaughter, had kept it to herself.

But now, lying back on her pillow, her eyes closed, she just sighed and said in a weak but very Scottish voice, "Och, *what* did you give her a name like that for?"

Those were the last words I remember her saying to me. And, looking back, they are oddly comforting, as if my mother were going out with all her instincts and character intact. Her girlhood had been spent by the seashore and hills of the Western Highlands, and she lived almost the whole of the rest of her life in one of the dreariest parts of East London, a slave to the doorbell and the phone. In some ways, and in the light of what she might have expected when marrying a doctor with a brilliant university career, her life had been tragic. Not tragic in a grand sense, but in the loss of what might have been. We had been a happy family, but from Mother's point of view it was a happiness imprisoned in bleak duty, resigning herself to my father's needs, and to his unwillingness – or inability perhaps – to move to a practice that might have been more congenial to her. Mother was not a snob (although nowadays she might be thought one), but she found few people around her at Plashet Road with whom she felt able to socialise without condescension. And then, when at last her dream of a house in the country had been achieved and they had finally got through the disruption of moving and settling in at Walnut Tree Farmhouse, the cancer came back. As she said herself, it was 'unfair'.

I had hardly got back home after that visit when, early the next morning, my father phoned: Mother was in a seriously bad way. He did not say she was dying.

I remember that when, for the second time in less than eighteen hours, I reached and was opening the gate of Walnut Tree Farmhouse Father appeared from the kitchen door and, in the manner of a Roman emperor signifying that a gladiator was for the chop, gave me a thumbs-down sign. It seems in retrospect an inappropriately laconic gesture, but at the time I understood exactly why my father would wish to convey immediately, but without shouting it out, the news that Mother had died. He took me in to where she was, on her bed, with a handkerchief or scarf tied round her head and jaw.

"Poor Mother, she looks very severe, doesn't she?" said Father in a conversational tone. It was as if he were commenting on an exhibit in an art gallery.

In all my life I had never known him show emotion. Anger, scorn, humour (to the point, sometimes, of helpless laughter), sympathy, yes; but rarely a suggestion that his composure could be shaken by sentiment. It was only at the funeral, in the Ipswich crematorium some days later, that his studied urbanity ever so briefly wobbled. As Mother's coffin glided slowly into a glowing orifice and disappeared from sight, Father beside me gave a great, gulping sob. Just once, that was all.

26 – ROME

I started my new Rome-based job in April 1965, and was at first lodged in the Woodcock pensione (later renamed Lancelot) in the Via Capo d'Africa, just off the Colosseum. This was an establishment well known to the numerous field staff of FAO who flowed in a constant stream of various technical expertise through its headquarters, either going out to or returning from assignments in countries throughout the world. Via Capo d'Africa was almost a cul-de-sac, and the Woodcock was near the end of it, a blandly ugly four-storey building with a small courtyard protected by cast-iron gates, and hemmed in on either side by equally ugly buildings whose most prominent features were the drainpipes that stared back at you whenever you pushed open the shutters of a window. On the other side of the street was a bar, not very well patronised during most of the day; a greengrocer with boxes of tomatoes, artichokes, melons, etc., piled out on the pavement; and a shop that sold nail scissors, toothpaste and things like orthopaedic supports – all, including the greengrocer's disorderly cornucopia, rather grubby and cheerfully Italian. Although right in the centre of the city, it was a quiet street.

    The Woodcock Gravina (to give it its full name, which nobody did) suited me well for the three or four months while I was settling down and looking for somewhere suitable for us to live. The pensione had a friendly family atmosphere. It was owned and run by Contessa Gravina, known simply as the Contessa, assisted by three or four very hard-working maids, a male cook, and a porter whose main activity seemed to be doing first-aid jobs on the plumbing. Finding my room at the end of a maze of corridors and stairs with the lights economically turned off was an art I soon mastered; and as for lumpy beds, after a good meal with plenty of wine I could forgive anything. The Woodcock was famous for its evening meal. It was served on the dot at seven o'clock; we all had to be there, seated eight to a table, and anyone foolish enough to be late missed out on the soup or antipasto, or whatever course the meal started with. Wine flowed throughout, with flasks constantly replenished; and the sound of conversation in various languages would be deafening. I never knew who I'd be sitting next to: on my left might be a Chinese water engineer from Malaysia on his way out to Ouagadougou, in Burkina Faso; on my right a French plant pathologist, going home after two frustrating years in Guatemala. The following morning at breakfast I might be trapped by a Sikh project manager who would bore me stiff describing with great intensity the technicalities of oilseed milling.

Another advantage of the Woodcock was its proximity to FAO – a pleasant fifteen-minute walk, past the Colosseum and the backs of seminaries and various other ancient ecclesiastical buildings, along a grassy dedicated tramway above the traffic of Via di San Gregorio, and then finally negotiating a life-threatening intersection of major roads in front of the FAO building itself. Known in Rome as La Fao (pronounced as in 'foul'), this is a vast eight-storey block of four white stone-clad interconnected buildings whose blank sides are monotonously punctuated by hundreds of identical windows.

Apart from a tidy arrangement of gardens at the front, and an occasional display of the flags of all its member nations, the Palazzo della Fao is utterly devoid of ornamentation. Yet it occupies what is probably the finest site in Rome. On my first visit, John Abbott took me up for a beer on the roof terrace, which almost casually (since nobody else was looking at the view) offers a magnificent panorama of the city. To the left is the sandy length of the Circo Massimo (where chariot races were held at the time of the Roman Empire), the River Tiber, and the ancient quarter of Trastevere. To the right are the ruins of the Baths of Caracalla; and straight ahead, beyond the shrubberies and teeming traffic of the Piazza di Porta Capena, is a jumble of monastery walls, roofs, and secluded gardens with their dusty oleanders and clusters of round-topped conifers typical of the Italian landscape – and, impossible to miss, the grey ancient stones and arches of the Colosseum, massively surviving the centuries, battered but still almost intact, at the far end of the Roman forum.

My first meeting with John Abbott – tall, tanned, good-looking, straight fair hair brushed back – was when I arrived in Rome for briefing prior to my assignment in Mauritius; he had come down to the foyer to conduct me personally up to his office. In the labyrinth of lifts and corridors it was certainly necessary to have a guide, but he need not have done it himself. Yet it was typical of John that he did: he was one of the most considerate people I have known – indeed, for one's chief, considerate to a fault. He would hardly ever *tell* you to do something. A summons to his office would be "Do you have a moment, Alan?" An order was almost always a suggestion: "Do you think it would be a good idea if . . . ?" he would say, or "Why don't you just . . . ?" Yet he was a complex character, and one was never in any doubt that failure to respond precisely to his hinted requirements would incur a black mark in a private register at the back of his mind. Although he was exceptionally diffident and defensively shy of self-revelation (as many of us are), at a party, or other social occasion lubricated by alcohol, layers of inhibition would drop away and John Abbott became quite a different person. He had a wife, but she apparently lived in California as a research scientist, trying (it was said) to produce a featherless chicken that would revolutionise the economics of broiler production.

John presided over a marketing branch that was largely his own creation. He had a PhD from California and had done research at Oxford in the same institute where I had been a student; he was very much an expert in his field. He had three professional staff when I arrived (making the fourth): Hans Mittendorf and Robert Ellinger, both German; and Hubert Creupelandt, Belgian. Hans I have already introduced, as the man who tried to shunt me off to a post in Latin America. Ruddy-faced, fair curly hair – flaxen we should say, to make it sound Teutonic, because he was definitely cast in the mould of the Übermenschen – almost always with a cheery countenance, Hans exuded confidence, 'positive thinking', and what I can only describe as ruthless bonhomie. To my embarrassment, one of the first tasks I was given to do by Hans (who was second in command to John) was to write a paper, for publication in the official FAO journal, on 'Freeze-drying Agricultural Products'.

I had to confess, "I'm very sorry, Hans – I'm afraid I don't know anything about freeze-drying."

Hans looked at me in astonishment. "Ellen," he said (that's how he always pronounced my name), "you don't need to *know* about it. Just go down into the library and read it up. Do some *research*."

This was my introduction to the occasionally dubious quality of some of the FAO expertise that was authoritatively disseminated throughout the world. In the organisation's extensive library, by dint of digging around in the literature on the subject and scouring current specialist magazines, I was eventually able to cook up a draft which was then circulated to my colleagues for 'peer review'. The article which finally emerged, in three languages, from this fairly rigorous process of discussion and criticism, although I say it myself, was pretty impressive. I hadn't dreamed I could know so much about freeze-drying.

Robert Ellinger, very tall and dark, married to a Canadian, was a different type of German altogether. If Hans was in the tradition of Goethe and Wagner, Robert would probably have seen himself more in the spirit of Thomas Mann and Günter Grass. It was easy (though probably unfair) to imagine Hans, comfortable in his nationality, as an enthusiastic member of the Hitler Youth, but definitely not the questioning, ironic, cosmopolitan Robert Ellinger. He had come to FAO from the Paris-based OECD and, ever restless, was later to move on to the World Bank in Washington. He invited Beryl and me for a meal at his apartment (as flats were invariably called in Rome) on the Via Flaminia, shortly after the family had joined me, and was startlingly frank in criticising the working procedures of FAO, which I was still dutifully, and at that time fairly uncritically, doing my best to master.

"We are in a golden cage," he said, "and we can't get out."

Seeing Robert on his home ground, with his charming piano-playing wife and two young boys fluent in three languages, I could not easily understand why he should be so discontented.

Hubert, the third member of John Abbott's little team, had been my 'subject-matter officer' in Mauritius, the linkman at headquarters with whom I had corresponded, and to whom I had looked for advice and assistance. I'd had no complaints on that score: in my lonely post at the other side of the world, his friendly letters had been a continual source of reassurance and comfort in my daily frustrations. Now he was even more helpful to me: he was, among all his colleagues, the best-integrated into Italian society. FAO professional staff and their families tended to make their social life with each other – unlike the numerous secretaries, who quickly found Italian boyfriends and, outside office hours, disappeared into the local scene. Hubert – and his wife, who positively refused to speak English – were among the few who had mostly Italian friends. An engagingly animated character, he was nevertheless one of those egocentric individuals who are really interested only in matters that concern themselves. A physical-fitness fanatic, he could spend ten minutes in my office enthusiastically describing his excellent progress in workouts or distance jogging, but would make his excuses, saying he had 'something important to attend to', as soon as I tried to talk about something else.

I doubt whether it was Hubert who directed me towards Parioli to find a suitable apartment; he was a brash 'modern man' and had little time for the snobbish conceits of who your neighbours might be. For, although not perhaps the smartest part of the city, Parioli, where we first lived, was associated with 'old money'. The Via Giuseppe Mangili, near the zoo, is a quiet winding street shaded by trees on either side, flanked by the dull shrubbery of small gardens and old abutting walls; and No. 32 was unusual in being a three-storeyed house, not the typical apartment block. Our compact but pleasant two-bedroom apartment on the first floor had parquet floors, and its salotto, or living room, gave on to a terrace that ran round three sides of the building. Our landlord, a bald-headed *ingegnere*, treated with great respect by his dragon of a housekeeper, lived on the ground floor; his daughter, a very smart red-headed woman of nocturnal habits (she was rarely seen during the day), had the top-floor apartment. My first attempt at written Italian was a note to her complaining of the clack clack clack of her footsteps above us at unearthly hours of the night, and politely requesting that she wear carpet slippers after ten o'clock. Whether my request was incomprehensible or merely ignored, I never discovered; but the clacking continued, and I was either too cowardly, or didn't find an opportunity, to confront her in person.

We never discovered the name of Ing. Bruschelli's housekeeper (probably Maria – that sort of person nearly always was): she was simply a baleful presence to be observed (or, more usually, sensed) as we climbed the stairs to our apartment, or descended on our way out. But there was never any doubt of her hostility: whoever had formerly occupied the middle floor of the Bruschelli family home, we were, so far as 'Maria' was concerned, an unwholesome filling in the domestic sandwich. There was an early argument over Jeremy's bicycle, which he had just learned to ride without falling off, and which we insisted on parking in what we thought was a suitable space, tucked unobtrusively under the stairs in the entrance hall.

"No! *Non si puo!*" said Maria, wagging her finger in front of her nose like a windscreen wiper (a typical Italian gesture of negation).

But Beryl was not to be intimidated – well, nor was it possible to lug a bicycle, however small, up the stairs with a baby and the shopping, she responded with spirit in her own inimitable and then still rudimentary Italian.

Maria, totally flummoxed by a *straniera* daring to stand up for herself, retired glowering but shrugging her shoulders, as if to say, "You'll be sorry!"

As indeed we were. A few days later the bicycle was stolen from under the stairs.

Yet in spite of these disagreeable early encounters with the two women of the household (which evolved, as the days passed, into mutually cool indifference) I had a perfectly cordial, though definitely businesslike, relationship with Ing. Bruschelli. What counted with him was solely my suitability as a tenant: on that score, being employed by FAO was in his eyes recommendation enough. For our part, so long as he was happy to have us, we were content to remain there.

I would regularly walk to work across the Villa Borghese park, which in most weathers was delightful in the early morning, with men watering the flower beds and few others about, save for the silent grey statues and busts of Italian heroes and persons of historical significance, impassively ignoring me as I cut across under the trees towards a dark little path which led to the top of the Spanish Steps (later in the day to be crowded with tourists). From there it was a short distance through the narrow Via Condotti (Rome's Bond Street, where the likes of Gucci and Armani displayed their ridiculously priced objects of high fashion) to where I boarded a tram in the Via del Corso. This narrow, exhaust-choked canyon of a street is, to my mind, the epitome of Rome. Starting where the old Roman road to the north meets the city walls at the Piazza del Popolo (formerly a fashionable meeting place for the well-to-do, but now better known as a forum of flag-waving megaphone party politics), it runs in a dead-straight line to the Piazza Venezia and its enormous white marble 'wedding-cake' monument to Victor Emmanuel, first king of unified Italy. My tram skirted the Roman forum and the Colosseum, and then took the same, almost rural, track that I used to walk when billeted at the Woodcock. Getting to work in Rome, even after we moved from Parioli, was on most days an enjoyable experience, quite unlike the tiresome drudgery of commuting into London.

Getting to school – although it would not have been characterised by Jeremy as an enjoyable experience – was at least very convenient. Apart from its pleasant location, a main reason for settling on the Via Giuseppe Mangili was its proximity to St George's English School, where Jeremy was enrolled shortly after Beryl and the children joined me (Hilary was still little more than six months old). St George's occupied an old ducal mansion, or palazzo, which had been converted into a school for mainly expatriate children, by no means all of whom were British. (The headmaster informed parents in one of his reports that their number comprised forty nationalities.) Many of the staff seemed to be young teachers attracted by the idea of living in Rome for a year or two – very agreeable for them, no doubt, but I think it may have been this constant 'churning' of staff which ultimately led to a crisis in parent–teacher relations. I remember attending one PTA meeting at the school, chaired by

David Willey, the BBC Rome correspondent, which practically turned into a riot: parents standing on tables, shouting at the tops of their voices, and teachers yelling back with equal ferocity. That meeting was utter mayhem, and not at all what might have been expected of St George's English School.

Yet these ructions and rumblings of discontent appeared, oddly enough, to have little effect on Jeremy's schooling; his classwork proceeded normally, so far as we could tell. He had his little friends, most of whom seemed to be rather more streetwise than he. Luka, for example, was a graceless oaf famous for having inadvertently – and almost fatally – swallowed an orange whole (peeled, admittedly). Luka, invited to one of Jeremy's birthday parties and having gorged himself on the jellies, cakes and ice cream, etc., would spend the entire party-games time, until his parents came to collect him, reading a book in Jeremy's bedroom. And there was the boy who one day relieved him of his 100-lire pocket money. Jeremy was not particularly upset, but we were outraged.

"Who was this boy? We must make him give it back to you."

Jeremy, puzzled by this strange reaction on our part, hastened to reassure us: "It doesn't matter," he said. "He told me he *needed* it" – as if that were a perfectly reasonable explanation. He added, as further reassurance, "And anyway, it was an old one."

Some children develop a love for money from a very early age; Jeremy never did. He was as happy to give it away (if he had any) as to spend it.

We had not been long settled into the Via Giuseppe Mangili when my father, driven over by Hamish, arrived for a Christmas visit, and was so enchanted by the Italian climate that he stayed on for three months into the new year. Ever urbane and outwardly cheerful, Father showed little obvious evidence of the effect on him of my mother's death. Yet in a married lifetime blessed with hardly any close personal friends, she had been his sole intimate companion for more than forty years; and I think it may perhaps have been an inward premonition he might shortly be following her that contributed to my father's serenity during what was indeed to prove the early part of his last year alive. He liked nothing more than to sit out on our long balcony with its wrought-iron railings at treetop height, soaking up, and marvelling in, the winter sunshine. He had always been a sun worshipper, and being able to sit out in shirtsleeves in December, reading yesterday's English newspaper – or as likely snoozing with it on his lap – was, for him, perfect contentment. He enjoyed Beryl's cooking and the Italian cuisine with its, to him, unaccustomed liberalities of wine; and he definitely appreciated the ready availability of his favourite White Label whisky, which I was able to obtain (duty-free) from the FAO commissary.

When he first arrived we would take him out to see 'the sights'; and Father dutifully allowed himself to be so taken to St Peter's and the Vatican, where he gazed at their splendours with an expression of resigned good humour, as if to say (though he didn't), "Yes, yes, marvellous. Now what about lunch?"

I believe Father would have been quite happy to stay on with us indefinitely: the prospect of returning to an empty Walnut Tree Farmhouse in winter was bleakly unattractive to him, I imagine. But situated as we were, with only two bedrooms – Hilary in with Beryl and me, and Jeremy in the *cantina* (box room) – accommodating a guest necessarily involved a degree of inconvenience to ourselves. Besides, Father was not at all one to muck in; he had his little jobs at home, but it would not have occurred to him to help in someone else's home; and, as ever with him, children were only good-naturedly tolerated so long as they were not a nuisance. So perhaps it was not surprising that Beryl eventually began to see her father-in-law as beginning to show signs of becoming something of an incubus. Yet he was a man of his time – we all of us will seem strange creatures to our grandchildren – and I was moved with pity and self-guilt when finally I saw Father off at Fiumicino Airport, unmistakably feeling that he had been eased out.

Father's departure was soon followed by the arrival of Beryl's mother – an altogether different kind of grandparent, who positively scooped up her grandchildren and enfolded them in matriarchal affection. There was nothing she liked better than to wheel Hilary out in her pushchair, into the Villa Borghese park, or listen contentedly to Jeremy's chatter when he got back from school. Although more appreciative of Roman churches than my father, Mrs Mungavin's consuming interest was her family; and whether she was in Glasgow, Calcutta, Western Australia or Rome, it was all much the same to her. They were part of God's world.

After a year at Villa Mangili, having had time to become more familiar with Rome – and perhaps a bit fed up with the atmosphere chez Bruschelli – we decided to move to an apartment in the Via di Villa Betania, a small street off the Via Aurelia Antica, one of the old Roman roads to the west. Although well inside the outer reaches of the city, the Via Aurelia Antica had a delightful feeling of being almost in the country. Crossing the river, you wind through the narrow, cobbled streets of Trastevere and up on to the hill of Monteverde (again, old houses and trees, much like Parioli) into the Via Aurelia Antica. You pass through a Roman arch with tufts of grass and small bushes growing out of its ancient stonework, and for the first third of a mile or so this is a narrow road, completely shut in on the left-hand side by the high walls of the Villa Doria Pamphili, and for halfway along on the right-hand side by the walls, dark shrubberies and railings of the Russian Embassy. Beyond these was church land, now sold off for the building of modern apartments, spaced out in well-maintained gardens, especially attractive to foreigners. Our building did not have much by way of landscaping, but, being initially on the ground floor, we did have a small private garden; later, when the opportunity arose, we moved up to a better apartment on the second floor with a large terrace overlooking the Villa Doria Pamphili. Unlike the Villa Borghese, which is a public park, the extensive grounds of the Villa Doria Pamphili are private and, from our viewpoint, gloriously left to the rule of nature: the trees, rough parkland and scrub looked much as they might have been for the past two or three hundred years. Yet from this prospect of a rural idyll it now took me little more than fifteen minutes to drive to FAO.

We were very happy at the Villa Betania. Hilary was able to attend a local convent school for infants quite close by; and Jeremy continued at St George's, using the school bus service. After one or two inevitable false starts, Beryl managed to find an excellent 'daily', Gina, and a succession of au pairs or nannies – which gave her time to pursue what eventually was to become an almost full-time occupation as the first secretary of the Rome branch of Oxfam.

As is the way of such things, the Rome branch of Oxfam was started up by the wife of a former British ambassador, through the agency of a member of the Italian aristocracy – in this case the Marchesa Virginia Proto, who became its enthusiastic and devoted president. I hardly knew Virginia Proto, but her name and the names of the other few members of the committee were a constant thread in Beryl's news of the day, after I got back home – rather more entertaining as a counterpoint to my own boring chit-chat. Starting completely from scratch, these admirable ladies threw themselves into the tasks of recruiting a membership, building up stocks of the usual cast-off clothing and bric-a-brac, and taking turns to run a cramped two-room Oxfam shop in the Via del Babuino, no more than 200 yards from the Spanish Steps. I lived with every twist and turn of that saga mercifully at one remove, but Beryl was there in her element. She loved organising things, and for three or four years was the driving force of the Rome branch, as its secretary – but actually, I think, willing-horse-in-chief would have been a more accurate title.

For a large capital city, Rome was surprisingly easy to get out of, and in the early days we would often go to the seaside, although the beaches within easy reach – apart from the popular *stabilimenti*, which are crowded – were typically unattractive, black sand littered with garbage and dreck, the lack of public lavatories everywhere evident. So, later, we would more often take the children out into the countryside to picnic or perhaps eat at a village or roadside trattoria; and it was on these weekend expeditions that we gradually found ourselves, as often as not, in one of the small towns around Lake Bracciano. This is an old volcanic crater, about twelve miles all the way round, in a part of the Lazio region somewhat off the beaten track. The Romans referred to the area disparagingly as '*rustica*', meaning it was unfashionable – OK for peasants, but not the sort of place smart people would want to be seen in; Romans are mad about *bella figura*. Yet it was charming, and the lake big enough to respond visibly to all the changing moods of the weather: sometimes completely calm, reflecting perfectly the sky and surrounding low hills; sometimes, under lowering clouds, flecked white by winds that set small waves crashing on to the shoreline. The country around was mainly vineyards and olive groves, with coppices of sweet chestnut interspersed on difficult hillsides by patches of wild broom, brilliant yellow in season. Bracciano itself, with its ancient castle overlooking the lake, was the main town, the business and municipal centre; Trevignano was where most of the olive-oil pressing was done; and Anguillara, the third of these old Italian towns, which seemed to have grown organically out of the brown volcanic soil, was further along the border of the lake and roughly equidistant from the other two; it had a restaurant famous for eels, from which its name derived.

The quiet simplicity of life at Bracciano appealed to us so much that, when an opportunity arose, we bought a plot of land on the lake shore, less than a mile from Bracciano itself and, at that point, well away from the country road which encircled the lake. It was an old vineyard which had been bought by an architect with the intention of building a house on it. A drawback was that the planning authority (a bit of a joke in Italy) was to expire in two years, after which, under a new law, all building within 200 metres of the lake shore would be absolutely forbidden. Our agent, an engagingly crafty old countryman whose office in the cobbled town square was next to the Bracciano municipality, assured us that, so long as foundations were laid within the two-year period (already partially expired), we could take as long as we liked to complete. This seemed reasonable enough, so we went ahead, engaged an architect and got a local builder to lay substantial foundations about three feet deep. At the same time, we had him put up a boathouse of similar material – tufa blocks. These are large sun-dried bricks of volcanic soil which in the course of time harden to the consistency of rock. Houses built of tufa look comfortably part of the landscape; and our unauthorised boathouse with its traditionally tiled roof blended in nicely. It had large steel doors, admittedly, but they faced the lake and were painted green (and anyway, occasional jarring notes in Arcadia are typically Italian).

Once the boathouse (which we did intend eventually to use as such) was completed, we spent many of our weekends down at the lake. With an excellent stone fireplace, and two storerooms at the back, it was quite comfortable, even in cold weather. Apart from the derelict vineyard (which in the course of time I uprooted, together with its tangle of wire and rotting posts) there was a large fig tree near the shore, four mature olive trees, and, up by the gate to our property, a tree that bore the most delicious cherries I have ever tasted (provided we got to them before the birds or – surely not? – our neighbours). For the children, swimming or rowing about in their rubber boat, it was a release into paradise – as indeed it was for us, too. I have always enjoyed physical work outdoors, and Bracciano, as we rather grandly referred to our half-hectare of land, gave me a marvellously satisfying opportunity to do my own messing about – hacking back a thicket of undergrowth and reeds down at the shore's edge, planting shrubs and trees, mowing grass – and, astonishingly quickly in that fertile soil, eventually gave our little weekend retreat by the lake quite a homely appearance. From the bustle of life in Rome, Bracciano was a haven of warm sunshine and peace – usually.

We discovered the dangers of the shore when Hilary one day trod on a broken bottle in the shallow water, badly cutting her foot. Fortunately, the first-aid facility at Bracciano was astonishingly good: two nurses came practically running to the car as I drew up at the Bracciano *pronto soccorso*, carried Hilary inside, and immediately, without any fuss, had her on a couch for a tetanus jab and stitches – all done in a most efficient and sympathetic manner, and without any of the bureaucratic procedures we had come to expect of Italian officialdom.

Less welcome Italian kindness with children was exhibited on another occasion when Jeremy and Hilary were taken off for a sail by complete strangers. The children would often go over to the neighbouring farm near the road to see the animals and play with the dog; and they were up there one day when an Italian family, in a car towing a yacht on a trailer, stopped by the farm. The children got into conversation and probably looked enviously at the yacht, whereupon they were cheerfully, innocently – and foolishly – invited to "Come along with us." And off they went, miles away to the other side of the lake!

When, sometime later, we walked over to the farm to see what they were up to and why they hadn't come back, we were told, "Oh, they went off with their friends."

"Friends? What friends?"

The question was met with shrugged shoulders, upturned palms, raised eyebrows and the pop-eyed expression that Italians adopt when calmly facing one of God's great mysteries that will no doubt be revealed all in good time.

"Do you mean to say . . . ?"

It was a heart-stopping moment. But no point wasting time asking more questions the farmer's daughter couldn't answer – we dashed up to the Bracciano police station, bitterly blaming the children for being so foolish and ourselves for heedless lack of proper care. I think it was before the time when John Paul Getty's grandson – who was also a pupil at St George's – was kidnapped, but it was easy to imagine it having happened to Jeremy and Hilary. Who else could possibly have taken off two children, ten and six years old, without speaking to their parents? Certainly the police sergeant of the carabinieri took the matter much more seriously than colleagues of his had done on three previous occasions when I'd reported theft (Jeremy's bicycle in Parioli; Hilary's pushchair, carelessly left behind on a beach; and Beryl's handbag, whipped off her shoulder by a speeding moped rider in Trastevere) of articles, admittedly much less important than *two children*.

Of course, it all turned out well in the end. Accompanied by the police car, we arrived back at the farm to find Jeremy and Hilary's 'friends' bidding them a fond farewell after their pleasant sail on the lake. It was a family much like ours – father, mother and two children – whose smiles of kindly pleasure were, I'm afraid, swiftly wiped off their faces by the police sergeant, who gave the parents a suitably severe dressing-down. It was so severe, in fact, that we, overwhelmingly relieved at a safe reunion with our own children, did not find it necessary to add to their discomfiture by pitching in ourselves.

The farmland, which was mainly rough pasture with a few large nectarine trees here and there, ran down one side of our own land. On the other side was a vineyard tended by a red-faced *contadino* (a smallholder, I suppose we would say) named Franco – a thickset, friendly chap, whose pale-ginger (possibly albino) colouring was more English than Italian. Franco was bemused by my meticulous grass mowing with an ordinary rotary mower, but it was one of the few things on which he *didn't* venture to offer an opinion. Like Uncle George's old farm helper, Wilfred Knock, Franco was a countryman who took it for granted that people who lived in the town knew absolutely nothing about the countryside. When I told him I was going to plant some vines for table grapes he at once gave me explicit directions on the depth and spacing of the planting holes, which I followed to the letter. Came the day for actually putting in the cuttings, and there was Franco, leaning on his hoe, looking at me beadily through the chain-link fence between us.

"You're putting them in upside down," he said.

I thought, 'Surely not?' but had to acknowledge he was the expert. . . .

Well, not a single one of those bloody cuttings rooted! I do genuinely believe that this was his neighbourly way of ensuring that (in his estimation) my likely-to-be-ill-tended grapes did not contaminate his own vineyard. More fool me.

Our ownership of land at Bracciano as often as not encouraged others to join us for the day. Our closest friends were Alec and Wanda Zemaitis – Lithuanian Americans. More Lithuanian than American, the Zemaitises were themselves a landed family (Alec said he was a prince, and had a coronet on his business card to prove it) who had become refugees during the war, fleeing from the Russians into Western Germany, where Alec attended Bonn University. He then did three years at Oxford before moving on to America to join Macy's department store in Chicago, employed as I don't know what. But whatever it was, Alec's main idea anyway, in going to America, had been to acquire US citizenship – which eventually he duly did, serving in the Korean War and gaining a war-wound Purple Heart in the process. While Alec (Alexis actually) was going through this graduation and civic apprenticeship, Wanda had been busy producing American citizens-to-be, so that by the time they all arrived in Rome, about two years after we did, there were five smaller Zemaitises, the youngest of whom was still a baby and the eldest, another Alec, about three years older than Jeremy.

There was an earthy, almost peasant directness and simplicity to Alec and Wanda Zemaitis which appealed to us. They had something of a Molly and George quality about them: uprooted characters who have gone cheerfully through hard experience in unusual places, but remain nevertheless anchored in a secure tradition that spans more than a single lifetime. Beryl and Wanda at once hit it off together, and have remained friends ever since. Alec and I had many interests in common, but it was in eating, drinking and carousing – of which, over the years, there was a great deal – that we spent most time together. If there is one person that I associate most with my time in Rome, when I think back on it, it is Alec Zemaitis.

Alec, tall, bearded and good-looking (as he would be the first to acknowledge) was a fascinating character whose carefully cultivated sense of his own significance was mitigated by an engagingly sardonic view of the world and of his fellow man – with whom he was often comically at odds. Wanda and Alec would shout at each other in Lithuanian, and the children – part American, part Lithuanian – would be rude to each other in any one of three languages. Their household was a mixture of ideal home and Gypsy caravan: framed photographs of Alec and Wanda resplendent in robes of the Knights of Jerusalem (or possibly it was some other order of knights of the Cross) in the living room; young Paulus lying fully clothed on an unmade bed, eating biscuits out of the packet, in a bedroom. They were a delightful family, and their friendship was a large part of our life in Rome.

It was not long after my father's return to Walnut Tree Farmhouse that he began to exhibit the first signs of the cancer that was to be his final illness. Hamish, who managed to stay at Bacton with him on most weekends, wrote to me to report of Father, who had been, as usual, watching the evening news: 'a sudden jerking of his right arm', followed by severe pain. I don't think a brain tumour was actually diagnosed at the time – or the suspicion of it may have been merely withheld – but in any event the disease, so far as the family were concerned, followed a distressingly typical course. There were days when he seemed much better. He would write encouraging letters to us – in rather scrawly handwriting – saying how good his appetite was and how he was managing to potter about doing little things, like 'feeding Trigger'. Trigger was a large, boisterous springer spaniel that had belonged to us at Cone Hill, but which we had gladly handed over to my parents when we were posted to Mauritius. As with Joey, the budgerigar at Plashet Road, Father developed a bond of affection with Trigger, and his last days would have been sadder were it not for the companionship of that affectionate and sometimes exasperatingly energetic animal.

But then came another stroke, after which Father partly lost the power of speech, and it became evident that, although able to be up and about, he could no longer safely be left to look after himself. He still had Edith, who came in to 'do' for him, and old Jack in the garden (who taught me, while on one of my 'working visits' to Walnut Tree Farmhouse, how to keep a bonfire of damp garden refuse going for days), but part-time help from the village could not be expected to look after an invalid. So George and Molly, who by then had little else to do, nobly came over from Ireland to stay with him.

When Jack's Farm finally failed – it must have been one of the first of the old English small mixed farms which even government feather-bedding could not save – they had sold up and, with whatever small sum remained after paying off their overdraft, bought an old house near Clifden in Galway; and there, by the river, George and Molly had opened a licensed bed-and-breakfast establishment, advertising it in America as the perfect place in the Emerald Isle to come for the fishing. Sure it was, wouldn't you know! Well, although Molly's cooking could be surprisingly good when she felt like it, her housekeeping standards were likely to have remained much as they had been at Burridge Heath; and while George would have been perfectly happy behind the bar, Mother used to say (on what evidence I don't know, as she never went there – possibly past experience) that he spent too much time sociably carousing with his guests. Unfortunately, an agreeable barman and the occasional half-decent dinner could not compensate for damp mattresses, or desiccated traces of yesterday's meal adhering to one's fork at breakfast; and there is a limit to the tolerance that rich Americans will allow for the idiosyncrasies of old Ireland – especially if they come without an Irish accent. In the end, therefore, that venture into the tourist industry became, after about three years, yet another of George and Molly's enjoyably interesting failures; and so they moved off to County Cork, where they bought a hovel without a roof, mended the roof and kept goats. That is what they were doing when they answered the call to come and stay with Father (leaving the goats to the care of their daughter Betty and her birdwatching husband, Joe).

Father did not die at home; and to this day I do not know why he had to be moved to the hospital in Ipswich – perhaps for tests; we were no doubt guided by his doctors. But I look back with sadness on his last day in that old house, where he and Mother had at last found peace – alas, for so short a time. I had flown over from Rome for the weekend, and was sitting with him in their bedroom with its low beams and narrow windows looking out over the fields of the Suffolk countryside.

Father had never spoken to me of his addiction to morphine, until – I think it must have been two or three weeks previously, on an earlier flying visit – between the long silences (he could barely speak) he had said, apropos nothing, "Well . . . you know I gave it up . . . the morphine."

I wish I could have made a fitting response, but I was unable to make any reply. After so many years of unacknowledged reticence about the elephant in our drawing room, I was too emotionally buttoned up against it to respond adequately. Yet Father knew me well enough, I believe, to be satisfied simply to have made the declaration – and know that I had heard it.

But now, on that last visit, we were waiting for the ambulance to take him to the hospital. He was coughing a lot, his chest wheezy with phlegm which I literally had to pull from his mouth with tissues. Although in retrospect I find this image revolting, at the time it felt quite natural; which says something about the way we behave in extremity. I remember speaking enthusiastically about yoga, which I was beginning to take up.

I said to him, "You know how sometimes you feel imprisoned within your ribcage? Well, the yoga method of breathing allows you to escape from the cage."

Father looked at me intently, with great understanding, and I wondered whether he was thinking I might have hit on something that he had himself been seeking, but had the misfortune to find by another route.

Then the ambulance arrived, and two burly attendants clumped up the stairs with a canvas stretcher, their sudden presence in the room a graceless intrusion (Molly or George must have let them in). Father gave a little moan of protest, but with a few routine jollying words ("Don't you worry now, you'll be all right," or something equally comfortless) and remorseless professionalism the men pulled back his bedclothes and carefully rolled him on to the stretcher, which they then manoeuvred down the narrow staircase as if what they had come for might just have been a valuable carpet going out for cleaning. I saw Father's distressed face as they took him down and out into the ambulance, and wretchedly felt his anguish. I travelled with him in the back of the ambulance to the hospital and, with Hamish, followed while he was trundled down corridors and into quite a pleasant little single room by himself. I don't think we stayed long. I remember kissing him on the forehead – something I'd not done since I was a child – and leaving for Rome with a heavy heart, knowing that I might not see him again alive.

And nor did I. It can't have been more than about two weeks later that Hamish phoned to say Father had died, quite peacefully. As it happened, I was at the time taking part in a production of the FAO theatre group (an after-hours activity) which was due to open for three performances on the nights immediately preceding the funeral. Father could hardly have chosen a more awkward time to go. Our producer was aghast at the prospect that I should pull out (sans understudy) at the last moment. We were playing *The Cocktail Party* by T. S. Eliot, and I was Peter, a young man who (offstage) goes out to a tropical country, where he is eventually crucified by the natives. Had it been any other kind of play, I couldn't have gone ahead with it; but the 'seriousness' of this one was oddly appropriate, and, since Hamish was making all the arrangements at Bacton, I allowed myself to be persuaded to stay with the cast and play the part.

Strangely, I have no recollection at all of my father's funeral – perhaps because it was in the same church as Mother's, and I confuse the two.

27 – FAO

For an FAO staff member, Rome was the plummiest of plum postings: all the amenities, with the fascination of an ancient capital city only two hours from London; and instead of having uncertain employment on a fixed-term project, I now had a permanent contract. So far, my relations with Rome had been little different from the long-distance links with Dar es Salaam when I was in the Colonial Service, posted out to Songea or Mbeya.

The Food and Agriculture Organisation (FAO) as an agency of the United Nations was established after the war, in 1945, to help its member countries tackle the scourges of hunger and malnutrition. It had started off in Washington, with a craggy pipe-smoking Scot, Sir John Boyd Orr, as its first director general; and then, on receiving from the Italian Government an offer of accommodation too good to refuse, it had moved to Rome. An impressively large building had been erected on a prime site shortly before the war by Mussolini, as a suitably grand headquarters of his intended new Roman Empire. So now, with no empire remaining to a defeated Italy, this massive building was occupied by an FAO headquarters staff of about 1,200 international civil servants, having roughly another 2,000 'experts' (such as I had been in Mauritius) stationed out in 'the field'.

The director general when I joined it was B. R. Sen, a distinguished Indian diplomat who was obsessed with the nightmare of impending world starvation – an understandable obsession, bearing in mind his personal experience of the seething millions of the poor in India who genuinely were in that condition. As it happened, the 'Green Revolution' advances in plant breeding (chiefly of wheat and rice), by permitting vast increases in crop yield, in the event largely averted that catastrophe – at least on a worldwide scale. Nevertheless, when I joined the organisation it was the spectre of world hunger that dominated a huge range of its activities. These ran from 'hands-on' things like the international Desert Locust Campaign (tracking swarms and destroying their breeding grounds), irrigation projects, land reclamation, animal husbandry, plant production, storage and processing, and extended to forestry and fisheries as the wider implications of rural development became evident. The corridors and meeting rooms of FAO teemed with politicians and boffins from all over the world.

My post at headquarters, when I joined it, was in the Economic Analysis Division, whose director was a chain-smoking Englishman named Barter. Dr Barter, who looked rather like Eric Morecambe (of Morecambe and Wise), had been a senior civil servant in the British Ministry of Food during the war; a languidly clever man, he presided over a division whose senior staff were almost all British – rather odd, you might think, in an organisation that recruited from virtually all the countries in the world. Yet that was how things worked when I first joined FAO. If economics had been cornered by the Brits, nutrition, for example, was a preserve of the French, and statistics a happy hunting ground of the Indians. The field programme (that is, all the projects out-posted from Rome) was also run very much on an old-boy basis. A project would be cooked up – or 'formulated', as we would say officially – by somebody in one of the technical divisions keen to improve his (rarely her) standing with his superiors, who, if impressed by the number of noughts after the dollar sign, would then have to convince one Karl Olsen, FAO's chief of 'programme co-ordination', that the project was feasible. In the mind of the eager headquarters progenitor, 'feasible' meant 'Will New York cough up the money to finance my brilliant scheme?'

In the mind of Karl Olsen the question was more likely to be 'Who is this guy, and does he know what he's talking about?'

Olsen was an Americanised Swede, or Swedish American, a tall, lean man with an engagingly pleasant manner and an amazing capacity for work. With two equally hard-working secretaries, he performed a function in the organisation which, five years later, would occupy the attention of two whole divisions. Of course, corners were cut; they *had* to be cut when literally *all* the projects submitted to New York for funding were channelled through one man. You'd get a call to go with your chief to Olsen's office, and there he'd be, sitting behind his desk in his stockinged feet (he hated wearing shoes), talking to somebody on the phone in Laos or Afghanistan, or Upper Volta, perhaps. While this was going on, he'd be looking through the papers on his desk; and then, with the phone hardly put down, he would immediately launch into an animated discussion of your project with as much authority as if he had drawn it up himself – in fact, with *more* authority, as he was quite likely to know more about the country in question than you did.

If Karl thought the project was OK he'd send it on with his comments to one Myer Cohen, a senior executive officer of the UN Technical Assistance Board in New York. I don't know what sort of a staff Cohen had in New York – probably, in those days, not much more than Olsen in Rome – but incredibly, bearing in mind that he had to deal with proposals coming in from many of the other UN agencies (ILO, WHO, UNESCO, etc.), Cohen would have an opinion or comment to offer in return, before approving the necessary funds. 'Dear Karl' and 'Dear Myer' were not exactly inspired amateurs, but they recognised no limits to the depth of interest they were prepared to take in the details of project proposals that streamed uniquely through their offices for their personal scrutiny. It was these two men, operating quite informally, without any bureaucracy, who masterminded the release of literally millions and millions of dollars for FAO's programmes throughout the world. But the days of control by dedicated professionals and a few omnifarious administrators were about to end.

Between 1968 and 1970, there was a great upheaval in the UN system. The old-boy network (which in some ways had worked well) was broken up, and the 'managers' were brought in. For FAO, this meant that, instead of John Abbott being responsible for all the UN agricultural marketing projects in the world, he would now be responsible for *none* of them: he and his staff would merely provide technical support to a headquarters administrator who would look after *all* the agricultural projects in one country. This sort of 'managerial revolution' is well known: the BBC had it with John Birt's hated reforms; the National Health Service has it with its hated managers telling the doctors what to do; British Rail got fat-cat accountants instead of engineers to run trains. Thus it was, in the first stage of FAO's version of this 'efficiency enhancement' makeover, that I drew the short straw in the Marketing Branch, and, instead of being a marketing specialist, I now became a hated manager – in FAO-speak, an 'operations officer'. In this capacity I was charged with headquarters responsibility for all 'rural institutions' projects in English-speaking Africa and francophone North Africa, only a few of which had I visited before.

My new chief was Don Kimmel, an American 'good ol' boy' (with an English wife), who presided over weekly meetings (no such formalities with John Abbott) with great joviality and good nature. He had a great booming voice and, unintentionally, put on a fair impersonation of John Wayne (in more amiable mood). He made great play of 'kicking ass' when things went wrong, but was really a bit of a softie, and his 'world' team (about eight of us) was given – for all the regular weekly 'reviews' – a pretty free rein. Rural institutions comprised things like farm management, agricultural extension, credit, marketing, storage, etc.; but apart from a project in Uganda, which I shall mention shortly, I now recall little of the technical aspects of my work at that time. It is the countries themselves, their people, and the FAO staff that served in them, that I shall always remember, many of them with much affection. This was a period when most African countries were exulting in a recent achievement of political independence; for most of them it was a period of huge optimism and relative peace. Yet looking back now, after more than fifty years, during which something like three generations of Africa's politicians have held their countries' destinies in their own hands, the present reality in many of them – of poverty, war and disease – contrasts dismally with those hopes.

Ghana was the first British colony to get its independence, in 1957. Ten years later its first president, Kwame Nkrumah, was deposed in a military coup, leaving behind him a veritable herd of 'white elephants' – ambitious agro-industrial projects (modern abattoirs, canning plants, etc.) completely out of kilter with the country's needs – whose ruinously expensive failure to achieve their objectives our man on the spot, Eberhard Reusse, took an almost sadistic delight in analysing in exhaustive detail. I too, it must be admitted, took a self-indulgent pleasure in the (as I now feel it must have been) somewhat arid correspondence that we batted back and forth between Rome and Accra; and when Reusse was himself later posted to Rome, we became quite friendly. With his red and straggly beard, there was an engagingly Bohemian quality about Reusse (educated Germans don't use Christian names with each other) which I found attractive – *simpatico*, as the Italians would say. And for all his German intellectual fastidiousness, he seemed to devote much of his often mysterious social life to indulging a prodigious appetite for food and women. Jeremy innocently made a disconcertingly apposite comment – which children have a habit of doing – when Reusse was at lunch with us one day.

Intently watching the spectacle of a bearded Reusse spooning up soup opposite him at the table (and after some thought) our ten-year-old son solemnly told him, "You eat like a dog."

Politically correct behaviour – even if, as on that occasion, it did not apply to every member of one's own family – was nevertheless most strictly enjoined upon all UN civil servants. Words or deeds likely to offend anyone of another nationality or race were the FAO equivalent of swearing in church. Former Colonial Service officers, such as I was, were sometimes felt by their very presence to be offensive, by reminding formerly 'subject people' of their previous lowly status; so we had to be especially careful. On my first and only visit to Nigeria, when it was on the verge of descending into the calamitous war of Biafra's attempt to secede, I was tactfully reproved by our senior FAO representative there, a Dutchman named Van der Meulen (himself an ex-colonial), for wearing shorts. In East Africa we had almost always worn short trousers with long stockings; and in Lagos, where the climate was even hotter, I had sensibly continued the habit. But no: in West Africa, shorts, however comfortable, were a symbol of colonialism. And indeed it seemed they were: Africans in the first flush of new authority were incredibly thin-skinned.

A typical feature of newly independent countries was a servile press. Politicians were deferred to, and members of the government given vast quantities of column inches for whatever routine public duty they happened to be performing. As for the President, his photograph would appear daily, his every pronouncement reported at length and praised in the leader columns as if it were the word of God Almighty (as, in some respects, it might as well have been). It was often pretty nauseating stuff, but UN staff were supposed to take it all as a matter of course. One FAO man in Nigeria didn't, and paid the price. Reading a local paper one day in his office, this chap was so incensed by the sycophantic rubbish he was reading that he crumpled the offending rag into a ball and flung it with an oath of disgust into a corner of the room. That momentary act of fury was observed, and within days the unfortunate man was declared persona non grata and expelled from the country.

In most Arab countries, for 'colonialism' substitute 'Israel'. Syd Galpin, an FAO marketing specialist charged with setting up a canning plant for tomatoes in Libya, found that the job required him to operate from a caravan, and that the best place to park it was an oasis in the Libyan desert. This was shortly after Colonel Gaddafi, at the head of a military junta, had deposed King Idris; and the sight of one laconic Englishman living out in the desert under the palm trees, on the pretext of canning tomatoes, excited extreme suspicion – albeit that he was there under an official arrangement with the government. Spies were sent to investigate and, to Galpin's surprise and embarrassment, discovered in his rubbish pit . . . empty cans! Unfortunately, these were not ordinary cans – or, at least, not all of them were ordinary cans – for on the base of at least two or three of them were stamped the fateful words 'Made in Israel'. It was enough. Galpin was unable to explain how the cans got into his rubbish pit. All he could say was that he had certainly not ordered anything from Israel, cans or canned products. All in vain. The government wanted Galpin out, and out he was brought. Whether he was set up or merely unlucky, we never knew. The merest taint of Israel in an Arab country was implicitly understood by FAO to be regarded as insulting, and there was no point in arguing.

For the most part, though, FAO staff integrated well with their host countries and were often accorded privileged status – not always entirely deserved. In Algeria, after the French had been kicked out, but before the country had descended into a virtual civil war with dreadful massacring of innocents, we had quite a big project devoted to the training of what were known as agricultural technicians. The project manager was an Irishman named Kehoe, whose previous experience had been as agricultural correspondent for an Irish newspaper. A man of learning and cultivated tastes, he was a delightful fellow, if somewhat at sea in the brash political climate of Algeria (though he spoke good French). He gave the impression of being happier to talk about the works of W. B. Yeats or James Joyce than, say, audiovisual assistance to animal husbandry, which was part of his project's remit. Well, Kehoe's wife most regrettably ran into an Algerian cyclist one day, killing him outright; apparently the poor man rode out of a side road straight into the path of her car. Mrs Kehoe being French, the police apparently took some satisfaction in confiscating her passport and informing her that she was to be charged with manslaughter. Weeks and months passed without anything happening; the impending court case hanging over his wife's head was causing them both increasing worry – until the day when Kehoe's administrative officer, a Syrian Armenian of legendary resourcefulness, came into his office and, with some pride, handed him the confiscated passport.

"That cost you two bottles of whisky," he said.

And the court case?

"Let's just forget it: the police now agree the man committed suicide."

Sierra Leone, Liberia and Somalia, while they were in my sphere of duty, were, like Algeria at the time, perfectly peaceful countries; yet within just a few years all three were also to be ravaged by dreadful warfare and carnage. Sierra Leone's capital, Freetown, standing up from the seashore, still had, with its trees and colonial-style buildings, a comfortable atmosphere of the old British administration. I went with our marketing man there, an elderly Israeli named Zur, to a rice project upcountry, and apart from the suffocating heat it might have been in East Africa. Perhaps an augury of the later breakdown of civil order, Zur, poor chap, had just had his house broken into. The burglars had made off with his entire wardrobe, leaving him only the clothes he stood up in. Though obviously upset, he wasn't making much of it. It was a mark of seasoned UN staff philosophically to accept conditions in their country of post as they were. You could become exasperated; you could – and sometimes did – have a stand-up row with your government opposite number (known as one's 'counterpart'); but, if you were of the right material, you did not inveigh generally against the country and its people. I was later to meet Mr Zur in happier circumstances when, on a conference trip to Israel with Hans Mittendorf, we were invited for a meal at his house in Haifa, and to meet his wife, who had not been with him in Sierra Leone. It was not unusual for FAO staff to leave their wives at home, especially on less salubrious postings.

Liberia, further down the coast, while topographically similar to Sierra Leone, bore distinct signs of American influence: natural enough, as it had been virtually a colony of the Firestone rubber company. Vast swathes of land were given over to rubber trees, and occasionally you'd come across a pleasant clearing with tidy lawns and red-tiled buildings belonging to the company. My business, though, was with the University of Monrovia, where we had a team helping to establish a faculty of agriculture and forestry. It was a project in which Don Kimmel, appropriately enough, took an especial interest – its project manager was a close friend, the venerable Dr Ma from Taiwan, virulently anti-communist, whose doctorate was from Berkeley, California. Dr Ma was not only venerable and a friend of Dr Kimmel; he was also famous, and had been in Monrovia for the past seven years. He was, therefore, one of that rare breed of project managers whom nobody, but nobody, presumed to tell what to do. In 1980 Liberia's government was overthrown by a military coup and the country descended into bloody civil war; but by that time I imagine Dr Ma would have been safely out of the country, his mission accomplished. I hope the faculty of agriculture and forestry has survived.

If Africa's post-independence rivalries had not at this time yet broken out into bloody civil conflict, the continent was on the other hand very much an arena where another kind of war was being played out: the Cold War between a hard-line Soviet Union and the West – and nowhere more so than in Somalia (a country the Americans were not quickly going to forget). A land of proud nomadic tribesmen whose wealth was counted in camels, sheep and goats, it did not in itself have a great deal to offer; but situated as it is on the Horn of Africa, I suppose it was strategically important. And for me, too, Somalia strikes several oddly persistent chords of memory, centred mostly on Mogadishu, the tumbledown port that serves as the capital of what had been Italian Somaliland. Partly, I have to confess, it was the seashore and the UN beach hut (with a bar, sort of) where staff members and their families would congregate in the afternoons. After a sweaty day of meetings in government offices, or bumping about in over-sprung Japanese four-wheel-drive vehicles, it was delightful to go for a swim followed by a walk up and down that long open strand, practically deserted except perhaps for a few lithe Somalis splashing about in the waves; then just to lie back in a deckchair with a beer, idly observing the well-fed Russian families promenading up and down the beach in their wasp-striped bathing costumes. Although they were apparently forbidden to talk to westerners, one or two brave souls did occasionally exchange a few words.

That at least was an improvement on the Chinese, who were (rather charmingly, I thought) building a 'national theatre' for the Somalis – although their manner of doing it did not win them any friends. Chinese foreign-aid projects had a character all their own. There was never any question of working with counterparts: for the Chinese there was to be *no* communication with *any* foreign nationals – not even those of the host country. *Everything* was to be done with Chinese staff. In that spirit, thousands of Chinese labourers had been shipped over to East Africa to build the 'Tanzam' railway between Dar es Salaam and Zambia; and here too, in Mogadishu, the theatre was being built wholly with Chinese labour billeted within the Chinese Embassy. Every morning, the gates would open and fifty or so Chinese masons, carpenters, plumbers, tea boys, etc., would march out to the building site; and in the evening they would all march back and disappear within the walls of the embassy compound, until the next day.

Our main project in Somalia was to set up a grain-marketing organisation, mainly for sorghum produced in the Baidoa Plain; and potentially also for imported rice, as an agent of the World Food Programme. Our project manager was Richard Kelly, one of the most interesting men I have known, who was to become a good friend. He had been general manager of the Rice Board in Malaysia, so his appointment to a considerably less important (though equivalent, and possibly better paid) job in Somalia was something of a comedown. It was characteristic of Richard that this did not weigh with him in the slightest; massively self-contained, he was the essence of imperturbability. I met him first in Rome, when he was a candidate for the post in Somalia: a tropically yellow-tanned man of medium height who, with his prominent chin and nose, looked rather like Mr Punch. He entered my room with a sort of slow, loping gait. Although it was I who was sizing him up for the job, his demeanour, looking at me under veiled eyes, with an expression somewhere between faint amusement and contempt, was that of a spectator, only mildly interested in the outcome of our meeting. Regrettably for his reputation at FAO headquarters, Richard's attitude to his project in Somalia appeared to be similarly disinterested. One felt he had a profound understanding of the Somalis – indeed, in many ways he admired them – and he knew exactly what had to be done to get his project operational, but he also knew why it might fail and, unforgivably for an international civil servant, he wasn't inclined to accentuate the positive. Getting a reputation for being negative in FAO was fatal for one's prospects.

In a limited sense (it did not stick) I too once had a 'negativity' label attached to me. I was asked to attend a meeting with the chief of FAO's link with the World Bank – a beefy no-nonsense Greek – to brief him on investment possibilities in Mauritius. What they didn't tell me was that this was an interview for my possible assignment to that group – which I would have welcomed, had I known about it. Quite a bit of the conversation, I remember, was about Graff's disastrous scheme for milk, and that probably coloured the impression I conveyed. In any event, Hans told me afterwards that Henry Ergas, the World Bank link, found me 'too negative'. This was a pity, because that assignment would have got me a little sooner out of the tedium of administration.

I did, though, sometime later manage to arrange for myself a small project which got me back into my own field for a couple of months. I had been looking for a consultant to make recommendations for the development of cotton-ginning in Uganda, and after several possible appointments had fallen through, for one reason or another, I thought, 'You can do this yourself – why not?' Being away from headquarters for three or four weeks on duty travel was quite normal (two of us worked in tandem, covering for each other as necessary), so it only needed a little persuasion to get Don's agreement (and my opposite number's resigned acceptance) and I was translated to Kampala for two fascinating months. Based there in a spartan room near the noisy swimming pool of a Greek-owned hotel, eating pawpaw, tasteless bacon, India-rubber eggs and half-burnt toast for breakfast, I again felt completely at home.

Although I knew little about cotton when I arrived in Uganda, the industry was organised on the same lines – through cooperative societies under the general direction of a marketing board – as in Tanganyika. Uganda had achieved independence in 1962 – one year after Tanganyika – and the new African government, having shuffled off most of its remaining British Colonial Service officers, was beginning to chafe at the continuing economic power of its relatively large and long-established Asian population. Virtually all Ugandan business – with one important exception – was owned and operated by Indians, Sikhs and Muslims whose ancestors had been brought over from India and what is now Pakistan, to work on the pioneering railway from Mombasa to Jinja, on Lake Victoria. The exception – or exceptions, rather – were the farmers' cooperatives. Uganda had two main cash crops, of which cotton was one (the other was coffee), and the farmers resented having to deliver it to ginneries (to separate the seed from raw cotton) owned and operated by Asians. They were demanding, with increasing vehemence, that all the ginneries should be taken over by the cooperative unions. My task was to see how that might equitably be achieved, but the report I submitted at the end of this assignment, proposing, as I thought, an elegant solution, was already too late.

The tragedy of the Ugandan Asians, who about five or six years later were to be expelled en masse from the country in which most of them had been born, was still ahead of them; but the prejudice and animosity they excited among the African population were everywhere evident. And, it has to be admitted, for the most part they did not do much to make themselves liked. A ginnery, full of noise and dust, typically a large corrugated-iron building stuck out in a cotton-growing area, might be managed by a single Asian, living a spartan existence alone in an African village. Completely isolated and miles from any possible assistance, he would nonetheless find it natural to yell at his labourers in much the same way as Chummy Lockwood shouted at his in Songea. Valuable as their entrepreneurial talents were in East Africa, you could understand why the Asians were disliked: on the whole (there were exceptions, of course) they had little respect for Africans; and so long as their relationship with them remained that of boss and worker, most Asians saw no reason to change an opinion of their employees as a pretty shiftless lot who didn't have the gumption (as *they* had) to do better for themselves. The redeeming feature, though, was that the Asians weren't *racists*; their contempt was merely that of one human being for another, and had nothing in common with the poisonous disregard, in South Africa, of Boer for 'kaffir' (which didn't even have a capital letter to give it dignity).

Lesotho is one of those little 'enclave' countries – entirely surrounded by South Africa. To get there one had to fly to Johannesburg and then, normally, proceed from there by road. At the time, South Africa was still under its rigid apartheid regime, and UN agencies were looked on by the Nationalist government with extreme disfavour. Anyone travelling to Lesotho whose nationality made them persona non grata with the Boer authorities – for example, anyone from a communist country, or foolish enough to travel using a UN laissez-passer – was forced to fly into Maseru, the capital, by charter plane, rather than contaminate the soil of South Africa with their filthy presence. Lesotho was legally an independent country, but in practice it was totally subordinate to

South Africa, where a large proportion of its male population found employment in the mines.

The Ministry of Agriculture people in Maseru had, with touching consideration, booked me into a hotel on the South African side of the border, just a mile or so from it; but the first night there was enough. The 'race' atmosphere was palpably threatening: it was not just that all the guests were white and all the servants black (that was common enough in Africa); it was the cold, disregarding, impersonal attitude to the blacks that I found literally intolerable. So, instead of, absurdly, commuting daily across the border, I shifted to less comfortable but much more congenial quarters in Lesotho's university at Roma, whose simple single-storey buildings in a rough, grassy campus were a modest symbol of the ambitions of an independent country. From there, I remember going out sketching. The country is scenically beautiful, with lowlands, foothills and mountains; and many of the people, with wide-brimmed hats on their heads, ride about on horses, more like South America than Africa. I forget what I was supposed to be doing there – a promising idea for developing a mohair wool industry occupied some of my time – but I remember being shown, on a remote hillside, the foundations and half-built stone walls of what was to be a vast observatory. This was the probably never-to-be-completed life's work of a Swiss missionary – an obsessively single-minded man with obvious talents in fundraising and masonry, but otherwise clearly demented. I was told he wanted to get an advance look at God in heaven before eventually arriving naturally in His presence. Africa was perfect territory for eccentric hermits.

These snapshot references to some of the countries I was dealing with in that vast, and now sadly disregarded, continent are intended simply to give an impression of my field of duty while I was working as a country project officer. For most of that first stint in Rome, however, under the rumbustious leadership of Don Kimmel, I was a bureaucrat, in contact with them but far from the scenes of action: constantly on the phone, dictating memoranda, attending meetings, chasing targets. Apart from intermittent, fairly short country visits, it was mainly my correspondence with 'the field', and the refreshing visits of project officers 'passing through', that offered glimpses of what all this was in aid of, so to speak. Some people thrive in an office environment – the bureaucratic tidiness of dealing with a variety of different matters in a uniform way, according to prescribed regulations, appeals to their sense of order. And it has the distinct advantage that you are within spitting distance of 'the seats of power': the ladders of promotion are almost entirely located at headquarters. But I have always approached work in a critical spirit with a view to doing things, as I thought, better (grit in the oyster, or sand in the machine; decide for yourself) and in spite of the material advantages, I was never wholly comfortable simply to busily beaver away while waiting for my Buggins' turn to achieve a grade step-up.

So when, one day, Don asked me, quite out of the blue, "How would you like to take Hudson's job in Tehran?" I should not have been quite so surprised.

Not that I think Don wanted positively to get rid of me: Claude Hudson was project manager of the Centre for Agricultural Marketing Development in Iran – a post very much up my street from a professional point of view. I wondered what Beryl would think of going out to live in Tehran, and said I'd check first with her, because I would definitely not have agreed to go out alone. At the time we were very comfortably settled in our apartment on the Via Aurelia Antica; Beryl was happily occupied with her Oxfam work; Jeremy, after a rather miserable first term, was now at least philosophically reconciled to boarding at Betteshanger prep school in Kent under an excellent headmaster (Gerald Peacock); and Hilary was, in turn, herself now at St George's. I put the proposal to Beryl that evening much as Don had put it to me, and she immediately welcomed it with enthusiasm. Everyone was surprising me.

The next day I told Don Kimmel, "Yes, OK. I'll go."

28 – IRAN

In Tehran I was taking over from Claude Hudson, an august Canadian professor, who had started up the project about a year previously but now concluded he preferred the pastures of North American academia to the hassle of dealing with Iranian government departments. As a greenhorn project manager myself, I was therefore fortunate in finding already done most of the spadework of getting the Centre for Agricultural Marketing Development on the road, so to speak, and a nucleus of the project team recruited and in place. We were not short of advice, therefore, when, installed for the first few weeks in the very Persian Hotel Keyhan, it came to looking for a suitable house to rent. I think it was probably Susie Etebar who was the guiding hand which led us to settle on the Tehran home of Dr Kianpur, at that time Governor of Esfahan. Susie, whose carefully made-up face, hooded eyes and languidly thin figure conveyed a suggestion of the femme fatale, was the project manager's secretary and herself, as the daughter of a former government minister, a person of some consequence in the circle of people surrounding the people surrounding the Shah.

Dr Kianpur's was a two-storeyed flat-roofed house within a walled garden, with poplar trees running along one side and a tangle of high climbing roses on the other. It was fairly typical of the new houses then being built by the more prosperous Iranians in the huddle of traditional villages to the north of the city. Looking out on the garden from a covered terrace, to the right was a small lawn, and to the left – an unlooked-for luxury – a good-sized swimming pool. This house, on a dusty unmade road through the village of

Gholhak, on the lower slopes of the Elburz Mountains above Tehran, was to be our home for the next three years.

We – Beryl, Hilary and I – had driven out by car: a fascinating and, in the mountains, occasionally hair-raising six-day journey through Greece and Turkey. With only a primary English school in Tehran, we'd had to leave Jeremy behind at Betteshanger prep school, under the care of Gerald Peacock, its headmaster. Poor little chap, Jeremy had not at first taken at all kindly to being (dumped?) at boarding school; but it was a system through which both Beryl and I had been ourselves brought up, and which we – perhaps inconsiderately (since I could perhaps have ordered my life otherwise) – regarded as an ineluctable choice. Hilary, meanwhile, was enrolled at the Tehran English School and conveniently picked up in the mornings by a school bus, leaving Beryl alone in the house to acquire an education of her own from our maid, Batua.

Iran is a big country: to travel by road from the border of Russia's Azerbaijan province in the top left-hand corner of the map, to Chabahar, near the mouth of the Persian Gulf in the bottom right, is a journey of more than 2,000 miles. It is also a very old country, with a recorded history of more than 2,500 years. So for me, coming to it for the first time, it was a revelation to discover the strong cultural identity of the people (who are *not* Arabs, except for some in the south-west) and how secure they are, as a nation, in their ways. As Beryl very quickly learned, in Iran you do not tell your maid how to do her work: *she* tells *you* how it is done. It was in the course of picking up this lesson that we lost our first domestic help – a dominating woman, who quite soon resigned from our employment in exasperation. Batua, who followed her, though equally disinclined to be taught how to do her job, was a gentle and altogether pleasanter character, and she quickly established a good relationship with the mistress of the house. We have had many servants during our time abroad, but, uniquely in my experience, Iranian servants insisted on moral equality with their employers – yet without challenge to the status of either. In that, they exemplify what is probably a characteristic of feudal society: for the exploited 'lower orders' to refrain from rebellion, and serve their lord and master faithfully and cheerfully, they have to be given at least *dignity*. And in Iran, for all that the Shah had inaugurated what he called the White Revolution, which had introduced an element of land reform to the country, it was still at that time essentially a feudal society: many villages – and virtually also their inhabitants – were still owned by rich landlords.

Having a brief that covered all agricultural activity in Iran, the project gave me an opportunity to travel frequently – although an early trip out of Tehran to Gorgan, in the province of Mazanderan, was not typical: over the Elburz Mountains (passing newly developed ski slopes on the way) and down by the Caspian Sea. As it happened, I was accompanied by Richard Kelly, who had been transferred from Mogadishu. Mazanderan is quite different from the other regions – you could almost call it Iran's riviera – with paddy fields, cotton, tobacco and tea plantations, mulberry (food for silkworms), olive groves and citrus orchards. It was not at all the Persia of Omar Khayyám (apart, perhaps, from caviar and the silkworms) that I had imagined. It was a surprise, also, to find that many producers in the north of the country were big farmers, with settled estates of many hectares, which put me in mind of late-nineteenth-century Russia as described by Tolstoy and Turgenev. We were aiming to gather information about cotton production in the area (government statistics were hopeless) and stopped at one large farm known to Richard – a cluster of ancient buildings and tall trees among an expanse of fields, where a binder rather like my Uncle George's was harvesting maize, its sails turning against the sky. Although quite unexpected, we were immediately invited in for lunch.

There must have been about fifteen who sat down to the meal around one enormous table. Our host, who with his son spoke good English, was joined by what was probably all the significant male household – some family, some senior estate workers. Most of the women were bustling about, bringing a great array of food and serving at the table, though an ancient mother and a daughter-in-law (French, apparently) were seated with us. I was struck by the great variety of what there was to eat: large platters with mounds of rice, some with saffron, some plain or mixed with raisins and pimento nuts; tureens with lamb or chicken stew; bowls of sabzi (green vegetables); dishes of different relishes; basins full of the most delicious yoghourt I'd ever tasted; and of course, without which no Iranian meal is complete, vast quantities of freshly baked bread. It was a veritable feast, yet in its simplicity and atmosphere of relaxed hospitality appeared to be a perfectly ordinary occasion. Our presence – apart from the courtesy of English being spoken to us by those who could – seemingly made very little difference to what would have been a normal midday meal in that establishment.

Looking back now on that scene of feudal domesticity – masters and workers alike at table (I was to find that sitting cross-legged on a carpet was more usual), both high and low exchanging conversation and banter with each other on terms of easy familiarity – it is sobering to think that, only eight years later, their whole society was to fall apart with the most devastating consequences for the character of the country and Iran's relations with the rest of the world. At the time of our arrival in Tehran, in 1971, Muhammad Reza Pahlavi, Shah of Iran, was at the peak of his power. An urbane, relatively youthful-looking man with a beautiful wife (his third), he considered himself – and was generally considered by Western governments – to be an enlightened and progressive monarch. Yet he was an autocrat; his government (including our landlord) hand-picked cronies, the majlis (parliament) filled with placemen. What made the charade 'acceptable' was the Shah's diplomatic skill in managing to stay on good terms with both America and Russia, his powerful neighbour to the north. And socially he was a very smooth customer, friendly with the royal families of Europe – including our own – and as comfortable in the south of France as he was in his various palaces at home.

We in the UN knew very well what sort of society this was: my project was established within a government ministry; our co-workers (our counterparts) were Iranian civil servants. These young, recently graduated men and women were attached to us in an in-service training capacity, and through them we learned a great deal about the great sham of 'progressive' Iran. Speaking in English to foreigners, many of them felt freer to open up to us than they might, perhaps, even to their friends. They had good reason to be cautious: the elite which ruled Iran was generous in its benefits to the middle classes (from which our counterparts were mainly recruited), but utterly ruthless towards any suspected political opposition. The polished sophistication of the Shah's court was underpinned by the steel of Savak, his feared secret security service, some of whose methods of dealing with 'subversive elements' I cannot bring myself even to write down.

I got to know something of this on my first trip out of Tehran, accompanied (apart from my driver, Nikfarjan) by a young man named Haddad, who was regarded in the project as being amiably ineffective, but who spoke quite good English and was easily spared to act as my 'familiarisation' guide. Haddad was the son of a Tehran carpet dealer and had a slyly ingratiating manner which might have stood him in good stead if he'd been working for his dad, but which had given him the reputation of being an obsequious toady with most of the UN staff. On our first evening, after supper at the modest country guest house where we were staying, Haddad surprised me by suggesting we go for a walk; but it became evident he was less interested in taking exercise than 'filling me in' about the sort of government we were both working for. As we walked along a deserted track in the darkness, with an almost conspiratorial Haddad pressing against me rather too closely for comfort, he spoke of his superiors and the whole system of power in Iran with an intensity of feeling that was almost venomous. At the time, although surprised by the vehemence of this normally ineffectual young man, I assumed his display of reckless confidence was probably his way of sucking up to the new project manager. Many other counterparts, equally critical, were later cautiously to reveal that they were not fooled by the hypocrisy of the Shah's regime, but you'd never hear any open criticism; the tentacles of Savak reached everywhere.

It was widely believed that no office of government was without its Savak agent, and we amused ourselves by trying to guess who it might be was the Savak sleeper in *our* project. By general consent we concluded it was almost certainly my secretary, Susie Etebar. With her lank hair and a gash of red lipstick emphasising the pallor of her skin, I would not have called Susie attractive; and her world-weary manner, American accent and carefully made-up appearance were, on first meeting, faintly off-putting. Yet, without question, Susie was a tremendous asset to our project. When so much in

Iran depended on personal relations, the machinery of government could be infuriatingly obstructive. No one had authority to make decisions; to get anything done one *had* to go to the top. You could never rely on the word of a mere underling (even one in a relatively senior position). I used to say that trying to get a decision out of the government was like fighting your way through cotton wool: soft and comfortable, but ultimately suffocating. That is where Susie was invaluable.

As members of an extremely long-civilised society, Iranians have well-developed qualities of charm and apparent candour in their dealings with foreigners which are both beguiling and frequently misleading. Our counterparts would fall over themselves trying to do what they thought would please us – and especially so, it sometimes seemed, when they knew it would be impossible of achievement. In that respect Susie was different: educated abroad, she understood our impatience with 'the system' and, as a member of a family close to the Shah, she was able to pull strings in mysterious ways that cut through the normal frustrations of government bureaucracy. The discreetly efficient project manager's secretary would have been good cover for a Savak agent. Nevertheless, Susie thought it useful occasionally to demonstrate her personal significance rather more ostentatiously. Once a year, she would invite the whole project team and a few of the more favoured Iranian staff (about twenty-five of us) out to her 'estate' for a day in the country – a day spent lounging on the lawns surrounding her large swimming pool, or sitting in the shade of trees, eating and drinking an impressive variety of local food and drink prepared by Susie's servants. It was slyly said that her village was deprived of water for a week while the swimming pool was being filled; and no doubt Susie *was* showing off, but in doing so she rather acceptably made the point: "As you see, I am not just a mere secretary." Still, there were limits to her influence, and she, too, would on occasion become part of the cotton-wool merry-go-round.

I had been wanting to see the Minister of Rural Affairs to get some definite decisions that only he, apparently, could make, on matters connected with our work programme. My co-manager had said yes, of course he would arrange it. Days passed.

"When am I going to be able to see the minister?"

"Ah, well, you see, the minister has been away in New York, but he should be able to see you soon."

Weeks passed. What was happening? Well, nothing apparently. One allowed oneself to become slightly testy: "WHEN is the minister going to be free to see me?"

"Well, er, would next week be convenient?"

"Perfectly."

A date would be fixed – and cancelled. Another fixed – and cancelled, but with profuse apologies . . . until, eventually, Susie, put on her mettle, said *she* would arrange it through her personal contacts. And, sure enough, remarkably quickly, I received word from the minister's office that he would see me the following week. Unfortunately, when I duly turned up at his office – or, rather, *tried* to turn up – I found the whole area barricaded and bristling with armed police.

"What's all this? I have an appointment with the minister."

"Nobody comes in: the Shahrina is visiting the ministry."

I realised later the date and time of my appointment had been deliberately set to give the message "Stop pestering."

When I did eventually see the minister – at a date and time of *his* choosing – he blandly greeted me: "Ah, Mr Hall, I believe you have been wanting to see me."

Dr Shakhpur* was one of the darker forces underpinning the Shah's smoothly autocratic regime. Before becoming a minister he had been the head of Savak, a position akin to that of Beria in the Soviet Union or Himmler in Nazi Germany. I was to meet him several times – a short man with a military moustache and, unusually for an Iranian (though appropriately enough for the boss of Savak), completely lacking in charm. I'm afraid to say he never gave me the impression that our project research had any effect on the policies of his ministry (it was not he but his predecessor who had inaugurated our project). We had meetings with officials of the government's Plan Organisation; we produced many volumes of background information with detailed recommendations; and we definitely struck sparks with many of the younger civil servants. But

---

* Not his real name, which I have conveniently forgotten.

the government itself – in the shape of the Shah's ministers – met almost anything new with typically Iranian bland waffle intended, it seemed, merely to keep us happy while changing nothing. In practice they proved totally unwilling to change direction in any respect other than where large sums of money were involved. Nevertheless, so long as we did not rock the boat, the minister was happy to give us a free hand to travel about and produce reports whose recommendations would then be treated as a worthy exercise in the casting of seed on stony ground. In that respect our project was perhaps little different from many United Nations Development Programme (UNDP) projects, which is not to say that international assistance is a waste of money (though some of it undoubtedly was) but that its ambitions are frequently set far too high, and tend to underrate the good qualities of much local practice.

Let's not forget, the Persians (as we used to call them) were selling produce and all manner of merchandise in the souks of Tabriz, Esfahan and Shiraz at a time when our ancestors were still hacking out forest clearings and chasing wild boar for their supper. Yet one of our project objectives was 'to improve' the Iranians' marketing of fruit and vegetables; and when I arrived in Tehran an American, whose sole experience had been in the Californian citrus industry, was busy setting up a pilot tomato-packing plant in Pishva, a village on the outskirts of the capital. This was to be a demonstration of an 'improved' way of marketing 't'maytas'. There would be no more of just throwing them in a box – big, small, ripe and half-ripe, good and bad all mixed together; now the tomatoes would all be sold by 'grades', washed and waxed, with each grade commanding a different price, so there would be a cash incentive for farmers to aim for high-quality produce. Well, that proved to be fine – so long as the packing station was paid for by our project, and so long as the farmers got paid subsidised prices to get the thing going. What Tom Bennett, our energetic Californian, failed to take into account was that, in Iran, 'grading' is done by the housewife, who, when buying from the market, selects only the best from a heap on the trader's stall; and during the course of the day, as the poorer stuff gets left, so the trader lowers his price accordingly. A packing station, from the Iranians' point of view, merely added to the cost. Ironically, it was more a lesson for *us* than for them. Yet, keen to please the Shah by introducing 'modern methods', the minister at the time (a retired army general, not Shakhpur) was highly impressed by the packing station, and had himself photographed by the press beside boxes of beautifully graded and waxed tomatoes, proudly standing there as if at a passing-out parade of recruits in dress uniform. It was a boost for his political image (and reputation at court), but that was just about all.

I still ask myself why the UN spent millions of dollars in Iran on projects which, as an important oil producer, it was quite rich enough to commission from its own resources. The answer probably is that *every* government – even our own when we were in the European Union – will make a bid for 'development funds' on the principle that if the money's going, grab it. There were something like twenty-five or thirty UN projects in Iran when I was there – not all as big as mine, but involving perhaps 200 international staff, co-ordinated and backed up by the office of the UNDP under its resident representative, Sidi Shallom (again, not his real name), who was in effect the UN's ambassador in Iran.

Shallom was an Egyptian Copt, a Christian and long-service staff member whose whole working life had been with the UN. A tall, lean, always well-groomed man, fluent in English, French and Arabic, his suave manner concealed a fervent belief in the aims and ideals of the UN. This became almost embarrassingly apparent on the occasion – I think it was the twenty-fifth anniversary of the signing of the UN Charter – when Shallom became so emotional during the course of his speech that he almost broke down. He was later said to be outraged by the apparent inability of most of his audience (including the UN staff) to be as demonstratively moved as he. But if he *was* offended, he probably misjudged at least the UN staff, most of whom, in my experience, were equally idealistic, but in the course of duty had seasoned their idealism with a down-to-earth appreciation of the difference between aspiration and realistic ambitions.

World public opinion expects far too much of the UN, yet, ironically, looks on it with contempt. Nevertheless, like religion to the heedless, the UN is valuable simply for being 'available'. It is there as a resource for humanity; and if it wasn't there the world would be even more of a jungle than it already is.

Unlike the foreign businessmen in Iran, whose equally well-paid representatives tended to work through westernised local agents, UN staff were much more involved with Iranian people on their own ground. Based as we were within a ministry of the government, we were daily exposed to the same regime – quirks, frustrations, privileges and all – as the Iranian civil servants with whom we worked. When in Tehran, our daily routine would be constantly refreshed by continual supplies of tea, delivered scalding-hot in small glasses, without milk but with rough lumps of sugar through which to suck it appreciatively. We ate our midday meal, the same food as the Iranian civil servants, in the ministry canteen, and enjoyed all the holidays associated with the many Shia religious festivals. We even worked by the Persian calendar, which meant that our 'Sunday' was on Friday, and the year began (much more sensibly than ours) in the spring. I see from my work diary of 1974 that *Now Ruz* (New Year) was a four-day holiday from 21 to 24 March. As a special concession, the project's UN staff were (grudgingly) permitted to celebrate 25 December – a date of no significance in Iran.

The UN field staff may have been unromantic about their role as 'experts', but those who had been in the field for any length of time, and had learned to cope with the endless frustrations and delays that foreigners encounter who try to introduce new ideas abroad, those seasoned field officers acquired the inestimable quality of *cultural sensitivity* – the opposite of chauvinistic bigotry. (A few years later, on the staff at Farnham Castle, it would be my job to promote cultural sensitivity in the minds of British ODA staff, business executives and their wives – in five days flat!) Being culturally sensitive doesn't mean that you're necessarily going to like the ways of foreigners, but it does equip you to be instinctively prepared to recognise those quirks of nature and the weight of history that have made people what they are – in much the same way as one accepts without question that the soil and climate of a country affect what's likely to grow there. There's no point arguing with the weather;

you just have to get on with what you've got.

As it happened, the UN staff on our project were, untypically, a pretty homogeneous bunch: apart from an ex-Pakistan Canadian and a Brazilian with an English wife, we were all 'European' (in the sense that includes North Americans). We may have come, as we did, from twelve different nationalities, but we were a band of brothers who worked together remarkably well – although, oddly enough, it was the Americans who tended to have most difficulty in adjusting to the laid-back style of the Iranian way of doing (or not doing) things. I exclude Carl Newman from that observation. Carl was our computer programmer – an engaging young bullshitter who dressed like a hippy and walked about with a large wallet half sticking out of the back pocket of his jeans. He wasn't with us for long and I never fully understood what he was supposed to be doing on the project: we didn't have any computers, and the only equipment he brought with him was an enviably professional-looking guitar. Carl would probably have gone native had he stayed with us longer.

America was 'big' in Iran at that time. When President Nixon made a state visit, there was a great flurry of unaccustomed activity to ensure that the great man was impressed by what he would see – which wasn't a great deal, of course. The main road from Tehran's Mehrabad Airport was resurfaced all the way up to the Shah's palace at Niavaran; and any building which looked dirty or shabby (in some districts quite a few) was given a compulsory coat of whitewash on walls fronting the processional route! Our (not shabby) offices were actually on this tarted-up thoroughfare; but as orders had been issued that no one was to occupy any room with windows overlooking it – and soldiers were actually posted in the building to enforce the prohibition – we were all herded into back rooms and saw nothing of Nixon and the Shah as they swept past in their motorcade. Indeed, the only people who did get to see Tricky Dicky were specially vetted 'irreproachables', media cameramen, and hundreds of schoolchildren lining the route waving little flags of the Stars and Stripes.

Although none of us knew at the time – or even suspected – how shaky was the Shah's hold on power, he himself must surely have known he had mortal enemies within the country, to say nothing of the grim old Ayatollah Khomeini, menacingly impotent in Paris. Savak wasn't just to keep an eye on restive young civil servants. But a second line of the Shah's defence was his cultivation of powerful friends abroad. The year 1971, the year we arrived in Tehran, was the 2,500th anniversary of the founding of the Persian Empire, for which the Shah had arranged a super-grandiloquent celebration to be held by the ruins of the ancient city of Persepolis. Luxuriously appointed tents had been erected for the royalty, presidents and potentates of the world who had been invited to grace the festivities; and strict security surrounding the event made sure that the people of Iran got nowhere near the Shah-emperor and his exalted friends enjoying the occasion.

The pageant went off very well, apparently; and after the dignitaries had gone home (suitably impressed, no doubt), lesser mortals – but still not the hoi polloi – were allowed to visit the tented city and what remained of the exhibition. So, accidentally on purpose, while on a visit to the southern city of Shiraz accompanied by a senior man from the ministry, I had the uninvited honour of a private visit to the now almost deserted site which only a few weeks earlier had been commanding the world's media attention – a visit in rather more comfort, I imagine, than stiff formalities would have permitted even the Shah's most esteemed guests to enjoy. However, shorn of the atmosphere of the occasion, the things that I remember were not those His Imperial Majesty would have wished to be the lasting impression – the slashed rents in some of the tents, for example, ripped by vandalistic knives in the night: a mute display of the fury provoked among common people, unspeakably affronted by a national display from which they had been excluded, people who had no political voice. Yet none of this would ever appear in the local press, and would not have been noticed anywhere else in the world.

Typical of the Shah's news management were the Ministry of Agriculture's exhibition statistics of the production of clover. Clover?

"Er, well, er, opium, actually," said Mr Doroudian, my ministry companion, a civilised and engagingly frank man who had previously performed duties at court, and was therefore not expected to be so indiscreet. "Opium is of course grown legally under licence," he explained, "but the quantity is quite large and people in Europe and America tend to get rather excited about it; so the minister probably didn't want to embarrass His Majesty."

To say nothing of the Shah not wanting to be embarrassed in front of the world!

One other small incident during that first trip to Persepolis sticks in my mind. We had stopped overnight at a brand-new five-star hotel; erected for the benefit of tourists, its first well-catered-for customers had been journalists of the world's press assigned to cover the Great Event. That night, however, it had been virtually taken over by members of the majlis, Iran's parliament – at that time an utterly supine body which merely rubber-stamped whatever decisions the government required it to agree. But even yes-men need to be stroked and kept happy – especially those who had not been invited to the main party. So there they were, about forty or fifty of what we would probably call 'obscure backbenchers', all, after two or three days of lavish entertainment, in a roistering party mood. I remember leaning on a banister rail overlooking the banqueting hall where these loyal majlis foot-soldiers of the Shah were talking, shouting, drinking and laughing noisily among the remnants of their meal. Beside me was Yazdan Pannah, my lean, ascetic-looking co-manager. He was looking at the scene below with an expression of such obvious disgust that I was quite startled.

"And *these* are the people who govern us!" he said very softly, with a curl of his lip.

What made the tone of this cryptic remark surprising was that Yazdan Pannah had not been at all a man to confide in foreigners; unlike most of the counterparts (his subordinates) who were friendly, indiscreet and eager to learn, his demeanour towards the FAO staff normally varied between reserved and surly. He was a difficult man to work with – a young man with attitude. Yet for a brief instant his reserve had dropped, and I realised for the first time that disaffection within the government service went deeper than the student left-wingery of junior ranks. In retrospect it is likely that part of Yazdan Pannah's morose attitude came from his feeling that we were 'collaborating foreigners', helping to shore up the system – as, of course, we were, I suppose.

I would be giving a misleading account of our lives in Iran if I were to leave you with the impression that we were much concerned with the omens of the country's wholly unforeseen revolution. These were merely the background to our lives; only in retrospect do they stand out as immensely significant. During our nearly four years there I travelled the length and breadth of the country – from the Russian border in Azerbaijan (with its sinister watchtowers spaced out above the trees) to the arid mountains of Baluchistan in the south-east, a remote and craggy moonscape; and from the holy city of Mashad, in the north-east, down to the sweltering heat of the Persian Gulf. In those days there was no hostility to foreigners. Staying in the same, usually rather grotty, hotels as Iranian merchants, civil servants and family travellers; taking our breakfast at nearby coffee houses (goats'-milk cheese, pickled garlic and delicious flat bread hot from the oven); and preferring the local bathhouse to the dribbling shower in our hotel – by the end of a long and dusty trip I nearly always returned with a satisfying feeling of having managed to get just a little closer to the people of an extraordinarily interesting country.

During the time that we lived there, Iran was ruled by an autocrat friendly to the West. Now it is governed by clerics and the stifling disciplines of doctrinaire Islamic sharia. Iran has been branded by America as part of an 'Axis of Evil' (a crassly meaningless epithet), yet the Iranians are still the same people we knew in the early 1970s, and whom I now look back on with affection. They are a people a bit like the Irish: courteous, friendly, generous, sometimes unreliable, whose occasionally infuriating disengagement from the serious business of the world is redeemed by a beguiling poetic sentiment – and perhaps by a better understanding of the human condition than we have here in our own secular consumer-oriented society.

29 – BACK TO ROME

About the end of 1973 we received unwelcome news that our landlord, Dr Kianpur, having been appointed Minister of Information and Tourism, was returning to Tehran and wanted his house back. There was nothing for it but to look for somewhere else to live – at rather short notice. Now, however, it was more a question of finding a convenient perch for our remaining time in Iran. For, as it happened, we were about to start the last year of the first phase of our project, and I had already decided not to continue beyond that first phase. Jeremy was about to change schools, and Hilary, too, was at a stage when a move up would shortly become necessary.

We missed the swimming pool and garden, but the two-bedroom flat that we found in a quiet street in the centre of the city was much nearer the ministry building, and Hilary could still be picked up by a school bus. My work and our social life – to a large extent with the families of the project staff, themselves scattered throughout the upper parts of the city – continued much as before. The main difference, so far as I remember, was that the local American forces' television channel became more intrusive in our flat.

We travelled more as a family throughout Iran in those remaining months of 1974/75, so Beryl, and both children too in the holidays, got a wider experience of the country than was offered by busy modern Tehran – at least compared with the fascination of cities such as Tabriz, Esfahan and Shiraz, which much more exemplify the character and traditions of an ancient civilisation. Or was it, perhaps, that on our family travels we tended to spend more time as 'tourists', in the mosques, souks and interesting places to eat?

Iran has a rich cultural history, and much time was spent in galleries and carpet shops, buying with abandon. A journey by train round the southern end of the Caspian Sea to Gorgan was the last we did together before Jeremy started at his new school, Millfield, in Somerset on 11 September 1974.

At the end of March, the following year, Beryl and Hilary returned to the UK and settled back in Cone Hill. Hilary joined St Lawrence Primary School, about 150 yards up through the woods behind our house – very convenient (though Hilary apparently stood out, perhaps uncomfortably, as the only child there without a Kent accent), but it was only a temporary arrangement before she, too, started as a boarder at Cobham Hall, a girls' school near Rochester.

I was left to clear up in Tehran and hand over to my successor, Bob Hood, already present as our meat-marketing specialist. Although the project was to be extended into a second phase, it had settled into what had now become a somewhat boring routine of churning out reports, which, while involving, for us, much interesting travel throughout the country, nevertheless were rarely given by government the attention we felt they deserved. The reason for this apparent lack of interest was almost certainly (and this was characteristic of virtually all FAO reports to government) the fact that they were at that time necessarily produced in one of the three standard languages – in our case, English. Our attempts to get one or two papers translated into Farsi proved to be time-consuming and diverted staff from their real work. Besides, it could not be guaranteed to be accurate. Nevertheless, it was the training of the local counterpart staff that was the project's main purpose, and in that I believe we did achieve useful results. My nearly four years' experience in the country had been, for me, immensely stimulating, and rewarding in many ways – chiefly, I think, through our influence on our young counterparts. But I was now ready to go.

I had opted to return to headquarters, to be nearer the children's schooling, and perhaps also to advance the progress of my career. Our first preoccupation on getting back to Rome, however, was to find somewhere for us to live; and by chance I happened to learn that Kei Harada, the Japanese chief librarian of FAO, was offering a house to let in Trevignano, one of the three villages round Lake

Bracciano. Although this would involve almost an hour's slow train journey daily into the city, we had been so fond of the area (where we still had that land by the lake) that I jumped at the opportunity. So the heading of this chapter, 'Back to Rome', is accurate only so far as my professional life is concerned. As a family we were to live on the Poggio delle Ginestre (literally Hillock of Broom), in a two-storeyed house with a good garden of fruit trees and a balcony overlooking the lake. Kei himself had built another house on the same big plot, and so we had him and his English wife, Jeanette, as our sole neighbours for the next two years. They were friendly, having us over from time to time, as we did them, but mostly they kept themselves to themselves. Nevertheless, Kei and I took it in turns to drive daily the short distance to the Bracciano Railway Station, and for two years he was my friendly travelling companion; yet, oddly, we never became close: in spite of his English wife, his Japanese reserve never verged on familiarity.

Much had changed in the intervening four years since we left Rome for Iran. The city, of course, was still the same charming, chaotic place; but FAO itself had by now shaken off its old, comfortable informality, and had become noticeably different. It was a creature now of the new, post-Jackson* reforms: impersonal, bureaucratic, driven by targets and wonderful procedures for achieving efficiency (see Chapter 27). Yet perhaps, on reflection, it would be more accurate, and not totally unfair, to say that, in what were to be my last five years with it, the organisation was still wallowing about in properly coming to terms with the *real* changes it had to confront, arising from the newly assertive demands of most of its member countries, luxuriating in their first flush of independence from colonial overlordship.

Personifying the new dispensation in the FAO Agricultural Operations Division was a new chief: in place of Don Kimmel (who had moved on) we now had Dr G. C. Juneja as head of the Asia and Pacific Branch (to which I was now assigned). Juneja had a brisk military manner – a reminder of his background in the Indian Army. What other experience got him into FAO I don't know; but he was a knowledgeable and kindly boss, and he kept

---

* Sir Robert Jackson, author of the 1969 'Capacity Study' for UN reform.

strictly to the rules, however exasperating he also found them – an exasperation he would share with engaging frankness with his team at our regular weekly meetings. I was now responsible for rural institutions projects (marketing, credit, extension, etc.) in Indonesia and Bangladesh, and later in India, Nepal and Bhutan – all new to me and of tremendous interest. Looking back, I count myself very lucky to have had the opportunity to travel widely in them and meet, both professionally and socially, many of their people during these remaining years of my FAO service.

Indonesia is a large country of 13,000 islands – or 8,000 (depending on which authority you consult). I remember, on a flight to Papua, passing over numerous small islands (blue sea, palm trees, golden sands) and thinking to myself, 'I'll have that one . . . no, *that* one.' They were so totally untouched by human life and away from the world, primal and pure as God made them. But, of course, the people of Indonesia do not indulge such ridiculous flights of fancy and are crowded mainly into the large islands of Java, Sumatra, Sulawesi and the largest (southern) part of Borneo, known as Kalimantan. And crowded is the word. One of our projects, strongly pushed by the government of President Sukarno, was an attempt to alleviate overpopulation in Java by organising a system of transmigration, by the wholesale transfer of people to underpopulated areas of Sumatra. Whether this was achieved voluntarily or by administrative fiat, I never discovered. Our British project manager, David Butcher, was satisfied the arrangements for resettlement in Sumatra were sufficiently attractive not to require coercion.

I myself on one occasion found myself making an involuntary stay in Sulawesi, being marooned at Ujung Pandang (on the west coast) for a week longer than intended, owing to my determination not to pay the bribe apparently needed to get on the plane back to Jakarta.

"Very sorry – full up."

"But there are hardly any passengers!"

"Too much freight."

Fortunately, the check-in clerk did not attempt to try the same story again when the plane came in the following week. My stopover at Ujung Pandang had been pleasant enough, but I wouldn't have called it a holiday – in contrast to my visits to Bali, where our animal-husbandry project treated me, most generously, less as a visiting headquarters official and more like a tourist, which, frankly, I believe they may have thought I might prefer.

I must confess that on our duty trips abroad there was always a narrow line between achieving its official objectives and taking the opportunity to see as much as possible of the cultural attractions in each place we visited. Indeed, we would have been pretty moronic not to have done so.

I remember Dr Juneja saying to me, when I was leaving on a trip to India, "Be sure to stop over at Agra (on the way to a project at Jhansi) to see the Taj Mahal." I strait-lacedly thought this a rather improper suggestion, and priggishly stayed on the train when it stopped briefly at Agra, and then moved on to my destination at Jhansi, a city of little interest to me and, as it happened, I stayed in a pretty crummy hotel too. I must be one of the very few people who have passed through Agra without going to see the Taj Mahal (though Beryl and I did go there as, indeed, tourists after my retirement). Professionally, though, India was a country where the locals were definitely in charge. One went there not so much to check on how things were progressing (though one did that, diplomatically) as to be told what the government wanted, indeed demanded, from FAO.

The Nepal government was equally demanding and, during one of my visits to Kathmandu, made plain its dissatisfaction with FAO's performance. Discussion of this allowed me to draw attention to a problem that was common to many international projects. As I wrote in a report at the time, there was 'a tendency of the Government, without itself providing adequate resources in support, to push FAO into attempting objectives that are in practice beyond the project's powers to achieve. . . . The lesson to be learned is that FAO should insist on clear project objectives [in the Plan of Operation]' and the question of what was needed to achieve them 'must be squarely faced at the time those objectives are specified – and not left simply to emerge as a result of "unsatisfactory performance".' Peter Myers, the British project manager of a Hill Agriculture project on the end of this sort of criticism, relieved some of his frustration by taking headquarters people, like me, on long walking treks in the hills, with the object of proving what softies we were. Fortunately, I was equal to the task and positively enjoyed the exercise in the beautifully clean and bracing mountain air.

That landscape description could equally apply to Bhutan, which some say is the nearest place to heaven on earth. I went there for the first time in 1978, after a night in Calcutta and an early morning drive through a slum district that might equally have qualified as the nearest place to hell on earth – women and children scrabbling about in huge rubbish tips, looking for anything that might still be edible or of some sale value. Bhutan was still at that time several years away from having an airport – or indeed anywhere a plane might land – and to get there required special authority to pass through the North India security zone to Phuentsholing on the border, where (after a night's stop at the rest house) a Land Rover would drive you up a spectacular and occasionally terrifying mountain road – 'track' would be more accurate – to Thimphu, the capital. Here I stayed at the government hotel, where a complimentary bottle of Johnny Walker Black Label whisky was hospitably placed by my bedside.*

I have to restrain myself from rhapsodising about Bhutan, a largely Buddhist kingdom, high in the Himalayas between India and China. It has never been colonised, and its, one might almost say, complete independence from the world is everywhere evident in the style of its decorated houses and the Dzong architecture of walled fortresses. The government administrative buildings and the country's monasteries are practically indistinguishable from each other: their almost silent courtyards, with pigeons and prayer wheels, have more the atmosphere of an old university college. But for all their hospitality, the Bhutanese, who go about in thick stockings, boots and dressing-gown-like garments, are fiercely protective of their country's independence and singular character (a favourite sport is archery). The government had a strong disinclination to accept long-term experts. So far as we were concerned, short-term consultancies were much preferred.

"Tell us what you know, then go" was the unspoken message.

* In those days I didn't drink whisky, and left it untouched.

Down in the deltas of the Ganges and Brahmaputra, and the intersections of many smaller rivers, Bangladesh is, to my mind, the opposite in many ways of Bhutan. It is one of the most densely populated countries in the world, and is terribly vulnerable to climate change: about a third of the land is flooded in the monsoon rains. One of our projects was to promote the digging of tube wells for drinking water, only for it to be later discovered that many of them have become contaminated by arsenic from the soil. Most of my memories of Bangladesh are sad: of its swirling rivers crossed by ancient ferries, of being pestered on them for coins by pitifully clad children, of the FAO staff member bitten by a rabid puppy (he survived), and of being present in September 1977 when a Japanese airliner was hijacked and flown to Dhaka. I could see the plane clearly while negotiations went on for a ransom and release of the passengers. It was an eerie experience, being so close yet quite apart from the drama that had the whole world in thrall. (It was ultimately resolved by the Japanese Government caving in to the hijackers' demands.)

These visits to our out-posted field staff probably occupied little more than a quarter of my working life; most of it was spent behind a desk in Rome or attending meetings of one kind or another throughout the house. Some of these were meetings where all member nations were represented, many by internationally well-known figures, and it was noticeable that the British were often prominent among them. Barbara Castle, who was the Minister for International Development in Harold Wilson's Labour government, gave the keynote address, to great applause, at one of FAO's annual conferences; and I observed, strolling on the roof terrace, in deep conversation with somebody, the chief economic advisor to the same administration, Thomas Balogh – an unprepossessing man, I thought. (He had been described as 'a macaw among mandarins', a man with a conspiratorial nature who made many enemies.)

Apropos well-known British characters, I must just mention John Cairncross. He was not a visitor, but, when I knew him, was working as a close assistant to the director of our division. I say I knew him, but I did not know John Cairncross at all well – and certainly did not know he was the 'fifth man' of the notorious Cambridge spies. Nor, indeed, did anyone else (other than MI5, whom he had outwitted under interrogation, when they rumbled him after Burgess and Maclean's 'disappearance' in 1951). But we would frequently pass each other in the long corridor where we each had a room, and one day he suggested we take lunch together. I merely knew him as a rather odd sort of chap, who was remarkable among the mostly well-dressed FAO headquarters staff for looking, with his baggy trousers, pale face and unkempt sandy hair, more like an untidy senior schoolboy than an international civil servant. He would usually give an amiable fluttering wave of the hand as he went on his way, almost always alone. Nobody seemed to know exactly what he did, other than, it was said, read books that the director general ought to know about. When Gunnar Myrdal, say, or von Hayek produced some weighty tome, Cairncross would reduce the guts of it to a single sheet of A4 for the director general's edification – an unobtrusively influential job, when you think about it.

Retrospectively, I sometimes ask myself whether he was perhaps checking me out, assessing whether I might conceivably be an undercover MI5 agent keeping tabs on him. What does remain clearly in my memory, though, is what a disgusting eater he was, sloshing his food about and taking ages to complete each mouthful while maintaining a more or less continual flow of conversation – conversation that would not have been out of place at a college high table, but was completely above my own doltish head. Indeed there must have been an element of deliberate cruelty in what was virtually a monologue seasoned with references to Racine, de Maupassant and goodness knows who else I'd never even heard of, let alone been able to discuss intelligently (as he must have known very well).

Yet, after lunch, as we were promenading back and forth on the top-floor terrace, our conversation turned more to our shared line of business: the world's diminishing natural resources. It was during those brief ten or so minutes that John Cairncross gave me what I subsequently realised was a preview of the 'Club of Rome's Limits to Growth' – about two years before it was published.

Country project officers, such as I now was, each had their own office and a personal secretary who kept things in good order, and to whom one dictated letters and memoranda. My predecessor, Alec McCallum, had died in office, and I had inherited his dragon of a secretary, Dorothy Wotton, who was clearly unhappy with Alec's replacement by me. Dorothy was undoubtedly efficient – so much so that it seemed Alec had left her to deal with much of the work independently, without needing detailed guidance or instruction from him. Dorothy liked it that way, and resented my constant questioning about how things were done. I remember one occasion when she put something in front of me.

"What am I supposed to do with this?" I asked.

"Just sign it!" she thundered.

What Dorothy didn't take into account was that I was already by now a well-experienced FAO man, and had my own definite views. I was just unfamiliar with the new systems at headquarters.

Having 'sandwiched', in Mauritius and Iran, periods of work in the field with my earlier time in Rome, I had become, in particular, intimately aware of the precarious nature of the employment conditions under which our field staff operated. Working on fixed-term contracts, they never knew when or where their next assignment might be – nor, indeed, whether they would get one at all. It entirely depended on a post in their specialisation being required at a time when they happened to be available. And even then their ultimate appointment to it would have to struggle through the occasionally capricious nature of the respective governments' clearance procedures. (Dorothy's reassignment – at her own request – was managed smoothly, however.)

When I became aware of a proposal being cooked up by some enterprising staff of the agricultural engineering section – headed by a burly Australian named Al Faunce – to establish a Field Staff Association (FSA), I immediately became interested, and had no difficulty in joining their self-selected committee. We were to be, in effect, headquarters staff batting for the field staff. After a bit I found myself elected as secretary, and later, for two years, chairman of the association. The policy which eventually emerged from our discussions comprised several proposals which we urged upon the management of FAO at ADG level. In particular we wanted the organisation to make forecasts of future requirements of staff in different specialisations, so that cadres might be available and ready for deployment with less of the customary delays and uncertainty – on all sides: government, staff and FAO. Permanent appointments, we argued, should not be limited to headquarters staff, and there should be a serious attempt to rotate people between headquarters and field.

None of this was particularly ambitious – except possibly the proposal for headquarters/field rotation. Headquarters staff tended to stick to their posts in Rome like limpets, and would have been fully in accord with the sentiment in Gilbert and Sullivan's *HMS Pinafore*, where landlubber naval officers were cheerfully advised:

> Stick close to your desks and never go to sea,
> And you all may be rulers of the Queen's Navee.

In the end, I think the main benefit of the FSA was to make our outposted field staff feel less neglected by an impersonal headquarters leviathan. Yes, they had their 'subject-matter' officers, and many of these were personally helpful; but subject-matter officers did not speak for the organisation, and nor did they have an answer for the employment insecurity of fixed-term contracts. It was the FSA that let the field staff feel that someone was speaking up for them – and getting answers. They did not always give us what we were asking for – in fact, they rarely gave us what we were asking for – but we had many meetings with 'the administration', and, in my time, we had one with the director general; we did nibble away at the edges of procedural difficulties, and we definitely made the personal circumstances of field staff better understood by 'personnel'.

At home, meanwhile, we continued living comfortably in the rural peace of Trevignano; and I would commute daily with Kei into Rome, leaving my wife . . . twiddling her fingers in the countryside. Apart from Jeanette, who was a pretty self-sufficient individual with a life of her own, there were no neighbours, and Beryl, who had previously enjoyed her busy and useful activity with Oxfam in Rome, now found it impossible to reintegrate herself there. Apart from the distance, several of her fellow workers at the shop had changed and, from being a big wheel, she now found herself merely a visitor. She was not happy. We still had friends in Rome who would come over, usually at weekends, but mostly Beryl's company during the week was shared just with our Cairn terrier bitch, Scally. Beryl herself was also quite self-sufficient; but after a year or so at Trevignano, the loneliness began to pall, and she pressed for us to move back into the city.

As it happened, the Haradas had a flat in Rome that they were keen to let. No. 38 Via Francesco dall'Ongaro was by no means as swell as our previous apartment at Villa Bettania, but, situated in Trastevere, on the other side of the Tiber from FAO, it was convenient – at least for me. So, still with our boathouse and land at Bracciano, we eventually swopped tenancies and moved back to Rome. That was when small things led to unplanned consequences. We had bought Scally* as a companion for Beryl in the country, which she was; and although many Romans did keep dogs in flats – as often as not leaving them out all day on a balcony – it was *not* a life for a sentient animal. So, after keeping her with us for a few weeks, we decided to send her back home, which necessarily involved six months' quarantine in England (we had brought her out as a puppy in the car – over the Simplon Pass – without asking whether the Italians had similar regulations to the British). Those six months conveniently postponed a decision on what to do when Scally was released. Perhaps we had, at the back of our minds, that Jeremy, who was about to leave Millfield, might look after her. Or, more likely, I was not properly thinking about it. Beryl, however, probably was. Not that she had it in her mind to up sticks and base herself in England, but it had not taken long for her to discover that she didn't much like 38 Via Francesco dall'Ongaro.

The FAO staff cooperative organised a regular system of charter flights to London, which meant that British staff members and their families could easily and cheaply hop over for a weekend or longer. We, and especially Beryl, naturally took full advantage of

---

* Her registered name was Supercali (from *Mary Poppins*), which we thought ridiculous.

this, to see the children at half-term, and also now to check up on Scally in her quite comfortable but definitely unwelcome (to her) quarantine prison not far from Sevenoaks. Cone Hill was not at that time let, so it was like going from home to home. I forget how things evolved, but gradually Beryl's journeys back became more frequent and extended to more than a few days. I was not too happy about it, but put up with it partly because some of her visits were indeed necessary, and partly because I, too, would quite frequently be away on duty travel. That was the way of our life.

I think it was in December 1978 that I went off the rails. Beryl was in England and there was a divisional Christmas party in Rome, at which I was master of ceremonies. I spent much of the evening, when not full of myself with a microphone and wine, dancing with one of the secretaries, a curly-headed girl whom I'll call Ruth. 1 had not known her previously, merely seeing her occasionally in the corridor further along from my office. That evening I rather quickly got to know her better. Just about the last to leave the party, I ended up by taking her home – and, yes, spending the night at her flat. That was the beginning of a new pattern of my out-of-office activity.

We would eat out at restaurants and occasionally go to concerts together. Ruth had a good voice and was a soloist in the FAO choir. I remember in particular *The Beggar's Opera* and – I think it would have been the Christmas time following our first encounter – Handel's *Messiah*. As often as not we would go back to her flat, and occasionally to ours – though obviously not when Beryl was in Rome. I tried to limit the degree of my unfaithfulness by telling Ruth plainly, at an early stage, that there was nothing wrong with my marriage – partly in the hope that she would not get too emotionally attached – but that obviously was not true, and anyway did not have the desired result. Ruth clung to our relationship with a passion that owed something to a previous unhappy affair, from which she had an unplanned baby that her family had more or less forced her to place for adoption. When she showed me a photograph of the man in question, clearly much older than she was, something in my expression when I looked at it must have led her to take it back from me – and immediately tear it up! It was a dramatic statement, intended, it seemed, to demonstrate the transfer of her affections wholeheartedly to me. That was the kind of girl she was.

I say girl, but Ruth was probably about twenty-five. On another occasion, when on our land at Bracciano, although the weather was cold, she wanted to go for a swim. Not having a costume was no problem: she stripped off and plunged naked into the lake. I did not join her. Nor, though I was fond of her and enjoyed her company, could I abandon myself emotionally to the same extent. Nevertheless, for more than a year Ruth was 'the other woman', to be taken up or put aside as Beryl came and went. Ruth accepted that, content merely to have me to herself as and when possible. I entirely accept that my behaviour was reprehensible. I justified it to myself because I was irritated by Beryl's unwillingness to live properly with me in Rome. I don't know how she eventually got to know about my egregious dalliance (to describe it more lightly than is strictly accurate). Although not a gossip, John Abbott was at a concert I attended with Ruth and he almost certainly would have seen us together. Wanda Zemaitis, too, had her ear to the ground, and it was more likely she who alerted Beryl.

However it was, at a time when I was home in England, Beryl asked me direct – she already knew of Ruth's existence – had I slept with her? I made a clean breast of it and acknowledged, yes, I had.

Although Beryl had clearly prepared herself for my answer and accepted it calmly, simply saying, "Of course I will have to divorce you," that was a defensive shield for the utter devastation she genuinely felt and which she later gave into the same day. She wept uncontrollably and for days asked innumerable questions about every detail of my fall from grace: When? How many times? Where did you do it? How *could* you? I don't think the question of divorce was ever seriously considered, but of course I had to promise to stop the affair forthwith; and to cement my fidelity, Beryl insisted that I tell the children. I did not find it easy, yet Jeremy and Hilary took it well – partly, I think, because they had some sympathy for my embarrassment.

When Beryl was joining in the explanation of my confession,

Jeremy said something like, 'All right, Mum – don't rub it in," for which I was grateful.

I still had to tell Ruth, which I did shortly after my return to Rome. I took her for a last lunch. Oddly enough, it was harder to break the news to her than it was, for a different reason, to Beryl. For Beryl there was to be a reconciliation and recovery of our marriage; for Ruth it would be, and was, another of life's smacks in the face. I have never ceased to reproach myself for it.

Disentangling myself from Ruth did not, however, lead, of itself, to much improvement in the facts of my family life. Although Beryl recognised that she was not wholly blameless in leaving me to wander astray, we did have the two children in England, who had half-terms and exeats that one of us at least had to be there for; and I myself was, anyway, often on the other side of the world, or kept late in the office owing to an increasing pressure of work arising from bureaucratic innovation at headquarters. To be honest, I had to recognise that life for Beryl at 38 Via Francesco dall'Ongaro was pretty dreary on the best of days. Another factor was that Jeremy had completed his time at Millfield and was at a bit of a loose end. In January 1980 he had gone off to Israel to work on a kibbutz. For a number of reasons, therefore, I agreed with Beryl that I would take early retirement, as was possible when I reached the age of fifty-five. Quite apart from the Ruth question, I was becoming fed up with the labyrinthine bureaucracy of our procedures – the fruitless attempt to keep on top of multifarious activities going on simultaneously.

The essential nature of my work as a country project officer was to help develop and then keep an eye on the activities of different projects in the countries for which I was responsible. This meant, in collaboration with the government and participating FAO divisions, defining their objectives and the resources needed to achieve them; getting all that legally specified in a plan of operation to be agreed jointly by the government, FAO and UNDP (United Nations Development Programme); and then organising the provision of FAO's contribution to the project. As I put it in a memorandum to the deputy director of our division, Chris Bonte-Friedheim:

> There is one aspect of our work which is constantly mentioned, frequently discussed, and never to the slightest extent improved: it concerns our old friends 'feed-back' and 'follow-up'. It will be clearer if I put this in concrete terms. . . .
>
> On any day you care to choose, the average CPO [country project officer] has only a vague idea what (if anything) is going on in respect of all current activities [in his area of competence] – eg. project formulation and approval, recruitment of staff, selection & ordering of equipment, organising fellowship training programmes, etc. To get to know, for (say) thirty projects, he has to ask (roughly) 400 questions of one to six people – say an average of 1200 questions daily.
>
> This process of questioning is known in this division as 'follow-up'. In practice it is the most time-wasting procedure that could possibly be devised, since at least 95 percent of the questions make no difference to the speed or otherwise of performing the activities in question; they merely interrupt the person being questioned from doing his or her work. Strictly speaking, it is not a procedure that has been devised at all: it is a frantic and hopeless attempt on the part of the CPOs to try to keep on the ball, in the absence of a proper feed-back system to keep them informed.

I continued fulminating for another couple of paragraphs, and concluded:

> There are a number of ways in which current information could be systematically made available, the most economical of which might possibly introduce 'fail/safe' checks, so that activities that were *not* being performed within a given time were automatically signalled back to the CPO. Alternatively, senior management could possibly be convinced of the undoubted fact that any significant expansion of FAO's field activities depends upon its willingness to computerise all delivery functions, with Operations Services able to extract information at will.

I did not highlight the last sentence, but in retrospect it is obvious that this is what was missing at the time. In November 1979 (when I wrote my memorandum) the furthest my division had got in the way of office technology was in the use of a single word processor. Bonte-Friedheim was himself a reformer, so to some extent I was pushing at an open door. Far from resenting my rather outspoken criticism, he suggested I write down some of my thoughts about the field programme, from the different points of view I had seen it during my service with the organisation. I did eventually do this, but much later, when (there then being not much point in sending them to him) in response to a call for contributions to the UN Career Records project, I submitted a paper on the subject, taking a wider view of it,* and later included a summary of it in a memoir I wrote as an edited version of these memoirs, for the benefit of colleagues in my pensioners' association, 'Grit in the Oyster, or Sand in the Machine'.

---

*'The Administration of FAO Field Operations – 1963–1980. Headquarters and Field Viewpoints', a paper by A. S. M. Hall submitted in 1992 for the UN Career Records project, in the Bodleian Library, Oxford.

30 – THE CENTRE FOR INTERNATIONAL BRIEFING

What I remember best about Cone Hill, especially every time I came back to it from Rome, is the birdsong on waking in the morning – a heavenly chorus all the more delightful for the complete lack of any competing noise of traffic. Of all the places we have lived, Cone Hill is where I think back with a tug of emotion, and regret at ever having left. It would have been nice to have just retired in September 1980 and devoted myself to improving the woodland and garden, and, with two reasonable pensions, I might easily have done so (only Hilary was now at school). But fifty-five was still too early to call it a day. So, while still at Rome, I had been scouting out further opportunities of employment. Up popped – I forget where – an advertisement from the Centre for International Briefing, at Farnham in Surrey, seeking an organiser of courses for government and business people going out to Asia and the Pacific Islands. What made this position especially interesting was that the Centre was located in a castle – a former palace of the Bishops of Winchester that dated back to Norman times.

I didn't know anything about the Pacific Islands, but Asia was right up my street, and I applied for the post. Never in my previous experience had events moved so quickly as they did after that. There was only one day's enjoyment of Cone Hill's birdsong following our final return to England before I was phoned by the Centre. Could I come for interview? Tomorrow? Seemingly my experience was exactly the kind they were looking for, and they had been eagerly awaiting my return to see whether I would, in the flesh, measure up to their expectations. I, of course, equally eager, agreed to come over the following day, with my wife, who, although not part of the package, was likely also to be weighed in the balance. I was correct in that assumption, because the Centre for International Briefing, prominently situated in the ancient castle above the town, had a character that was, of its essence, 'homely'.

The idea of briefing courses for people going out to foreign lands had started with a man named Harry Holland, who was previously a missionary doctor in India, and had been present during the British handover of power in 1947. He was one of the earliest to recognise that this was the beginning of a movement that would ultimately extend to all the colonies and dependent territories of the European powers, and that it would necessarily entail a fundamental shift in the relationship between Europeans and the people of their formerly dependent countries. He was also clearly a dynamic character who was able to do something about it. He did so through the Colonial Office and the British Council of Churches, roping in the Archbishop of Canterbury for good measure. From small beginnings, holding overseas-employment briefing courses in makeshift accommodation in different large houses in the south of England, Holland, with his small staff (often husband-and-wife teams), eventually came to a mutually beneficial arrangement with the Church Commissioners to lease the whole of Farnham Castle (otherwise largely unused and decaying) for a peppercorn rent.

On arrival we were greeted with exceptional friendliness by a girl at the desk – a reception I was later to discover was not put on especially for us, but was part of the Farnham Castle culture: consideration, thoughtfulness, knowing the names of strangers. It was evident as soon as we stepped in the door that this was a community that valued personal relations. Beryl was led away by somebody while I was shown to the director's office, a pleasant room looking out on to a wide lawn in front of the castle. Patrick Lloyd had been a senior executive of Shell International and clearly regarded that company as having almost blue-blooded status abroad – it was certainly very well paid in its upper echelons. I must have been with him for at least two hours – an interview I thought was never going to end. He was cordial enough, but remorselessly probed into every aspect of my life; and then, when he must surely have become bored with the conversation himself, he asked if I could come over later to meet a member of the board of governors. Beryl and I were then given a tour of the castle. That day Patrick (all members of staff were known by their first names) must surely have formed a pretty reliable opinion about me, as indeed had I about him: amiable, shrewd, fastidious, and definitely cautious in coming to a settled decision.

A few days later, my (much shorter) meeting with the board member duly accomplished, Patrick phoned me to say they were happy to take me on – if I was still available! I was, and on 27 October, barely a month after leaving FAO, I was enrolled on the current five-day course, as an ordinary course member, to get an idea of what I was myself going to face as the course organiser for Asia and the Pacific Islands. In the early days of the Centre most of the staff lived 'in house', but the policy now was for them to find their own accommodation. This was not something I could do quickly, so Peter and Barbara Aylet, who had a big house very near to the castle, offered me a room (to rent) until I could get something of my own. Peter, who had formerly worked for the Iraq Petroleum Company, was the deputy director and organiser of the Middle East courses; Barbara was the course assistant for that region. It was a strictly business arrangement. I had my own key and did not intrude at all on their domestic lives, having all my meals, including breakfast, at the castle, along with the students. At the weekends I went back home to Cone Hill.

I met the man I was taking over from in his last two weeks at the castle. I forget his name, but he was clearly leaving under a cloud, arrogantly at odds with the Centre's way of doing things and bitter at his failure to get his ideas for improvement accepted. I was warned that the unpleasantness of his departure would probably be reflected in his handover. And it was. His wife, who had been his assistant, would be leaving at the same time, and Patrick had already lined up, but not yet employed, a replacement to work with me in that capacity. With typical consideration, he arranged for me to meet Vera Attwooll before finally signing her up, to make sure I was equally happy. Vera had been in an administrative position at the Bank of England and was one of the many unfortunates who found themselves now without a job, after Mrs Thatcher's Stock Exchange Big Bang, and throwing-open of the currency markets. I took to her (Vera, not Mrs Thatcher) immediately, and for the next five years we occupied the same office on the third floor of Fox's Tower, sharing every detail of organising and conducting the Asia and Pacific Islands courses.

It took me about two months to find and then buy a small house at 20 Dollis Drive, as a convenient place to live during the week. From there it was about fifteen minutes' walk through Farnham Park to an obscure 'back door' in the castle wall, to which I was given a private key. I felt very privileged doing that: so far as I know, no one else used that door. Work at the Centre was organised around five-day courses for about twenty-five to thirty people – mostly husband-and-wife couples about to be posted to one of the countries of a particular region. Occasionally courses about the UK would be conducted for foreign business people coming to Britain. Typically, therefore, we course organisers would have three or, occasionally, four weeks in which to prepare a course and one to actually conduct it. You may think that was a pretty relaxed schedule, but it wasn't.

What made the Centre unique in the country (and possibly the world) was that each participant had a course designed specifically for himself or herself: a man going to Delhi would obviously get much the same briefing as one going to Calcutta, but not entirely the same; nor indeed was it quite the same as their wives'. A banker going to Bangkok would have very different requirements from those of a missionary going to Kuching in Sarawak. Although I got a rough idea, from my discontented predecessor, of what the setting-up of a course required, my first one – about three weeks after my arrival – was an experience of being thrown in at the deep end, since Vera, too, though quick on the uptake, was also new to the game. In a way, though, getting one's guidance from a man who didn't give a damn about the job he was being kicked out of was an advantage, as it allowed me to think through the system of work for myself.

What happened in those first three weeks (and would be typical for most of the preparatory work) is that we had before us details of the thirty or so people who had applied for the upcoming course:

their names, job and place they were going to, spouse if they had one, and things they were particularly interested in (for example, fishing, music, swimming, climbing mountains, etc.). How to feed enough information to these people to help them avoid a feeling they were jumping into a great unknown? Some of the talks for the region or country were standard, of course (for example, the geography, history, political scene and, especially important, cultural identity of the people). Well, we had a few boxes of well-thumbed index cards with the names of people who had experience of a particular country or countries in the region, and some indication of their background and interests – for example, 'former headmaster in Kuala Lumpur' or 'was a personal friend of president Sukarno' or 'knows a lot about snakes'. Whether the snake expert was available for the course – i.e. alive and still in this country – had to be ascertained by phoning him up on a dial-up phone. This was an infuriating procedure when I or Vera had to do it many times a day (it was at least three years before I was able to get a push-button phone). We were lucky if the person phoned was in and even luckier if he was able to come for the course. Fees were never discussed: speakers got what we gave them (about £20 and travel costs); family visitors (i.e. those who just came for an informal chat about their experience in a country) just got a decent meal, as did the speakers. If the index cards yielded nothing we had to phone around: to the BBC (a good source), university departments or people who knew people who might be able to help.

Course assistants were previously known as 'hostesses', a homely and perhaps more accurate title, though later discarded as perhaps not very businesslike. But in that role Vera was an ideal counterpart to my own role as designer of the courses. Not only did she undertake much of the phoning to 'regulars', but she had, among the course members, social skills that I entirely lacked. Much of the time, in coffee breaks, meals, and in the evening, was occupied in chat and general intermingling, where I was pretty useless. Vera, on the other hand, was in her element, knowing their names without having to look at their name tags, and generally making sure that each and every one was happy. She had a nice sense of humour and a good memory. I was fortunate in having her company in Fox's Tower for more than five years. We have met only three times since leaving the castle, but have kept in touch.

Another prominent member of the staff was Karin Sherrington, head of the Resources Centre – the remodelled library, which had not only books but an array of audiovisual equipment, including copies of all recent BBC and ITV foreign-country reports. Compared with today's touch-of-the-button online information, it was perhaps a bit clunky, but Karin's quite spacious domain in the castle was a welcome retreat and mine of information, where the course members could 'interleave' with the talks and lectures of the course by the twenty or so different speakers. Karin's husband had been on the staff of the British Council, on a plane in the Far East hijacked by terrorists, which they suicidally caused to crash, killing all on board, leaving Karin a widow with three children. She was sharp, clever and amusing. I admired her.

So my life continued, with a fairly regular progression of courses, one after the other: five days at the castle and 20 Dollis Drive, and two (and three nights) at Cone Hill, devoted mainly to gardening and improving the landscape of its outstanding position above the Weald of Kent. Jeremy meanwhile, having left Millfield and, after Israel, spending a year or so plucking pigeons and pheasants at a place that did such things in Sevenoaks, decided he really ought to decide what to do with his life. He opted for a course in Farnborough having something to do with chemistry and matters connected with the environment. So he stayed with me during the week for about two years before, after graduating, he joined the GLC (Greater London Council) staff. After that, it was Hilary's turn. She had decided to do her sixth form at Farnborough College, and, for her too, 20 Dollis Drive was a convenient perch during the week, conveniently after Jeremy got his GLC job.

Patrick, as director, had been an administrator: apart from an introductory talk and concluding 'feedback' sessions with course members and, separately, with the staff, he had taken no part at all in the conduct of courses. Although I had been on fairly good terms with him – I was made deputy director on Peter's retirement – he had almost secretively kept the business side of the Centre to himself. On my first appointment, he had asked me to attend a governing board meeting. That was it. Never again. Yet, to give him his due, he was an excellent custodian of the building.

In Patrick's time a huge amount of work was done to repair and enhance the fabric of the castle, including the roof and the three-quarters of a mile of its walls. But there was no question, with him, of being one of the crew; he was very much the captain and, although friendly to everyone, seemed to consider himself somewhat above the rest of us socially, as well as being our boss. Partly, I suppose, this was because he did work closely with our board of governors, many of whom were indeed very important persons in the Civil Service, BBC or business companies.* I think he was probably more interested in the castle than he was in the work of the Centre. This could lead him astray. Fairly early in my employment he arranged for a group of about twenty Metal Box† middle-rank employees to attend a special course for people bound for South Africa – and then he went on holiday, leaving me in charge, to 'welcome' them. The attendance of this group caused tremendous consternation among the staff, who quite reasonably asked why were we helping a company that was proposing to send British people to South Africa to do jobs that its own (African) people should surely be trained to do. When I took this up with Patrick on his return, he was a bit surprised, but saw the point, and we did no more courses for whites undercutting opportunities for black labour.

I have to confess that I had not myself recognised the political twist to that course until it was pointed out to me. Two of the course assistants were demonstrably left wing, and it was Barbara Broer, herself a South African, who drew my attention to it. Barbara had two children and an ex-husband, and was later to become a Labour MP and marry Ken Follett, a famous novelist apparently. Being a Labour MP nevertheless didn't prevent her from swanking in her husband's Rolls-Royce on a return visit to the castle. The other radically tinged assistant was from one of the South American countries, and had got on the wrong side of a military dictatorship.

* Lord Sherfield, a former ambassador to the USA, was chairman of our board, and Johnny Wilkinson, secretary of the BBC board, a member. Shell and Phillips were also represented.

† Metal Box plc was a big FTSE 100 canning and packaging company, later absorbed into other companies.

She was a staunch supporter of Amnesty International and enlisted me to do letter writing to government ministers of countries holding named political prisoners. It was said that receiving hundreds of such letters did sometimes have the effect of securing their release or at least improving the conditions under which they were held.

Staff at the centre were required, normally, to retire at the age of sixty. However, as it happened, Patrick's retirement was also on the horizon, and I was asked to stay on for an extra year. I was happy enough to do that, but Beryl, back at Cone Hill and believing that I might be getting rather too happy among all the female company in Farnham, was strongly against it. So, with some reluctance, I settled for staying on simply until a new deputy director could be recruited. Hilary, meanwhile, had completed her education at Farnborough College and was installed as a trainee nurse at Maidstone Hospital; so, 20 Dollis Drive no longer being needed, I was able to sell it – at a decent profit – and return finally to Cone Hill. Although that was the end of my 'working' life, retirement was still going to be fairly busy.

Cone Hill's three acres, although mainly woodland, still offered opportunities for improvement, and I was never happier than when digging, cutting, burning and composting. The vegetable garden got more attention than before, but I was always more interested in plants, shrubs, lawns and landscaping. We had only three neighbours, none of whose houses could be seen from ours: Maureen and Trevor Jones and their three children, much the same age as ours; the vicar, Donald Lynch (who had been a chaplain to the Queen), and his wife Jean; and down below at the bottom of the hill, David Woodgate and his wife (name forgotten). David had taken advantage of our absence abroad to shift the boundary between us – to his advantage. There was a definite bulge into our land which I didn't notice until we had lived with it for some years, and David insisted that was how it always was. He may of course have been right, and that was how it was when we bought the place. But our civil relationship with him always recognised that he was a crafty old sod. With the other two families we were good friends – in the case of one, because we were good churchgoers; and the other because of the children. Otherwise we didn't have much of a social life. Partly this was because we had previously been short-term inhabitants, never staying long before we were off again abroad; in Cone Hill we never fully got back into our new life in England. Partly, I think, Beryl always had itchy feet, and, being from an Anglo-Indian family, felt a bit of a stranger in this country, no matter that this was where she lived, on and off, for most of her adult life. Now, with me freed from Farnham Castle, she was thinking of moving nearer to her family in Scotland. I did not immediately buy into the idea.

Nor was Beryl immediately pressing it. She was actively pursuing her interest in the Mungavin family history, which involved frequent visits to the Public Records Office in London and, more often, to the British Library, where most of the British family records from India are held. I accompanied her as her willing assistant. It was fascinating work. The result, after many months scouring box files and video records, is, I think, an interesting document ('*Mungavins of the Raj*') recounting the lives of the descendants of an Irishman who joined the British Army in the nineteenth century and was posted to India, where he married and spent most of the rest of his life – as did his progeny from two marriages.

I had joined the Council for the Protection of Rural England and was hoping to do something with them (it never came to anything), and we both joined the Tunbridge Wells branch of the United Nations Association. Both Jeremy and Hilary had settled into their new jobs in England and, although they were now living separately from us, we saw them frequently. Two things influenced my eventual agreement to move to Scotland.

Hilary, in addition to working diligently at her nurse's training, was also getting to make new friends, and one friend in particular. His name was David Vale, a young man, carpenter by trade, who was working in the building firm of his father and an uncle, at Tatsfield, near Westerham. I can't recall any previous boyfriend. Anyway, Hilary didn't let the grass grow under her feet, and in fairly short order she had accepted his proposal to marry. There was a whirlwind of preparations. I had wanted the reception to be in a marquee on the lower lawn at Cone Hill, but Hilary shot down the idea at once.

"I'm not having my reception in a TENT!" she said.

There was no argument about the church, of course. It was

obviously going to be St Lawrence's, little more than 100 yards through the woods behind our house. Hilary and David were married there by Donald Lynch on 16 August 1986. It was a joyous occasion and the St Lawrence bell-ringers did them proud, and so also, I suppose, did the Post House Hotel at Wrotham Heath. But I still would have preferred that 'tent' in our garden.

After their honeymoon, the newly weds settled first in a cottage in Hawkhurst; then, less out of the way, a house with a precipitous garden in Biggin Hill; and finally in David's home village, Tatsfield, where his parents still lived. Jeremy, meanwhile, bought a flat in Thamesmead – surely one of the dreariest parts of London.

The second reason I came to accept that we should move to Scotland was because, on a visit north, we took the opportunity to have a look at Gatehouse of Fleet, a small town in Dumfries and Galloway in the south-west of Scotland, where Beryl's sister and brother-in-law, Phyllis and George, and their several children – ultimately five – were accustomed to go on caravan holidays by the sea. They spoke ecstatically of its out-of-the-way charm, and strongly recommended it as a place to live. Originally a small village, it was developed in the nineteenth century by an enterprising businessman named Murray – mainly for cotton mills using the waters of the River Fleet, the single remaining mill being a museum in what is now a small town. We approached it via Laurieston, about eight miles from Gatehouse on a single track through conifer forests and open hill country occupied mainly by sheep and the occasional deer. Shortly before reaching the town, we saw, up on the left-hand side of the road, one or two cedar-wood houses, each in quite a substantial garden. I must be a sucker for the environment, because that is what impelled me (Beryl already primed) to seek out an estate agent in Kirkcudbright. Were there any other similar houses on the Laurieston Road?

And yes, the cedar-wood houses we glimpsed on approaching Gatehouse were part of a housing development designed by the local laird, Mrs Murray-Usher, a descendant of the original Murray. There were approximately twenty houses, all of cedar wood and well spaced out on the hillside south of the Gatehouse of Fleet Golf Course, and the Kirkcudbright estate agent told us there was indeed one up for sale. He warned us, however, that there were quite severe conditions that a potential buyer was compelled to accept, regarding maintenance of the house and upkeep of the garden; on selling, one's buyer would be similarly bound. We weren't put out by that, though the legal document, when we got round to reading it, was pretty fierce in its penalties for non-compliance. Mrs Murray-Usher and her estate office were definitely in charge.

Toftingal, which we arranged to see that very day, was quite a large single-storeyed house on a gently sloping site with a beech hedge and silver birch along the lower side of the grounds – a bit more than half an acre. It had an excellent view over the river valley to the hills beyond. Behind us, beyond the boundary stone wall, was the golf course. The house had a good, big kitchen and two bathrooms. We didn't haggle over the price, and ultimately moved in in August 1987. It was not the only property we bought that year.

In January we had taken the first of what were going to be regular winter holidays in Cyprus. This was at a hotel in Limassol; but later, when we had travelled more widely on the island, we always stayed in Paphos, on the south-west coast. Over the years, Cyprus has succumbed to the degradation of holiday-island hedonism, catering for drunken parties and loutish behaviour – often British. But at that time the original old-fashioned 'British' character of Cyprus was still strongly evident: nearly everyone spoke English and was amazingly friendly. And it was that, plus the beguiling salesmanship of Messrs Lordos, a property company that specialised in selling flats and villas to foreigners, which, after a few seductive lunches and tours around the Paphos area, ended up with us buying a two-bedroom flat in a small development known as Kingsgate (with a pool) immediately opposite the Tombs of the Kings. On the second (top) floor, the flat had a balcony looking out to the sea beyond. Below us were Thetis and Evagorus Pantelides, Cypriot Greeks expelled from Famagusta by the Turkish invasion in 1974, understandably bitter, but making the best of their situation by running a friendly bar in the counterpart of our living room. So we did not lack company in the evenings; and because the site was at that time virtually isolated, the clientele were mostly regulars and middle-aged people like ourselves. It was almost a club down there.

31 – GATEHOUSE OF FLEET

The removal to Scotland of our effects – which included several of my useful stock of railway sleepers – was completed on 20 August 1987, when we were at last installed at Toftingal. There were a further few in-hock-to-the-bank weeks before Cone Hill could be finally sold and handed over to its new owners – just days before the great storm of 16 October devastated the area of Sevenoaks and its environment. We had got out just in time. Our unfortunate buyers could not have timed their purchase worse. As we heard later, half the trees on what had been our land were blown over, and the drive to the house was blocked for several days. It was an awful experience for the poor man. Yet, when speaking later to our erstwhile vicar, Donald Lynch, who had of course himself lived through the full force of the hurricane, he was quite relaxed about it.

"They'll grow again," he said.

God brought the wind, and God would provide the seeds of recovery.

We naturally hoped that Cone Hill had survived intact, but at the time we were much more interested in looking around to see more closely where it was that we had now ourselves so impulsively landed. Gatehouse of Fleet, being on a loop road off the A75 from Gretna to Stranraer, was a quiet town, attractive to retired people, many of whom appeared to be English – which tended to mean that its inhabitants were slyly regarded either as 'incomers' (however long resident) or 'locals', who perhaps had a more legitimate right to be there. To some extent this was reflected in the churches: Church of Scotland for the Scots and the Episcopal Church for the likes of us.

Coming up from England, what struck me most as soon as we reached the A75 was the sparkling clarity of the air: it made me realise how air pollution is taken as a matter of course in the south; we don't think about it. But here, on the Laurieston Road estate (some little way out of the town) with a big, already well-developed garden, I gloried in the space, the views, and the feeling that I could turn my hand to almost anything I wanted. Beryl rejoined the Red Cross, and we gradually got to know people.

In the house there were sufficient rooms for me to have a study to myself, where I had bookshelves built in by Mr MacInnis, a local joiner – which reminds me that he was working on that job when I returned from an appointment with our doctor, Dr Armstrong. I had consulted him about a cyst on the inside of my thigh.

"Mrs Thatcher likes us to do that sort of thing ourselves," said Dr Armstrong, a keen young man, and in short order he had me on his couch, cut out the cyst and sewed up the wound.

I strode out of his surgery and, getting out of the car back home, burst the stitches. Blood everywhere! I took off my trousers and lay on the kitchen floor just as Mr MacInnis was about to leave.

He took one look at me, gasped "Oh Gawd!" and bolted – whether in terror or to seek aid I don't know.

I shouted "It's OK, Mr MacInnis!" after him.

And it was, more or less, after a bit of mopping. But it rather made a mess of Dr Armstrong's handiwork.

St Mary's Episcopal Church had a small but regular congregation of about twenty-five, and shared its rector with the church in Kirkcudbright. At the time of our arrival there was an interregnum, the previous rector having been dismissed for, it was said, petty pilfering. His ultimate successor, Claude Broon, with his wife, Janice, later became well known to us: he was a bit of a pedant in church matters, having been a student at Brasenose College, Oxford. Janice was equally the expert when it came to Czechoslovakia, where she had developed contacts with 'opposition' people. John Clark, who had been a London stockbroker, and his wife (Mary?) were regular attenders from our Laurieston Road community, as were Geoffrey and Marjorie Mercer. Geoffrey, a gruff Lancastrian, had been a school teacher of Greek and, although they didn't go there now, knew Cyprus well.

Our Laurieston Road houses were strung out on a private road that ran roughly parallel to the Laurieston Road itself. Someone who had been a top man in MI5 or MI6 lived at the far western end (appropriately enough, I can't remember his name; he was to die while we were at Gatehouse), and Mr and Mrs Longfield – he had been a police commissioner in one of the Borneo countries – were at the eastern end. Opposite us were Jack and Barbara Veitch. He was a retired farmer, very lame. Next to the Veitches was a retired Dutch rose grower.

These were the sort of people we had now landed among. The remaining thirteen households were of similar vintage: almost all were retired husbands and wives. There were no young children – not one – and they were mostly English. I can remember only two who were Scottish: the Veitches and a rather unpleasant Ayr solicitor who came after us and used his house (our immediate neighbour) merely as a weekend holiday home. Two or three years after we arrived I was asked to be secretary of the residents' association – not a very demanding job. We had annual meetings to discuss our common facilities: mainly upkeep of the road, sewage (sometimes a major preoccupation – for example, when the pipes blocked), and the water furrow! The furrow did not run through everybody's garden (we didn't benefit from it), but the quality of the flow depended very much on whether you were at the upper or the lower end. On the whole, we all got on remarkably well with each other; but the furrow was, for a few, a matter of grumbling discord.

Both John Clark and John Longfield were excellent oil painters. At that time, although I had briefly attended a course in London using oils, and had cursorily painted in Africa, my painting materials had been entirely forgotten in a cupboard. But Kirkcudbright was well known for its Scottish painters, and in Gatehouse was a young chap, Jeremy Carlisle, who held watercolour painting classes in his own home. I signed up with him and, in time, improved somewhat on the standards set by Mrs Taylor of King's Leigh. In good weather we would go out and paint en plein air. On at least two occasions we held exhibitions of our work in Kirkcubright. Jeremy knew a man who not only framed pictures, but had an eye for the kind of frame to show off a particular painting. I didn't manage to sell anything, but my bedroom walls still have two of my well-hung efforts from that time.

A surprise discovery in Gatehouse was when I learned that my godmother, Dr Isobel Brown, who had, after my childhood, almost completely disappeared from my life, was now, in her late nineties, living in Castle Douglas, about fifteen miles away on the A75. She was still, when we first arrived, living alone.

"Did ye think I was deid?" she asked when I phoned her.

Aunt Isobel, as I called her, had been a fellow student with my father in Aberdeen. She was now almost blind and very deaf, but still very bright and in full possession of her other faculties. It was fortunate that she had a niece, Isobel Bell, with whom she had always been close, living at Borgue, near Kirkcudbright; and she did eventually move in with the Bells. We often visited her and she would chat away about current affairs with as much interest in them as we had – I especially.

But it was Beryl's relatives to whom we had now hove into closer proximity, and we would quite frequently be found shuttling up to Ayrshire to see Phyllis, George and their five children, who were all living near their parents. We also saw more now of her clergyman brother, Gerald, and his wife, Margaret (their four boys were all scattered hither and yon). Both Gerald and George had retired early, though Gerald still conducted the occasional service. Both families (minus children) came to stay with us in Cyprus after we had sold Kingsgate and bought a villa at Zelemenos, just north of Paphos. Brother Patrick's Glasgow family (wife Deborah and six children) was a danger area we steered clear of; and Beryl's elder sister Laura (her husband, Frank, and five children), who, I gather, had been a bit of a martinet to the younger Mungavins in India, was now living in Paisley, but we only saw them occasionally – mainly at funerals and weddings. Beryl's brother Jack (his wife, Joy, and, abstemiously for a Mungavin, only one daughter) we had left behind in London.

Apart from my secretarial duties with the residents' association, I was also roped in as secretary of our church council and at the same time, with entirely different people, area secretary of the Galloway Scout Council. I had never been a Scout and this job didn't involve any actual Scouting: I was merely in charge of handling the surprising amount of bureaucracy the Scout movement involved. The area commissioner was John Firth, a retired army officer, and it was he who had asked me to take it on. He was a very pleasant, easy-to-get-on-with, good-looking man, about my own age, who lived in a big house near Borgue, but seemingly on an insufficient army pension – because he supplemented it by working as a house painter, mainly for his friends. Later he became a salesman for some kind of proprietary medication, which he pressed on all and sundry over coffee – very difficult to refuse. Our honorary president was a member of the local gentry, Mr R. W. Rainsford-Hannay, who lived, it seemed to me, just in three rooms of an enormous house near the sea. He was only wheeled out on special occasions, as when visited by the Chief Scout.

On the subject of money: on a visit to us from Bristol, Hamish – who, since our days of playing Monopoly at Plashet Road, was well into squirrelling away wealth – introduced me to the stock-market activity of 'traded options'. What you do is to make a contract to buy or sell so many shares of a company at a price two or three months ahead. For this commitment you are paid a commission, the amount depending on how many shares you are committing yourself to buy or sell. In the Colonial Service I never had much money, but the UN paid well – to the extent that I was able to live on half my salary and pay the other half into an account in England. So I had a few thousands to play around with. When buying a 'put' option, you had to make sure you had enough money in the bank to buy the shares put upon you if the price you were 'committed' to would prove, at the end of the two or three months, to be higher than the actual market price. Similarly, when selling an option to buy, you had to already own the same shares (or the money to buy them), ready to sell at the contract price. Naturally, when selling a 'put' you hoped the future market price would be higher than your bid – in which case you simply pocketed the commission; and when contracting to buy shares (which I rarely did) you hoped the future market price proved to be lower than the current price. The delightful thing about traded options at that time was that you received from the stockbroker a cheque in the post (for me, normally about £200) for the commission every time you made a contract. For about two years I engaged in this, what proved to be, quite lucrative activity, mostly selling 'puts'. Even when getting shares put upon me, I consoled myself by at least adding to my small portfolio of investments. My interest in this activity waned* when my stockbroker (Stock Beech) stopped sending cheques (merely crediting my account – not nearly so gratifying) and Stock Beech, including the pleasant young lady I dealt with, got taken over by a larger, more impersonal firm.

All these, though, were peripheral interests. My main activity at Gatehouse was gardening – a rewarding occupation which suited my temperament and kept me physically active.

I have also always taken a perhaps eccentrically close interest in current affairs: not so much in UK politics, which are often tediously partisan, as internationally. This was an interest which, for the whole world, was galvanised on 21 December 1988 when an American plane was brought down by a terrorist bomb at Lockerbie, only about twelve miles on the other side of Dumfries from us. As with my experience of terrorism at Dhaka, it was almost dehumanising to be so close to it yet not feel personally affected. Indeed only a few days after that tragedy, which obliterated the lives of all 243 passengers and sixteen crew of Pan Am flight 103, we were blithely flying off to Cyprus (where we were later joined by Hamish) for our regular winter holiday.

We returned in March and were almost immediately taken up with the preparations for Jeremy's wedding to Sally Chiverton, whom he had met through her brother Colin, a fellow student at his Farnborough College. Most of the arrangements, of course,

* Just as well I stopped: I'd be on the street selling the *Big Issue* now, if I hadn't.

were handled by the bride's family, who got permission for the reception to be held at Farnham Castle. It was a day (15 April 1989) marked by joy, but also sadness: Sally's father had been suffering for some months from terminal cancer. He made a supreme effort, in his wheelchair, to attend the wedding, but couldn't make it to the reception meal, and died the following day. A brave man.

In September the same year we made our first trip to Ireland, and in County Longford tracked down my Aunt Molly. Uncle George had died of a heart attack some years previously, and she was living with their daughter Betty, now married to Joe, a birdwatcher who (on no other evidence) we suspected might be an IRA spy. I say 'living with'; actually, Molly was living in a caravan in Betty and Joe's farm-like garden. She was still the same old Molly, now *very* old but remarkably hale and hearty. She greeted us with enthusiasm and quite took a shine to Beryl. The feeling was mutual: Beryl tended to like eccentric people.

In September 1992 we made a trip to Russia – which, because it was almost pioneering at the time, deserves a chapter to itself, drawn mainly from notes I made at the time.

32 – RUSSIA

For the ordinary tourist, travel in Soviet Russia had always been difficult to impossible, but after the cataclysmic fall of Communism throughout Eastern Europe in 1989, and the ultimate hauling-down of the hammer and sickle flag over the Kremlin, when Mikhail Gorbachev handed power over to Boris Yeltsin in December 1991, the atmosphere had markedly changed. The authorities were now making efforts to encourage foreigners to visit the country. One of the tours being promoted was for a river cruise along the Volga. Such trips had always been part of Communist Party benevolence towards its favoured apparatchiks: several cruise ships already existed; now many of them were to be at the disposal of people like us. We decided to go, eager to see something of a country that had been, for all our lives so far, almost completely shrouded to Western eyes.

7 September 1992
We disembarked from the plane at Sheremetyevo, Moscow's main international airport, much as any other on first sight, only shabbier; then entered a large, gloomy reception area: brown marble effect and glass screens – apart from our flight, shuffling along corridors and steps, virtually deserted. Initially, rather like entering a cathedral. That impression is swiftly dispelled as we encounter the first obstacle: immigration. The place suddenly becomes populated by a multitude of passengers queueing to get their passports scrutinised and stamped by immigration officials who seemingly hadn't been re-educated to *perestroika*

and *glasnost* procedures. Baggage collection from a rickety carousel: a period of half an hour's stomach-churning anxiety; then into about six queues which gradually narrow down to two as it became clear that only that number of customs desks remained open. Welcome to Russia!

Our group eventually reassembled outside, to be greeted by a smiling Ludmilla.

"Call me Luda," she says, and shepherds us onto a coach. Pouring with rain but very mild – and dark. Three hours (half an hour on the journey, two and a half to clear the airport) before we reach the landing stage on the Moscow river, where MS *Russ* is berthed. Efficient check-in at the key desk, where we are given a 'registration card' and assigned our cabin and table in the dining saloon. Our cabin was surprisingly good, but there was little time to relax there because we're already late for the evening meal.

At the table we met the three other people who were to be our dining companions for the next two weeks: a retired British naval officer and his wife, who rather reminded me of my brother David and Liz, and a single American lady – very sharp and amusing – none of whose names can I remember.

8 September

Off we went by bus to Zagorsk, 43 miles away. Nothing much of interest on the way: we were mostly on dual-carriage roads lined with many trees, mostly conifer and silver birch, with stretches of untended grass. The occasional buildings were mostly gloomy, high-rise blocks, but here and there little country cottages, broken down and neglected looking. Some had little, sad-looking allotment gardens, but after a very dry summer, perhaps to be expected. Our guide, Rosa, told us that conditions in Russia for ordinary people had much improved in the last two or three years, and (if that was not entirely convincing) certainly since ten years ago. Our driver, for example, gets 5,000 roubles a month – that's equivalent at today's exchange rate, to 25 US dollars – and, she said, "He can manage on that." The old age pension is 1,000 roubles a month. This obviously was more an indication of an unrealistic exchange rate and the very low (rouble) prices in Russia. Rosa agreed that the poor and unemployed were very badly off, and that 'privatisation' was being brought in corruptly. Warming to her subject, she went so far as to say that in Russia there was "corruption from top to bottom", the difference now being that newspapers can reveal it. [I wonder if that still applies in Putin's Russia.]

Zagorsk is actually Sergiyev Posad, renamed after a Communist hero of the 1917 Revolution. But, home to the most important Russian monastery and spiritual centre of the Russian Orthodox Church, it was neglected and actively vilified by Stalin. It was founded in 1337 and throughout succeeding centuries added additional churches, seminaries and cloisters until it is now almost a village, a veritable blancmange of onion domes of different sizes, some gold, some blue. Very impressive from the outside. But Orthodox churches (of which my first experience had been in Cyprus) are mostly dark, gloomy and cluttered (to my mind) with icons, ornaments and hanging vessels. I have yet to see one that has anything of the *grandeur* of cathedrals in Western Europe.

Outside was a cheery market, with stalls selling all kinds of mementos: dolls, amber jewellery, lace, paintings, books. Along with several beggars that were hanging about, we noted the dignity and superior bearing of many of the stall-holders – good-looking young men, perhaps students, speaking some English. Currency changing, illegal here, was easy.

In the afternoon we were back in Moscow to see something of the Pushkin Museum of Modern Art. I can't remember anything of it now but I noted at the time that it was 'fabulous'.

9 September

Breakfast: black or white bread, cheese, jam, porridge, cheese pudding with raisins, apple juice, tea or coffee.

Lunch: good, hot consommé with diced potatoes and meatballs, grated carrot & cold fish (bones), spaghetti and sliced beef with melted cheese on top, three small plums floating in thin juice, tea/coffee.

Dinner: sliced cucumber and tomato, chicken with rice, cake, ice cream, tea/coffee.

That was pretty typical throughout. OK if you were hungry but hardly ever really enjoyable.

In the morning we were taken to the Tretyakov gallery, a world-famous collection of Russian art assembled and enlarged from 1856 by a Russian merchant, Pavel Tretyakov, who donated it to the nation shortly before it was to descend into political upheaval and chaos. Amazingly it survived the revolutionary years and two world wars. There was time to see only a very small part of the collection (still being added to) but it was enough to recognise that Soviet Communism had not totally destroyed its Russian heritage.

Still not started on the Volga journey, we were taken in the afternoon to the Red Square: impressive for its wide space and view of the Kremlin on one side and the multi-domed St. Basil's Cathedral at the end (the GUM department store on the other side attracted nobody's attention). Shaking off the importunities of gypsies who surrounded our bus, we entered the cathedral (15 roubles = 4p) and at once found ourselves climbing up a narrow, wooden-floored spiral staircase into what proved to be the first of nine chapels, the central one with a soaring roof. It was dark inside and a maze of interconnecting passages and stairways. Some of the flower frescoes have been restored, but generally the building is gloomy inside and seems neglected – quite different from its flamboyant exterior.

1.30 p.m. – Back on board MS *Russ*, we move off up the Moscow river and into the canal connecting with the Volga. Magnificent lock gates! Does one ever say that of lock gates? But these were: huge, and surmounted by large bronze galleons in full sail.

6 p.m. – The Captain gave a presentation to us in the main saloon, via an interpreter: "Dear passengers . . ." introducing everyone we'd be coming into contact with: the purser, the 'cruise director', two bands (evening floor-show and dining room), the aerobics instructor, who gave us a brief cavorting exhibition accompanied by deafening disco music (the Captain looking on impassively), the hair-dresser, a massive masseur, the head of catering and, finally, the programme organiser.

10 September

We have now joined the Volga and, after a talk on Peter the Great, the ship moors at nowhere in particular so that we can stretch our legs in the neighbouring countryside, typical of much that we have been passing through: here groves of silver birch, silent, peaceful, seemingly untouched by the bustle of daily life.

Next stop Uglic, famous in Russian history but which appears to have suffered from neglect during the Communist period. We were surrounded by little boys like a flurry of flies, trying to sell post-cards, guide-books and old medals. A pleasant river-side walk into the town: very open: wide roads, a few miscellaneous buildings but no character other than a uniform dinginess. The wide market square with a few forlorn kiosks led onto the kremlin – what remains of it, now mainly the Cathedral of the Transfiguration of our Saviour, with its separate bell tower; the Church of Demetry [son of Ivan the Terrible] on the Blood; and a remaining chamber of the Palace of the Princes of Uglic, the oldest building of the kremlin to have survived. All almost heart-stabbingly evocative of a long-gone age.

11 September
Our stretch of the river is roughly halfway along the Volga, travelling upstream in a south-easterly direction. Now we're at Kostroma, in a small church – white, overlooking the river – where a service was in progress: mostly women. We noted a number of wooden houses, intricately ornamented – mostly in a poor state of repair; but, set in their straggly gardens with apple trees and other fruit, they gave the area a pleasantly traditional appearance. In the centre of the town several of the older houses have been 'classified' (much as we do with some of ours) and may not be altered. In the impressively large central square we gingerly entered the convent Church of the Resurrection, where a service in full panoply of metropolitan bishops, etc. was taking place: very beautiful and moving singing by nuns with sonorous male accompaniment.

12 September
Held up by fog, we missed our turn through the locks, but arrived at Nizhny Novgorod (Gorky) in bright sunshine. We had a geography lesson on Russia, and our first Russian language lesson. Then by bus to the kremlin, beautifully situated on a hill above the harbour. Only one church remains in the kremlin – now, it seems, little more than a museum – but impressed by the singing by three women, of Russian religious music, we bought a tape [which proved, on our return, to be disappointingly dreadful]. Then to the centre of the town, which

is quite handsome: wide main road with shops, all very dingy and hardly anything for sale; but some imposing architecture in a sort of heavy Italian style.

Gorky had been virtually cut off from the world – a forbidden city, so to speak – in the socialist era, because of the important armaments and military aircraft industries there. We passed the KGB building, an enormous, forbidding block of offices. Our guide says "They are still working there, but I don't know what they do. They have no effect on our lives." Then on to another church, one of the few working churches in Gorky, badly neglected but being renovated. No sign of living religion but a small choir regaled us with 17th–18th-century sacred music: the tone and harmony of those few voices, echoing in the vast vaulted roof, was wonderful. It is probably true that they were performing for us, to get donations for the reconstruction, and that made it rather sad. Nevertheless, these small church choirs are the equal (and in some respects more deeply spiritual) of the very best in Britain. We are amazed and profoundly impressed that Russian musical traditions have survived and outlived the stultifying period of Soviet communism.

In the evening: fancy dress and fun and games aboard ship. I learned today that our Russian lecturer was a member of the KGB who had been expelled from Britain (nothing personal – he was probably part of a quota of expellees).

13 September
We arrive in the afternoon at Kazan, capital of the Tartar Republic. As the guidebook says, it's a unique blend of Moslem and Christian architecture. Visited the kremlin and its museum and picture gallery – well worth seeing, including ikons up to modern Russian paintings. Best of all, we attended a concert put on especially for us by the Kazan school of music: up a stone staircase into a magnificent (19th-century) auditorium. All very talented children, some outstanding, but I was struck by their unsmiling reception of our applause – clearly the opportunity to perform before a group of foreign tourists didn't appeal to them. Then a quick tour of the university buildings, Russia's third oldest apparently.

As one goes further from Moscow, poverty seems less and 'change' less. But the urban landscape through which, these past few days our ship has been making its way, was almost uniformly a picture of desolation: rusting cranes, abandoned warehouses, piles of forgotten stores or factory waste, with vegetation growing unchecked, lines of ancient railway engines silently going nowhere. Hardly a sign of human activity in these deserts of industrial decline. They, more than anything else we saw in Russia, were a stark picture illustrating the failure of Russian Communism.

14 September
Ulyanovsk, birthplace of Lenin and the last port of call before the boat turns round and retraces our journey. Our guided tour today (in rain, looking through the misty windows of the bus) was a bit in what I imagined was the pre-glasnost mode: a pleasant but not very fluent guide pointed out all the public buildings and monuments, carefully spelling out the dates of birth and death of each poet, historian, etc., commemorated, with Lenin getting star treatment. Like many in Russian towns, the streets are wide and characterless, the difference here being the evidence of municipal efficiency: many trees and well-maintained flower beds. We visited the school, now a museum, that Lenin attended (getting the 'Silver Prize') and saw the hall in which he sat his examinations ('with outstanding success'). We trailed through the rain to a museum filled with the art, furniture and treasures of local noble families, from whom they had been confiscated after the Revolution – a fairly mixed collection, as one would expect.

Finally, we came to the main hotel (disgusting lavatory) where our three bus-loads of tourists were disgorged into the Ulyanovsk Beryozka for some souvenir shopping. The 'rouble' shop next door had a good range of cheap art objects: eg. one could buy a very decent painting, fully framed, for as little as £2.50 (equivalent). Ironically, it seems that where glasnost has disrupted lives least – i.e. where communist practices continue much as before – the lives of the people are better. There are less signs of poverty. Our guide told us that prices were still subsidised. Perhaps the lesson here is that 'change', even towards something better, is always initially destabilising, especially for the poor.

15 September
Cheboksary, on the way back, is the capital of the Chavash

Republic. Our guide was a young medical student, who proudly emphasised the cultural distinction and separateness of this small republic of the Russian federation (pop. 1.25 million: about five times the population of Brighton). It almost reminded me of the Ealing Studios film *Passport to Pimlico*. Small though it is, it still had its full quota of squares, statues, avenues, etc., named after honoured poets and revolutionary leaders – including Lenin, Stalin and the first head of the NKVD (later KGB). "They are part of our history. Why should they be removed?" said our guide somewhat defensively. We stopped near the garden memorial to the dead of WW2, and trooped through to the imposing monument with its perpetual flame. It was a splendid site, overlooking the city and the Volga.

Back to the bus and on to the new (1987) theatre, looking rather like a marble grain silo from the outside; but it, too, occupying a splendid site, with spacious walks and promenades around it. Inside, an orchestra was beginning to assemble for a rehearsal, but could not be prevailed upon to play anything for us – in spite of the endeavours of another guide, an elderly man who was nauseatingly obsequious to "our American friends". Cheboksary apparently has five theatres.

More touring of streets – the wide boulevards, too densely planted with trees, are typically lined with featureless blocks of buildings: dull, unimaginative, depressing: everything on a large, not grand, scale, diminishing the people who live or work in them. Yet, in some areas, the pre-revolutionary buildings, however tatty, are refreshingly different, as are the little old wooden houses that you see in some of the older streets, sometimes wedged between larger monstrosities on either side. We pause outside the modern art gallery (but disappointingly did not enter); then to the museum: very ho-hum and dark. Finally, to the cathedral, being renovated after 70 years of neglect. One becomes a bit blasé about Orthodox cathedrals, we have seen so many, but it was magnificent inside, nevertheless.

16 September
The Volga is not only the longest river in Europe, it also carries a vast amount of water. Indeed, on our way back, with little more to do than observe our boat's passage, there were times when it seemed we were passing through a lake, the banks were so

distant. We stopped briefly at Nizhny Novgorod again. I climbed up a winding flight of steps to a wide terrace overlooking the harbour: a splendid view but unfortunately very misty.

17 September
A full day at Yaroslavl, the most attractive city we have seen on this tour. There is a good tree-lined esplanade or promenade above the river and running parallel with it. Behind it you can see through the trees a number of substantial houses that formerly belonged to rich merchants of the town. Yaroslavl is said to be the oldest city on the Volga, being founded by Yaroslavl the Wise about the same time as William the Conqueror invaded Britain. It became prosperous as a trading link from Moscow both north and east.

We first visited the Monastery of the Transfiguration of the Saviour, once immensely rich but now (as the guidebook accurately says) somewhat forlorn. You enter the white-walled grounds through a fine arched gateway and, were it not for the 'museum' aura of the place, would find the old buildings set among trees peaceful, and evocative of the age they were built (from 1516). As it is, we couldn't enter the cathedral and ended up at a group of shabby kiosks selling books and mementos. Then a tour of the town, well laid out with parks and gardens; few buildings higher than two storeys, which is now apparently the limit. The Church of Elijah the Prophet is a working church presently under restoration. We were fortunate to be allowed in. Every inch of its walls and ceilings is covered with frescos illustrating biblical scenes.

Then half an hour wandering through the outdoor market – full of activity – and the nearby department store: large, gloomy and ill-stocked. In the afternoon B and I forwent a guided tour of the folk museum, and wandered back through the town on foot, to get a better feel of the place. Yaroslavl is apparently twinned with Exeter. The weather, hitherto rainy, was much improved and we much enjoyed strolling through the park avenues, full of trees and flower beds. We sat for some time on an old-fashioned bench in the sunshine in the Ploshchad Volkova (the central 'circus') and just watched the people and traffic go by. Placed a candle in a little church near the KGB building. Wandered into various shops, dark and scruffy, with little more in them than you might find in an East African *duka*. Prices, on the whole, very cheap, and food in better supply than we had come to expect. Then back to the ship, pausing to do a bit of trading with the good-natured boys (and a few adults) selling old coins, watches, postcards, Red Army hats, paintings, etc., and ended up buying a jar of caviar for $4 (roughly £2 then) and a bottle of (very good) Russian champagne for $2.50.

18/19 September
By this time the tour organisers, who had been remarkably efficient in arranging our sightseeing days, seem to have run out of steam and assumed we would be happy enough just taking in the view on our way back to Moscow. Probably fair enough: we'd certainly had our fill of Russian history and culture: a truly majestic story which in many ways had been a revelation to most of us. Our last stop, before re-entering the Moscow Canal, was to moor at what they termed an 'evergreen grove', not strictly accurate, since it was a vast area of almost wholly silver-birch woodland; but it was oddly appropriate: the quiet and stillness among those trees as we walked among them, which seemed to go on for ever, somehow perhaps touched us with the soul of Russia.

33 – GOODBYE TO GATEHOUSE

Two days after returning from Russia we found ourselves just in time to attend the annual reunion of the British Association of Former United Nations Civil Servants (BAFUNCS) at Harrogate. Although I was an early member, joining Shirley Phillips, the man who started the organisation off in meetings in his own house some years previously, I don't much enjoy these large annual gatherings of people, most of whom one doesn't know, but who themselves seem to be having a whale of a time.

Still in 1992, on 23 December Aunt Isobel celebrated her 100th birthday. Niece Isobel, dispensing tea and cakes in one room, marshalled the visitors, while Aunt Isobel received them – including the Lord Lieutenant – in her sitting room, in ones and twos. And that, with her still looking as bright as ever, was the last we saw of her. Three weeks later we were off to Cyprus for our winter holiday, Hamish joining us for a couple of weeks. By this time we had sold the Kingsgate apartment and bought a two-bedroom villa (as they were called in Cyprus) further up the hill above Paphos, in an amazingly well-designed development still being worked on by the indefatigable Messrs Leptos. We had open country before us, looking out over the sea, another (usually unoccupied) villa on our left, and preparations for a third intermittently threatened on our right. Our garden, which had provision for a swimming pool, had been considerably neglected by the bulldozers, and was a jumble of rocks, weeds and wild flowers, of which the asphodel is the only one I remember.

Aunt Isobel died on 7 March 1993, shortly before our return.

Having reached her century, according to niece Isobel, she decided that was enough and just peacefully passed away.

In April the following year, after a prostate operation, I had the most traumatic experience of my life: I think it was occasioned by a delayed reaction to the anaesthetic. I woke up one morning with a feeling of the most appalling depression, very difficult to describe, but life from that moment seemed to be utterly pointless. Vitality had drained from me and the very act of getting up, washing and dressing was a nightmare of uselessly going through a customary routine for no reason. But I still had enough sense to know something was very wrong – I shouldn't be feeling like this – and I told Beryl almost immediately. She decided at once I must see Dr Armstrong, and, as I was unsafe to drive, she drove me to the surgery. So far as I remember, no appointments were required; it was first come first served. When he saw me, Dr Armstrong decided this was just another case he was accustomed to deal with occasionally and prescribed I think it was Prozac – which I duly took for one day.

The following night, totally overcome by depression, I resolved to kill myself as the only way to obtain relief. With Beryl sleeping, I got up and wrote her a brief note, which I left on my desk, apologising for what I was about to do and asking her to forgive me: life was no longer endurable. I had already decided what to do. I took a roll of broad sticky tape, went out, in my dressing gown, to the garage, and proceeded to wind the tape round my face, covering my nose and mouth as tightly as I could . . . until I lost consciousness.

The next thing I knew, I was lying on the floor of the garage, breathing with difficulty through a gap in the tape, which must have become dislodged in my fall – and saved my life. Incredibly as it must seem, my immediate feeling was of profound relief that I had failed. Somehow I had been shocked back into momentary sanity. With difficulty I cut off the tape and stuffed it into our garbage bin. When I went back to bed, Beryl was awake and, still heedless of anything, I told her what I had done.

I don't have much memory of what happened after that. I was still hopelessly depressed and simply allowed (if that is the right word) events to happen to me. To cut it short, I was admitted almost immediately to the Glencairn Ward of the Crichton Royal Hospital in Dumfries. This was said to be 'the grandest of Scotland's royal asylums'. It was founded privately in the nineteenth century by Elizabeth Crichton, a wealthy widow, and originally opened as the Crichton Institute for Lunatics (they called a spade a spade in those days). Nevertheless, under the direction of a leading psychiatric doctor at the time, the institution (renamed) ultimately acquired an international reputation, and with Mrs Crichton's money was developed in a park of eighty acres, with practically every facility for a self-contained existence, including a magnificent church capable of holding a congregation of several hundred.

I dwell on the history of the Royal Crichton because its early philanthropic and pioneering spirit was everywhere still evident. The Glencairn Ward, when I was there, had no more than about fifteen patients – nearly all elderly psychiatric cases, not lunatics – looked after by a team of perhaps eight nurses (not all on duty at the same time, of course). Most of us had our own room, but, as we were not physically unwell, tended to congregate in a large living room looking out over the park. Here we had our meals also, on tables of four. I remember there was a mature cherry tree in blossom immediately outside. The nurses spent most of their time just chatting to one or other of us, helping us to do jigsaw puzzles or drawings (art was encouraged throughout the hospital, including the wards for the actually insane). There was hardly any conversation between the patients themselves; most of us were wrapped up in our individual hopelessness. We saw doctors from time to time, who tested the balance of our minds. All of us were under medication. On most days we were visited by outside volunteers, who did their best to shake us out of our self-absorption by playing games like 'I spy with my little eye something beginning with . . .' or hunt the slipper. One lady took me out in her car for a drive into the countryside around Dumfries, chatting away in a friendly manner.

One Sunday I was asked if I would like to go to church. I must have been getting better at the time and said yes. I was to be accompanied by one of the male nurses (I knew all their names, but have forgotten them now). Why I should have been accompanied I don't know, as I was always free to walk out by myself in the park. Perhaps he, too, wanted to go to church. If so, it was rather strange because, although the service was held in that enormous church, it was immediately clear that this was a service for just a few clergymen, one of whom played the organ, around which we gathered; there was no other congregation. Some hymns were sung, prayers were said, and one of the clergymen delivered a little homily – hardly a sermon. In retrospect, though, what struck me most memorably after the service was the matey conversation of these clerics with each other and including also my nurse-minder. I was totally ignored; it was as if I was merely a dog on a lead. This cliquishness of some church people, which I have often observed, is perhaps no more than a feeling of community, a reflection of who we now are, in a country whose population is for the most part totally indifferent to religion. Nevertheless, that doesn't excuse those men of God, who obviously did not regard me as capable of sensible conversation.

I think I was at the Royal Crichton for about three weeks, during which, with all the stimulus and expert care of the staff, and Beryl's regular visits, I did slowly begin to see the world in a better light. On most days the weather was good and I would go walking by myself in the well-tended park, with its lawns, flower beds and mature trees. I might even find myself exchanging a few words with one of the gardeners. But what eventually convinced me that I was indeed getting better was in one of the regular meetings we had with a 'committee' of the doctors, when I was asked how I was and replied that I thought I was getting better.

"How do you know that?" one of them asked, rather sharply.

"Because my appetite has improved," I said. "I'm beginning to enjoy my food."

Did I think I was ready to go home? As it happened, both Hilary and Jeremy, dropping their jobs, had come up together some days previously. That had been a tonic and reminded me that being down in the dumps is sometimes self-indulgence and not fair to those nearest and dearest to us. I replied that yes, I did think I could now go home.

It was Hamish who drove me back to Toftingal (he too had come up) and my life did slowly begin to return to normal. (I was told by the doctors that these 'episodes' were often temporary and to some extent self-healing.) Perhaps a month later I was virtually back to my old self. The previous month had been ghastly, but now it was over. And, thank God, I have never since had a recurrence.

In June 1995 Beryl's brother Jack, the retired Pakistan Navy admiral, born the same year as me, died in London. We had often visited him and his wife, Joy, at their flat in Balham. He was, in my experience, the most outgoing and rumbustious of the Mungavin clan, and in his service life he had acquired much the same bearing and manners as his fellow officers in the Pakistan Navy. I remember one occasion when he had invited us to lunch at a fairly smart restaurant: after a short time at the bar, we moved with our drinks to our table – but not Jack, who handed his to a flunky to carry there for him. Even Beryl found this amusing. Poor Jack – his last couple of years were dreadful: a stroke left him virtually paralysed.

Of course it was the Mungavins living in Scotland that we saw most of, with the 'children' now adult and getting married or divorced, and having children of their own. Meanwhile down in England, Jeremy and Hilary had been producing families of *their* own. Hilary and David, naturally enough, marrying first, got in first with son Jonathan (now known as Jon) and daughter Katherine. Jeremy and Sally's sons, Richard and Hamish, were born either side of the Vales' Eleanor in 1992.

Very sadly, Sally lost a baby girl, Alicen, very late in her pregnancy – I will not forget Jeremy's heartbroken voice on the phone after trying more than once to get through: "We've lost our baby."

So now the family tug was coming from the south. Beryl began to talk of moving back again.

Had it been left to me, we probably never would have left Cone Hill in the first place; but now the opportunity of seeing much more of our grandchildren easily outweighed my aversion to a life of constant uprooting (which is what it always has been). We began scouting about for a new home in the area around Sevenoaks (which we knew best), and eventually decided on a bungalow called 'Outfield' in the village of Leigh. Sandwiched between a B-road and a railway, as it was, it might not sound attractive, but the road was not busy and the railway at the end of the garden was in a cutting; so all we would hear would be the swoosh of the relatively few trains that occasionally passed along it. Actually, it could have been much worse, as at the time that railway was being hotly debated in Parliament, regarding whether it should be developed as a main line to 'piggyback' lorries from the north, and thus reduce congestion on the roads. That threat had the incidental benefit, to us, of reducing the price of the house. We took a no-doubt foolhardy gamble that the project would be rejected – as it ultimately was.

As the house-sale laws are different in England and Scotland, there was no chain to be completed before moving; so we had an expensive few months when Outfield was bought before the Toftingal sale was completed. This had the incidental advantage of allowing us to make a start on our plans for a loft conversion and other changes downstairs. We would spend the occasional week sleeping on the floor of our new house, pigging it in the kitchen while (in the daytime) the friendly workers of a – very good – local building firm were pulling the place apart to meet our plans for its refurbishment. Almost the whole of 1996 was therefore a hiatus, until, in December, with Outfield finally sold, and Toftingal in a condition to receive it, we were able to load up our furniture and say goodbye to Gatehouse.

I left with mixed feelings – it was goodbye to our beautiful garden and the clean air and hills of Galloway, goodbye to the friends we had made in the past ten years. Yet now we would have the inestimable benefit of seeing much more of Hilary, Jeremy and the grandchildren. And, if I'm honest, downsizing at that time was probably a good idea.

34 – LEIGH AND THE WORLD BEYOND

Although Leigh – eccentrically pronounced Lie – is said to have derived from a thirteenth-century hamlet, it had barely increased in size over the following 800 years. It is still little more than a collection of houses round a large village green, and a straggle on the B-road from it to Penshurst. Our house was almost at the end of the straggle. The land had been owned, for three or four hundred years, by the Sydney family of Penshurst Place, and there still was a lingering tinge to Leigh of its feudal past associations.

It was not until the end of 1996 that we were able to vacate Toftingal and install ourselves in Outfield; and it was a few more months before the last of the builder's men finally took leave of us. They had done a good job. Beryl had an excellent well-lit bedroom and bathroom in the loft, where she could begin her mornings in comfort, undisturbed by me. I had the garden and a useful workshop outside to keep me physically occupied. Our lives settled down into the uneventful routines of the comfortably retired: supermarket shopping, grandchildren at weekends, occasional holidays abroad. We became regular attenders at the eight o'clock Holy Communion service at the thirteenth-century church, St Mary's, where I eventually found myself enrolled as one of the two who took alternate Sundays to read the epistle.*

---

* The other was a man named Gibbs, who happened to be a son of Sir Humphrey Gibbs, the penultimate governor of Southern Rhodesia, who was not recognised by the illegal government of Ian Smith after its unilateral declaration of independence (UDI), and remained virtually isolated in his gubernatorial mansion.

I was also beginning to interest myself in new technology and signed up for what turned out to be, for me, a quite unsuitable course on computer graphics, put on by the Tonbridge local authority. However, as it was based on the Apple computer, and I was impressed by its 'elegance' I plumped for that, rather than the market-dominating Microsoft, when deciding to progress from my clunky Amstrad and buy a beautiful green model of the first 'bulbous' Apple computers. In spite of keeping pace with the technology, since then, I have never become properly computer-savvy, and have to rely on my children and grandchildren to get me out of 'glitches'. Nevertheless, such basic skills as I do have are a useful complement to a close interest in current affairs, as it allows me, Pooter-like, to fire off emails to the press without all the old-fashioned business of writing a letter and sending it through the post.

My newspaper of choice, which began with the *Manchester Guardian*, then *The Independent*, has now settled on *The Times*, as the former two became, for my taste, too school-teacherly left wing. I supplement this with *The Spectator* at weekends, a decidedly Conservative-leaning periodical, for which I once cancelled my subscription in exasperation, but then restored it as it keeps my critical juices working. Apart from one year I have never belonged to any political party, nor felt any inclination to; politically I am a cross-bencher; and, in a letter I wrote to a *Times* columnist*, in August 2015, I gave him the benefit of what I called a 'Floating Voters' Charter', to which I gave him exclusive access:

> *Income disparities* – The gulf between the incomes of the very rich and the rest of us (not just the poorest) is scandalous and an indictment of our society. All incomes above £100,000 (for example; put it higher if you think that's too radical) should be matters of public record, within which the recipients would be required to state how much they have given to charity and, for each donation over, say £1,000, who or which charity gets it.
>
> *Immigration* – OK, immigration enriches our society, but too many coming too quickly damages social cohesion and must be countered – in three ways: proper control of our borders and points

---

* Philip Collins, who did not deign to reply.

of entry; active policies of 'integration' (multiculturalism should be tolerated but not encouraged); recognise that bad governments and civil conflict in, primarily, Africa, the Middle East and South Asia, are the 'push' behind migration – so the overseas aid target should be vigorously defended and directed especially to promoting local skills and employment, rooting out corruption and imposing sanctions on local despots.

The Economy – Stop talking about 'the Deficit' as if it were a disease that has to be cured by nasty medicine labelled 'Austerity'. Say how much we (the government, the people) are borrowing, how much we are paying in totally unproductive interest, and do we really want to pass this on to our children and grandchildren while we go on gaily living beyond our means? The answer and remedy are obvious.

Housing – There's enough brown-field land on which to build a million houses (apparently). Let's put a cracker under the backsides of the builders; put a tax on all undeveloped land they have owned for more than two years. Get local authorities to start building again, borrowing to do so, if necessary (debt for investment is OK isn't it? Gordon Brown says so).

Defence – Greenham Common and Lefties have given anti-Trident a bad name in polite society. Nevertheless, have the courage to say that Trident is little more than an unrequired membership ticket to the 'top tables', world-walking politicians' 'Bling'; and we can't bear the thought of the French having it and we don't. Think how much more credible (and creditable) we would be as a nation if the Trident billions were spent instead on properly equipping our fully manned (and womened, if you insist) armed forces. In supporting Trident, our generals, admirals and air-marshals are shooting themselves in the foot.

Health – So long as all parties support the NHS there's no political axe to grind; it's a matter of efficient administration, and party political point-scoring is a total voter turn-off. Stop doing it: you all want the same thing.

Education – Point up international comparisons (to our disadvantage). Lay responsibility for improvement squarely on school Heads. Get private schools (in return for their charitable status) to interact more with state schools.

Government – Reform of the House of Lords: just get on with it. Recognise that nettles have to be grasped and that you will be stung, no matter how you do it. Keep the 'great and good' element (which does not necessarily include bishops and ex-MPs), and stop the prime minister deciding who to send there.

Party relations – Stop talking about (a distortion of) the other party's policies. We know you don't like them. Just shut up about it, unless there's an obvious need to comment or rebut. We want to know what *you* are proposing.

I doubt whether most of the people we knew in Leigh would have signed up to much of that. There was an occasion when our local MP, Sir John Stanley, held a meeting in the village hall. It was, he said, a non-political meeting simply to get to know his constituents and listen to their concerns. That may have been his intention, but, as questions were asked by those present, it very soon became evident that his audience were pretty solidly Conservative – as, of course, was Sir John himself, who quickly grasped the mood of the meeting, which from then on became a Conservative Party rally.

In the 1997 general election I probably voted for the Liberal Democrats under Paddy Ashdown, demonstrating my general ambivalence rather than positive support for that party. In the event, the country was pretty well knocked sideways by the avalanche of the Labour victory; and I, too, was carried along with the general euphoria after the lacklustre end of eighteen years of otherwise triumphant Tory rule. John Major's leadership had been fatally undermined by his party's right-wing zealots, much as Labour's left-wing zealots fatally weakened James Callaghan's government in the 1978/79 'Winter of Discontent'. "Kick the rascals out!" had been the rallying cry that led to Margaret Thatcher's eleven years in power; now it was "Oh, for God's sake, we've had enough of these bloody Tories!" rather than any positive enthusiasm for Labour under its then relatively unknown Tony Blair. Nevertheless, Major was, and is in my opinion, a sensible, level-headed politician, whose somewhat prissy manner led him to be caricatured unfairly by the media.

What was missing from my 'Floating Voters' Charter' was any reference to 'green' issues, which certainly would be there were I to write it today. To some extent the question has been muddied by global warming, about which I think there is room for debate on the extent to which we humans play a significant part. The world has experienced ice ages in the past, and subsequent re-warming, without the agency of man. Yet our pollution of the atmosphere in the past two or three hundred years is incontestably a unique factor that increasingly affects the quality of human life, if not of the planet itself. The trouble is that concentration of the discussion on global warming, which, if we can do anything about it, is essentially a house-cleaning problem, diverts us from what is likely to be a really significant looming calamity: exhaustion of the world's finite resources in our pursuit of ever greater prosperity. Because that is happening relatively slowly over a human lifetime, and many millions in the world are still living in abject poverty, the need for 'growth' has been virtually unquestioned. We are back to the first point in my charter . . . and pie in the sky. I am not at all optimistic that *Homo sapiens* is sapient enough to share out more equitably the fruits of our unique world.

In spite of that, I have to confess that I have been mostly unthinking about green issues. My political antennae have been much more closely directed towards world current affairs. In March 2003, when America, with Britain in close support, invaded Iraq, things had boiled up so much that I decided, no doubt eccentrically, to keep a diary of the war. I wrote as an introduction three years later:

> This diary is an attempt at history in slow motion. I began writing it because I felt, along with very many other people in this country, that the invasion of Iraq in March 2003 was likely to prove disastrous. Even if Saddam Hussein did have weapons of mass destruction (and I was prepared to believe our prime minister that he might well have them) there seemed to be no reason he would be any more likely to use them aggressively than Soviet Russia had been during the 'cold war', when it, too, was faced by the infinitely greater power of America. Yet, while I agreed with those who said the war would unleash all manner of tensions and inter-communal hostilities – not only in Iraq but throughout the Middle East and against ourselves – I would, given my relative ignorance of the facts on the ground, have been hard-pressed to defend my own puny opinion against the supposed expertise available to the

British government. I decided therefore to keep a record, day by day, as the events and effects of the war unfolded before us on our television screens and in our newspapers – and on the internet. How exactly does a predicted disaster occur? I wanted to find out.

Below I reproduce the first two entries from my 'Armchair Diary of the War in Iraq':

30 March 2003
This is the eleventh day of the war, and I am becoming convinced that the decision to start it was a catastrophic error. I am not proposing to show this diary to anyone else; but I shall leave it among my effects as a record of the events of the war and its aftermath as seen from the point of view of an ordinary citizen of this country, derived simply from reading the newspapers and watching television. It will not be of much interest to anyone who might read it today – the story is being lived out and reported round the clock as I write. But in fifty or a hundred years' time (if this diary and the world survive) when all the lies and controversy will have been shaken out by history, it may be interesting to see how it all looked at the time. I am typing it out in the evening pretty much as thoughts come into my head.

But first, a bit of background. It seems as if the 'hawks' of Washington were hatching thoughts of finishing off Saddam Hussein soon after the Kuwait war [August 1990 to February 1991] only half did the job (for reasons that were perfectly respectable at the time). Pretty well everyone else in the world viewed these hawk people as dangerously irresponsible, but their ideas were so lunatic as to be disregarded. Then came the hijackings of 11 September 2001 and the cataclysmic destruction of the two World Trade Centre towers. We were in Dublin at the time and saw the pictures on the television in our room at the Royal Marine Hotel – the scenes of the two planes crashing into those buildings were played over and over again. The effect was extraordinary: strangers shared their sense of shock with each other – in the bank where I first saw a screen (tellers, customers all staring up at it), in the street outside, in shops; it was as if all humanity in the world had suddenly been drawn together. And indeed it had. But then it became apparent that the reactions, perhaps naturally, were very different from what they were in most of the rest of the world. The superpower's unquestioning confidence in itself was terribly shaken, but it was determined to fight back. It did not wish to ask itself WHY nineteen apparently sane Arabs would wish to kill themselves in this insane project of destruction and murder of nearly 3000 innocent people. How could hatred go so far? Beyond hitherto invulnerable America, the rest of the world recognised that injustice to the Arab 'nation' – pre-eminently, but not exclusively, the oppression of Palestinians by Israel – led desperate men to resort to terrorism. But this attack demonstrated that the scale of it had now reached such terrifying proportions that every country almost without exception (North Korea?) was prepared to sign up to a 'War on Terrorism'.

The war which actually followed, in Afghanistan, aiming to destroy the Taliban government that was sheltering the al-Qaida terrorist network led by Osama bin Laden (held responsible for '9/11') was widely supported. America had been grievously attacked and was fully entitled to exact retribution. Yet the hawks were not satisfied with defeating the Taliban and scattering al-Qaida. Without any evidence that Iraq had anything to do with 9/11 or al-Qaida, America ratcheted up the pressure on Saddam Hussein, on the grounds that he still had 'weapons of mass destruction' (WMD) and that he was consequently a threat to his neighbours and indeed to the whole 'free world', including Europe and America. It had become clear, after George W. Bush's (challenged) election, that the hawks had taken over the White House and were determined to have the war that the US President's father had not (in their eyes) properly finished. America began assembling its forces in the Middle East; Tony Blair tried to get the action legally done through the United Nations. An attempt was made to discover, by means of UN inspections, whether Iraq really did have WMD. The weeks passed; American and British forces continued to build up in the Gulf; Saddam Hussein played his usual tricks. America lost patience and went to war anyway eleven days ago, taking Britain with it.

31 March 2003

America has invaded Iraq without UN sanction. It seems there are only two ways a country may *legally* make war on another: 1. if it has itself been attacked (Iraq has not attacked America); 2. if war is formally approved by the UN (It has not been). But I don't oppose the war on the sterile (and disputed – as every legal question is) ground of its illegality. I oppose it, first, because it introduces a new and perilous idea, that a pre-emptive war may be justified when you simply *believe* that an unfriendly state *might* attack you. Secondly, I oppose *British* participation in the war because it does not have the support of British public opinion. Thirdly, most importantly, I oppose it because I believe that, even if *we win this war*, the dislocation it will cause, and the hatred it will raise up against us in the Middle East will lead to an increase in terrorism rather than a reduction of it. And finally, I believe that Tony Blair, by giving absolute priority to Britain's alliance with America, has badly damaged our relations with core countries in Europe – this at a time when America is being governed by a hard-line, right-wing administration.

I rigorously maintained my armchair diary for the next three years, covering every twist and turn of the war until 21 May 2006, when, with a new Iraqi Government precariously installed, I felt the questions raised at the start of the war had been well and truly answered.

Going back to our early years in Leigh (my excursions into politics and world affairs have led me to get rather ahead of myself), a chance event led to a resumption of my painting activity. It probably says something about me that I need some kind of stimulus to make any kind of change to the even tenor of my life; without that, I just trundle along, doing what I've always done. Beryl usually provided the stimulus, but on this occasion it was Hamish (he combined visits to us with appointments with his dentist in Sevenoaks). We were walking past a shop that had an artist's easel for show on the pavement.

"That's very cheap," I said.

"I'll buy it for you," said Hamish, and he did.

Were it not for his spontaneous gift, I probably would not have taken up oil painting again. Now I had to do something with that easel.

Way back, at Plashet Road, I had first been introduced to painting in oils at a class I attended in London. Two paintings survive from that period: *Chianti Wine Bottles* and *Vase of Tulips*, neither very good, but examples of my first efforts. Then followed the watercolour painting in Jeremy Carlisle's indoor and open-air classes. Although I enjoyed and benefited from them, watercolour is, in my opinion, a subtle and difficult medium to master: once you apply paint to paper you can't change it. Although there still exist a few of my watercolours from that time, none of them do much more than acceptably fill a space on a wall – mainly owing to them being very well framed by a local man who knew his job.

I owe my reintroduction to oils to my son-in-law, David, who told me about a South African artist who conducted classes at Tatsfield, where he and Hilary lived. Adrienne Parker, known simply as Adie, is an amazingly versatile artist, and quite a ball of fire in her enthusiasms for different techniques – occasionally a bit over the top, but artists are allowed to be. I joined her group of about twelve to fourteen mostly pension-age amateur painters, who met once a week in St Mary's Church Hall – all very informal and jokey. Adie's system was for her to provide a painting 'reference', which she would herself paint in stages, alternately with her pupils, whose efforts she would then constructively criticise individually. These classes ran for about twenty-five or thirty weeks in the year, over three terms (I think it was), during which our little group became quite friendly. We eventually decided that we would continue to meet, ourselves alone, interleaving with Adie's classes. The net result was that I would be painting on nearly every Wednesday of the year, producing eventually more than fifty oil paintings, some of which are quite good – for an amateur. At any rate I have had no difficulty in disposing of most of them among the family, and even managed to sell five (three, admittedly, at knock-down prices).

35 – GETTING A NEW HIP

In September 1999 I went into the Kent & Sussex Hospital in Tunbridge Wells to have a replacement hip operation. I was there for a week and spent part of the time keeping a diary of what happened.

I was surprised to find myself not merely in a mixed ward, but in a mixed *bay* – with three men (including me) and three women, not in any way segregated. There was no requirement for me to get immediately into bed, so for the first few hours I simply exchanged an armchair in the day room for an armchair by my bed. It was an opportunity to see who I was 'in' with. This was more difficult than might be imagined, as the room was by now thick with visitors. A notice at the entrance to the ward had sternly insisted that patients were allowed – 'not more than TWO visitors at any one time' – but it was clearly not being enforced.

There was one ninety-three-year-old woman (as I learned) who, with her two female visitors, were literally dominating the room: not only were they talking at the tops of their voices, they were *intending* to be overheard by everyone else. This was Dorothy, who had been for many years the secretary and inspirational force of what sounded to be a formidable Tunbridge Wells society devoted to the arts. She was an interesting woman, fluently intelligent (quite exceptionally so, considering her age), with a dry wit, but off-puttingly arrogant. The four other patients were either surrounded with (relatively quieter) visitors, or simply comatose.

Shortly after eight o'clock, visitors gone, supper was wheeled in, kept hot in the same sort of trolley as used on airlines, except about four times bigger and with wheels that move like recalcitrant supermarket trolleys, needing two strong nurses to fight it round the wards. Patients normally get a menu to choose from – except on their first day, when they get the choice of the person who has just vacated their bed. Meals occasionally get mixed up and patients then also have to take what they get. On the whole, though, I was to find the food quite good, if never hot enough.

It was after supper and in the mornings that the nurses sprang into action. Just as I'd think it was about time for a bit of shut-eye they'd come bouncing in with thermometers, blood-pressure things and an array of tablets and potions, the result or disposal of which they'd meticulously tick off on lists, and enter on charts at the foot of the beds. Nothing for me though, at first – except a notice hung above my bed: 'NIL BY MOUTH'. Apart from (somebody else's) supper, that was the first sign that I was more than a spectator there. And indeed, as if he had only been waiting for 'NIL BY MOUTH' to be posted above my bed, in came my consultant, Mr Nicholl, trailed by the duty junior doctor, Dr Debika Chakraborti, and the ward sister, Helen Kedge. Mr Nicholl was a young man, who could not have had a great deal of experience. Still, he had given me a good half-hour consultation on our first meeting ten months ago, and had explained the whole thing in great detail. I had no qualms. Now he was fairly brisk (it was about nine in the evening, after all), and we exchanged a few conventional words.

"All ready, are we? Now, it's the left hip, isn't it?" he asked, and, taking a felt-tip pen from his pocket, he marked a big arrow, pointing up, on my left thigh.

That disposed of a small, almost laughable, element of doubt: I suppose they'll remember which leg it is.

"Good. See you tomorrow, then."

And he was off, followed by his little retinue.

As it happened, I *didn't* see him the next day, but I did see a succession of people, including the anaesthetist, a rather untidy young man with designer stubble; a nurse, who measured me for elastic stockings; another who handed me a ludicrously small operating-theatre smock and sent me off to have a shower; and then Dr Chakraborti, who carefully explained to me what had already been explained umpteen times before. The NHS can keep you waiting about for ages, but once you are accepted into the system the flow of information is more than generous.

Dr Chakraborti was one of those doctors you read about in the newspapers: always on duty, it seemed, whether early in the morning, throughout the day, or late in the evening, her chubby face always smiling, her white coat always open – looking indeed as if she would have difficulty in closing it even had she tried.

"When is my operation likely to take place?" I asked her.

"You're down for the afternoon," she replied.

So I got on with my book.

Meanwhile, two of my fellow patients were wheeled off. Two stolid-looking porters (more correctly, 'orderlies', I suppose) would troop in, like removal men coming for a sofa, briefly check the name beside a bed and then busy themselves with levers and foot pumps to convert it into perambulatory mode.

"All right, Frank?"

"OK, George."

And one of my neighbours, still recumbent in her bed, would be floated off out of the ward to her appointment in the operating theatre. The tea lady, Josie, known as Jo, came round and I had a visit from a physiotherapist. The inconsiderate nonagenarian called loudly more than once throughout the morning for a bedpan, necessitating each time the arrival of two nurses with a wheeled commode, a swishing of curtains round her bed, and a great deal of conversation and accompanying noises as the performance, or lack of performance, proceeded.

Nurses came to take my temperature and blood pressure. Lunch arrived: none for me. I wasn't nervous, but I didn't feel like lunch anyway. The anaesthetist paid a brief visit and checked the records at the foot of my bed.

"We'll give you an injection which should make you feel a bit drowsy." A pat on my thigh and he was off.

The injection was administered and I settled back, prepared to feel drowsy, but I think it was more a 'relaxant' I was given – not especially long-lasting, I was beginning to feel, as the afternoon wore on with no 'removal men' looking for *my* address. . . . But then, out of nowhere, they were at my bed, pulling levers, putting up rails, bumping me down like a car after mending a puncture.

"All right, Frank?"

"OK, George."

And I felt myself effortlessly wheeled off, out of the ward.

The view as one lies supine on a moving trolley is wondrously novel: it is almost like seeing the world through the eyes of a baby, and my short-sightedness corresponded to the unfocussed gaze of an infant in his pram. The ceilings slid past, we turned corners, bumped through swing doors; the decor changed from cream to pea green; then more bumping, scraping and squeaking . . . into a very small, dark room (a lift actually) which shuddered down to a lower floor . . . more ceilings, and I became conscious of a sudden change of atmosphere as we entered what seemed like a small tent, and the bustle of corridors had given way to a quiet, clinical hum. I became aware of green-robed figures, one of whom was probably Mr Nicholl.

Somebody said, "All ready, are we?"

I said, "Yep," and indeed I felt quite relaxed.

There was no hanging about: a mask was placed over my face.

"Just breathe normally."

And I wondered how many . . .

"Yes, all done! D'you feel all right?"

A nurse was bending over me, smiling at my astonishment that the operation should have been done in the twinkling of an eye. A few more cheery words and again the ceiling swirled above me as I was wheeled out of what I suppose was the recovery room. There was no pain; I had a feeling of euphoric lassitude – the morphine, probably. I remember waving out with my free hand (the other impeded by a drip feed) in grateful farewell as I was borne back to the ward.

For the rest of the afternoon I dozed contentedly. Visitors arrived, including Beryl and Hilary. I had not expected to see anybody so soon, and was delighted to see them. They were surprised to see me so 'chirpy'. Did I need anything? Grapes? No, thanks, but I thought prunes would be a good idea.

Next day there seemed to be a general clearing-out of the ward. Patients who had come in for operations the previous week were being discharged, and a fresh intake would not be expected until the Monday. Over the weekend the ward would be only half full. The nurses took the opportunity to unscramble the mixed sexes, and there was a general process of what might be described as musical beds, in which I managed to insist that, if I was going to be moved, at least I should retain my place by a window – not so difficult to achieve, as nobody else seemed to mind where they were put.

My main recollection of that first day of the 'move', while I was still getting used to the restraint of tubes in my left thigh, a drip feed in my left wrist, and the cosseted feel of a large, numb leg at the end of the bed, is of an injured rugby player brought in late, accompanied by two or three of his friends, all of whom were half intoxicated. They seemed to be quite unconscious of being in a hospital ward. What annoyed me especially was that the nurse who was booking in this late-night casualty was obviously enjoying the company of these noisy young men and joined in the laughing and joking. I endured their uninhibited bantering rowdiness with mounting indignation. My fellow patients were silently recumbent, either asleep or amazingly indifferent.

It was the nurse's flirty abetting that finally snapped my patience, and, to my own surprise, I barked out, "Will you please make less noise? We are trying to sleep!"

There was a sudden hush, and a voice said, sheepishly, but with restrained mirth, "Sorree!"

I could imagine them looking at each other like schoolboys called to order by a master. There was no further noise. The nurse completed her logging-in and the out-of-hours visitors soon shuffled off, leaving their chum to nurse his broken collarbone by himself.

As it happened, he wasn't with us more than a day; nor were his visitors really the most noisy. That accolade I award in retrospect to those of my immediate neighbour, Lionel Bartholomew. Although most of us were called by our Christian names, he was invariably addressed as Mr Bartholomew. The formality in his case was strangely appropriate, and reflected the staff's civilised attitude to the more helpless of those in their charge. Mr Bartholomew had been a farmer all his life, but had been forced to sell up and retire seven years previously when Alzheimer's disease made it impossible for him to continue. Latterly he had been in a home, and it was there that he had fallen and broken his hip: hence his arrival in hospital, where, physically, he was now on the mend – except that he refused to eat.

He had a high whining voice and would pipe out "Naow, naow, it's agony, agony!" whenever anyone tried to coax him to eat.

His wife, a wonderfully patient woman, told me, "He just puts it on, you know."

She, and a whole troop of his relations – sons, daughters, sisters, nephews, grandchildren – regardless of visiting hours spent every afternoon and evening with him, mainly talking to each other, but intermittently jollying him along, telling him how well he looked and what good progress he was making.

This would sometimes spur him to articulate the glimmer of memory he still held of his former life: "When I was on the farm, I wouldn't . . ." and his voice would trail away. Then he would try again: "When I was on the farm . . ."

"Yes, we know all that, Lionel; you were a worker, you were," they would say soothingly.

During the evenings, he would have five or six family visitors round his bed, chatting away as if at a convivial wake.

The mornings were the time when most of the hospital activity took place, such as morning tea and the elaborate washing of those unable to leave their bed. That included me for little more than a day, whereafter my various drips were removed, and all I needed were the washing of my feet and changing of the long white surgical stockings, as obviously I couldn't do that for myself. For the rest, I was on my feet a couple of days after the operation, rather shaky, with the assistance of a Zimmer, but astonished I could actually make my own way to the bathroom for the rest of my ablutions. It was a precarious journey nevertheless, keeping an anxious eye on faster-moving traffic, such as speeding nurses and porters' trolleys; and on arrival there was the additional hazard involved in keeping the bathroom door shut. Of the two bathrooms, one had no lock and the other had a bolt that fell off the door if anyone tried to open it, so it was worse than useless. In response, I developed a way of jamming my Zimmer between the washbasin and the door handle, which proved to be quite effective. Later, when I had progressed to using crutches, I would sit on the throne with one of them poised to ram, if necessary – which occasionally it was.

My surgeon had been round to see me, trailing his retinue of acolytes – mainly, it seemed, to check that my legs were both the same length.

"You may laugh," he said, "but that is the most difficult part of the operation."

I imagine he said that to all his patients as a joke, since, whatever the length of the leg, it was obviously now too late to do anything about it. Mr Nicholl was normally a rather supercilious young man. He wore a blazer and somewhat overacted the 'great man' before he had properly graduated to that august status.

I had two physiotherapists, both young and very fit. Helen was the physio proper, who got me out of bed and put me through an exercise regime; Hilary was the 'home' physio, who had a lair of her own in the bowels of the hospital, full of appliances and rehabilitation aids, including a fully equipped kitchen, in which she invited me to boil a kettle, peel imaginary potatoes and wash up imaginary dishes at the sink. All this helped pass the time. Being an eager learner, I probably overdid the exercising, quickly dispensing with the Zimmer, and taking some satisfaction in walking up and down the corridor with my two sticks. Among all the advice I was given, nobody warned me that, doped up as I was with painkillers, the normal function of pain as an alert to go carefully would be to some extent in abeyance.

The last patients to arrive before my departure were both young lads. One, a golden-haired, spoilt-looking youth, had broken a bone in his foot. Although completely lively and alert, he showed absolutely no interest in anyone else in the ward, but spent long periods chatting away to his girlfriend, who was a constant visitor. The other boy was wheeled in late on the night before my release.

He had broken an arm – in a car accident – and was in considerable pain, crying and moaning continuously until, after being given a painkiller, he eventually quietened down. Next morning he was up, sitting on the side of his bed, talking cheerfully to his neighbour. I could hardly believe it was the same boy who had been sobbing like a child in the night.

Mr Nicholl had cheerfully said "Why not?" when I told him I was ready to leave; but he hadn't, apparently, passed on an instruction. So I did it for him.

Dr Chakrahorti looked doubtfully at my swollen knee. "It looks rather swollen," she said, but didn't question that I was to be discharged.

I said goodbye to the nurses and thanked them for their kind ministrations. Apart from the frivolous girl with the rugby group and a couple of rather officious women, I had no complaints, and only praise for their friendly professionalism.

David arrived. I said goodbye to my fellow patients. Mr Bartholomew managed a faint "Goodbye", benevolently open-mouthed and a look on his face which seemed to say, "I've seen this fellow somewhere before."

The man in the corner said, "Cheers, mate."

I declined the offer of a wheelchair, and carefully made my way out into the open air.

36 – WINDING DOWN

We lived in Leigh for a little over ten years, but were perhaps a little too 'elderly' to fit easily into the well-established local community. Although quite capable of holding her own in social gatherings, Beryl was not by nature sociable – unless she herself was organising the society. I, too, as the reader may have gathered by now, am not particularly sociable. The people we saw most of during our first year in Outfield were the builder's men, and I see from my diaries that this was the only year, while living in Leigh, that we never got away on holiday. The anticipated pleasures of seeing our grandchildren growing up were, however, amply fulfilled. Hilary and David were amazingly attentive in bringing Jonathan (not yet Jon), Katherine (never Katie or Kath, but sometimes Kitkat) and Eleanor (not yet Ellie, at least to us) over most weekends. We saw less of Jeremy and Sally's two boys, Richard and Hamish (never corrupted, so far as I know, to Dick or Ham) – inevitably, as they were further away at Farnham.

We also continued to meet up with our old Songea chums in annual reunions in different, usually Kent, pubs, and I was always intrigued to see how, over the years, they had changed. Bob Wise, who had been a lanky, clean-shaven district officer, was now a crusty retired solicitor (following his father, apparently) with a homely wife. Stan Dryden, another young district officer, who used to be ribbed for having a crush on a dishy (female) UMCA missionary teacher, was now a retired schoolmaster with a horsey wife. And I hardly recognised Bill Hay, who had acted in loco parentis for Beryl at our wedding: who was this bald-headed old chap who was greeting me so warmly? Thank goodness I grasped it in time, as I recognised his voice, which was much the same old Bill. His wife, Sheila, who had been my drinking companion on the *Kenya Castle*, and on her way to marry Bill, was no longer with him. After most unfortunately contracting and living many years with polio, she had now died, as had Jock Scott, our old district commissioner, and also, I heard, my old bête noire, George Baker.

UN pensioners' reunions were rather more formally organised: internationally, nationally (with the clunky acronym of BAFUNCS) and regionally. We started off in the Scottish region and ended up in Kent & Sussex, where I was for a few years its treasurer – not a very demanding job. I think we attended only two of the national meetings, which are held over two days – one, I believe, in Edinburgh and the other in one of the Oxford colleges. Probably fewer than ten per cent of members attend these gatherings, which rely on the efforts of a few willing horses to keep going.

I think I should mention that for two years I acted as auditor of the national association's accounts. After the second year they said thank you and asked somebody else to do it; I think the (long-standing) treasurer didn't expect the auditor to say more than 'I have examined the accounts and found that they represent a fair view of the financial situation of BAFUNCS.' Having previous experience of working closely with auditors in Tanganyika, I didn't recognise that constraint.

Beyond these infrequent excursions into our former days, our lives retreated to the humdrum. Beryl became an avid supermarket shopper; and as she no longer drove, I necessarily accompanied her. She was also expert at involuntary games of hide and seek in the aisles, which I sometimes found exasperating. When not in the supermarket, she would be in the charity shops, looking for bargains. Unlike our children, we never stopped for coffee at the likes of Costa and Café Nero. That part of modern culture never reached us. At home, Beryl had certain television programmes that she would always watch: *Coronation Street* and *Bargain Hunt* – and the news, of course: I was not the only news junkie in the family. On the whole, we were pretty much in agreement on world affairs and politics. If anything she was perhaps a bit more left wing than I was, but not in a predictable way.

Our occupancy of Toftingal coincided almost precisely with Tony Blair's premiership (May 1997 to June 2007). We both welcomed the end of the long period of Conservative government, and evidence that Labour might have something new to offer. Blair's reputation is now, sadly, for ever damaged by his ardent support for America in the Iraq War, and our own military entanglement in it. Yet he is the same man who led the way to the Good Friday Agreement in Ireland, and spoke for the country on Princess Diana's death. I believe that were he to admit he was mistaken in backing America in that ill-advised war, he might yet redeem himself. But he won't.

The underlying question of the time was (and still is) Israel/Palestine – underlying the '9/11' bombings of 2001 and thence underlying the origins of the continuing war in Afghanistan and much of the sporadic terrorist activity in Europe and America. With the Iran Revolution thrown into the Middle Eastern cauldron, it seems now almost impossible to find an acceptable way forward that would allow its people to live peaceably together. In the past, the directly affected internecine powers would fight it out among themselves, and the strongest, such as the Ottomans in their day, would establish a system that prevailed, and the weaker would recognise the limits of their ambition. One is tempted to ask what would happen if America and Europe simply withdrew from the contest? Israel has 'the bomb', which in the last resort would protect it. But without America behind it, would it not perhaps be more accommodating in its negotiations with the Palestinians? In April 2000, with no political end in view, Beryl had been on a visit to Israel, in a party led by Bishop Nasir-Ali, of Rochester.

In February the following year we went to Belgium, and Mechelen in particular, where Beryl's ancestor linking Ireland with India finally died. Major James Bruce Mungavin, having signed up in the army of the East India Company as little more than a boy in County Clare, had returned in 1857 to his native land with two of his grandchildren. How was it that he ended his days in Mechelin of all places? Our earlier discovery of a document confirming his death, at a specific address, led us to a narrow winding street leading into the centre of the town. The original house, sadly for us, had been demolished: all we saw now was a bland building with shops on the ground floor – nothing to stimulate the imagination. We were reduced to tramping through the local cemetery, where James was recorded as having been buried: a quiet, out-of-the-way place of ancient tombs, monuments and gravestones – but none for him. In Holland they reuse burial sites, digging up old bones and incinerating them, making way for the more recently dead.

I do not wish to give the impression that Beryl was obsessed with her family history, but of all the living Mungavins in her line, she was certainly the most diligent in digging into it. In the course of helping her, I too found the exercise fascinating and did not at all grudge the time we spent on it. In September we flew to Dublin, rented a car, and toured the south of Ireland – Limerick, Cork, Dun Laoghaire – where it seems most of the Mungavins originated. It was an interesting trip, talking to people who knew something of the Irish past in those parts; but, at the end, it was completely overshadowed by the terrorist attack on those towers in America.

In November we went back to India, this time more to visit the game parks than to visit old Mungavin stamping grounds – though we did that too. As I kept a good diary of the trip, it will get separate treatment.

37 – INDIA DIARY, 2001

14 November, Imperial hotel, Delhi
Excellent room, with enormous bathroom, but antiquated plumbing left something to be desired. After an all too brief rest and a mix-up over 'lunch', we were re-embussed for an afternoon tour of Delhi: the Red Fort, Jama Masjid mosque, and Raj Ghat, where Ghandi was cremated. Impressive, but only moderately interesting to us (we had seen them before). Last visit to a Kashmir carpet-weaving sale room – mainly a sales pitch, which kept most of the party hanging about while one couple entered into serious haggling.

15 November
Early breakfast and well-organised start of a trip to the Corbett game park (journey time 8 hrs +). Lodge pleasant and airy, but very basic facilities. Reminded me of an East African rest house, albeit on a grand scale. Evening drive (standing up) bucketing about on a Jeep with an excellent guide, who pointed out Langur and Rhesus monkeys, Sambar deer, Spotted deer, Wild boar; birds – kingfisher, robin, kite, black stork, hornbill (heard only), egret . . . and several others I didn't manage to record. The Corbett national park, in the foothills of the Himalayas, is famous for Jim Corbett and 'the man-eaters of Kumaon'. But we didn't see any tiger.

16 November
Early drive, this time with a useless guide: four of us on the Jeep had to take charge of the driver, who seemed to know more than the guide. The tracks are through forest and mostly dense undergrowth. In the afternoon, waded across a shallow river and walked on a 'birding' expedition. Most of the group are keen bird-

watchers. We saw four grey hornbills – great excitement among the twitchers – and many other birds, identified and forgotten, that I observed through binoculars but didn't make notes.

17 November
Long drive to Agra, partly cross-country avoiding the main roads: most interesting views of rural India and the ant-like activity in smaller towns, through which our bus had to crawl at the pace of bullock carts, pedestrians, motorised rickshaws and ramshackle vehicles belching poisonous fumes to an accompaniment of shattering noise and a cacophony of horns. I was fascinated by the variety of artisan and small-trading business along the roadside: carpenters, bicycle repairers, potters, blacksmiths, baskets-weavers, bakers, barbers, makers of beds, sellers of ghee, fruit, vegetables, pulses. Among them, the endless tides of humanity that we observed with curiosity through the windows of our bus – shuffling, shouting, running, loitering, bargaining, jostling – resolve themselves, here and there, into individuals that momentarily command attention: a man on a bicycle with an almost two-foot high stack of (full) egg trays, balanced precariously on the rack above his rear wheel; a fat babu asleep on a hammock slung under the awning of a stall displaying some kind of sweetmeats (and flies); a man getting a haircut in a yard where animal hides are stretched out on wooden frames to dry. Journey time 12 hours.

19 November
A visit to the Taj Mahal in the early morning, at that hour its park shrouded in mist (or smog). There are trees, ornamental water gardens, and a great feeling of freedom and space. But where is the Taj? Our guide enjoys our mystification, and leads us to a vantage point within a raised cloister: and there, far away, distanced by the mist, as if in the clouds, are the famous white minarets and dome of the Taj – almost literally a vision of heaven. No photograph does justice to it: truly a wonder of the world. We spent an hour or so walking about its halls and terraces, balconies of carved stonework overlooking the river (Yamuna or Jumna), taking photographs nevertheless.

After breakfast, it was Agra Fort, still used, apparently, by the army as barracks; so we could only see about a tenth of it. Even that was a lot to cover, the fort is enormous and virtually a city within a city. The 'Hall of Private Audiences' used to hold the 'Peacock Throne' that was taken by the Persians for *their* Shah. (It is now in

Tehran, where we saw it when we were there in 1971–75.)

Here we disengaged from our group. The afternoon was the point around which we had organised this tour: when Beryl had arranged to visit her father's grave. A battered Ambassador taxi turned up at the hotel and we climbed in. Off we bumped and jolted through the traffic, windows open to let in the heat, smells and noise of the city. The military cantonment, when we got there, was, in contrast, an oasis of calm: straight, tree-lined streets, and every so often a guard house at the gates of some army unit or barracks. Only once were we stopped and our driver interrogated: the sentry stared at us in the back, but we were waved on. Although Beryl had been there two years previously, with her brother Gerald, we still made some wrong turnings before eventually arriving at the crumbling gateway of the cemetery, through which was a vista of ancient gravestones and monuments within a sea of yellowed grass and scrub.

Amazingly, someone was actually scrubbing the stone slab above the grave we had come to see; our arrival was clearly expected. Of course, it should not have been so surprising, as B had written to Trevor Rosemeyer, the local representative of BACSA [the British Association for Cemeteries in South Asia] to say we would be coming that afternoon. But to see the cemetery attendant in his tattered, dusty clothing, dutifully awaiting her arrival, after so many years had elapsed since her departure from India, was oddly moving. The man had cleared the area round the grave-stone and had placed a few sprigs of bougainvillea on top of it, almost the only attention it would have received over the past half century. B had brought some clothing for his children but, in the poignancy of the moment, forgot to give it to him (we sent it on later). Thanking him for his attention, Beryl communed with her father's spirit, and we left to visit her old home. The house no longer existed, demolished, and now replaced by the Clark Shiraz hotel; but the garden, she said, was much as it had been in her time, fifty years before: wide lawns and shaded by trees, but little colour.

20 November

We had been scheduled to fly to Khajuraho, but owing to the sharp fall in tourist numbers following the 11 September attack on the World Trade Centre [we benefited from the resulting lack of competition from other visitors throughout our tour] our plane had been cancelled, forcing our party to go on by train to Jhansi and thence by coach. This exposed us to a hazard of travel in India from which tour operators normally try to shield their clients: pestering by hawkers and beggars. In my experience there is nowhere else in the world where poverty, destitution and human wretchedness are so apparently tolerated as a normal condition, as [they are] on the subcontinent: to be regretted, deplored even, but resignedly accepted as a fact of life.

So we filed into the station pursued by a crowd of gesticulating postcard sellers, old men on crutches, little boys insisting on cleaning our shoes as we walked, women with babies pathetically holding out their hands and pointing to their mouths as evidence of hunger – while our guide and his assistant counted off our bags and martialled eager porters in a chaotic caravan of precious luggage on wobbly trolleys into the station and on to the platform: bags lined up and counted again. An enterprising seller of padlocks appeared and did a good trade with those of our group whose luggage was not fully secure.

On the train I found that my reserved seat had been occupied by a young woman who airily waved an arm, suggesting I find somewhere further up the carriage. I firmly declined this invitation, pointing out that I wished to sit next to my wife. There was quite an altercation, during which both of us kept our temper, but each refusing to budge, until she seemed to realise that this 'tourist' was not going to meekly accept that he was a 'guest' who ought to behave and do as he was told. She gathered her belongings and left without rancour, as much as to say 'well, it was worth a try'. Indian women can be pretty tough, and especially young, educated ones.

At Jhansi a coach was waiting to take us on to Khajuraho – a six hour journey over dreadful roads. But there was to be no rest for us – we were still assumed to have arrived by plane – the Temples of Khajuraho had to be fitted in before dark. Guides and guidebooks make much of the 'erotic' carvings, and no doubt a prospect of seeing the uninhibited depiction of 'life in heaven' is an excellent tourist draw; but the small weather-worn figures on the sides of these thousand year-old temples required excellent eyesight and a good deal of imagination to discern what on earth they were up to. Our guide drew attention to a man "having sex with three women at the same time", yet even those of our party with binoculars were unable to work out how the performance was actually being achieved. For my own part (Beryl had sensibly decided to forego the visit) I found the ambience of the park itself, with five or six of the larger temples within sight, spaced out among the ornamental trees and enormous clumps of bougainvillea, like immobile dinosaurs encrusted with the barnacles of innumerable carvings, wonderfully, almost awesomely, poetic: as if one were transported to a time when Man and Nature and God – or gods, if you were a Hindu – had come together before the Fall.

21 November
An interesting and scenically beautiful but exhausting 11-hour drive to Bhandhavghar – only 230 kms but over mostly dreadful roads; should have been done by 4 × 4, not coach – where we are lodged at the 'Jungle Camp', in tents. It is dark and we do not yet know what our surroundings are like. We find our way back to our tent by torchlight.

22 November
Called at 5.30 for a six o'clock game drive. Bandhavghar is spectacularly beautiful in the early morning: still misty and the sun level with the horizon, glistening on the dew of tall grasses. Our six Jeeps set off one after the other but soon lose each other, and then we are alone. Scouts on elephants are already out looking for tiger. We could see wild boar, spotted deer and, of course, lots of monkeys. Then, at a bend in the track, we came upon three large, dirty-looking elephants saddled with grubby blankets and sacking, onto which ancient wooden howdahs are tied with old rope. Our guide whispers "Tiger!" as the driver stops and turns off the engine of the Jeep. At a signal we clamber up onto one of the howdahs; the mahout clamps a metal bar between us and the ground (to stop anyone falling out, as four of us sit back to back, two on each side) and immediately we start lumbering out into a sea of elephant grass. It is tremendously exciting, being ten feet up on this great beast, our eyes unaccustomedly observant, no-one speaking a word but full of eager anticipation. Not having had any breakfast also seems to sharpen the senses. As we learned later, the scouts had already located a tigress and two cubs at a kill, so the mahout, guided by their calls, knew where to go – although we did not see them until we were virtually upon them: the grass was so high and dense, they were well camouflaged in it. But suddenly, there she was, the tigress, right below us, cradling the remains of a spotted deer, with her two cubs rolling about beside her. All three looked pretty satisfied and took no more notice of us than if the elephant had wandered past on its own. After staying several minutes, taking photographs from different angles, we left them to finish their breakfast and returned to the Jeep for our own at the camp.

A less fruitful drive later in the day, but the bird-watchers were satisfied. Tribal dances in the evening – very much a 'tourist' thing.

23 November
The best morning drive yet. Had an excellent driver, who could drive and spot tracks at the same time, and it was not long before he found recent pug-marks of a tiger. From that moment he handled the Jeep as if we were on our feet, charging through the undergrowth between trees, stopping, listening, then charging off in a new direction. From time to time the scouts could be heard from a distance making a sound like some jungle animal, which signalled where the tiger was, or in which direction it was moving. The driver switched on the engine, and off we would go again, bucketing through grass and trees, four of us standing up at the back, hanging tightly onto the handrails, contributing nothing to the stalk – if indeed this chase through the bush could be called stalking – but with our primitive hunters' instincts fully alive. After each stop and change of direction the driver became increasingly excited (for our benefit no doubt) and his handling of the vehicle more reckless, until finally, like the conductor of an orchestra he led us in a crescendo of swerves and rushes, down into an almost dried-up river bed, beyond which, almost invisible but unmistakable against thickets of bamboo, was a magnificent male tiger.

Much more exciting than the previous day, when our 'kill' had been more or less found for us and was ready waiting, this was the real thing. Although helped by the invisible scouts, we were the first of our party to find the 'prey' and very satisfactorily shoot it with our cameras. So long as one stayed on the Jeep (and we were of course forbidden to get out at any time) animals and even birds took little notice, treating us as part of the fauna of the forest. We stayed with the tiger for about 15 minutes while it prowled through thickets and grass, sometimes getting as close as five yards to it. Fifty or sixty years ago, we'd have had guns, not cameras to shoot it.

24 November
A brief game drive in the morning – surprisingly cold before the sun gets up – then off by coach on what was supposed to be a six hour drive to the Khana national park, but actually took eleven hours. We stopped on the way to get a closer look at a village market: crowded and colourful. Wandering about among the stalls, I was surprised that, as with the animals of the game park, we aroused little interest; yet these villagers can surely not have seen many westerners at close quarters. It was pleasant being able to jostle among the people without being trailed by beggars.

25 November
Game drives in Khana: savannah grasslands, hills and forest. Saw a small herd of Gaur (buffalo) grazing peacefully in swampland, but considered to be among the most dangerous animals if they get too near. Up on an elephant again, we find a male and female tiger resting in a dense thicket. We are getting almost blasé about seeing tiger, but apparently have been especially lucky.

26 November
Drive to Nagpur where we get an excellent meal before taking the plane for Mumbai (Bombay). Here we leave the tour group (who return to the UK this evening) and check in to the Oberoi Towers hotel. After roughing it in jungle camps and rest houses for the past ten days or so, it's great to luxuriate in the opulence of the best that India can offer.

27 November
In the morning we have a guided tour of the city. Negotiating the traffic in an air-conditioned taxi is surely the only way to do it without enduring intolerable stress. The street scenes are full of interest and fascination, teeming with people and vehicles: Ghandi's house (now a museum), the Crawford market, the Jain temple on Malabar hill, and the Pherozeshah Mehta hanging gardens. We ended up at the end of the Colaba causeway, to visit the memorial church of St John the Baptist. Commonly known as 'the Afghan Church', it was built as a memorial to the British soldiers who died in the first Afghan War. At the end of a quiet street with dusty old trees and virtually no traffic, its tall steeple and stained glass windows looking from the outside very English, the church inside is a veritable mausoleum of the British Empire. It is simply stuffed with marble plaques, inscriptions and rolls of honour commemorating the officers and men (especially the officers) who lost their lives in the service of the Queen Empress a hundred and fifty years ago. Although I write this somewhat flippantly, the atmosphere of faded glory set off tingles at the back of my neck.

We took a number of photographs, including one of the font where a Mungavin ancestor had been christened; bought some postcards from the ancient attendant in the otherwise deserted church; popped a contribution into the 'Restoration Fund' box that he pointed out; thanked him and left.

In the evening we meet up with Dr Gupchuk and her husband, both professors at Mumbai University (he, apparently, vice-chancellor in his time). She is writing a history of Bombay's

St Thomas's cathedral and had been in correspondence with B about it. They took us for a meal at the Gymkhana Club, a relic of British India, but still, with its membership now almost exclusively Indian, maintaining the traditions probably much as they were in the time of the Raj. Perhaps unwisely, I asked Dr G to explain the Kashmir dispute. He expounded the Indian position most fluently and cogently; but, although as a guest I did not presume to argue with him on such an emotionally charged subject, I still do not see why the question may not be decided by a plebiscite – which India refuses to countenance.

28 November
We fly to Pune, where our most efficient agent has a car waiting to take us to Le Meridien Hotel. The Delhi and Bombay hotels had been sparsely occupied, but this one was like arriving at a party at the wrong time. Your host hastily exchanges his slippers for shoes and greets you as if the sight of you was the happiest event of his day. Indian servants are always attentive, but those here, the receptionists, porters, waiters, etc. are exceptionally helpful: we had their almost undivided attention – perhaps inevitably, as there were hardly any other guests at the hotel.

The tall windows of our room look out over the marshalling yard of Pune railway station, but the clanking, rumbling and occasional whistle of the trains is thankfully muffled. In the bathroom the towelled bathrobes have an elegantly printed notice attached to the hanger:

'This bathrobe has enjoyed considerable success among our guests, to the extent that some particularly enthusiastic customers have become "collectors of Le Meridien bathrobes". While we recognise that this initiative helps spread the reputation of our establishment, we nevertheless urge our most fervent supporters to separate themselves from this admittedly endearing garment when they leave. (Alternatively, a bathrobe may be obtained for a nominal charge.)'

A rather nice way of saying: 'Don't steal the bloody bathrobe!'

In the afternoon we searched out, and eventually found, the cemetery of the Holy Sepulchre, where one of B's ancestors is known to be buried: a wide, parched, yellow-ochre expanse of old gravestones interspersed with a few trees. We pulled up at the entrance, a stucco archway leading to a long avenue between the graves on either side, most of them mere bumps in the ground, or distinguishable only by the vestiges of long-neglected memorials. Just a few remained whose inscriptions could still be made out, recording for a posterity that would never read them the birth, life and death of those servants of the British Empire – and their wives and children too – who were ever to remain where duty had placed them, far from home, wherever that might have been. In its peaceful desolation, set apart from the noise and bustle of the city – and ignored by it – it was a place of almost heart-rending sadness.

By good luck, the cemetery custodian was in his office. Unfortunately, he was just off for his lunch, he said; but with great good will he delved through a pile of tattered documents in one of his cupboards, in search of the name that B gave him, and miraculously found it and a grave reference. Spirits raised, we set off in search of the spot, accompanied by a grave-digger, who appeared from somewhere. Unfortunately, the stone markers had, in the course of time, either become indecipherable, or had disappeared altogether. Nevertheless, we continued casting about in what was virtually scrub, vainly trying to read ancient inscriptions, while the custodian eagerly sought out new areas ahead of us. We were beginning to feel guilty: surely he should be going home for his lunch? But no, he had the bit firmly in his teeth and continued scurrying back and forth like a gun-dog searching for a winged pheasant, while we, both hot and tired of trailing after a man who had clearly lost the scent, sat down on the edge of a recently constructed concrete fountain . . . the warm water of which, comfortingly yet imperceptibly, overflowed onto the seats of our pants. It was only on standing up that we realised our trousers were wringing wet – an embarrassment that might have been worse, were the cause of it not immediately obvious. At any rate it put an end to a search that we decided was anyway going to be fruitless. Our driver resourcefully produced a blanket to protect his garishly opulent back-seat covers. We thanked the custodian and grave-digger for their efforts, duly rewarded them, and departed, leaving Beryl's ancestor, wherever in that hallowed ground he is resting, to remain there in peace.

29 November

A fascinating but terrifying drive through the Western Ghats to Satara. We have a skilful driver, who is determined to pass everything, and has us white-knuckled in the back most of the time. He speaks not a word of English, which is a disappointment since we now have no guide. This deficiency becomes acute when, on arrival at Satara, he proves to have as little knowledge of the town as we have. "Cem-et-ery," we said; "CEM-ET-ERY." How do you mime dead and buried? How about Church? "Church?"

The driver stopped and asked a passer-by: "Chaach . . ." plus an animated conversation in Hindi and much pointing in different directions. After several of these fruitless enquiries and purposeful drivings-off, first in one direction, then another, Beryl suddenly spotted a dusty signboard (everything in India is dusty) with 'Methodist Church' written in English. "Stop! Stop!" we cried, with vigorously appropriate sign language; then climbed out and, as we were casting about for someone we might at least be able to communicate with, a man drove up on a moped and stopped at our side. Incredibly, he proved not only to speak English but also to be a Christian. As B said later, it was as if an angel had suddenly appeared. This was "Samuel", an angel with an Errol Flynn moustache and an open neck shirt. "You have met the right person," he said. "Follow me." He hopped back on his moped, turned it round from where he had been going, and led us, via his home (where we briefly met his mother, who insisted we return later for some refreshment) not just to one cemetery, but eventually to two – one more like a field, with here and there the remnants of monuments and broken gravestones; the other much smaller and visible only through rusting, padlocked gates – both surrounded by crumbling, unrepaired walls. We wandered over the larger cemetery, which seemed to have been tended over the past fifty years only by browsing cattle, the Empire's dead peacefully neglected beneath arid clumps of grass and thorny bushes, disturbed now, it seemed, merely by a snorting breath or the occasional plopping cow pat. Impossible to find any trace of a Mungavin; only by a stroke of luck might a name have survived on the remains of one of the more substantial blocks of stone: 'Captain John Ogilvy, 2nd Bn. Black Watch, beloved husband of [indecipherable]; Into your arms, Oh Lord . . .'.

Then Samuel led us to the church, still used by the Indian Christians but now very shabby, yet showing nevertheless signs of a congregation doing its best, with limited means, to maintain what had obviously once been a prosperously endowed place of worship; and again everywhere, plaques, inscriptions, rolls of honour, memorials . . . so many memorials.

We were taken to meet properly Samuel's mother, Leila (I think it was) who, to our surprise, proved to speak better English than her son (although it should not have been surprising, as it was she rather than Samuel who had been in closer contact with the British). Originally a nurse, she had now turned her house into an infants' school. Before sitting down, we had first to make a tour of all the classes. How much more docile and well-disciplined they are in the 'developing countries'! Everything very shabby and makeshift, but the little children all in their uniforms and staring at us with round eyes as we made conversation with their teacher, much in the manner of a royal visit. Later, drinking fruit juice in Leila's little parlour, with its garden furniture and roughly-framed certificates of competence and pictures of Christ in Glory on the walls, she told us of the difficulty that Christians experience in Hindu India. She was obviously a woman of character, and it was humbling to understand how she and her son had managed to negotiate the quagmires of Indian bureaucracy (inherited from the British) to achieve the necessary authority to run a (secular) infants' school.

We shared our packed lunch with the driver on the way back to Pune, and mercifully arrived at the hotel later that evening, having miraculously survived several close encounters with death on the way.

30/31 November
We fly back to Mumbai, and after one night at Le Royal Meridian (that's how they refer to it) spent the rest of the day trying to arrange for a bouquet of flowers to be sent to Dr Gupchuk.

38 – MAN OF LETTERS

We lived in Leigh for almost exactly ten years, by which time Beryl was again feeling her nomadic urge to move on. Apart from that, we were now both getting on in years: I had reached eighty and Beryl was only four years behind me; she had noticeably slowed down after a knee operation in 2005, and I was beginning to feel my years. There was therefore general agreement between us that we should move to smaller accommodation in Sevenoaks – a town well known to us already. After some searching about, this proved to be a flat in a quiet street near the railway station: 12 Clarendon Place, on the second floor, had everything we needed: a good, big living room with a balcony overlooking a common garden shielded by trees, two bedrooms and bathrooms (we each had our own), a hall big enough for me to use as a study, and a very small but adequate kitchen off the living room.

You may wonder why I should feel I needed a study. Partly, I suppose, because I am a reader and am comfortable in the company of books. A study is one's own private world, where you can, if so inclined, indulge your thoughts about the world, and occasionally put it to rights in letters to the press. Actually, for most of the time I would not be doing that: I would be in our living room, looking at the same television programmes as Beryl. But my preferred persona would be as a student of current affairs, refreshed by a study of history. Part of that, of course, we did get from the television programmes we shared, but *my* interest was 'geeky' – I had a feeling that I needed to get a handle on the leading questions of the day and put my own spoke in, however futile. That, I have to confess, does indeed put me in the 'Pooter' box – with the difference that, although I take my own ideas seriously, I do not take *myself* seriously. I advance that as a saving grace, when inflicting on the reader examples of the letters I was writing, and the questions that stirred my interest. At the time these chiefly concerned the never-ending war in Iraq and the reputation of Iran after its 1997 revolution. The first one is to a writer, Ferdinand Mount, for whom I actually have a lot of admiration:

2 January 2007

Ferdinand Mount Esq.
c/o *Prospect* magazine

Dear Mr Mount

May I congratulate you on your most interesting, and stimulating, article "Lost Legitimacy" in the current (January 2007) issue of *Prospect*: stimulating, because although I agree with much that you have written, and acknowledge that you do take account of much that is new in world affairs, the geography, so to speak, of your analysis seems (in spite of your up-dating of George Kennan) to remain securely in the twentieth century.

You point out, what is manifestly true, that since the 'anti-communist rationale' melted away 'western leaders have failed to construct an alternative strategy that would bear the heat of public scrutiny'. But your revised stance – that of the West confronting its adversaries with hard or soft power (according to taste or perceived necessity) – is little different from the post world war II anti-communist line-up, except that the Western world view now has a multiplicity of adversaries to contend with. Yet, given your recognition that a 'national will to resist' is forged by foreign invasion, I am puzzled how you could accept philosophically 'the brutal consequences' of a war in Iraq, so long as they were the inevitable result of an 'unwavering aim' to liberate its people. One is tempted to rejoin: that may be good enough for you, but is it good enough for the people of Iraq? And why should we not do the same thing for the wretched people of Zimbabwe? – indeed you imply that such an intervention would be legitimate. But the answer is surely clear: because we know very well that there would be the most almighty howl of protest from most other African countries, which would damage our standing in that continent much more than we might subsequently gain from the plaudits of history.

Here in this country we fall over ourselves in trying to adapt the ways of our society to the presence among us of many new immigrants; we compromise, both sensibly and ridiculously. Yet when it comes to dealing with foreigners in their own country, even senior representatives of it, our leaders' sensitivity to personal dignity and patriotic self-respect is far too often coarsened by political playing to the home gallery. In an age when ten men can do as much damage as a small army that is simply idiotic.

Iran, Iraq and Syria have much closer, and arguably more legitimate, interests in the middle east than do Britain and America. It is merely our democratic and superior economic credentials (and the dubious value of our historical associations) which allow us to cloak crude economic concerns with an appearance of respectability. Is it not obvious – to others if not ourselves – that however coherently we present the 'narrative' of our foreign policy strategy, it will be at best self-serving, and at worst hypocritical. Rattle your precision weaponry at Iran; convene consultations with North Korea; fulminate against Iraq; attempt, uselessly, to isolate Burma; get shamed into breaking with Uzbekistan; cosy up to Egypt and Saudi Arabia; forgive Libya; dither about Zimbabwe: the only consistency in any of that is bluster and bluff. In the chancelleries of the West, however, they are pragmatic responses to real world situations: "What would *you* do, old boy?" they might reasonably ask.

The bone of my contention with your article (as you will have guessed if you have had the patience to read so far) is paragraph 8 of your instructions, where you extol the 'demonstration effect' of successfully applied military force as, in some circumstances, a necessary part of your brief. Up to a point I have no argument with that; but it is clear that you do not restrict it to *defence* – although, in the long sweep of history, you may argue that removing despots and standing up forcefully in the defence of human rights makes the world safer for all of us. Don Quixote had the same idea. In the long sweep of history any good event may be traced back to something deplorable. The Peace of Westphalia established the principle of nation states; it took the Thirty Years War to do it, and was categorised by C V Wedgwood as "an object lesson on the dangers and disasters which can arise when men of narrow hearts and little minds are in high places".

My feeling (which may be unworthy) is that you are trying to have your cake and eat it. You draw up an admirable blueprint for twenty-first century statesmen and yet wish to shoe-horn into it a defence of the Iraq war. If we wait long enough, and the world endures, some good may indeed eventually arise; but whether from it or from some intervening cause, God only knows.

Yours sincerely,
Alan Hall

Ferdinand Mount replied to that:

Many thanks for your long and thoughtful letter. I am sorry to be so slow in replying. It took some time to reach me.

Yes, of course my line of argument could be used to justify invading Zimbabwe. It could also be used to justify not invading Iraq and leaving Saddam to stew, in the hope that in the long run his dictatorship would wither into something less menacing both to his own people and the outside world. The costs and benefits of all such choices cannot be simply read off automatically, but I do think we need to have a clear set of principles to work with.

With best wishes, yours sincerely,
Ferdinand Mount

Both Ferdinand Mount and Charles Moore, to whom my next letter was addressed, are Conservatives: Mount was for two years head of the No. 10 Policy Unit when Margaret Thatcher was prime minister, and Moore is a former editor of the *Daily Telegraph*.

10 April 2007

Charles Moore Esq.
c/o *The Spectator*

Dear Mr Moore

For some weeks I have been half-meaning to write to you about an entirely different subject, but your (I thought) unnecessary little paragraph about Norman Lamont* in 'The Spectator's Notes' of this week's edition has finally irritated me into taking up my 'pen'.

---

* Chancellor of the Exchequer in John Major's government, Norman Lamont is chiefly remembered for pulling Britain out of the EU's Exchange Rate Mechanism on Black Wednesday. At the time of my letter he was chairman of the British Iranian Chamber of Commerce – hence Moore's snide 'unnecessary little paragraph'.

It seems now *de rigueur* – even for those who regard Iran as a seriously dangerous force in the Middle East – to pay lip service to the country's long history and rich culture (lest anybody should doubt their qualification to have an opinion on it worth listening to) and your reference to "a much misunderstood country" sounds, I'm afraid, to anyone with some acquaintance of it, gratingly ironic. I served four years in Iran, working in one of its ministries (whose minister for most of that time, as it happened, was a former head of Savak; this, of course, was in the time of the Shah). Iranians, in my experience, are rather like the Irish: charming, hospitable, romantic, unreliable, and sometimes infuriating – and they have minds of their own. Do not be fooled by TV pictures of excitable crowds chanting "Death to America!" The Shah's men were equally capable of putting on a show, and his hidden cruelties were not so different from the open cruelties of the mullahs. I do not believe that Iran is a greatly different country from what it was in the early 1970s, except that the power of the mosque has now extended from the rural areas into the cities, and that the people now have recent memory of the terrible experience of war. The big change, so far as we in the West are concerned, is that the government is no longer our friend.

And why is that? Two reasons mainly, I believe: we didn't like the tone of Khomeini's Islamic Revolution (which in reality no more affects us than does the tone of Mubarak's Egypt); and, after the American hostages episode, Uncle Sam's absurd (though characteristic) difficulty in burying the hatchet. Does Iran, our ex-friend, really have aggressive intentions in the middle east? Neo-conservatives love to parrot the quote from Ahmadinejad about "wiping Israel off the map", but anyone who has the slightest grip on *realpolitik* knows perfectly well that, even if Iran did have nuclear weapons, it would be suicidal even to *threaten* to use them (much safer to bluster to one's own supporters about wiping Israel off the map). While America spends its time and resources destabilising Iraq and squaring up to Iran, all in the name of fighting Terrorism, the really dangerous country is Pakistan: a peril we foolishly ignore because Musharaf (like the Shah in *his* time) is our friend. The terrorists are in Iraq because we put them there; they have been in Pakistan all along – and Pakistan has nuclear weapons. We have forgotten the assistance given by Iran to America when US forces were fighting the Taliban in Afghanistan, while the same Taliban were being given covert assistance from some of Musharaf's security services.

As for Iran's covert intervention in Iraq, is that much different from United States' earlier intervention in, say, Guatemala? Where national interest is involved, one helps one's friends. Has Iran less of an interest in neighbouring Iraq than America? I'm sorry, but the huffing and puffing about the malign influence of Iran in Iraq strikes me as hypocrisy.

I do genuinely believe that Iran would like to be on friendly terms with Britain and America: Iranians are among the most instinctively ingratiating people I have, in quite a wide experience, encountered. To put it crudely, they like buttering, and being buttered, up. The present American posture is utterly counterproductive (Ours is merely ignominious).

I regret this long letter may appear disproportionate to the short paragraph which evoked it, but I felt you were saying more than you actually put into words. I do indeed feel that Iran is misunderstood – and no, I do not have any financial interests in Iran, nor for that matter any previous great admiration for Lord Lamont.

. . . With apologies again for the length of this,
Yours sincerely
Alan Hall

Moore replied:

Thank you for your interesting letter about Iran. I am sure you are right to draw attention to the complexity of the question and to point out that there are many continuities between the country before and after the Islamic Revolution. You must also be right that we should not be surprised that Iran wishes to advance its interests in Iraq – it has always tried to do so.

I must strongly disagree with you, however, when you suggest that Iran presents no danger either to us or its neighbours. The doctrines of the Islamic Revolution are dangerous and they are universalist. Ever since Khomeini's victory Iran has been important in promoting terrorism in many parts of the world. Its revolutionary role is comparable to that of the early years of Bolshevik Russia. I do not think it is reasonable to expect the world, let alone Israel itself, to brush off remarks about 'wiping Israel off the map' as mere bluster. You may be right that Iran will not in fact use nuclear weapons, but the level of hatred promoted in Iranian political and religious utterance is surely significant and intolerable.

I do not know what the solution is. You say that the American posture is 'utterly counterproductive' and this may be so, but so is the EU position. It seems to me to be perverse not to be worried about a country whose rhetoric and ideology are intensely hostile developing greater military power.

By the way, you are surely right about Pakistan. I have written to this effect myself.

. . . . With best wishes, Yours sincerely
Charles Moore

15 May 2009

To: *letters@spectator.co.uk*

Sir:

Charles Moore's atavistic juices seem to have been excessively stimulated by the parliamentary expenses scandal (The Spectator's Notes, 16 May). But really! His apparent yearning for a return to the world of Anthony Trollope is preposterous. The idea that MPs don't need to be concerned about their remuneration, or (what 'really does shock' Mr Moore) feel the need actually to work at the job (if 'job' is not too irredeemably dreary a word for what looks to be more like *noblesse oblige*) is no doubt attractive when viewed through rose-coloured spectacles, but is likely to be unconvincing or downright objectionable to the electorate. On the other hand, Mr Moore's proposal that all MPs should submit themselves for reselection before the next election is an excellent idea, and should be adopted by all parties, regardless of their particular modes of candidate selection.

Alan Hall

5 May 2010

To: *letters@spectator.co.uk*

Sir:

In the first paragraph of her 'Welcome to the Age of Irrationality' (1 May) Melanie Phillips sets up a few clearly absurd Aunt Sallies, which she then proceeds to demolish with equally absurd ferocity. As a critique of the Western mind (which in this instance, appears to exclude America and Israel) her article seems little more than a diatribe giving vent to her own personal hates – and, no doubt, publicity to her new book. Nevertheless, I am surprised that *The Spectator* should consider fit to publish such hysterical drivel.

Alan Hall

2 October 2011

To: letters@telegraph.co.uk

Sir –
　Your correspondents who, with most Americans, take our (part-) national title of 'Great Britain' to be a hang-over from the British Empire (and thus no longer appropriate?) are mistaken. "Great" here has no political – far less vainglorious – connotation. 'Great Britain' is a geographical expression denoting the island of Britain and its surrounding dependent small islands, and therefore always strictly correct – even though we colloquially tend to use, simply, 'Britain' ourselves when referring to our nation, and would not dream of suggesting that the inhabitants of Mull were any less British than those of London (many, perhaps most of whom, are not). Illogicality is a valuable British quirk: the Queen is still head of a Kingdom. Politically correct feminists haven't got onto that one yet.
　　Alan Hall

1 May 2015

To: letters@thetimes.co.uk

Sir,
　With due deference to the informed opinions of your high-ranking correspondents who have argued so forcefully for the retention and up-grading of our nuclear deterrent, may an ordinary citizen, who served in the last war, however humbly, get a word in? For how is it that these generals, admirals and air marshals can so blindly support billions of expenditure on Trident, and thus, in effect, deny themselves the proper weapons, technology and personnel that are now, by their own asseveration in other discussions, presently inadequate for the defence of this country?
　We know why our politicians are so strong in support of Trident: they could not bear to see France as the only European country striding in, as they see it, the exclusive chambers of world influence and power. As Germany knows (and the United Nations may not) that is a shallow reading of what counts in the world today. We expect better of our military commanders, who should be preparing for the possibilities of an actual attack on these islands.
　　Alan Hall

While I seem to have had something against diatribes, I did not for a moment think that my letters or emails to these people (and there were others, who did not bother to reply) would have the slightest effect in changing minds. I did it more as a mental discipline, to keep my hand in, so to speak, and because I like writing. With much the same end in view, in 2007 I signed up for a one-year Open University course, 'An Introduction to the Humanities'. Covering literature, history, politics, art and much more, it spanned almost anything from Rachel Carson's *Silent Spring* to 1914–18 war memorials. I found it immensely stimulating. My course tutor wanted me to continue for the full degree, and had I done so it would have been in history. But I decided not to for a reason I some years later explained in an email to Vera (who did complete an Open University degree course – as, indeed, did my brother Hamish some years earlier):

> The biography I was trying to remember yesterday [we had been having lunch together] was of Thomas Cromwell by Diarmaid MacCulloch – to illustrate the reason I did not go on with the full Open University History course. It (the biog.) came out last year and has been widely praised as the *definitive* biography, even by Hilary Mantel [author of a three-volume novel about Cromwell's life]. It is a historian's history, in which every sentence is supported by the evidence of a known document, and every known document remorselessly presented and evaluated: a bit like presenting a beautiful Rolls-Royce by describing its mechanical components. MacCulloch (for me) reduced to dry as dust a character that Mantel is memorably illuminating in her novel. . . . I was afraid (you may be able to correct me) the OU course would involve wading through evidence-based history, sucking the life out of it, so long as it could be justified as 'accurate'.

So I prefer to get my history from biographies and, to a lesser extent, autobiographies, and from writers like Antony Beevor and A. N. Wilson. Charles Moore, in his *Spectator* column terribly right wing and fussy has nevertheless written a truly magnificent biography (in three volumes) of Margaret Thatcher. In my time I have probably bought or otherwise acquired twice as many books as now remain on my shelves. Our successive moves have seen the more ephemerally valued ones disposed of to family or Oxfam – a process of weeding which means most of those that remain are, in my opinion, books of merit. I have catalogued most of them, and like to think I may get round eventually to actually reading some of those still unread.

39 – BERYL

In January 2009 we had what was to be our last holiday in Paphos; the following year it would be Marrakesh, with my Open University course in between. Although Beryl was increasingly lame, she was still indefatigably keen on foreign trips, and in 2012 we were booked to spend a couple of weeks in Gibraltar, but had to cancel when I developed serious pains in my neck and shoulders. Was it a psychological protest at all this gallivanting about involving the hassle of airports (where Beryl now required wheelchair assistance) and domestic dislocation all in favour of a tourist experience I felt I could now do without? If so, it was, albeit involuntarily, very selfish of me, because Beryl positively thrived on it. Having now a fairly cloistered life at home, she relished the opportunity of something new being served up to her in comfortably welcoming surroundings, in warmer weather than England's winter. In retrospect, I wish I had been strong enough to allow that holiday in Gibraltar to go ahead, for it would have been her last.

In August Beryl had a wisdom tooth extracted. Although her whole face and jaw became swollen and painful, she typically bore it stoically; but it disorientated her, and was probably responsible for a bad fall at home. It was the middle of the night and I was woken by a loud thud. I got up . . . to hear Beryl snoring. I thought 'Thank goodness!' and then practically tripped over her. In falling, she had hit her head on the wall of the passage outside her room, and there was a lot of blood. The phone was within a few feet of where she lay, barely conscious. I dialled 999, got through, and then engaged in an exasperating conversation, in which I was asked to do things with her – which I could not do at the same time as staying on the (not mobile) phone.

"We need an ambulance," I said.

"The ambulance is on its way."

Apparently, they send it as soon as you tell them the address, and *then* go on to ask all those, to me, exasperating questions. And indeed the ambulance arrived commendably quickly.

Beryl was taken to the brand-new hospital at Pembury, near Tunbridge Wells. After being patched up and thoroughly checked, she was discharged a day later, and for another month her life – apart from a follow-up visit – returned to what had now become routine: late rising, but still doing the cooking of lunch (I prepared the vegetables). It was summer, and we had the opportunity to sit outside in the afternoon or – what had become almost a hobby of Beryl's – she was still able to spend some time in a supermarket, followed by lingering in one or two charity shops. In the evening we would watch the occasional television programme together, and sometimes played a game of Scrabble.

Although unfit, Beryl was not one to play the invalid, philosophically accepting her lameness, high blood pressure and diabetes as now part of her normal life. But one evening she suddenly became very weak, began vomiting, and collapsed. I called for an ambulance and she was again taken to Pembury Hospital. That was on 29 September. When I saw her after she'd been assessed and taken to her own small room, which was standard for Pembury wards, she was looking remarkably calm and relaxed – almost amused that this was becoming, well, 'here we go again'. But it was not to be 'again'.

Three days later I received a phone call from a nurse to say, "Your wife suffered a relapse and has been taken into intensive care."

I at once phoned Jeremy and Hilary, and then drove to the hospital. Hilary and David joined me in Beryl's now empty room; Jeremy and Sally arrived from Farnham less than an hour later. There was not much more news to tell them. The two sympathetic duty nurses (whose names we used, but have now forgotten – let's say Suzy and Thelma) knew little more than that Beryl had needed immediate attention. Now they told us she was being returned to the ward – not a good sign. A few minutes later, Beryl was wheeled back in, still breathing but not conscious.

We were ushered into a separate room nearby, which seemed to be intended for visitors, and told that a surgeon would be coming to speak to us. They offered us tea. It seemed to be a procedure they were accustomed to. The surgeon, a tall, thin man, turned up after about quarter of an hour, and didn't beat about the bush.

"Your wife has suffered a brain haemorrhage and must be expected to die within the next twenty-four hours."

Both Hilary and Sally, as nurses themselves, had known what to expect when we were told that intensive-care treatment was to be discontinued. My own feelings I held in abeyance. We went back to Beryl's room. She was lying there in her hospital gown, eyes closed, breathing unevenly.

"Hearing is the last thing to go," said Thelma. "You can speak to her. Would you like us to call a priest?"

I said yes, knowing it was what Beryl would have wanted.

After a bit of one-sided conversation, Hilary suggested, "We'll leave you with Mum for a bit, Dad," and all three went back to the visitors' room, leaving me with her – Beryl Veronica Mungavin, who had been my wife for fifty-six years of my life; fifty-six years of *her* life too.

I told her I loved her, that I always would love her, however much she might think I got on too well with women. It's true, I do. But apart from Ruth (when I felt Beryl was almost as much to blame, though in a negative sense) I was never so much as tempted to stray from marital fidelity; I just prefer the company of women. Talking about sport or motor cars, or indeed men talking about women, is a complete turn-off for me. The 'Veronica' I met on the *Kenya Castle*, whose laughter and easy conversation at the dining table enchanted me, was in spirit still there on that hospital bed. What characterised her throughout her life was integrity. She knew perfectly well that drinking and joshing at the bar were what one did on a boat. But not Beryl Mungavin. Not that she disapproved – it was just not her scene and she didn't do it. The rows we had in our married life were, at bottom, often due to our disagreement about what was 'the done thing'. I am much more inclined to go with the flow. Not Beryl.

An Anglican clergyman arrived, introduced himself and, as we returned the introductions, irritated me by engaging in friendly chit-chat before getting down to business, so to speak. But of course it was good of him to come along at all (though I think he was accustomed to such priestly duties, and was probably on the premises at the time, he came so quickly). Addressing Beryl as well as us five, he said a few prayers and invited us to join in the Lord's Prayer. A final blessing and, shaking hands all round, he was off. Very shortly after he had gone, almost as if she had been waiting for the final benediction, Beryl's breathing became slower and slightly noisier, and the gaps between each breath longer. The surgeon had said 'twenty-four hours', but it was much quicker than that. Beryl died at approximately 2 a.m. on 3 October, just two days short of her eighty-third birthday.

I must confess, my immediate feeling, on being told my wife had less than a day to live, was of relief – relief that, after eighty-three years, she was able to leave this life without a prolonged period of increasing debilitation or pain – which had been her future prospect. A greater confession: it was combined with a sensation of freedom – the possibility now of being able to live without having constantly to trim everything I did to Beryl's requirements. For another thing that characterised all three of the Mungavin sisters was 'control'. The brothers, oddly enough, were much more relaxed domestically. Like her sisters, Beryl dominated her family – i.e. me and our children. Because we loved her, we mostly accepted it as the way things were. Only later was there occasionally a bust-up also with Hilary or Jeremy. Reconciliation was always achieved because we recognised that love bound us together – and that love could sometimes be a source of discord.

I have mentioned already that it may have been Beryl's early life in India that made her feel not fully 'at home' in Britain. Even in India, her family had been constantly moving from one 'station' to another. Her early education had been as a boarder at Barnes School in Deolali, near Bombay – a school built on ancient foundations, but, after the First World War, established on lines similar to those of an English public school as it was intended mainly for the children of Anglo-Indian families. Its eight 'houses' – four for boys and four for girls – had a strong Christian ethos and good facilities for sport. Beryl often spoke with affection of her, and her near-age siblings' time at Barnes – mostly during the Second World War. She remembered many of her teachers' and fellow pupils' names, and many times told amusing stories of their escapades, which seemed for ever imprinted on her mind. After leaving India, Beryl's subsequent life would never settle. Although that was how she liked it, I believe her sudden uprooting from an Anglo-Indian social scene, and the almost simultaneous unexpected death of her father, had given her a feeling of insecurity that she never wholly lost. And because I loved her for her steadfastness, I rarely challenged her vulnerability.

The funeral was at St Luke's Church, only 200 yards from our flat, where every Sunday without fail we had attended the eight-o'clock service of Holy Communion, using the traditional Book of Common Prayer rather than the modern version that seems now to be preferred by most Church of England congregations. Jeremy spoke the eulogy well, breaking down only over the final sentences, which Mark, our vicar, kindly spoke for him.

Later, at the graveside, Beryl's soul was commended to God. It had started to rain as we each threw a handful of earth on the coffin.

Hilary gave me a great big hug and said, "I love you so much."

As long as I live I will never forget that moment.

40 – TATSFIELD

About two months after Beryl's death I was in a different hospital for a hip operation to the other leg; and it was when returning from a check-up afterwards that I had a car smash – amazingly, very close to where we had lived in Leigh. It was at a blind corner, and the police decided no one was to blame. Neither driver was seriously hurt, but I was thoroughly shaken, and carted off by ambulance, strapped up like a trussed chicken. Fortunately, I was no more than badly bruised: the seat belt had done its stuff, but my car was a write-off. At the age of eighty-seven, I decided that was to be the end of my driving days – I would not buy another car. That was all very well, of course, but it took the loss of a car to make me realise how dependent I had become on having my own transport always ready at the door. Yet as I was living within the town this was not now a big problem; indeed, perhaps it was useful in making me take more exercise than I would otherwise.

Some months later, at the flat, I had another annoyance: damp caused the ceiling to collapse in Beryl's unoccupied bedroom, and there was a lot of hassle with the flat-management people over the root of the problem and whose insurance was liable. Not only was the room in a mess, but I had workmen in, seemingly for days on end, spending half the time discussing what needed to be done rather than getting on with it. All the while I was expected to conceal my irritation and be pleased to see them when they turned up – and serve them tea and biscuits!

I forget the exact sequence of events: whether David and Hilary proposed it after the car smash, or whether the recounting to them of my daily frustrations led them to suggest that I might come to live with them. After the death of his wife, Audrey, in 2006, David's father, Reg, had made over to him the house he had built in Tatsfield, but continued living there for another six years or so. Yet at the time of my accident Reg was actually in a retirement home, where he'd be for the last few months of his life. Much had been done meantime to vastly rebuild the interior of the house to accommodate David's family with three children, while leaving Reg's accommodation intact in an annex with its own kitchen and bathroom. Sadly, he was never to come back to it. Reg died in March 2013, and I moved into his refurbished quarters – new carpets throughout and a brand-new kitchen – the following August.

Tatsfield is a village with a population of just under 2,000, fairly spread out in three main streets, configured in an H, and several smaller streets or lanes, mostly unmade, snaking away from them, mostly in woodland. This gives it a pleasantly rural feel, enhanced by the fact that it's not on the road to anywhere else. One of the first things I did, on settling there, was to make a map of its roads and footpaths so that I didn't become hopelessly lost on walks – which were my main form of exercise (that and a bit of pottering about in the garden). My weekly painting sessions – much nearer now – continued much as before, thanks to Hilary or David's willingness to ferry me to the church hall and back. I went with Hilary to an exhibition of Veronese paintings at the National Gallery, joined the Royal Academy as a 'friend', and on occasion went up to London alone to see other exhibitions – something I would not do now.

The main event of 2014 was the wedding of our grandson Jon (i.e. Jonathan) and Alex (Alexandra) Price, which was a grand ceremony held at Hever Castle. They had met at Exeter University, and had relatively soon decided to tie the knot. In due time, all our grandchildren were to form partnerships, and, as I write, Katherine, Ellie, Richard and Hamish are each now living separately with a partner – a practice that would have been frowned upon in my earlier days, and would have scandalised my parents. Yet I think most people, including me, now accept that a steady partnership is a sensible way of properly getting to know whether you really will want to spend the rest of your life with that boy or girl you are presently so mad about. That was not the only thing I changed my mind about.

Because my working life had involved so much world-travelling, I could never equal Beryl's enthusiasm for holidays abroad; but, in my now quiet life at Tatsfield, I was able to look back and recognise how much those we took together enriched my experience. Apart from our wintering in Cyprus, and other holidays in Europe, I remember especially a 'round-the-world' trip we did while I was at Farnham Castle. This was 'duty travel', to meet, and sometimes stay with, former participants on our courses, to discover how they were making out, and later to feed back an up-to-date picture of life in their country of post. We had stopped for a few days each at Singapore, Hong Kong, Macao, Guangzhou (Canton), Taipei, Seoul and Tokyo, and returned home via Chicago, where we met up with our old friends the Zemaitises. It was a truly fabulous journey, by air, riverboat, hovercraft and train. I now realise what an old grouch I was as a reluctant holidaymaker, because I did enjoy the Farnham Castle trips, which were virtually holidays – once we got into them.

Hilary and David are also keen on foreign travel – usually in Europe, but in this country too. My own very last two holidays – I doubt I will have any more – were with them and all the family, which now included our first great-grandchild, Harry, and Alex pregnant with our second, Oliver (Ollie). The first (holiday) was in Devon, in a beautiful part of the Exmoor National Park; the second, in Dorset, was somewhere in the countryside near Corfe Castle, almost equally pleasant for walking – which was what we mostly did. I say 'we', but it was the others who did most of the walking. I did some sketching, but nothing worth keeping.

That first family holiday was remarkable for me, not so much for the change of scenery as for the declaration of a surprising result of the referendum that would decide whether or not Britain would leave the European Union. I hadn't stayed awake for it; I just remember Katherine coming down in the morning and saying, "We're leaving." I could hardly believe it, and at first thought she was pulling my leg, it was so improbable. At least *I* thought it improbable, because, along with most Members of Parliament, but not, apparently, a majority of the voting public, I thought – and still do – that leaving the EU was an insane act of national self-harm. As a legal challenge, later, required the decision to be ratified by Parliament, rancorous debates in the House of Commons continued for more than two years. After following them closely, I wrote down my own opinion of Brexit:

> 1. Everyone is arguing about whether Brexit is: (a) a glorious opportunity, or (b) an unmitigated disaster. But surely that's not the problem. Nearly all the countries of the world are NOT in the European Union; only 28 countries *are* in it (of which the UK is, or was, one). Countries outside it are, more or less, doing much the same (better or worse) than countries *in* the EU. It's not the final state, in or out, that matters most: it's the act of CHANGING from one to the other that's proving so disruptive. It's like deciding to change from driving on the left to driving on the right. Maybe one side *is* better than the other; but, having decided [on which side of the road to drive], it would be merry hell to now decide to change over. And that's what is happening with Brexit. Our whole economy and much of our legal system have been tied up and intertwined with the EU for the past forty years. Disentangling it and reordering our machinery of government (and customary ways of thinking and working by our civil servants) is proving to be a nightmare – and it's not a dream! It's not so much that being outside the EU would be a disaster (though I believe it does stupidly underplay our influence as an EU member): it's the decision to *change* from IN to OUT.
>
> 2. How strange, therefore, to find that it is dyed-in-the-wool, right-wing Conservatives who are, in this case, the revolutionaries – people whose whole philosophy is to welcome the slow maturing of society, and to abhor revolutionary change. A revolution, nevertheless, is what they are now fanatically embracing.

As I write, although the decision to leave the European Union has been ratified by Parliament, the terms of our future relationship are still up in the air.

We returned from our Dorset holiday via Bristol, where I was dropped off to spend a week with Hamish, who, having lived there for the previous forty-odd years in a flat, had very sensibly decided to settle finally in a comfortable retirement home that still allowed him to live an independent life, but with all necessary services at hand. Like David in the navy, and me, he had spent much of his working life abroad – in his case, Kuwait, Nigeria and Holland. So, although we had seen each other briefly from time to time, our relationship with each other had markedly changed from our childhood to later life. Perhaps that is natural in most families, but being in different countries accentuated the difference in our case.

When we were boys, Hamish, being the youngest – if only by two years from David – was always treated as the baby of the family. David and I would go roller skating in the park, leaving Hamish at home, very much the mummy's boy. That was before his accident. And it was perhaps indicative of our relationship that, even when Hamish took up canoeing, it was to David and me that he lent his canoes, rather than accompanying one of us himself. Yet, when physical ability and the difference in years between us ceased to be significant influences, I discovered much more of my thinking to be in common with Hamish than with David, who, having absorbed the ways of the wardroom, married into, and then lived among, a Lancashire family of a different culture to our Scottish-based one. He adopted, reasonably enough, their ways rather than ours. That I did not adopt the Mungavin culture, harking back to their five generations of life in India, was probably due to not living among them in Scotland.

David died from a sudden heart attack in 2003, at the age of seventy-seven – earlier than he might have done, had he given up his pipe and the enjoyment of a full English breakfast. Now Hamish and I were the only survivors from the family of 49 Plashet Road. Chewing over old times with him was a particular pleasure, even though our conversation would occasionally revert to fraternal bickering. On two or three occasions, when visiting his dentist in Sevenoaks, Hamish would stay with me – which meant complete turmoil, as he was unable to manage the stairs of the house, and a bed had to be brought down into my cosy living room. We still talk on the phone, but I doubt whether we will ever see each other again.

In 2016, still reasonably active myself, however, I was returning by bus from a visit to the neighbouring town of Oxted – or I was about to return. The bus was full of schoolchildren, one of whom offered me a seat just as the bus was moving off . . . and then suddenly the driver jammed on his brakes, catapulting me headlong on to the floor. The police later maintained, with the driver, that he had *not* braked, but I believe they were relying on the evidence of the on-board camera, *which would have braked at the same time as the bus*, so it was only myself that actually appeared to move. As I wasn't inclined to make an issue of it, the net result was a broken hip, needing a replacement of my earlier replacement. That slowed me down.

Not content with that, two and a half years later I had another fall, this time on the path to the church hall. It was entirely my own fault: I was pulling my shopping trolley full of painting materials with one hand while trying to keep a canvas clear of drizzling rain with the other, and I toppled over, cracking my right arm. It's never recovered full mobility. From not really feeling my age, I have now begun to recognise that I'm getting old.

Although Hilary had retired from nursing about the same time as I joined them in Tatsfield, she is nonetheless actively engaged in local social work – organising a London food bank, church duties, running a local ear clinic, visiting housebound people or ferrying them for hospital visits. David retired from the police in 2017, but, wanting to stay active, took a pleasant-enough handyman job at an airfield near Reading. After a couple of years, when that got a bit boring, he rejoined the police in a civilian capacity, handling things like population events and road traffic control. So until recently I would find myself, as often as not, alone in the house with Freda, their exuberant, very talkative, schnauzer.

You may note that I begin to adopt the present tense; and, indeed, most of what follows will now be more in the nature of a fragmentary diary than an autobiography. I write today on 4 May 2020, when the whole world is in the middle of the coronavirus pandemic upheaval. Everyone in the country, if not in an essential job that cannot be done from home, is required to isolate themselves at home, or if out on necessary shopping, must maintain a distance of two metres from other people. Yet I am in the curious position that, while nearly everybody else's life has been turned upside down, my own, with two exceptions, continues more or less as it was before. I always did do my shopping online, with home delivery. What I *am* missing are the weekly sessions of our Millennium Art Group (that's what we call it) and the Sunday church services, both of which have been discontinued with no idea yet of when they might be resumed. I can't go out for a haircut either, but here Hilary has stepped into the breach with some new electric clippers, very efficiently giving me a 'short all over', which is how I like it.

Missing church is, of course, much more than missing the social coffee get-together after Sunday service; but I may as well confess now – and very near the end of my life is a good time to do it – that my religious belief is not 100 per cent in line with your average vicar's idea of it. Five years ago I wrote a letter to Matthew Parris, a *Times* columnist and an avowed atheist, in which I argued against what I believed to be his false idea of religion, and attempted to outline my own faith and belief in God. Most of it ran as follows:

> In *The Spectator* of 19 October 2013 you threw down what I took to be a challenge: 'Religious sceptics deserve better enemies'; and I put your article aside, with the intention of giving you a double-barrelled response . . . and then, after drafting a few notes, forgot about it. . . . But now I see you are at it again. . . . The subjects of your two articles (Miracles and Wishy-washiness respectively) are different, but your criticism of Religion as a matter of belief, and [in the case of the Church of England] infirm belief at that, boils down to what I believe is your *misapprehension* of Religion. Am I giving the game away from the start, if I say you are fighting a myth? But religion is not what you say it is. If I had to define it, I would say that religion is the poetry of the human condition. Poetry is not just one poem; nor does religion have just one faith. Of course, religion has its fanatics; aesthetes can be equally fanatical: but the quality of a religion should be no more defined or judged by its zealots, than Art by its pretended connoisseurs. Yet, if that is so, why do we adhere, sometimes fanatically, to one particular religion?
>
> The answer, I think, lies in my definition: our subject is not simply 'Nature', Love, Beauty, War, Peace, and whatever else

inspires our muse: it is *all* these things bundled up within an attitude of mind that allows those who take the trouble, to see poetry in our existence. It is not surprising, therefore, that to make any kind of sense of our philosophy of life, – whether we acknowledge it or not – we find part of our brain (our soul?) reaches beyond the limits of pure reason (as in poetry) and, if we have the inclination, we quite reasonably (yes, reasonably) latch on to an exposition of the meaning of life (and death) that is near at hand, and conveniently in accord with the norms of our society [themselves, as I might have added, formed by an evolution of religious thought].

So far, so utilitarian, you may say. But just as humour stops being funny when you try to explain it, so in the same way, religion stops being inspiring if you submit it to pure reason: surely that is a dry-as-dust guide to the well-spring of our lives in the world.

Or perhaps you just can't get over the idea of 'God' in the first place, an idea common to all religions – sometimes a plurality of gods – and especially over the utterly inexplicable failure of a loving and all-powerful god to stop bad things happening in the world; or indeed why he (nearly always 'he', though today's feminists are pushing for 'Mother Almighty' – another slide down the slippery slope?) why, dammit, why he *caused* them to happen. A very reasonable ground for perplexity. The problem is we are just so cocksure of humanity's overlordship in the world that we have lost sight of our roots in the primal swamp. The lion and the antelope have equal rights to life, liberty and happiness. Is it therefore wrong for one to kill and eat the other? "Why does God permit this wickedness?" the antelope may reasonably ask.

Humanity is evolving. It is much more 'humane' than it used to be. So also is the Christian religion. It no longer burns heretics at the stake, or conducts crusades in the middle east (it leaves that to its secular brethren). Christians were prominent in advocating the abolition of slavery, and no-one, so far as I know, regarded its churches as slipping down a slippery slope, when they later conceded that slavery was not part of God's natural order. So also with the anathematising of homosexuality and women priests. It is not a question of God's will being 'found to have been revised', as you put it, but the church's recognition, *as it has always recognised*, that our understanding of the ways of God is imperfect.

Of its nature, a church has to be dogmatic if it strives for coherence, and it may well be argued that, in this respect, the Church of England does far too much thinking aloud. Islam does not seem to have this failing, but we should beware of judging it by its knife-wielding jihadists who suborn it for political ends. The idea of God – so easily mocked, and often portrayed, as an old man with a beard sitting up in the clouds – undoubtedly suffers from too much metamorphosis; but it is typically the best we can do to give substance to the wonder of the organic nature of the universe, wherein God is an expression of its fundamental unity: the action of a butterfly's wings setting up an earthquake in Mexico, for example.

The ultimate morality is harmony.

I did not dent Parris's scepticism, but at least made him suck his teeth. In reply, he wrote:

Thank you for your letter of 4 June.

Your point about the ineffability of religion, and God's ways, makes for a good riposte. However, I think you'll agree that this pushes the argument to the question of belief – prior belief is a necessary condition of accepting that the ways of God are mysterious to man. This obviously goes beyond the territory of reason. This is fair enough, but frequently organised religions try to give reasons to *begin* believing, they do not assume that their arguments are dependent on this already being the case.

Furthermore, were prior belief necessary the power of religious institutions would only extend over those who actively believed; this is not quite the argument the Irish Catholic church was making.

I would also counter your suggestion that aesthetes can be equally as fanatical as religious devotees: for example, though a stickler for form and style, the great literary critic FR Leavis never blew up a bus because people wrote bad poems.

Thank you for your thought-provoking argument. Yours sincerely,
Matthew P.

Having made my point, I wasn't going to pursue the argument (which would no longer have interested him). But Parris's reply – that you've got first to believe in God to be able to say His ways are mysterious – didn't recognise my definition of God. For me God *is* the mystery, the wonder of the universe; and my use of the masculine third person, 'His', is simply a Christian convention that I am happy to accept, because I am a Christian, a believer in the teachings of Jesus as he delivered them in parables, and specifically in the Sermon on the Mount. Yes, of course, I believe them because that is how I was brought up by my parents, and also because they accord with my own experience. You may say, why then believe all the 'Christian' palaver? I go back to my definition of religion as poetry, and to what I wrote to Matthew Parris in conclusion: the ultimate morality is harmony. Jesus called it Love, but recognised that we are self-centred animals who often fall short in benevolence to others, and always doing what, in our hearts, we know to be right. The Bible calls that failing 'Man's sinfulness', an expression which doesn't often ring a bell in this day and age.

That, I believe, is why we need religion, a discipline that constantly reminds us, if we are truly honest, of our moral obligations in the world, and by which we can live with confidence and enjoyment, if not always a clear conscience. That some fanatics pervert it is no argument against belief. Belief – or perhaps Faith is a better word: both have enriched our lives throughout the ages and, whether you recognise it or not, have brought us to where we are today. They have inspired both the beauty of our cathedrals and the mosques of Iran; our church music and their response to the call of prayer. Charity is central to both our religions. So have been war and strife: our Crusades, their Terrorism. And just because ours was then and theirs is now, doesn't really let us off the hook: we're still the same old homo stupido. And don't think I think I'm not included: as a reader who has managed to get through to the end of this book, you will know that in many places I don't come out of it well. . . . That's life, I suppose.